SCHLEIERMACHER'S EARLY PHILOSOPHY OF LIFE
Determinism, Freedom, and Phantasy

HARVARD THEOLOGICAL REVIEW
HARVARD THEOLOGICAL STUDIES

Number 33

SCHLEIERMACHER'S EARLY
PHILOSOPHY OF LIFE
Determinism, Freedom, and Phantasy
Albert L. Blackwell

SCHLEIERMACHER'S EARLY PHILOSOPHY OF LIFE

Determinism, Freedom, and Phantasy

Albert L. Blackwell

SCHOLARS PRESS

Published by
Scholars Press
101 Salem Street
Chico, California 95926

SCHLEIERMACHER'S EARLY PHILOSOPHY OF LIFE
Determinism, Freedom, and Phantasy
Albert L. Blackwell

Furman University
Greenville, South Carolina 29613

Library of Congress Cataloging in Publication Data

Blackwell, Albert. L.
  Schleiermacher's early philosophy of life.

  (Harvard theological studies ; no. 33)
  (ISSN 0073-0726)
  Bibliography: p.
  1. Schleiermacher, Friedrich, 1768–1834— Ethics.
2. Ethics. 3. Free will and determinism. 4. Liberty.
5. Fantasy. I. Title. II. Series.
B3098.E7B55   170'.92'4   81-5830
ISBN 0-89130-507-6   AACR2

Printed in the United States of America

To Marian, Christopher, Jody, Jonathan, Karen, David,
Melanie, Andrew, and Kristin, without whose interruptions
and distractions this book would never have been possible.

Immer aber musste Schleiermachers
Studierzimmer in der Nähe von dem
seiner Frau sein, denn das, was andere
in ihrer wissenschaftlichen Vertiefung
gestört hätte, das Kommen und Gehen,
die Besuche und häuslichen Verrichtungen,
war für ihn ein Bedürfnis, eine Beruhigung.

Heinrich Meisner

Table of Contents

List of Plates

Acknowledgments

I wish to express my gratitude to the Danforth Foundation for contributing toward my studies and travel in the Germanies and Poland; to the Director and the staff of the Literatur-Archiv der Deutschen Akademie der Wissenschaften zu Berlin for their generous assistance during the winter of 1970–71; to Furman University for a grant and a leave of absence during the final stages of this book's preparation; to Richard Kemmler, who set my style on a greatly improved tack in the earliest stages of my writing; to Professors Roderick Firth, Gordon Kaufman, and Richard Niebuhr of Harvard University and Wayne Proudfoot of Columbia University, who gave assistance in an earlier version of this study; to Grace Friend Mullen for her incomparably fine typing of the manuscript; to Mal Brown, who read portions of the manuscript; to David Youngblood, who read Part I with great care and offered valuable suggestions and encouragement; and to Marian Willard Blackwell, who has given essential advice and support at every stage of my work.

I also wish to thank the following for permission to reproduce the figures which appear in this book: Walter de Gruyter and Company for Figs. A and B, which appeared in Wilhelm Dilthey's *Leben Schleiermachers I/1* (ed. Martin Redeker); W. Kohlhammer Verlag for Figs F, G, H, I, and J, which appeared in Carl Grommelt's and Christine von Mertens' *Dohnasche Schloss Schlobitten in Ostpreussen*; and the Literatur-Archiv des Instituts für deutsche Sprache und Literatur, Deutsche Akademie der Wissenschaften zu Berlin for Figs. M and N, and for permission to use the manuscript of Schleiermacher's *On Human Freedom*.

Abbreviations
(For complete data consult the Bibliography.)

Br. I–IV	Schleiermacher, *Aus Schleiermachers Leben in Briefen*, vols. I–IV (vols. I and II, 2nd ed.)
Braut	Schleiermacher, *Friedrich Schleiermachers Briefwechsel mit seiner Braut*, ed. Heinrich Meisner
"Denkmale"	"Denkmale der inneren Entwicklung Schleiermachers," an appendix to Wilhelm Dilthey, *Leben Schleiermachers*, 1st ed. (1870)
First *Kritik*	Kant, *Kritik der reinen Vernunft*, ed. Raymund Schmidt (standard pagination)
Second *Kritik*	Kant, *Kritik der praktischen Vernunft*, ed. Königlich Preussischen Akademie der Wissenschaften (1908)
Monologen	Schleiermacher, *Monologen. Eine Neujahrsgabe*, critical ed. by Friedrich Michael Schiele
MS	Schleiermacher, Manuscript of *Über die Freiheit des Menschen*
Reden	Schleiermacher, *Reden über die Religion*, critical ed. by George Christian Pünjer
Die Religion	Kant, *Die Religion innerhalb der blossen Vernunft*, ed. Karl Vorländer
Soliloquies	Schleiermacher, *Schleiermacher's Soliloquies: An English Translation of the Monologen*, tr. Horace Leland Friess
Speeches	Schleiermacher, *On Religion: Speeches to Its Cultured Despisers*, English tr. of *Reden* by John Oman
Werden	Schleiermacher, *Schleiermacher als Mensch. Sein Werden. Familien- und Freundesbriefe 1783 bis 1804,* ed. Heinrich Meisner
Wirken	Schleiermacher, *Schleiermacher als Mensch. Sein Wirken. Familien- und Freundesbriefe 1804 bis 1834*, ed. Heinrich Meisner

Prologue

This book follows the course of Schleiermacher's life from the end of his student days at the University of Halle in 1789 to his return to Halle as Professor of Theology and Preacher to the University in 1804. For this young man of twenty to thirty-five, destined to inaugurate a new era in western religious thought, these were years of vigorous intellectual energy. At the beginning of this period Schleiermacher innovated a deterministic world view that was to underlie his lifework. In the context of this determinism he elaborated a concept of human freedom rich enough to sustain his thinking in both ethics and religion. This concept in turn prompted Schleiermacher as a participant in early romanticism—one of the most refreshing anomalies in the orderly pageant of Teutonic thought—to bring phantasy forward and acclaim its liberating role in the religious, ethical, and scientific interplay of our mental capacities. And all this formative intellectual growth occurred amid repeated emotional upheavals in career, love, and friendship.

Schleiermacher's religious philosophy was pronounced heretical in his own day and has provoked controversy ever since. Doubtless it would have provoked more had the fact of its underlying determinism been better known. But Schleiermacher elaborated his philosophy of determinism in an early treatise that, for reasons I shall later indicate, has never been published. Thus the fundamental determinism of his world view has remained obscure to many of his readers. Part I of my book focuses upon this early treatise on determinism in the hope of penetrating some of that obscurity.

The argument of my book assumes that the themes of determinism, freedom, and phantasy in Schleiermacher's thinking are best appreciated in sequence, both logical and biographical. My method has been to reconstruct this sequence by examining Schleiermacher's early writings in the broad environment of his life and times. Two considerations have led me to concentrate on the early period of Schleiermacher's life and to adopt an approach combining analysis and biography.

First, though Schleiermacher is widely acknowledged as Protestantism's most influential theologian since John Calvin, no sustained study in English has ever devoted itself to his early career. This despite the fact that the first half of Schleiermacher's career is biographically the more interesting half, thanks both to the greater variety of his early experiences and to the more extensive documentation provided by his torrent of correspondence as a young man, numbering upward toward three thousand extant letters. These were also the years in which Schleiermacher disciplined his intellectual genius, the versatile exercises of which have secured his place in the history of philosophical, ethical, and religious thought. Many, even a majority of Schleiermacher's early writings, however, have never become available in English and are scarcely even commented upon in English secondary sources. Among these writings are three unpublished treatises from early in the 1790s, *On the Highest Good*, *On Human Freedom*, and *On the Worth of Life*; two early essays on Spinoza; the influential first edition of *On Religion: Speeches to Its Cultured Despisers* of 1799; a 1799 dialogue, *On the Respectable*; numerous early notebooks and book reviews; dozens of early sermons and sermon outlines; hundreds of early letters, scattered through scores of sources; and the dense but correspondingly substantive *Groundwork to a Critique of Previous Ethical Doctrine* of 1804.

My purpose in writing has been as much to render these primary materials more accessible as to develop an argument. As a result I have quoted extensively from Schleiermacher's original sources.[1] I have done the same from the writings of other German idealists and romantics of the 1790s — contemporaries of Schleiermacher such as Jacobi, Eberhard, Schiller, Fichte, Schelling, and the Schlegels. Although their era was one of the most fertile periods in western intellectual history, many of these philosophers and philosopher-poets have remained inaccessible to English readers. I can claim no mastery of these figures except possibly in their direct relations to Schleiermacher, but I have hoped through those relations to contribute something to their accessibility as well.

A second consideration, guiding the analytical and biographical approach of my book, is my conviction that Schleiermacher can be rightly appreciated only when his ideas are understood in intimate association with his life and times. Many students of Schleiermacher have thought this before me. Oskar Walzel writes in his *German Romanticism*:

> From the very beginning . . . romantic thought centered in the problem of how a person can find a relation to life. The final and most sublime solution of this problem was found in Schleiermacher's attempt to see mundane existence, the finite, as a reflection of infinity, and to love the infinite in the finite.[2]

Schleiermacher's stepson, Ehrenfried von Willich, testifies more simply to the truth in Walzel's assertion. "I have never seen anyone in whom knowledge and life were so in unison as they were in him," he writes of Schleiermacher, "anyone who so lived what he thought and knew."[3] At

---

[1] All translations from German are my own except as otherwise noted.

[2] *Deutsche Romantik*, 5th ed., II, 79. Also available in the English translation by Alma Elise Lussky, *German Romanticism*, 258.

[3] *Aus Schleiermachers Hause*, 26.

times von Willich's expressions of admiration for his stepfather tend to effusiveness, but we shall see that in this instance his opinion is echoed in the almost universal testimony of Schleiermacher's contemporaries.

An exception to prove this rule (the only exception I know) occurs in an 1822 review of the third edition of the *Speeches*, reworked by Schleiermacher in 1821. The reviewer, Karl Heinrich Sack, an old friend of Schleiermacher, closes his predominantly critical review with a word of praise for the author of the *Speeches* and cites Schleiermacher's "pure development of life" and "deep religious spirit . . . *happily not in harmony with their philosophical elucidation.*"[4] Sack's review is in some respects astute, anticipating by a hundred years certain criticisms of Schleiermacher raised by the neo-orthodox movement of our own century. But I side with the majority of Schleiermacher interpreters, and with Schleiermacher himself,[5] in disagreeing with Sack's conclusion. Schleiermacher's life and character, I believe, can be appreciated only through an understanding of their "philosophical elucidation," and this relation is equally true in reverse. Alongside his publications and manuscripts, therefore, Schleiermacher's beautiful personal correspondence and the circumstances and events of his life have provided me with resources for my discussion.

Schleiermacher's changing spheres of activity and the materials that express his developing interests have seemed to me to require a more analytic approach for Part I of my book and a more biographical approach for Parts II and III. I am aware that this procedure has produced differences in texture between these sections. I have not tried to smooth over these differences, as they appear to me to bear the genuine impress of Schleiermacher's own course of experience. Before his move to Berlin in 1796, Schleiermacher's intellectual productivity was analytic and isolated. After his 1796 entry into the Berlin circle of early romanticism, in contrast, his first publications were the rhetorical fruition of his suddenly blossoming social life. Such contrasts notwithstanding, I have attempted overall to combine analysis and biography. By regarding biographical materials from a particular philosophical point of view, I have tried to create an interpretative portrait of Schleiermacher as a young man— something that has been lacking in English up to now.

It has not been my interest here to argue that the philosophical point of view I have chosen for this interpretative portrait is uniquely significant. That is, I do not claim that determinism, freedom, and phantasy are the key concepts for an understanding of Schleiermacher's early career. It seems to me that such claims all too often invite a kind of historiographical hysteria. We see this, for example, in one strand of the

---

[4] *Heidelbergische Jahrbücher der Literatur*, XV (1822), 848. Emphasis added.
[5] See Schleiermacher's response to Sack in *Aus Schleiermachers Leben in Briefen*, IV, 304–6.

Calvin literature, where decades of debate over the "key concept" of Calvin's theology issued finally in two contradictory claims: that none of the proposed concepts is key, and that all of them are. The literature on Schleiermacher's early career (as I have indicated, most of it in German) is happily free from such polemical tail chasing, and I do not want to risk disturbing that condition.

What is more, a claim to have discovered the "key concepts" of Schleiermacher's thinking would violate the quintessentially romantic sense for infinity that wholly possessed Schleiermacher's own consciousness. True vision, Schleiermacher believed, is not restricted to any single, privileged point of view. True vision consists rather in the viewing of all things from all points of view. In what follows I have made no attempt to conceal my agreement with this principle of Schleiermacher's romanticism. I have hoped only to present determinism, freedom, and phantasy as clarifying concepts, for I believe that they afford certain undistorted insights into the inexhaustible subject of Schleiermacher's early philosophy, life, and times.

Part I. Determinism (1789–1795)

Chapter 1. Schleiermacher's Intellectual Awakening

I had a peculiar affliction. It consisted in an amazing skepticism, the origin of which I can no longer recollect.

From May, 1789, to April, 1790, Schleiermacher spent a solitary year in the small country town of Drossen (Fig. E),[1] near Frankfurt on the Oder, preparing for his approaching theological examinations. It was the year of the storming of the Bastille. In Versailles and Paris, the French National Assembly was debating political freedom. In Prussia, Immanuel Kant was completing the last of his three great *Critiques* of reason and thus effecting his own revolution in freedom, philosophically understood. Schleiermacher was twenty-one. He had just left the University of Halle, disillusioned with the hollowness of academic existence, yet impoverished and dreading the uncertainties of practical life that now faced him. Two years earlier he had been asked to leave the seminary of the pietistic Bohemian Brethren at Barby as a result of his doubts concerning certain Christian doctrines. Had Schleiermacher not taken the initiative in leaving the seminary, he would in fact have been expelled.[2] A friend of those days refers to Schleiermacher's departure from Barby as a "scandal."[3]

Schleiermacher's father, Gottlieb Schleiermacher, an army chaplain in the Reformed or German Calvinist church, had sought in his letters to quiet his son's doubts. He had not realized the depth of Schleiermacher's anxiety, however. The belief on which Christian salvation depends, Schleiermacher finally wrote to his father from Barby after a year's hesitation,

is now lost to me. I cannot believe that he who named himself only the Son of Man was the eternal and true God; I cannot believe that his death was a substitutionary atonement, because he never expressly said so himself, and because I cannot believe it was necessary. God, who has

---

[1]Now Ośno Lubuskie, Poland.

[2]Letter to his father, Feb. 12, 1787. *Aus Schleiermachers Leben in Briefen*, I, 50. Volumes I and II of *Br*. are available in the English translation by Frederica Maclean Rowan, *The Life of Schleiermacher*, where letters can be located by date.

[3]Letter from Johann Baptist von Albertini to Schleiermacher, Apr. 26, 1787. *Br*., III, 14.

> evidently created humankind not for perfection but only for the striving
> after perfection, cannot possibly wish to punish persons eternally because
> they have not become perfect.[4]

"So, it is finally out," he concludes, "this news that must so greatly shock
you." Schleiermacher's anticipation of his father's reaction was accurate:

> O you foolish son, who has bewitched you, that you do not obey the
> truth? . . . Turn back! O my son, turn back! Human virtue is not perfec-
> tion, but to turn back from the way of error. O Lord Jesus, thou Shep-
> herd of Humankind, lead back thyself thy strayed lamb! Do it for the
> glory of thy name! Amen![5]

A month later the father's pastoral imagery had grown more severe:
"That your teachers shun you to a certain extent is not surprising; it
must be their concern that the whole flock is not contaminated by one
mangy sheep [ein räudiges Schaf]."[6]

Schleiermacher was never to see his father again. But to his relief,
his father's attitude mellowed with the passage of the seven years of life
remaining to him. By the time of his father's death in 1794, the father
and son were on terms as warm as the distant exchange of letters might
allow.[7] Even in these first, heart-rending letters, however, his father
granted Schleiermacher permission to proceed with arrangements for his
transfer to the University of Halle, where he was to live with his uncle,
Samuel Ernst Timotheus Stubenrauch. The brother of Schleiermacher's
mother, Katharina Maria Stubenrauch Schleiermacher, Stubenrauch was
a professor of theology at Halle. His letters to Schleiermacher reveal a
wise and generous spirit, and Schleiermacher turned to Stubenrauch for
paternal support in these troubled years.[8]

In going to Halle, Schleiermacher was proving himself an offspring
of the Enlightenment. He was following the imperative which Kant, in
his famous essay of 1784, "What is Enlightenment?" had established
as the watchword of enlightenment: Sapere aude!, "Dare to know!"
Halle had at one time been a center of pietism, but in 1787 its
character was quite different. Somewhat in decline, the university
represented new trends of rationalism in academic disciplines, including
those of theology and biblical criticism. Schleiermacher's father was
right to fear its influence upon his son's already wavering pietism. In

---

[4]Jan 21, 1787. Br. I, 42–43.
[5]Feb. 8, 1787. Br. I, 46, 49.
[6]Mar. 19, 1787. Br. I, 59.
[7]For Schleiermacher's own account of his relation with his father, written just after his
father's death, see the letter to his sister Charlotte, Oct. 13, 1794. Br. I, 131–32. For his
account from a later perspective see the letter to Eleonore Grunow, Aug. 7, 1802. Br. I,
310–11.
[8]See Hermann Hering, Samuel Ernst Timotheus Stubenrauch und sein Neffe Friedrich
Schleiermacher, esp. 56ff.

fact, Schleiermacher was so acutely concerned to convince his father that he was not irresponsibly seeking new beliefs but rather searching for an opportunity to examine his old ones, that upon his uncle's advice he avoided direct exposure to Halle's theological faculty. It seems that he did not even attend his own uncle's lectures in theology. He limited his rather desultory work at Halle to philosophy and the study of languages, struggling with his religious doubts in the privacy of his uncle's library. At the same time, both father and uncle were advising Schleiermacher to consider a career in teaching rather than preaching, given the unstable condition of his religious beliefs.

So it was that when Schleiermacher nevertheless chose to follow his own proclivity to the ministry (he sprang from a long line of ministers on both his father's and his mother's sides, a particularly distinguished line in the latter case), he found himself ill prepared for the theological examinations prerequisite to ordination. With these examinations looming before him, Schleiermacher had concluded his studies at the University of Halle in the spring of 1789, visited Berlin briefly for the first time, and then again moved in with his uncle Stubenrauch, who in the meantime had left Halle for a preaching post in Drossen. Had an observer of the time somehow known that Schleiermacher was eventually to be recognized as a great dogmatic theologian, it would not have been difficult to predict that his theology would be novel, or even that it might inaugurate the most significant new era in theology since the Reformation. The young Schleiermacher was recognized by his contemporaries as gifted and brilliant, even to the point of "pride and conceit," as his mother wrote of him as a lad, three years before her death in 1783.[9] But except perhaps to Schleiermacher's lifelong friend Karl Gustav von Brinkmann, to whom Schleiermacher was communicating detailed thoughts on the need for reconstruction in dogmatic theology,[10] it might have seemed unlikely to an observer that this young man would ever become a theologian at all. The prospect of his appearance before the Berlin theological examining board was, to use his own word, "nauseating."[11] His preparations forced him to work his way back through the writings of dogmatic theologians whose technicalities he said he forgot faster than he was able to review them.

It may therefore have been in part simply to preserve his sanity that Schleiermacher worked during his year in Drossen on three philosophical dialogues concerning the subject of human freedom. These dialogues are not extant, except for a few fragments of notes apparently pertaining to the third of them,[12] but we know something of their

---

[9]To Stubenrauch, 1780. *Br*. I, 20.

[10]See the letter of Sep. 28, 1789. *Br*. IV, 28–30.

[11]Letter to Brinkmann, Dec. 9, 1789. *Br*. IV, 42.

[12]*Schleiermacher Nachlass*, Item #134, in the *Literatur-Archiv* of the German Academy of Sciences in East Berlin (see Bibliography).

content from a letter to Brinkmann that Schleiermacher wrote in 1789. He describes the first dialogue as an argument that "one must treat willpower just like any other" human power if certain incorrect notions of moral accountability are to be avoided. The second dialogue concerns several practical questions that result when one discards the illusory and "obscure feeling of undeterminable freedom of choice." Would the presupposition that all human actions are determined lead to moral inactivity or quietism, for example? Would the feeling of moral regret become a mere deception? Finally, Schleiermacher describes the third dialogue as an examination of Kant's doctrines of freedom and respect for the moral law.[13] Thus we find Schleiermacher in 1789 absorbed in a critique of Kant's concept of freedom and already sympathetically weighing the merits of a deterministic world view.

The preservation of his sanity was not Schleiermacher's only motivation in writing these dialogues on freedom. During the year 1791–92, he returned to their themes in a formal treatise, *On Human Freedom*. Schleiermacher had passed the first series of his theological examinations in the summer of 1790. With the aid of one of his Berlin examiners, the court chaplain and old family friend, Friedrich Samuel Gottfried Sack, he had then secured a tutoring position in the household of the East Prussian nobleman Count Friedrich Alexander Dohna. In the Count's beautiful country manor in Schlobitten (Figs. H–J),[14] among the Dohna family of ten children—six boys and four girls, one of whom, Friederika (Fig. G), became the object of Schleiermacher's first, secret love—Schleiermacher found himself more happily situated than he had been since childhood. He wrote to his father:

> Here my heart will be properly cared for and does not have to wither under the weeds of cold erudition, and my religious sensibilities do not die under theological broodings. Here I enjoy the domestic life for which human beings are intended, and which warms my feelings.[15]

Schleiermacher was under no obligation to produce a philosophical manuscript in Schlobitten. In fact, he was afraid that any he did produce might be blocked from publication by the Prussian board of censors, of which his church superior Sack was a member.[16] Thus his choice to write the treatise *On Human Freedom* seems to represent simply Schleiermacher's most immediate philosophical interest in 1791–92.

The treatise is extant among Schleiermacher's papers. It consists of over a hundred pages in his own handwriting, which, always miniature

---

[13]July 22, 1789. *Br*. IV, 18–19.

[14]Now Słobity, Poland. Photographs and a detailed description of the Dohna palace in Schlobitten are available in Carl Grommelt et al., *Das Dohnasche Schloss Schlobitten in Ostpreussen*.

[15]Aug. 16, 1791. *Br*. I, 94.

[16]Letter to Schleiermacher from Stubenrauch, June 20, 1792. *Br*. III, 46.

and cryptic, continually diminishes into what even the dean of Schleier-macher scholars, Wilhelm Dilthey, is forced to call "illegibility" (Figs. M–N).[17] On page 103 the manuscript breaks off abruptly and thus remains a fragment. The manuscript is without a title, though its four major subdivisions are labeled. These various circumstances, together with a prolixity that Dilthey correctly identifies as inviting condensation, account for the fact that the treatise has never been published in full. It has appeared only in the form of Dilthey's abridgement-paraphrase, to which he has provided the title *On Human Freedom*, and which is on the whole a reliable guide to the treatise's contents.[18]

For all its singularities, the manuscript is coherent and self-sufficient as far as it goes. Dilthey wrote of it in 1870, "This treatise was for a long time (though it unfortunately remained in obscurity) the only consistent investigation into human freedom from the side of determinism; even to-day it remains one of the most fundamental."[19] Schleiermacher states the purpose of his treatise as that of giving "a more exact elucidation of the Kantian theory of freedom" than any that has yet appeared.[20] From evidence internal to the treatise, one sees that it is in fact a vigorous answer to the doctrine of freedom developed in Kant's second *Critique*, the *Critique of Practical Reason*, which had appeared three years earlier, in 1788.

Schleiermacher's correspondence makes it plain that the philosophy of Kant had for some time occupied a central place among his interests. From Halle, at the age of eighteen, Schleiermacher had written to his father:

> With respect to the Kantian philosophy which you have recommended for my study, I have all along had very favorable opinions of it, simply because it leads reason back from the metaphysical wastelands into the fields that properly belong to it.[21]

As a seminarian in Barby he had read Kant's *Prolegomena to Any Future Metaphysic* (1783) — the companion volume to Kant's more massive first *Critique*, the *Critique of Pure Reason* (1781), which Schleiermacher began to study at Halle. There he also studied Kant's second *Critique* (1788), together with its companion volume, the *Groundwork of the*

[17]Dilthey, *Leben Schleiermachers*, 1st ed., the appendix entitled "Denkmale," 19.

[18]Denkmale, 19–46. The treatise in manuscript is *Über die Freiheit des Menschen*, Item #133 of the *Schleiermacher Nachlass*. Here I shall quote only Schleiermacher's original wording, following the MS whenever Dilthey's version is incomplete or, as sometimes happens, inaccurate. A good, brief summary of the argument of the treatise is provided by Friedrich Wilhelm Esselborn, *Die philosophischen Voraussetzungen von Schleiermachers Determinismus*, 2–6. Publication of Schleiermacher's early unpublished manuscripts has been announced as forthcoming in the critical edition of Schleiermacher's writings currently being prepared by Walter de Gruyter and Company.

[19]*Leben Schleiermachers*, ed. Redeker, I/1, 138.

[20]"Denkmale," 21.

[21]Aug. 14, 1787. *Br.* I, 66.

Metaphysic of Morals (1785).[22] His university studies of Kant went forward under the stimulation of Halle's vigorous anti-Kantian professor of philosophy, Johann August Eberhard, whom Schleiermacher both admired and increasingly criticized. After Halle, midway in his Drossen stay when his theological studies were going so badly, Schleiermacher reported to his father that he had again worked through, "*con amore*," a "great part of the Kantian writings."[23]

Writing *On Human Freedom* as he did in 1791–92, Schleiermacher did not enjoy the advantage of being able to interpret the *Critique of Practical Reason* in the light of Kant's later writings. Kant's *Religion within the Limits of Reason Alone* was not published until 1792–93, and it was yet another four years until Kant's *Metaphysic of Morals* appeared (1797). Kant's third *Critique*, the *Critique of Judgment*, had appeared in 1790, but there is no evidence that Schleiermacher was acquainted with it in 1792. Had Schleiermacher written his treatise later, his interpretation of Kant's doctrine of freedom might have been different. We shall encounter some evidence that at points Schleiermacher seems not to appreciate Kant's depth of insight. On the other hand it is a subject of frequent debate whether Kant's later writings merely clarify his two great *Critiques* of reason, or whether Kant altered his outlook with the passage of years. Interpreters of Kant may therefore find Schleiermacher's treatise of interest not only for its intrinsic value but also as a point of reference: the reaction of a close student of Kant's second *Critique*, written immediately after that book's publication and without our present advantage of hindsight.

But intrinsic value there certainly is, and Schleiermacher himself had strong views about the course of Kant's later writings. *On Human Freedom* is thoroughly critical of Kant's doctrine of freedom, and subsequent acquaintance with Kant's later publications only confirmed Schleiermacher in his criticisms. In 1802, well after the appearance of Kant's final philosophical writings, Schleiermacher wrote of his early Kant studies at Halle,

> With respect to Kant, whom I then . . . studied with pleasure and vigor, I had exactly the same feeling about his incompleteness, his confusion, his failure to understand both others and himself, as I have now with the most mature insight.[24]

There are strong arguments to be made in support of the feeling

---

[22] *Br.* I, 66; IV, 41, 5.

[23] Dec. 23, 1789. *Br.* I, 79.

[24] To Henriette Herz, Aug. 10, 1802. *Br.* I, 312. For a thorough discussion of the relation between Schleiermacher's mature views and the mature views of Kant, see August Dorner, "Schleiermachers Verhältnis zu Kant," *Theologische Studien und Kritiken*, LXXIV (1901), 5–75.

Schleiermacher expresses here. We shall later see that Schleiermacher's treatise is trenchant in discriminating specific weaknesses in Kant's doctrine of freedom. But there are three more general characteristics of the treatise that invite a word of comment before we begin our closer analysis of its content. First, Schleiermacher's treatise dates from a remarkably early period of Kant criticism. Second, Schleiermacher appears to have arrived at his criticisms of Kant with considerable independence from other Kant scholarship of the time. And finally, the issues Schleiermacher raised and examined in his treatise proved to be among the most persistent issues in Kant criticism during the 1790s and early 1800s.[25] Let us look at these three characteristics in turn.

German philosophy in 1791-92 was involved preeminently with Kant's new "critical" philosophy—that is, Kant's philosophical inquiry into the nature and limits of rationality. Eberhard, Schleiermacher's mentor at Halle, had established a new quarterly, the *Philosophisches Magazin*, published in four volumes from 1789 to 1792, devoted to criticism of Kant's philosophy. "It is our intention in this Magazine," Eberhard wrote in an editor's note, "to open a fundamental and deliberate public investigation of the basic principles of the Kantian critique of reason."[26] Schleiermacher was familiar with the *Philosophisches Magazin* and was indebted to its ongoing debates. But his treatise *On Human Freedom* goes its own distinctive way in criticizing Kant. The *Philosophisches Magazin*, even up to its final volume of 1791-92, concentrated almost exclusively on Kant's first *Critique*, which deals with rationality in its theoretical or "speculative" function. Schleiermacher's treatise of 1791-92 concentrates instead on Kant's second *Critique*, which deals with rationality in its moral or "practical" function.

The first and greatest apologist for Kant's second *Critique* was the professor of philosophy at the University of Jena, Karl Leonhard Reinhold. In 1786-87, Reinhold had published a series of *Letters on the Kantian Philosophy*, attempting to clarify important issues in Kant's first *Critique*. In response to these *Letters* Kant had written to Reinhold, "I have, excellent and kind Sir, read the beautiful *Letters* with which you

---

[25]Indeed the issues have persisted to the present. Writing in 1973, Robert Paul Wolff isolates the same central weakness of Kant's moral philosophy as we shall shortly find Schleiermacher identifying in his treatise of 1791-92: *"But since the entire elaborate resolution of the conflict of free will and determinism depended upon hypothetically applying the category of causality to noumenal action, Kant had* [in the first *Kritik*] *undermined the foundations of his ethical theory. Kant never faced this problem. Indeed, it seems likely that he never even knew it existed." The Autonomy of Reason*, 8. Wolff's emphasis.

[26]*Philosophisches Magazin*, I (1788/89), 334. It is perhaps a measure of Eberhard's success that he is today remembered chiefly as the only philosopher ever to have drawn Kant's direct polemical fire. See Henry E. Allison, *The Kant-Eberhard Controversy*, 10.

have honored my philosophy, and which nothing can exceed in graceful-ness joined with profundity. . . ."[27] In 1791–92, Reinhold published a second series of *Letters*,[28] this time clarifying, with admirable patience and lucidity, certain crucial issues in Kant's second *Critique*. In an ex-change of correspondence with Kant extending over five years Reinhold was never able to extract from the Königsberg master, now aging and hard pressed to complete the publications he had plotted out for him-self, any substantive evaluation of this later work in behalf of Kant's ideas.[29] The correspondence is poignant because Reinhold had discerned what he took to be damaging obscurities in Kant's discussion of the freedom of the will, and he very much needed to know Kant's opinion of his painstaking attempts at elucidation. This he never received.

What is of importance to us here is the fact that the difficulties of interpretation isolated by Reinhold in his 1791–92 discussion of Kant's doctrine of freedom are precisely the difficulties upon which Schleier-macher alights in his treatise written during the same period. Schleier-macher was aware of Reinhold's earlier publications.[30] Indeed he could scarcely have remained unaware of them, since Reinhold, as Kant's surrogate, was an object for attack in virtually every issue of Eberhard's *Philosophisches Magazin*. It is possible that Schleiermacher was also aware of Reinhold's second series of *Letters* dealing with Kant's second *Critique*, though we shall see in a moment that this is unlikely. But in any case, Schleiermacher's treatise presses the criticism of Kant's doc-trine of freedom far beyond the limits reached by Reinhold's apologet-ics. And whereas the criticism of Kant in Eberhard's *Philosophisches Magazin* look backward for its standard of comparison—to the seven-teenth century philosopher Gottfried Wilhelm Leibniz, and to his early eighteenth century systematizer at the University of Halle, Christian Wolff—Schleiermacher's treatise presses forward toward a novel philo-sophical position of its own. Though critical of Kant, Schleiermacher was nonetheless Kantian enough to recognize the truth of Kant's claim that David Hume's philosophical skepticism had once and for all awakened philosophy from the dogmatic slumbers of Leibnizian and Wolffian "rationalism"—which might be defined in this context as philosophy based upon the insufficiently examined assumption that reason is a true and sufficient source of knowledge about reality.

As for Kant's uncommunicated opinion about the obscurities of his philosophy which Reinhold had tried to elucidate, Paul Olivier has

---

[27] *Briefwechsel von Imm. Kant*, ed. H. E. Fischer, I, 367.

[28] The two series appeared originally in the journal *Teutsche Merkur*, 1786/87 and 1791/92. They appeared expanded and in book form as *Briefe über die Kantische Philo-sophie*, 2 vols., 1790 and 1792.

[29] Kant, *Briefwechsel*, II, 327, 342, 347, 370; III, 19, 65, 83.

[30] See *Br.* IV, 40. Schleiermacher makes one reference to a 1789 work by Reinhold in *On Human Freedom*, "Denkmale," 22.

demonstrated that in Kant's last attempt at clarifying his doctrine of freedom, the *Metaphysic of Morals* of 1787, Kant has in fact altered his terminology in the direction required by Reinhold's arguments,[31] and this means also in the direction required by Schleiermacher's criticisms. Not far enough in that direction, however. Schleiermacher's radical criticisms in *On Human Freedom* are not satisfied by the presentation of freedom in either Kant or Reinhold. (The question of whether Schleier-macher's radical criticisms are *justified* will be a subject of succeeding chapters.)

Certain biographical facts from the period of Schleiermacher's trea-tise *On Human Freedom* help to account for both the critical incisiveness and the tenacious independence of that early work. In April of 1794, at the age of twenty-five, Schleiermacher submitted an autobiographical statement to his Berlin examining board in connection with his second and final series of theological examinations. It contains a passage of particular significance to our study. Speaking of his early teens, Schleier-macher writes:

> I had a peculiar affliction. It consisted in an amazing skepticism, the origin of which I can no longer recollect. I hit upon the idea, namely, that all the old authors, and with them all ancient history, were forgeries. Indeed I had no other grounds for this than that I knew no evidence for their genuineness, and that all I knew of them seemed to me fictitious and unconnected. The reputation for intelligence which I always enjoyed, and which I did not want to disturb by any disclosure of what I believed to be my exclusively great ignorance and incompetence, had produced in me a reserved taciturnity. This accounted for the fact that I kept these strange thoughts, which greatly afflicted me, to myself, and I resolved to wait for whatever I could eventually discover on my own to confirm or refute them.[32]

Joined with Schleiermacher's intellect, there was always the skeptical strain that he mentions in this description of his youthful outlook. It impelled him to suspend belief until he could establish his own grounds for conviction, or, as we shall see in our discussion of Schleiermacher's romantic sensibilities, to suspend belief indefinitely when grounds for conviction appeared to elude finite human capacities. Schleiermacher's skepticism touched every element of his early education: the pietistic orthodoxy of his upbringing; the classical studies that were later to culminate in his monumental Plato scholarship; the dogmatic metaphys-ics of Leibniz and Wolff, which had already been an object of the skepti-cism of Hume and Kant; and finally the critical and moral philosophy of Kant himself.

---

[31] *Zum Willensproblem bei Kant und Reinhold*, 62–65.
[32] *Br.* I, 6.

Besides his skepticism, we see also in Schleiermacher's autobiographical sketch his awareness of the inadequacy of his formal education ("what I believed to be my exclusively great ignorance and incompetence"). Schleiermacher's family moved their place of residence repeatedly, and as a result the boy's schooling was discontinuous and erratic. From the age of ten to twelve he was not in school at all. "We still keep him at home," his mother wrote to her brother Stubenrauch in 1780,

> because he already knows enough for his age. We only wish that his heart were as good as his intellect is vigorous; his heart is already corrupted by the amount of praise which those in Breslau have bestowed on him on account of his intellect. . . . Had we left him in Breslau, he would certainly have been ready for the University by the age of fourteen, so well does he progress in everything.[33]

At home, his mother continues, "Fritz occupies himself with French and Latin translations."

In his letters throughout his career Schleiermacher repeatedly complains of what he calls his *angestammte Faulheit*, "innate laziness."[34] It seems a paradoxical complaint from one whose collected works were to fill thirty-one volumes, and who left a personal correspondence of hundreds upon hundreds of letters,[35] until one realizes that what Schleiermacher is referring to is not simply idleness — though in a self-deprecatory way that is part of his meaning. He is referring to his peculiar inability from childhood forward to discipline himself to formal, balanced organization of his studies. From Drossen he wrote to his father:

> You have asked me repeatedly about the apportionment of my time. With me, studying is too passionate, if I may say so, for me to keep certain arbitrary hours in which I busy myself with this or that, and then approximately with the striking of the clock to switch over to some completely different discipline of knowledge. I undertake everything with a certain vehemence, and I do not rest until I am finished with it — at least to a certain point.[36]

This intense but formally unbalanced procedure Schleiermacher called

---

[33] *Br.* I, 19–20.

[34] Letter of Feb. 17, 1798. *Briefe Friedrich Schleiermachers an August Wilhelm Schlegel*, ed. Elstner and Klingner, 589. See also, for example, letter to Herz, Apr. 14, 1799, *Br.* I, 217, and *Friedrich Schleiermachers Briefwechsel mit seiner Braut*, ed. Meisner, 149, 190, and 205.

[35] The 1910 report of the Berlin *Litteraturarchiv* numbered the total holdings of letters "to and from Schleiermacher" at 3,294. Heinrich Meisner and Erich Schmidt, "*Bericht der Litteraturarchiv-Gesellschaft in Berlin für die Jahre 1903–1909*," in *Mitteilungen aus dem Litteraturarchive in Berlin*, Neue Folge 3 (Berlin: Litteraturarchiv-Gesellschaft, 1910), 8. Meisner catalogues Schleiermacher's letters in the *Zentralblatt für Bibliothekswesen*, ed. Paul Schwenke, XXIX (Leipzig: Otto Harrassowitz, 1912), 542–51. Since 1910 numerous other letters have come to light. See Tice, *Schleiermacher Bibliography*, 29–39.

[36] Dec. 23, 1789. *Br.* I, 78.

studying *con amore*. During Schleiermacher's Drossen and Schlobitten years this intellectual "vehemence" was absorbed by the moral philosophy of Kant, even to the detriment of his theological examination grades,[37] and his tenacious attention *con amore* is reflected in the incisiveness of his critique of Kant in *On Human Freedom*.

Finally, the novelty and independence of Schleiermacher's critique of Kant must relate in part to what Schleiermacher in his autobiographical sketch calls his "reserved taciturnity."[38] Before his entry into the romantic circle of friends in Berlin in 1796, and in a certain sense even long afterward, Schleiermacher was a solitary thinker. From childhood onward his doubts about matters accepted as established by those around him turned his skeptical reflections inward and rendered him aloof and secretive. In an 1802 letter to a friend Schleiermacher provides a glimpse into his character as a student at Halle some dozen years before:

> Let me communicate to you a testimonial, or rather a sketch, which someone—I no longer know who—made of me for my father when I was at the University. My father communicated the sketch to me afterwards, and I still do not know who could have known me so closely in those days, since I associated with almost no one. I was, it says, very negligent in my appearance, had entirely the nature of a person turned inward upon himself, cynical in my whole mode of life, very frugal, but in society, and to please my friends, ready to sacrifice everything, even the most urgent necessities; industrious on my own, though only by fits and starts, and always a poor attender at the lectures, which I appeared to despise; moreover, seeking privacy almost assiduously, but upon coming among the aristocratic and rich, acting as if I were both in even higher degree than they; cold and proud toward all superiors, and especially toward my teachers and masters.

"Do you recognize me in this picture?" Schleiermacher asks his correspondent. "It has several strange features, it is true . . . , but there was also much resemblance in it. Only you must remember that at that period a great deal in me still lay deeply asleep."[39]

Schleiermacher's disposition to personal independence, so obvious to his anonymous observer at Halle, had been cultivated during his earlier years of cloistered schooling among the Bohemian Brethren.[40]

---

[37]Schleiermacher's examination grades have been preserved: on all subjects "good," "very good," or "excellent"—except dogmatic theology (*Dogmatik*), on which he was graded "fair" (*ziemlich*). Heinrich Meisner, *Schleiermachers Lehrjahre*, 48.

[38]See Schleiermacher's discussion of his taciturnity in the exchange of letters with his bride-to-be, Feb. 19 and Mar. 3, 1809. *Br.* II, 223 and 225.

[39]To Eleonore Grunow, Aug. 19, 1802. *Br.* I, 318–19.

[40]For an exhaustive chronicling of these earliest years of Schleiermacher's schooling among the Bohemian Brethren see E. R. Meyer, *Schleiermachers und C. G. von Brinkmanns Gang durch die Brüdergemeine*.

During his Drossen and Schlobitten years immediately after Halle, his disposition to intellectual independence was reinforced by the geographical isolation of those two towns. From Drossen, for example, Schleiermacher wrote to his friend Brinkmann, still at Halle:

> Here there are few bookish friends, and also few books, and the whole of Frankfurt has no real literate society and no book-lender. Thus one remains a long time unacquainted not only with the newest books but also with the newest happenings in the scholarly world.[41]

Later he wrote more specifically, "Besides the *Allgemeine Literatur-Zeitung* and the *Allgemeine deutsche Bibliothek*, I see here no critical journal."[42] This situation was if anything worse in isolated Schlobitten. Thus we can assume with some assurance that Schleiermacher did not know Reinhold's *Letters* on Kant's moral philosophy (above, p. 14), which were appearing in the journal *Teutsche Merkur* during the very months of 1791–92 in which Schleiermacher, in Schlobitten, was writing his treatise *On Human Freedom*.

With an extensive manuscript of *On Human Freedom* in hand and tentative plans to have it published, Schleiermacher left Schlobitten in May of 1793. The plans for publication were never carried through. Schleiermacher spent the summer in Drossen with the Stubenrauchs, then in September went to Berlin where he took positions in an orphanage and as an instructor in the seminar for teachers conducted by the famous Berlin educator Friedrich Gedike. In March of 1794, Schleiermacher completed the final series of his theological examinations[43] and was ordained as a minister of the Reformed Church. In April, 1794, he left Berlin to assume the position of assistant minister in the church of Pastor Schumann, brother-in-law of Stubenrauch and of Schleiermacher's mother, in the town of Landsberg on the Warthe,[44] not far from Drossen. There for two years he preached and taught the church's young people. There, too, with Pastor Schumann's daughter, Schleiermacher had his first experience of the emotional involvement with married women that we shall encounter as a veritable leitmotif throughout the early romantic movement, now beginning to ferment in Berlin.[45]

---

[41]July 22, 1789. *Br.* IV, 17.

[42]To Brinkmann, Dec. 9, 1789. *Br.* IV, 41.

[43]In this second series of examinations, as in the first, Schleiermacher's only undistinguished mark was in dogmatic theology. Meisner, *Lehrjahre*, 66.

[44]Now Gorzów, Poland.

[45]See Schleiermacher's account of his inexperienced involvement with his married cousin, Frau Benecke, née Schumann, in the letter to Brinkmann, Aug. 8, 1789. *Br.* IV, 22. For his later reflections on the involvement see the letter of 1801 in *Schleiermacher als Mensch. Sein Werden*, ed. Meisner, 225 and the letter of 1808 in *Braut*, 118.

In 1796, Schleiermacher was to leave Landsberg and enter the ferment of Berlin life. With some justification, Berlin's early romantic movement has the image of libertinism and lack of discipline, not only in matters of conjugal mores, but in philosophical thinking as well. It is therefore of the utmost importance for us to observe that Schleiermacher's participation in the freedoms and excesses of romanticism came after a decade of analytic philosophical preparation. By the time of his entry into the Berlin romantic circle—where Schleiermacher's horizons were to be extended by such friends as Friedrich Schlegel and his depths stirred by such companions as Henriette Herz—he had prepared himself for romanticism by years of almost ascetic philosophical concentration. This previous discipline entitled him, we might say, to his newfound romantic freedoms.

Our appreciation of Schleiermacher's developing romanticism must follow the same pattern. With his experiences in the Berlin of 1796, Schleiermacher's earlier philosophical preparations came to fruition. Only with corresponding preparation may we hope for the same result in this study. Thus we turn first to a philosophical analysis of Schleiermacher's treatise *On Human Freedom* and its Kantian background. The reader interested primarily in Schleiermacher's romanticism *per se* would be ill advised to proceed directly to the freer, more biographical materials of Parts II and III.

Chapter 2. Kant's Doctrine of Transcendental Freedom

The philosophy of Kant can be fully understood without more intimate occupation with his character and his life; Schleiermacher's significance, his world view, and his works require a biographical presentation to be fundamentally understood.

These words open Wilhelm Dilthey's monumental intellectual biography of Schleiermacher.[1] Doubtless there is oversimplification in Dilthey's assertion, but there is truth as well. As we turn to an analysis of Kant's doctrine of freedom, we now set aside explicitly biographical concerns for a while, except to recall here at the beginning a biographical fact presented in Chapter 1. An analysis of Schleiermacher's concept of freedom must begin with Kant, since that is where Schleiermacher's own philosophical thinking began. We must therefore try in this chapter to understand Kant's doctrine of freedom as Schleiermacher understood it. We cannot presume to exhaust Kant's doctrine here, probably not even to present it convincingly. We can only discuss as much of it as is necessary background for our study of Schleiermacher's reaction to Kant in his treatise *On Human Freedom*.

Both Schleiermacher in his treatise and Kant in his *Critique of Practical Reason* pose the question of freedom in "practical" terms, as contrasted with "theoretical" or "speculative" terms. That is, neither asks whether there is such a thing as human freedom, still less whether it can be proven in some theoretical sense that freedom is actual. They ask rather, How is freedom to be understood in order that we may clarify our experience of moral obligation? Specifically, Schleiermacher phrases the beginning ethical question of his treatise in the following terms: "How must the faculty of desire [*Begehrungsvermögen*] be constituted if it is to be consistent with an acknowledgement of moral responsibility?"[2] Kant is taking the same point of departure when in the Preface to his second *Critique* he says of freedom, "We do not understand it; rather it is the condition of the moral law, which we do know."[3] With respect to this practical point of departure, both Kant

[1]"Vorwort," *Leben Schleiermachers*, ed. Redeker, I/1, xxxiii.
[2]MS 16. Cf. "Denkmale," 24.
[3]Immanuel Kant, *Kritik der praktischen Vernunft*, 4. I usually follow the excellent translation of Lewis White Beck: Kant, *Critique of Practical Reason*. Beck's English translation

and Schleiermacher are moralists in the tradition of Aristotle. Early in Book I of the *Nicomachean Ethics*, which Schleiermacher was translating in 1789 as he worked on his three dialogues on freedom (see above, p. 9),[4] Aristotle observes in a famous sentence that "to be a competent student of what is right and just . . . one must first have received a proper upbringing in moral conduct."[5] In other words, the study of morals must presuppose moral experience. Harvard's Professor D. C. Williams used to tell of a burgher who, asked if he believed in infant baptism, replied, "Of course I do; I've seen it *done*." Our point here is that neither Kant nor Schleiermacher falls into the formal mistake of Professor Williams's burgher. The question is not whether there is such a thing as moral experience, but rather, given some kind of moral experience, how it is to be understood.[6]

Kant did not choose his practical approach to moral philosophy in the second *Critique* merely on the authority of Aristotle, of course. Kant's first *Critique* had demonstrated—to Kant's satisfaction, and to Schleiermacher's as well—that a theoretical inquiry into freedom, in contrast to a practical inquiry, is in principle impossible. The first *Critique* had left theoretical reason in an unresolved perplexity that Kant calls the "antinomy of freedom." Kant had shown in that book how theoretical reason inevitably becomes "entangled when attempting to think the unconditioned in a causal series."[7] What he means is this: as reasonable creatures we feel the urge to account in some way for the causal chains of events in which we find ourselves. Whenever we attempt to locate the beginning point of a causal chain of events, however, we find our thoughts disappearing down an infinite regress. No matter how far back we press our causal inquiry, any state of affairs in the causal chain must be thought of as preceded by still other states of affairs that have given rise to it. The chain as a whole thus remains unaccounted for, and so our rational urge to find final explanations is frustrated. We feel that "for every series of conditions there must be something unconditioned," Kant writes, "and thus a causality that is entirely self-determining." But we cannot understand what such a self-determining causality might be like or where to find it. "It is absolutely impossible to give an example of it from experience."[8]

Kant argues powerfully in the first *Critique* that theoretical reason is in principle unable to resolve this rational frustration. But he also argues that while a resolution is impossible for theoretical reason—that is, for

gives in brackets the pagination of the standard German edition which I cite here (*Königlich Preussischen Akademie der Wissenschaften*, vol. 5, 1908).

[4]Letter to Brinkmann, July 22, 1789. *Br.* IV, 19.
[5]Aristotle, *Nichomachean Ethics*, tr. Ostwald, 7.
[6]MS 12, 18, 27.
[7]Second *Kritik*, 3.
[8]Ibid., 48.

scientific reason, or reason in its function of understanding "phenomenal" events and objects as "appearances" in space and time—a resolution is not necessarily impossible for reason in some other function. Suppose there is some other realm of "events" and "objects" besides the phenomenal realm of appearances in space and time. Suppose there is some "noumenal" or "intelligible" realm, as Kant calls it—some realm of "things-in-themselves," somehow apart from their appearance to us in space and time. Reason in its theoretical function can only suppose such a realm, to be sure. But as it cannot demonstrate the possibility of such a realm, so theoretical reason cannot demonstrate its impossibility either. Thus it is at least not impossible that objects and events might somehow originate in such an "unconditioned" realm, and that such origination is what we mean by the concept of freedom.

In the second *Critique*, Kant summarizes this conclusion from the first *Critique* as follows:

> Since no absolutely unconditioned determination of causality can be found among the causes of things as appearances, we could defend the supposition of a freely acting cause when applied to a being in the world of sense only in so far as the being was regarded also as noumenon. This defense was made by showing that it was not self-contradictory to regard all its actions as physically conditioned so far as they are appearances, and yet at the same time to regard their causality as physically unconditioned so far as the acting being is regarded as a being of the understanding. Thus the concept of freedom is made the regulative principle of reason.[9]

In other words, Kant is suggesting that while theoretical argument can never prove the actuality of human freedom, there is nothing in theoretical reasoning to prevent our supposing on some other, non-theoretical grounds that as "beings of the understanding" we may exercise freedom, or "physically unconditioned" causality. "The reader should be careful to observe that in what has been said our intention has not been to establish the *reality* of freedom . . . ," Kant writes at the conclusion of his discussion of the antinomy of freedom in the *Critique of Pure Reason*. "It has not even been our intention to prove the *possibility* of freedom. . . . What we have alone been able to show, and what we have been concerned to show, is that . . . causality through freedom is at least *not incompatible* with nature."[10]

This, then, is where Kant's first *Critique* was forced to leave the matter. As he begins the second *Critique*, therefore, Kant has two

---

[9]Ibid.

[10]Immanuel Kant, *Kritik der reinen Vernunft*, A557–58. Kant's emphases. I often follow the translation of Norman Kemp Smith: *Immanuel Kant's Critique of Pure Reason*. Kemp Smith's English translation gives in brackets the standard pagination for the first *Kritik* which I cite here: that of the first edition of 1781, designated by the letter "A," or that of the second edition of 1787, designated by the letter "B."

openings into a possible resolution of the antinomy of freedom. First, he can at least suppose that human beings are something more than objects, and their actions something more than events, in the phenomenal realm of space and time. Just what that "something more" is, and whether or not its supposition can be justified, reason in its theoretical function cannot say. But—and this is the second opening—in the *Critique of Practical Reason*, Kant is examining reason not in its theoretical but rather in its moral or practical function. It is at least possible that reason in this new function may have something to add in support of the supposition of a realm of human action that is non-phenomenal, or, as Kant calls it, "noumenal."

Kant's procedure in the second *Critique* is to hold this question of a non-phenomenal realm in temporary suspension while he sets about investigating the practical question, How are we to think of human reason and actions in order to account for our experience of moral obligation? More specifically, Kant's form of the question is this: How are we to think of human reason and actions in order to account for our experience of obligation *to moral law*? The first thing Kant does in his second *Critique* is to assert that moral obligation means obligation to universal and necessary moral laws, laws that may be "taken as a rule for the will of every rational being . . . ,"[11] without exception, and without regard for each individual's own preferences and inclinations.

> A practical law which I acknowledge as such must qualify for legislating universally; this is an identical and therefore a self-evident proposition. Now, if I say that my will is subject to a practical *law*, I cannot put forward my inclination . . . as fit to be a determining ground of a universal practical law. . . . For the wills of all do not then have one and the same object, but each person has his own (his own welfare), which, to be sure can accidentally agree with the purposes of others who are pursuing their own. But this agreement is far from sufficing for a law, because the exceptions that one is permitted to make are endless and cannot be definitely comprehended in a universal rule. In this way a harmony may result resembling that meeting of minds depicted in a certain satirical poem as existing between a married couple bent on going to ruin: "O, marvelous harmony, what he wants is what she wants as well."[12]

This passage from the second *Critique* is notable not only for the touch of humor with which it ends—which one must gratefully acknowledge amidst the usual densities of Kant's argument—but because it contains the most central and influential assertion of Kant's moral philosophy. Schleiermacher's disagreement with Kant will eventually center in this assertion. It is the noble assertion that our moral experience is grounded in universal moral laws that obligate us to obedience, without exception,

---

[11] Second *Kritik*, 19.
[12] Ibid., 17–18, Kant's emphasis.

and regardless of our individual inclinations. Thou shalt not kill. Thou shalt not bear false witness. Such are moral laws that tradition has provided us. With heroic, persuasive force, Kant argues that without such universal laws morality is left resting only upon conflicting interests, and, like the married couple of his example, is harmonious only in being bent on going to ruin.

Kant goes on to specify just what the form of these universal laws of morality must be, the form expressed in his famous "categorical imperative." But that is what Kant labels "Problem II" of his second *Critique*. "Problem I" consists in granting for the moment the assertion that there are universal laws of morality and then discovering the nature of the human will that can account for our obligation to obey them. Kant states the problem this way:

> Problem I. Granted that the mere legislative form of maxims is the sole sufficient determining ground of a will: to find the character of that will which is determinable by it alone.[13]

Our course now will be to follow Kant's solution to this first Problem. Fortunately the solution takes a somewhat simpler form in the second *Critique* than it does in Kant's later writings, where he modulated his discussion of free will under the influence of his critics and of Reinhold's response to those critics in Kant's behalf. Three definitions will put us in a position to state Kant's doctrine of freedom.

The first is a definition of the term *faculty of desire* (*Begehrungsvermögen*). Near the beginning of his treatise *On Human Freedom*, Schleiermacher himself quotes the definition of this important term from Kant's *Critique of Practical Reason*: "The faculty of desire, according to Kant's definition, is the faculty of being, through its representations, cause of the reality of the objects of these representations."[14] In other words, Schleiermacher follows Kant in defining the faculty of desire as a person's capacity to "represent" or call forth in thought some object in such a way as to establish the person's desire to make that object a reality. The "object" here might be any intended goal, from the creation of some object of art, let us say, to the holding of one's tongue when provoked. In short, *faculty of desire* is the general term for a person's capacity to *intend*.

---

[13]Ibid., 28.

[14]"Denkmale," 22. Also Kant, second *Kritik*, 9n. I use "representation" to translate the German *Vorstellung*, as is commonly the case in English translations of Kant. "Idea" or "notion" would often read more smoothly, but the reader would more easily lose sight of the fact that a precise Kantian term is being indicated. I have tried to render every German term consistently by a single English equivalent in this way. The exceptions — *Gemüth, Seele, Geist, Eigenthümlichkeit* — I shall note when they appear. The best statement of the principles of philosophic translation I know is found in Allan Bloom's Preface to his translation of the *Republic* of Plato (see Bibliography).

If the intended goal is one to which a person is inclined by what Kant calls "empirically conditioned" or "subjective" motives, that is, by any motivation related to the realm of the person's senses, then the person's intention is being determined by the *lower faculty of desire* (*unteres Begehrungsvermögen*). If on the other hand the intended goal is presented to a person by pure reason alone—more precisely, by "pure practical reason," or pure reason in its moral function—then the person's intention is being determined by the *higher faculty of desire* (*oberes Begehrungsvermögen*).[15]

With these terms we are prepared for Kant's doctrine of freedom. If we are to account for our experience of obligation to moral law, Kant argues, then we must presuppose that we are capable of formulating our intentions under the exclusive determination of our higher faculty of desire. This presupposition is what Kant calls the postulate of *transcendental freedom*.

By the adjective "transcendental" Kant means that freedom, as he defines it, is an absolutely necessary postulate if we are to account for our experience of obligation to moral law. Now Kant knew perfectly well that most of our actions are ambiguously motivated. Usually our intentions are determined not by "pure practical reason" but by an interaction of our sensible and our rational capacities. But Kant was dauntlessly committed to his insight that we can be obligated to universal moral laws, disclosed to us by reason, only if we are free always to obey them. Otherwise we are able to rationalize our actions whenever we wish by arguing, "Yes, I see that reason demands that we must never bear false witness; for if I feel that I am sometimes justified in lying, then you may feel the same, and truth is nowhere to be trusted. But in this particular instance, my concern for the loved one who was protected by my false witness surely frees me from the usual obligation." No, says Kant. In such an ethical outlook "the exceptions that one is permitted to make are endless," and human morality is in fact annihilated. Moral philosophy cannot account for the obligation to be truthful, to reverence life, or to honor promises, so long as some of us feel morally justified in sometimes lying, killing, or practicing deceit—even if something as subjectively determinative as the unjust suffering of a loved one is at stake.[16]

So Kant insists upon his postulate of transcendental freedom, freedom always to obey the moral law. This postulate, with which we shall

---

[15]Second *Kritik*, 22.

[16]This argument will occur in its most vivid and condensed form in Kant's essay of 1797, *Über ein vermeintes Recht aus Menschenliebe zu lügen*. It is available in English as "On a Supposed Right To Lie from Altruistic Motives" in Lewis White Beck's translation of Kant, *Critique of Practical Reason and Other Writings in Moral Philosophy*, in the original hardback edition (University of Chicago Press, 1949), 346–50.

soon find Schleiermacher at odds, implies the following two conditions. (1) It must be possible that the representations determining our intentions can originate in pure reason alone, uninfluenced by our sensible experience. To put this another way, it must be possible that the representations determining our intentions can originate *a priori*, free from *a posteriori* influence. Kant's "moral laws" are *a priori* representations of this kind. Further (2) it must be possible that such an *a priori* representation of pure reason can be "sufficient of itself to determine" our intention. That is, it must be possible that a moral law can determine our intention without any admixture of empirical, or *a posteriori*, conditioning.[17] This *a priori* or "intellectual" determination of our intentions, then, is what Kant means by his term *transcendental freedom*.

Now to speak of something without any admixture of empirical conditioning is to speak of something non-phenomenal, something somehow outside the realm of causal connections, "outside" the realm of space and time. It is to speak of something in that "noumenal" realm which Kant's first *Critique* has allowed as possible but not established as actual. We can therefore see why Kant calls transcendental freedom a "postulate" of practical reason. Being somehow exempt from the conditions of space and time, the actuality of transcendental freedom can never be demonstrated by arguments of theoretical reason. It is not a hypothesis awaiting confirmation by empirical observation. In the first *Critique* Kant has argued with overwhelming force that theoretical reason is confined to the island of cause and effect relations. From the phenomenal perspective of theoretical reason, transcendental freedom is shrouded in noumenal fog, possibly illusory, certainly inaccessible. But for practical reason, for reason in its moral function, transcendental freedom is a necessary supposition. Without it, Kant argues, we cannot account for our experience of moral obligation.

Thus we are brought back to the first assumption of Kant's moral philosophy, as Schleiermacher understood it. Kant does not intend to prove that there are such things as moral obligation and freedom.[18] He intends only to discover how freedom must be understood if we are to account for our experience of moral obligation. The result of Kant's inquiry is the postulate of transcendental freedom. "No one would hazard the risk of introducing freedom into science," he writes, "had not the moral law and, with it, practical reason come and forced this concept upon us."[19]

---

[17]Second *Kritik*, 15.

[18]See Robert Paul Wolff's assertion that in the *Groundwork of the Metaphysic of Morals* of 1785, Kant does in fact argue for the inevitability of moral obligation, albeit obscurely. *The Autonomy of Reason*, 24–28. Wolff is probably correct, but this does not materially affect Schleiermacher's line of argument.

[19]Second *Kritik*, 30.

This does not mean, however, that Kant altogether neglects to apply scientific analysis to the concept of transcendental freedom. It is an exotic and tantalizing philosophical concept, inviting analysis to the limits of theoretical reason's capacity. In particular, Kant was disturbed by one very important question that appears to invite investigation by the science of "anthropology," which, as Kant defined it, included the study of psychology. The question is this: How exactly does transcendental freedom determine our intentions? Transcendental freedom is postulated in the noumenal realm, free from the necessities of phenomenal causality. Our intentions, on the other hand, operate in the world of space and time and causal connection. How can these two realms interact? How can transcendental freedom "determine" our intentions when they are already determined by their location in an unbroken chain of phenomenal causes and effects?

This question expresses a central difficulty in the interpretation of Kant's moral philosophy. It is the difficulty upon which we shall shortly find Schleiermacher's treatise *On Human Freedom* focusing. To understand the issue in question we must introduce one further Kantian term—though if Schleiermacher's interpretation of Kant is correct, in the end this term obscures more than it clarifies. It is the term *incentive* (*Triebfeder*), to which Kant devotes the chapter of his second *Critique* entitled "The Incentives of Pure Practical Reason." Kant defines incentive as "a subjective determining ground of the will."[20] Both Kant and Schleiermacher seem to mean by an incentive a representation together with its subjective means of influencing our intentions; and both seem to believe that the means by which a representation influences our intentions is always some form of feeling associated with that representation—that is, some form of pleasure or pain. My incentive to remain standing while resting in the woods is the pain associated in my mind with the recollection of earlier encounters with chiggers. The recollection of chiggers here is the "representation"; the recollection and its associated pain together constitute the "incentive" to remain standing.

The goal of Kant's chapter on incentives then is "to determine carefully in what way the moral law becomes an incentive and, since the moral law *is* such an incentive, to determine what happens to the human faculty of desire as a consequence [*Wirkung*] of this determining ground."[21] Immediately an obstacle presents itself. An incentive involves feeling as its means of influencing our intentions. But feeling is what Kant calls a "sensuous impulse," and we have already seen Kant's argument that the influence of the moral law upon our intentions must be *a priori* and not by any sensuous or empirical means. If moral

---

[20]Ibid., 72.
[21]Ibid.

obligation is not to be undermined, Kant writes, then we must postulate that "in a practical law, reason determines the will *directly*, not through an intervening feeling of pleasure or displeasure, even if this pleasure is taken in the law itself."[22]

> If a determination of the will occurs in accordance with the moral law, but only by means of a feeling *of any kind whatsoever*—a feeling which must be presupposed in order that the law may become a sufficient determining ground of the will, so that this determination does not occur for the sake of the law alone—then the action may claim legality but not morality.[23]

Thus Kant's question of how the moral law can become an incentive is highly problematic. Incentives involve feelings, and yet, if moral obligation is not to be undermined, the means of influence of the moral law cannot involve feeling "of any kind whatsoever."

Kant tries to overcome this obstacle by postulating a unique feeling which he calls "respect for the moral law." This respect, he writes, is a "positive feeling," and yet a feeling "not of empirical origin."

> This feeling is one which can be known *a priori*. Respect for the moral law, therefore, is a feeling produced by an intellectual cause, and this feeling is the only one which we can know completely *a priori* and the necessity of which we can discern.[24]

Kant maintains that the concept of respect—a feeling in a psychological class by itself—provides the resolution of his problematic question about how the moral law can become an incentive. Our incentive to do the moral thing is the moral law itself, together with the motivating feeling of respect for the moral law. Intentions resulting from this incentive have not only legality but also morality, because the unique motivating feeling of respect is not empirical or sensible but rather *a priori*. "Respect for the moral law," Kant concludes, "is the sole and undoubted moral incentive."[25]

We must now anticipate Schleiermacher's argument with Kant that will occupy us for the remaining chapters of Part I, for we have exposed what critics of Kant have perennially identified as a weak point in Kant's moral philosophy. The weakness consists in the fact that Kant's "respect" is a highly peculiar kind of feeling. We have observed that Kant places his concept of respect for the moral law in a psychological class by itself. But does it in fact belong in a psychological class at all? Kant's own anthropological analysis includes all of our psychological life in the phenomenal realm of experience, the realm of cause and effect interrelations in space and time. Kant's writings show him to be ambiguous in

---

[22]Ibid., 25. Emphasis added.
[23]Ibid., 71. Emphasis added.
[24]Ibid., 73.
[25]Ibid., 78.

his opinion of whether the causal operations of the mind can ever be completely understood, of whether psychology can ever become an exact science.[26] But in all three of his great *Critiques* Kant seems consistently to presuppose that our psychological states arise without exception from natural causes, including of course our own prior psychological conditions. And yet respect for the moral law, he claims, is "a feeling produced by an intellectual cause." It is not psychological in origin. Its origin is not from the phenomenal but rather from the noumenal realm.

Now if by saying that respect is a feeling produced by an intellectual cause, Kant meant to say only that respect for the moral law is produced in the course of our intellectual struggles with moral issues, Schleiermacher would certainly have been able to agree. Kant does in fact say that respect engages "in conflict with its subjective antagonists," namely, with other feelings, in our moral experience. But he makes it clear that respect as he defines it does not arise out of these psychological struggles. Respect is the incentive of the *a priori* moral law. As a concept, the feeling of respect "is the only one which we can know completely *a priori* and the necessity of which we can discern." Its origins are not *a posteriori* but *a priori*, not phenomenal but noumenal. The feeling of respect is not "subjective" but "objective," that is, a universal and necessary presupposition to any account of moral obligation.

Thus Kant's philosophical attempt to account for our moral experience leads him to regard human beings "as belonging to two worlds," the phenomenal and the noumenal, or "the world of sense" and "the intelligible world."[27] Persistently Kant struggles to clarify the relation between these two worlds. But his attempt remains a struggle. Just how severe a struggle it is becomes evident in the section of the second *Critique* dealing with the relation between the moral incentive of respect and the sensible incentives that are "its subjective antagonists." While Kant asserts at one place that "respect for the moral law is the sole and undoubted moral incentive," at another place the ambiguity of his argument forces him to equivocate. "Respect for the law is *not* the incentive to morality," he writes; "it is morality itself, *regarded subjectively as an incentive*. . . ."[28] That is a most unclear assertion. Furthermore, this equivocation is not an isolated instance. It is rather an example of the ambiguity in Kant's moral philosophy that has occupied both Kantians and their critics ever sinse.

When Kant says that the incentive to obey the moral law "is produced by an intellectual cause," that in his terminology is equivalent to saying that it is produced by an act of transcendental freedom. Kant

---

[26]See Wolff's discussion of this ambiguity in *Autonomy*, 19.
[27]Second *Kritik*, 87.
[28]Ibid., 78, 76. Emphasis added.

defines transcendental freedom as the *a priori* or "intellectual" determination of our intentions (above, p. 27). And so the questions with which Kant is struggling in these pages of his *Critique* are these: How can respect, as a "positive feeling which is not of empirical origin," enter into "conflict" with our empirical feelings, since the latter are bound up in their own unbroken chain of psychological causality? How can pure reason's moral incentive ever break into the causal continuum of our psychological activity? In an act of transcendental freedom, Kant writes, "reason becomes, in the field of experience, an efficient cause through ideas."[29] But how can this be, when the field of experience, as Kant himself defines it, is an infinite and unbroken fabric of efficient causality?

This central problem leads Kant to speak of the noumenal and the phenomenal in terms suggesting separate but parallel realms of reality. This contention will be a focal point of Schleiermacher's criticism, and Kant's clearest statement of this dualism in the second *Critique* deserves quoting in full:

> It may be admitted that if it were possible for us to have so deep an insight into a man's character, as shown both in inner and in outer actions, that every, even the least, incentive to these actions and all external occasions which affect them were so known to us that his future conduct could be predicted with as great a certainty as the occurrence of a solar or lunar eclipse, we could nevertheless still assert that the man is free. For if we were capable of another view (which, however, is certainly not given us, but in place of which we have only the concept of reason), i.e., if we were capable of an intellectual intuition of the same subject, we would then discover that the entire chain of appearances, with reference to that which concerns only the moral law, depends upon the spontaneity of the subject as a thing-in-itself, for the determination of which no physical explanation can be given.[30]

The "intellectual intuition" mentioned here is of course lacking to us. As we have seen, Kant maintains that we have no basis for a theoretical understanding of transcendental freedom. But, the paragraph concludes, the moral law nevertheless "assures us" that we may postulate transcendental freedom—"the spontaneity of the subject as a thing-in-itself"—in spite of the fact that neither the transcendental spontaneity nor the noumenal subject is ever to be met with in any possible experience.

For the determinations of transcendental freedom, Kant writes, "no physical explanation can be given." The means of its operation are ineffable:

[29]Ibid., 48.
[30]Ibid., 99.

> For how a law in itself can be the direct determining ground of the will (which is the essence of morality) is an insoluble problem for human reason. It is identical with the problem of how a free will is possible.[31]

Already in the Preface to his second *Critique* Kant has warned his reader of transcendental freedom's "complete incomprehensibility."[32] It would therefore seem that in specifying just where the incomprehensibility lies, our understanding of Kant's doctrine of transcendental freedom has gone as far as it may be expected to go. Transcendental freedom is ultimately a Kantian doctrine of belief.

[31] Ibid., 72–73.
[32] Ibid., 7.

Chapter 3. Schleiermacher's Analysis of Human Choosing

The activities of choice alter as richly and as quickly as only the flux of outer conditions can. Choice is in every moment called not only into life, but into superabundant, multifarious, and active life. Our fantasy, understanding, and reason leave choice never at rest. It lusts, selects, desires, resolves, and acts in every moment of its existence.

We cannot pretend that we now have before us a definitive account of Kant's doctrine of transcendental freedom. Chapter 2 has provided us with what we might better call a first approximation to Kant's doctrine, understood as Schleiermacher appears to have understood it from Kant's writings up through the *Critique of Practical Reason* of 1788. But to judge from the opinions of the prominent first-generation critics of Kant, it is a good first approximation. These contemporaries were in fundamental agreement with Schleiermacher's delineation of the weaknesses of Kant's moral philosophy. Beginning with his criticisms of Kant, however, Schleiermacher's moral philosophy then follows an independent course, and many have agreed with Dilthey's judgment that Schleiermacher's ethical originality constitutes his primary claim to genius. The foundations of Schleiermacher's moral philosophy in the treatise *On Human Freedom* of 1791–92 will occupy us for the remainder of Part I. At the same time, we shall be able to refine our Kantian first approximation.

We have seen that in the Preface to his second *Critique* Kant speaks of the "complete incomprehensibility" of transcendental freedom (above, p. 32). Yet in the same sentence he insists also upon the "indispensability" of transcendental freedom as a "problematic concept" in the "complete use" of reason in its theoretical and its practical functions.[1] Schleiermacher accepts Kant's first characterization of the concept of transcendental freedom, its incomprehensibility, but not the

---

[1]Kant, second *Kritik*, 7. "Problematic concept" has for Kant an exact philosophical meaning. He writes, "If the objective reality of a concept cannot be in any way known, while yet the concept contains no contradiction and also at the same time is connected with other modes of knowledge that involve given concepts which it serves to limit, I entitle that concept problematic" (first *Kritik*, A254). Thus the first *Kritik* prepares the way for the second, since transcendental freedom is precisely such a problematic concept.

second, its indispensability. Awakened into intellectual life as he was by
Kant's *Critique of Pure Reason*, Schleiermacher accepted the limits to
our knowledge established by Kant's critical philosophy. He was quick to
agree with Kant that a concept such as transcendental freedom must
inevitably remain incomprehensible to us. Kant at one point defines
transcendental freedom as a determination of our intentions, to which
"nothing is antecedent."[2] Of course, then, we can have no theoretical
knowledge of transcendental freedom. According to one of the central
contentions of Kant's first *Critique*, the possibility of theoretical knowledge necessarily presupposes our perceiving events as the effects of
causal antecedents. Kant argues with great persuasive power that there
is simply no other way to perceive. Causality is one of the essential
categories of all knowledge, without which our senses remain blind and
perceptual understanding is impossible.

Schleiermacher agreed with Kant in all of this. Throughout his
career he was what we might call a "strict constructionist" of the contentions of Kant's first *Critique* concerning the scope and limits of human knowing. That is, he not only accepted Kant's critical analysis of
the limits of our knowledge but applied it strictly in all his philosophical
thinking—in fact, as we are about to see, applied it more strictly than
Kant himself. Let us note first, however, that Schleiermacher's strict
construction of Kant's first *Critique*—in particular, of its demonstration
of causality's necessary role in all human experience—goes further
toward accounting for his commitment to a philosophy of determinism
than either the predestinarianism of his Calvinistic upbringing or his
familiarity with the philosophy of Leibniz, both of which are sometimes
mentioned as possible roots of Schleiermacher's deterministic predilec-
tion.[3]

It is in part because of the theoretical incomprehensibility of transcendental freedom that Schleiermacher finds it impossible to accept
what Kant calls the ethical indispensibility of that concept. It is clear
from the beginning of Schleiermacher's treatise *On Human Freedom* that
he rejects Kant's very idea of a noumenal realm, and with that idea, all
its accompanying concepts, such as things-in-themselves and transcendental freedom. Schleiermacher does not reject these notions because
he believes he can demonstrate the falsity of the idea of a noumenal
realm. He rejects Kant's noumenal realm because he does not believe
that its concepts are necessary to moral philosophy. He believes that the
question, "How may we account for our experience of moral obligation?" can be answered without recourse to Kant's incomprehensible

---

[2]Second *Kritik*, 97.

[3]On the influence of Calvinism, see Friedrich Wilhelm Esselborn, *Die philosophischen
Voraussetzungen von Schleiermachers Determinismus*, 9–10. On the influence of Leibniz, see
Dilthey, *Leben Schleiermachers*, ed. Redeker, I/1, 87.

concept of transcendental freedom, or to the equally perplexing notion of a person as a non-phenomenal thing-in-itself. Schleiermacher believes that ethical analysis can be regarded from a phenomenal point of view, that moral philosophy like theoretical philosophy can, indeed must, confine its sphere of operations to the limits of knowledge defined by Kant in his first *Critique*.

It is often remarked that Kant was led to the extreme of speaking of an incomprehensible, non-phenomenal realm by his profound sensitivity to the human capacities for dignity and for evil—capacities that are themselves ultimately incomprehensible to human understanding. It is often remarked also that in comparison to Kant, Schleiermacher was deficient in his appreciation of the human capacity for evil. There is truth in these remarks. Schleiermacher may perhaps be suspected of a lack of philosophical imagination, even a lack of moral sensitivity, in his phenomenological outlook. The charge is at least worth keeping in mind as we proceed. But be that as it may, Schleiermacher's point of view is clear. He felt that Kant's philosophy had unnecessarily abandoned the phenomenal perspective in favor of a problematic noumenal one, that Kant had too hastily stepped out of the world of sense into what Kant calls "the intelligible world."[4]

Schleiermacher's relations with certain of his contemporaries help to explain his difference of opinion with Kant. Both Schleiermacher's teacher Johann August Eberhard and the influential philosopher Friedrich Heinrich Jacobi, whom Schleiermacher was puzzling over at Halle[5] and whom in time he grew to love, had early focused criticism upon Kant's attempt to establish his philosophical dualism: his postulation of an "intelligible" world in addition to the world of time and space and ordinary experience. Concerning Kant's notion of the "thing-in-itself," for example, Jacobi had written in a shrewd epigram of 1786, "Without this assumption I cannot enter Kant's system, and with this assumption I cannot remain in it."[6] Three years after Jacobi's epigram, the fourth quarterly issue of the first volume of Eberhard's *Philosophisches Magazin* had carried an article keenly critical of Kant's first *Critique* for its problematic concepts of the thing-in-itself and transcendental freedom, which, as the author bluntly observes, are "not even in the world."[7]

Unquestionably, Schleiermacher's rejection of Kant's dualism was indebted to these earlier criticisms. Yet, as we have seen, Eberhard's *Magazin* looked backward, claiming that what Kant was attempting to do—namely, to rescue philosophy from the stranglehold of David

---

[4]Second *Kritik*, 50.

[5]Letter to his father, Aug. 14, 1787. *Br.* I, 66.

[6]"Beylage," *David Hume über den Glauben*, 304.

[7]J. Maass, "Über die Antinomie der reinen Vernunft," *Philosophisches Magazin*, I/4, 489. Maass was a co-founder of the *Magazin* with Eberhard.

Hume's skepticism—the philosophy of Leibniz had done already, and better, before Hume had ever set pen to paper.[8] Schleiermacher, however, was far more critical of Leibniz than he was of Kant. Schleiermacher greatly admired Leibniz's mathematical genius, but he left a small notebook, probably dating from 1797–98, filled with astringent criticisms of Leibniz's metaphysics. If Schleiermacher rejected Kant's noumenal realm as incomprehensible and dispensable, he dismissed Leibniz's "realm of monads" as an "elfin kingdom" (*Elfenreich*).[9]

As for Jacobi, the lesson he had drawn from Kant's philosophy was that no philosophy whatsoever can consistently account for our experience—neither the philosophy of Kant nor that of Leibniz. Jacobi believed that the only philosophy which may even lay claim to such consistency is that of Benedict Spinoza.[10] But Jacobi, like most thinkers of the eighteenth century, had to reject that seventeenth century philosopher as fundamentally in error because of his notorious naturalism and atheism. All that is left to us, Jacobi believed, is a *salto mortale*,[11] a "mortal leap" to faith: faith in the veracity of our sensible experience, and faith in the ultimate justifiability of our experience of moral obligation. "Every purely ethical, truly virtuous action," Jacobi writes, "is in relation to nature a miracle, and reveals Him who alone can perform miracles."[12]

Schleiermacher was a stranger, both temperamentally and philosophically, to Jacobi's notion of a leap of faith. At the age of eleven he had already found himself unable to make the leap to belief in orthodox interpretations of the Christian doctrine of Christ's vicarious atonement for human sins.[13] He was no more able to share Jacobi's sense of need for a leap of faith in the face of incomplete philosophical comprehension. And even Kant's vigorous attempt to demonstrate the necessity of "rational belief," postulated upon the basis of certain unavoidable "felt needs of reason,"[14] failed to convince him.

---

[8] *Philosophisches Magazin*, I/1, 26–27. Thus the satirical title of Kant's response to Eberhard, published in 1790, "On a Discovery According to which Any New Critique of Pure Reason Is Supposed to Have Been Made Superfluous by an Earlier One." See Henry Allison, *The Kant-Eberhard Controversy*, for a translation of and commentary on Kant's article.

[9] "Denkmale," 72.

[10] *David Hume über den Glauben*, 116.

[11] Jacobi, *Über die Lehre des Spinoza in Briefen an Herrn Moses Mendelssohn*, 59.

[12] *David Hume über den Glauben*, 121.

[13] See Schleiermacher's "Autobiography," *Br.* I, 7. See also above, p. 7.

[14] These phrases are from what is to me the clearest and most compact statement of Kant's justification for postulating concepts beyond those of phenomenal experience, his essay of 1786, *Was heisst: Sich im Denken Orientieren?* It is available in English as "What is Orientation in Thinking" in Lewis White Beck's translation of Kant, *Critique of Practical Reason and Other Writings in Moral Philosophy*, in the original hardback edition (University of Chicago Press, 1949), 293–305. My thanks to Professor Richard R. Niebuhr, who first acquainted me with this essay.

Schleiermacher was never able to accept Kant's division of human experience into two worlds. Instead he attempts to account for our moral experience by regarding us as beings wholly immersed in one world, the world of time and space. He thinks of the phenomena of the world as infinite in their scope and complexity. He shares Jacobi's sense that complete philosophical comprehension of the world will always elude us. But he does not share the heart's need for certainty which Jacobi satisfies by a *salto mortale* of faith, nor does he share the felt need of reason to "think the unconditioned in a causal series" (above, p. 22), which Kant satisfies by his postulate of transcendental freedom. Rather we see incipient in Schleiermacher's treatise of 1792 something we shall be encountering repeatedly in what follows, namely, Schleiermacher's willingness to live his life within the order of phenomenal causality, to make his religious peace and to seek his ethical vision within the realm of time and space. To be sure, the restlessness of finitude is a part of the dynamics of life. But in Schleiermacher it takes the romantic form of a yearning of the finite for the infinite, not a pietistic leaping to certainty or a rationalistic grasping for completeness. Even after the fading of the early romantic movement that was to bring Schleiermacher's "taste for the infinite" to its fullest expression, he never lost the sense of modesty he felt appropriate to the finite under the aspect of the infinite. Nowhere in fact are the effects of this modesty clearer than in Schleiermacher's scorn for all theological speculation that presumes to extend beyond our mortal placement in the world of time and space. One finds this sense of theological modesty clearly expressed in the capstone of Schleiermacher's mature career, his monumental theological work of 1821, *The Christian Faith*:

> In general the question of the origin of all finite being is raised not in the interest of piety but in that of curiosity; hence it can be answered only by such means as curiosity offers. Piety can never show more than an indirect interest in it.[15]

Such a remark is typical of Schleiermacher's outlook. Here as elsewhere he stands in the tradition of St. Augustine of Hippo. In response to the question, "What was God doing before He created the world?" Augustine rejects even the whimsical answer, "He was preparing Hell for those prying into such deep subjects," in favor of the simple answer, "I do not know."[16]

Before we turn to Schleiermacher's own ethical analysis, it might be well to summarize his most fundamental departures from Kant. Kant

---

[15] *Der christliche Glaube*, ed. Redeker, Proposition 39.1. I often follow the English translation of the edition by H. R. Mackintosh and J. S. Stewart: Schleiermacher, *The Christian Faith*.

[16] Augustine, *Confessions*, tr. Ryan, Book XI, Ch. 12.

calls his concept of freedom "the keystone of the whole architecture of the system of pure reason."[17] Schleiermacher believes that Kant's removal of this "keystone" from the realm of phenomenal experience is necessarily destructive of any philosophy that intends to account for the moral experience of men and women immersed in the conditions of space and time. Schleiermacher's agreement with a passage from Kant like the following is therefore highly selective. Kant writes:

> Doubtless there are intelligible entities corresponding to the sensible entities; there may also be intelligible entities to which our sensible faculty of intuition has no relation whatsoever; but our concepts of understanding, being mere forms of thought for our sensible intuition, could not in the least apply to them.[18]

Schleiermacher agrees with only the final clause of this passage: our concepts of understanding cannot "in the least apply" to Kant's intelligible entities. Kant's phrase "intelligible entities" includes both his notion of noumenal things-in-themselves and his notion of human beings regarded as inhabitants of a noumenal realm, gifted with the incomprehensible faculty of transcendental freedom. Schleiermacher is among the first-generation readers of Kant who were unable to agree that "doubtless there are" such entities.

It is a striking irony, as well as a tribute of a kind to Kant, that Schleiermacher's reservations regarding the Kantian moral philosophy are expressed so exactly in the famous figure from Kant's own *Critique of Pure Reason* (A235–36), the metaphor of the island of phenomenal experience in the beckoning but treacherous sea of metaphysical illusion:

> We have now not merely explored the territory of pure understanding, and carefully surveyed every part of it, but have also measured its extent, and assigned to everything in it its rightful place. This domain is an island, enclosed by nature itself within unalterable limits. It is the land of truth—enchanting name!—surrounded by a wide and stormy ocean, the native home of illusion, where many a fog bank and many a swiftly melting iceberg give the deceptive appearance of farther shores, deluding the adventurous seafarer ever anew with empty hopes, and engaging him in enterprises he can never abandon and yet is unable to carry to completion. Before we venture on this sea, to explore it in all directions and to obtain assurance whether there be any ground for such hopes, it will be well to begin by casting a glance upon the map of the land we are about to leave, and to enquire, first, whether we cannot in any case be satisfied with what it contains—are not, indeed, under compulsion to be satisfied, inasmuch as there may be no other territory upon which we can settle.

Kant eventually claims to have discovered that "other territory," namely,

---

[17]Second *Kritik*, 3.
[18]First *Kritik*, B308–9.

the noumenal realm of his moral philosophy; thus he ventures beyond the island of phenomenal experience. Schleiermacher, however, remains "satisfied with what it contains." For he finds that the phenomenal island in fact extends toward an infinite horizon, and that the experiences it offers are endless in their complexity.

So we pass now from Schleiermacher's criticism of Kant to his own account of moral experience, given in terms of phenomenal experience. His beginning point is the insight of his first dialogue on freedom of 1789 (above, p. 10), that "one must treat willpower just like any other." *On Human Freedom* focuses attention on the human power to choose, which Schleiermacher considers to be empirically conditioned like any other mental capacity—like phantasy, for instance, defined by Schleiermacher as the causally determined faculty of the association of ideas. The opening section of Schleiermacher's treatise is therefore a phenomenal description, or phenomenology, of what Kant has termed the faculty of desire (above, p. 25). He wishes to investigate "the conditions and grounds of particular activities of the faculty of desire,"[19] or in other words, to analyze the volitional operations that bridge the interval between mere representing, in the Kantian sense of that term,[20] and effective intending.

We may recall that Kant uses the term *incentive* (*Triebfeder*) to designate a representation together with its subjective means of influencing our intentions (above, p. 28). So we might say that Schleiermacher's purpose is to investigate the conditions and grounds of our incentives. But Schleiermacher feels that Kant has never adequately looked into these conditions and grounds. He feels that Kant's term *incentive* tends to collapse the very psychological process Schleiermacher wants to spread out for examination. It tends to reify in a single concept what is in fact a complex operation or series of operations. For this reason Schleiermacher's analysis of the faculty of desire proceeds in smaller steps than Kant's.

Thus Schleiermacher begins with only the root of Kant's term *incentive* (*Triebfeder*)—namely, with the term *Trieb*, which we may translate as *impulse*. Schleiermacher appears to have borrowed this basic term from the philosopher Reinhold, who also recognized the need for a more thorough analysis of the incentives of our choosing than Kant's moral philosophy had yet provided. Moreover, a few years after Schleiermacher's treatise, *impulse* will appear as the basic term of yet another moral philosophy which tries to advance beyond Kant's and which bears many resemblances to Schleiermacher's, though we shall later see that there appears to have been no direct relation between

[19]"Denkmale," 22.
[20]See footnote 14 of Chapter 2.

them. It is the moral philosophy of the great poet and dramatist Friedrich Schiller:

> Reason has accomplished all that it can when it finds and brings forth the law; the spirited will and living feeling must carry it out. If truth is to win the victory in its strife with other forces, then it must itself first become a *force* and bring forth an *impulse* [*Trieb*] as its agent in the kingdom of appearances. For impulses are the only motive forces in the sensible world.[21]

We shall occasionally find it useful to turn to Schiller's phraseology for clarification of Schleiermacher's ethical analysis. In Chapter 6 of Part II we shall examine the relation between these two thinkers in detail.

In defining this basic term *impulse*, Schleiermacher gives it first a more general and then a more specific meaning. "By impulse," he writes, "I understand in general: the activity of the representing subject, grounded in his nature, of bringing forth representations."[22] Impulse in general designates our capacity to give rise to mental content. It is then the work of the faculty of desire to single out specific impulses that will become objects of our intentions. So the question Schleiermacher wishes to investigate now takes this form: How exactly does the faculty of desire focus our general impulses to an intensity at which some particular impulse is kindled as an intention?

In response to that question Schleiermacher describes several modes by which our intentions appear to be determined, examining them in order of their increasing complexity. The first of them is *instinct* (*Instinkt*). Instinct can be observed whenever a single object is sufficient to kindle an intention.[23] The "object" here may be either external or internal, either material or conceptual. We might clarify Schleiermacher's definition of instinct by thinking of the way we spring into action whenever the telephone rings. This would be an example of what Schleiermacher calls an "instinct of sense." Or we might think of ourselves as homeowners, indoctrinated with the supposed moral law that cleanliness is next to godliness, who instinctively wipe polished surfaces with our sleeve as we pass. This might serve as an illustration of what Schleiermacher calls an "instinct of reason."[24]

A second and more complex mode by which our intentions appear to be determined is what Schleiermacher calls *choice* (*Willkühr*). Its

---

[21]Friedrich Schiller, *Über die ästhetische Erziehung des Menschen*, Eighth Letter. Schiller's emphases. In English, *On the Aesthetic Education of Man*, available in translations by Reginald Snell and by Elizabeth M. Wilkinson and L. A. Willoughby. I often follow Snell's translation.

[22]"Denkmale," 22.

[23]Ibid., 22–23.

[24]MS 15.

operation can be observed when our intention is kindled by a comparison of several objects of inclination. The telephone is ringing, but so is the doorbell; the piano is dusty, but my suit has just been cleaned. We may, of course, spend a while deliberating and ultimately choose to answer neither telephone nor doorbell. In connection with his definition of choice Schleiermacher refers with approval to the observation of the philosopher Karl Friedrich Jerusalem, that "human freedom consists in its faculty of postponing its actions."[25]

A third and final mode by which our intentions appear to be determined is *will* (*Wille*). As background for his definition of will Schleiermacher writes:

> If a choosing [*willkührlich*] faculty of desire is joined with understanding [*Verstand*] in a subject, then the understanding can form general concepts out of individual determinations of choice. By comparison of their outcomes it can develop judgments concerning their relative importance, and these judgments are thought of as rules for future cases, that is, as *maxims*.[26]

Then he gives his definition: a *will* is a faculty of desire in which there is an impulse to govern choice by the application of rational maxims. The will may therefore be thought of as a characteristic distinguishing human beings from animals. "A human being is capable of comparing not only individual objects of desire, but also maxims with those objects, and maxims among themselves."[27] We suppose that animals, on the other hand, are not capable of the last of these comparisons, and in most cases not of the second of them either—though Schleiermacher recognizes that we cannot know this with certainty.[28] Schiller in his discussion of the term *will* in 1793 will put the same point this way: "The animal *must* strive to be free of pain; the human being can decide to bear it."[29]

Both Schleiermacher and Schiller inherited the terms *choice* and *will* from Kant. But like Kant's defender Reinhold, both men recognized that Kant's use of these terms in the first and second *Critiques* is inconsistent and unclear. Under the influence of Reinhold, Schiller, and others, Kant tried in his work of 1792–93, *Religion within the Limits of Reason Alone*, to regularize and clarify his vocabulary.[30] In a footnote to

---

[25]"Denkmale," 23. Jerusalem's suicide in 1772 had given the impetus to Johann Wolfgang Goethe's *Die Leiden des jungen Werthers* (*The Sorrows of the Young Werther*), which we shall encounter below.

[26]"Denkmale," 23. Schleiermacher's emphasis.

[27]Ibid.

[28]MS 7.

[29]Friedrich Schiller, *Über Anmut und Würde*, 39. Schiller's emphasis.

[30]See John R. Silber's discussion of Kant's use of the terms *Willkür* and *Wille* in his Introduction to the English translation of Kant's *Religion within the Limits of Reason Alone*, tr. Greene and Hudson, xciv–cxxvii.

the opening pages of that book in its second edition of 1794, Kant refers to Schiller and graciously acknowledges the importance of his reservations concerning Kant's earlier discussions of moral obligation.[31] Neither in his *Religion within the Limits of Reason Alone*, however, nor in his *Metaphysic of Morals* of 1797 was Kant able to present a discrimination of these terms precise enough to satisfy his critics. Still less was Schleiermacher satisfied by Kant's vocabulary in the second *Critique*, hovering as it does between the phenomenal and the noumenal. He tries in his treatise to give Kant's terminology clearer outlines against the more stable background of his own phenomenology of human choosing.

But though he succeeds in making his vocabulary more precise than that of Kant, Schleiermacher insists that the various modes by which our intentions are kindled—instinct, choice, and will—cannot be thought of as discrete and separable. They can never be isolated, not even for the sake of observation.[32] They simply represent an attempt to designate ethically significant regions along the volitional spectrum, which as a whole we call the faculty of desire. In spite of his use of the word "faculty," as in *faculty of representation* and *faculty of desire*—phrases that were simply common coinage of German moral philosophers in the 1790s—Schleiermacher is not guilty of the analytic crudities that are sometimes the basis of criticism of "faculty psychologies." His treatise, in fact his world view rests upon the assumption of continuity from one volitional mode to another, the assumption of the indivisibility and interrelatedness of all human capacities. Already in his early treatise *On Human Freedom* we find the genius for meticulous psychological analysis that will serve Schleiermacher so precisely in his lectures on psychology, delivered at the University of Berlin from 1818 to 1834. But in both places we also find Schleiermacher's genius for analysis serving the larger purpose of appreciating the person's essential unity. At the opening of his 1830 lectures on psychology he writes:

> We presuppose the original unity of body and soul, and the equally original unity of all we can differentiate within the soul itself.[33]

The same holistic presupposition underlies his ethical treatise of 1791–92. Here again Schleiermacher anticipates the moral philosophy of Schiller, who was to write in 1793, "Human nature is in reality a more

---

[31]Kant, *Die Religion innerhalb der Grenzen der blossen Vernunft*, 10n. Hereafter cited as *Die Religion*, with the pagination from the second edition of 1794, provided in most German editions as the standard pagination. I sometimes follow the English translation of Theodore M. Greene and Hoyt H. Hudson: Kant, *Religion within the Limits of Reason Alone*, 18n. Hereafter cited as English tr.

[32]MS 7.

[33]Schleiermacher, *Psychologie*, 12.

united whole than can ever be revealed by the philosophers, who can make progress only by means of dissection."[34] What is more, we shall soon see that Schleiermacher and Schiller agree that the unity of human character is not only the presupposition of moral philosophy, but its goal as well.

In Schleiermacher's discussion of instinct, choice, and will, we come across an epigrammatic sentence which expresses the holistic presupposition of Schleiermacher's moral philosophy and which might serve as a motto for his treatise. Having just given his definition of *will*, Schleiermacher goes on: *Ein solches Begehrungsvermögen muss schlechterdings willkührlich sein*, "Such a faculty of desire must absolutely be a choosing faculty."[35] What he means is this. Even though a will is by definition found only in rational beings, endowed with understanding—that is, in human beings, who are capable of learning and generalizing from experience to develop rational maxims of behavior—still acts of will (*Wille*) are never separable from acts of choice (*Willkühr*). Our understanding is always bound up with our desiring. Our reasoning is always bound up with our inclining and disinclining.

Now Kant had claimed that in order to account for moral obligation we must suppose that our reason can influence our will "directly," that is, not by means of any "sensuous impulse" whatsoever. This claim led Kant to speak of his peculiar incentive of "respect" for the moral law—peculiar because it is said to be a feeling that, unlike every other, "is not of empirical origin" (above, p. 29). In this way Kant expected to overcome the obstacle of having to suppose that our wills can actually be effective, yet effective in the absence of any possible incentive that could join the representations of our reason with the determinations of our inclination. Kant's apologist Reinhold early recognized the difficulties inherent in Kant's attempt to keep the human will pure—to separate the rational determinations of our will from the sensible determinations of our choosing. One of the central preoccupations of Reinhold's second series of *Letters on the Kantian Philosophy* of 1791–92 was his attempt to rejoin the terms *will* and *choice*, which Kant had put asunder. Kant's concept of the "will's own law," Reinhold writes, is "indeed not incorrect, but completely undeveloped." To overcome the difficulties of Kant's presentation, Reinhold begins his reinterpretation by boldly defining transcendental freedom of the *will* in terms of *choice*:

> By freedom I do not understand either the faculty to act according to laws, or the faculty to do one's duty, but rather simply *choice* which is assured [*zugesichert*] by the law of the will.[36]

[34]Schiller, *Anmut*, 35.
[35]"Denkmale," 23.
[36]Karl Leonhard Reinhold, *Briefe über die Kantische Philosophie*, II, vii, viii.

If Schleiermacher knew Reinhold's second series of *Letters*, he must have approved of the direction in which Reinhold was moving in these redefinitions of Kant's terminology. But predictably, as Reinhold moved toward making moral decisions a matter of choice—not merely of will, purified from all sensible influences—he had difficulty maintaining Kant's "keystone" concept of transcendental freedom. Schleiermacher's course is different. He has no commitment to Kant's concept of transcendental freedom. Unlike Kant and Reinhold, Schleiermacher never speaks of the influence of reason on the will as being "direct." The influence of reason upon our intentions is by means of incentives, and the incentives of reason, like all other incentives, involve our feelings:

> The realization of a command of reason involves a feeling, and with it, an impulse [*Trieb*] relating immediately and solely to practical reason, which it represents in the faculty of desire. *This impulse must have exactly the same relation to the faculty of desire as every other.* Upon the existence of this impulse rests the entire possibility of the idea of responsibility, for it is through this impulse alone that reason is joined with the faculty of desire. In earlier moral systems one called this impulse the moral sense; in the more recent it is called esteem for the moral law.[37]

By his use here of the term *esteem* (*Achtung*), Schleiermacher may be deliberately avoiding identification with Kant's term for the incentive of the moral law, *respect* (*Acht*). He goes on to say that in a moral intention, the incentive of esteem for the moral law joins our reason with our faculty of desire, not directly, but simply "in a far more immediate and complete way" than other incentives.[38] In all our decisions the incentives of reason must be weighed along with other incentives. Rational and sensible impulses always combine to determine our intentions.

In summary, what the epigrammatic sentence from *On Human Freedom* means is that operations of our rational will are always joined with the comparing and inclining activity of choice. Schleiermacher believes this must be true if only because the rational will can never be called into operation unless suitable occasions present themselves to our senses, and deciding just what those occasions *are* involves choice.[39] This is yet another insight that Schiller was to express soon afterward: "So often as nature makes some claim and wants to overcome the will through the blind power of the affections, it falls to the will to order a standstill until reason has had a chance to speak."[40]

---

[37]"Denkmale," 25. Emphasis added.
[38]MS 17.
[39]MS 9.
[40]Schiller, *Anmut*, 40.

This then is the basic dynamics of moral choosing as Schleiermacher describes the process. Our moral responsibilities are manifold and unceasing:

> The activities of choice alter as richly and as quickly as only the flux of outer conditions can. Choice is in every moment called not only into life, but into superabundant, multifarious, and active life. Our fantasy, understanding, and reason leave choice never at rest. It lusts, selects, desires, resolves, and acts in every moment of its existence [*es gelüstet, wählt, begehrt, beschliesst und handelt in jedem Moment seines Daseyns*].[41]

The conviction implicit in this passage is absolutely fundamental to Schleiermacher's world view. Schleiermacher was convinced that human thinking and human desiring are joined in the most intimate, mutual, and indissoluble of unions. Our faculty of representation, he writes, "must always be active whenever some object of the faculty of desire comes into consciousness from without; and the faculty of representation in turn cannot be active without itself producing objects for the faculty of desire."[42] Probably Schleiermacher's baldest statement of this conviction occurs in some private reflections on the philosophy of Benedict Spinoza, dating from 1793–94: "In my theory, *the will signifies the understanding occupied with desire*."[43]

Here we come across the first of many similarities between Schleiermacher's ethical outlook and that of Spinoza. Spinoza differed from the classical Stoics in recognizing that it is never reason alone that motivates a person, but only reason coupled with the love of being reasonable.[44] The root of this difference is Spinoza's insight that emotions can be influenced only by other emotions: "A true knowledge of good and evil cannot check any emotion by virtue of being true, but only in so far as it is considered as an emotion."[45] To couch Spinoza's insight in the ethical language of Kant, we might say that it is never pure reason that determines our intentions, but only reason coupled with subjective incentives. Kant himself was acknowledging something like Spinoza's psychological insight when he coupled reason's *a priori* moral law with the feeling of respect, which serves an incentive function in the "higher" faculty of desire. But as we have seen, Kant's "respect" is an exotic and problematic bird in the psychological aviary, and one cannot imagine Kant saying with Schleiermacher that "will signifies the understanding occupied with desire." For Kant, the will is practical reason occupied "directly" with the *a priori* moral law.

---

[41]MS 21.

[42]Ibid.

[43]*Spinozismus*, ed. Mulert, 311. Emphasis added.

[44]See Frederick Pollock's discussion of this issue in his *Spinoza: His Life and Philosophy*, 252, 256, 279.

[45]Benedict de Spinoza, *Ethics*, tr. Elwes, Part IV, Proposition 14.

The congruence between Spinoza's insight and that of Schleier-macher appears clearly in the two unpublished essays Schleiermacher worked on shortly before and shortly after he wrote *On Human Freedom*.[46] The latter of the two is his fragmentary essay *On the Worth of Life*, dating from 1792–93. There we find Schleiermacher writing a rhapsodic passage, not simply in praise of truth and rules of reason, but in praise of "*pleasure* in truth" and "*pleasure* in rules of reason" (*Lust an Wahrheit, Lust an Regeln*).[47] The other essay, *On the Highest Good*, dates from Schleiermacher's final student days at Halle in 1789. Its editor, Dilthey, writes that it "documents the early maturity of an uncommonly sharp critical sense."[48] Like its companion, *On Human Freedom*, it is a response to Kant's *Critique of Practical Reason*. In it we find Schleiermacher, very much in the manner of Spinoza, criticizing the Stoic philosophers' "peculiar obscurity" (*Eigendünkel*) that made it impossible for them to see that "the law of reason can never determine our will immediately." Kant's pure practical reason, Schleiermacher writes, can determine "a will such as ours, not immediately, but only as mediated by subjective motivating grounds derived from the moral law."[49] What Schleiermacher means here by "moral law" will be our beginning question for the next chapter.

[46]Like *On Human Freedom*, both of these essays have been edited by Dilthey and published in "Denkmale."
[47]"Denkmale," 53. Emphasis added.
[48]Ibid., 6.
[49]Ibid., 12.

Chapter 4. Moral Law and Philosophical Certainty

I have always been far removed from system-mania. My thinking began in doubt; and for all that I have since read and thought for myself, for all my accustomed association with the stoutest adherents of this or that system, still I have remained at more or less the same stage, in theology as well as in philosophy. . . . Thus I look with tranquillity upon the joustings of the philosophical and theological athletes, without declaring myself for either side or wagering my freedom on one or the other. Yet I never fail to learn something from both.

It is perhaps already clear from the preceding chapter that Schleiermacher does not disagree with Kant's view that human reason can legislate to the human will. A passage from Schleiermacher's 1789 treatise *On the Highest Good* acknowledges his debt to Kant, and his even more fundamental debt to Plato, in this regard:

> If Plato does not set down for us a picture of the law of reason so completely or with such vivid colors as Kant, still with little trouble one finds its principal features in his art, and one sees that they were deeply impressed in his soul. The whole purpose of his so often misunderstood *Republic*, incontestably one of the most sublime compositions of antiquity, is to show that it is absolutely necessary for us to govern ourselves, and that this can happen in no other way than for us to submit unconditionally all the other parts of our soul to the governing faculty of reason.[1]

Schleiermacher shared Kant's reverence for the legislative authority of reason. In one important respect, however, he differed with Kant's interpretation of the moral authority of reason, and we need to appreciate what the difference is. It concerns the question of how complete or final our understanding of the moral law may be.

Schleiermacher agrees with Kant that certain absolute requirements of the moral law are clear to us. In moral philosophy as in logic and natural science, for example, the demands of reason must be free from self-contradiction. "The most original rule of reason is this," Schleiermacher writes, "that none of its propositions may contradict itself or its

---

[1]"Denkmale," 15.

fellows."[2] This principle is clear *a priori*. If the case were otherwise, reason would be self-annihilating, and we could not speak rationally of science or of morality at all. It is perhaps true that a thoroughgoing skepticism, maintaining that there is no such thing as rational discourse, is possible. David Hume had disturbed the slumbers of dogmatic complacency on that point, as both Kant and Schleiermacher well knew. But we must recall that Kant and Schleiermacher are pursuing not theoretical understanding but practical insight (above, p. 21). The question that motivates Kant's two *Critiques* is not "Are there such things as natural science and moral obligation?" but rather "What are the operations of reason that account for natural science and moral obligation as we know them?" It may prove true that in the end Kant's "critical" philosophy will fail in its attempt to find an answer to its basic question, and philosophical skepticism may be the result. But that is a possible consequence of Kant's philosophy, not its beginning assumption. Kant is searching for a rational basis for natural science and moral philosophy, and he is correct in asserting that one must begin with the principle of non-contradiction as an *a priori* assumption. If we are to find a rational basis for moral philosophy, then it must be true—"universally and necessarily" true, in Kant's famous phrase—that the moral demands of reason may not contradict themselves.

Schleiermacher recognizes that rational moral laws must apply "with the greatest generality."[3] But Schleiermacher's phrase "with the greatest generality" is not the same as Kant's "universally and necessarily," and in this difference of terminology we begin to glimpse a fundamental disagreement between Schleiermacher and Kant. It must be said here that Schleiermacher's attitude is not altogether clear from his earliest writings. It appears that he would agree with Kant that an obligation such as the obligation to be truthful qualifies as a moral "law of reason." It qualifies because it meets the requirement of Kant's "categorical imperative" (see above, p. 25):

> So act that the maxim of your will could always hold at the same time as a principle establishing universal law.[4]

The maxim "tell the truth" could certainly hold "as a principle establishing universal law." That is, it is not self-contradictory. What is more, any compromise of that principle—"lie if you wish," let us say—could *not* establish universal law. Rational truth could not thrive, nor even survive, where arbitrary betrayal of rational truth were a universal principle.

Schleiermacher, we are saying, appears to agree with Kant in all of

[2]Ibid., 10.
[3]Ibid.
[4]Second *Kritik*, 30.

this. Where he appears to differ from Kant is in giving far more emphasis to the term *maxim* in Kant's categorical imperative, and to the relation between maxim and law. In the vocabulary of Kant's moral philosophy, a *maxim* is the principle, idea, or representation governing a particular act of an individual's will. A *law*, on the other hand, is the universal principle to which all particular maxims should conform. Schleiermacher agrees with Kant that, as a law, "tell the truth" seems clear enough. As a maxim, however, it becomes problematic. Tell the truth, yes. But what constitutes telling the truth in particular instances? Am I everywhere and at every moment to tell all the truth I know? Surely not, for that is to speak of a sheer impossibility. How much of the truth am I to tell, then? And where and when?

From such questions it seems to Schleiermacher clear that we must continually be making moral choices in the process of telling the truth, and Schleiermacher's moral philosophy directs its primary attention upon these choices. A moral faculty of desire, his epigram runs, "must absolutely be a choosing faculty" (above, p. 43). We now see more clearly what that epigram means. The moral law may be clear and *a priori*, but we must be always engaged in choosing which formulation of the moral law is to provide our maxims for behavior, and when. The influence of the general judgments of the moral law upon the particular impulses of the will can never be "absolute," Schleiermacher writes,

> since the impulse depends solely upon the relation of the moral law to the faculty of representation, where the importance [*Werth*] of the moral law is not always the same. That is, the maxims under which an action is included will not always come to consciousness with the same clarity, nor always be thought through with the same thoroughness. Indeed, the consciousness that one has made this or that a maxim at all will not always be equally great. And any one of these conditions will modify the impulse of the will.[5]

Schleiermacher is saying that any formulation of the moral law—and the checkered history of interpretation of Kant's own categorical imperative must certainly bear this out—will be evaluated and applied differently by different people, and even by any one person at different times.

Thus Schleiermacher writes in his 1792 treatise *On the Highest Good* that rational laws must apply "with the greatest generality," but not that they must apply universally and necessarily. To speak of universal application is to speak of a sheer impossibility. Or better, it is to speak of a sheer ideal. In his treatise *On the Highest Good*, Schleiermacher explains this ideal in terms of a mathematical simile. We may think, he writes, "of the moral law as an algebraic function. Then we may think

---

[5]MS 22.

of the highest good as nothing other than that curve which is and contains all that is possible through that function."[6] This "highest good" is a curve of infinite extent. For us as finite mortals, therefore, the highest good must remain a sheer ideal. It is, in Kant's terms, a "regulative" idea, not a "constitutive" one—a goal regulating our striving for a perfection that will never actually constitute our lives. The most we can aspire to is the regulation of our maxims of behavior so as to bring the course of our moral lives into asymptotic proximity to the highest good along certain of its segments, or, perhaps for any saints among us, into contact with it at certain points along its unbounded length.[7]

We have said that Schleiermacher differs from Kant in this understanding of the moral law. One might want to argue that the difference between the two is simply a difference of emphasis. At points in his *Critique of Practical Reason* Kant seems to recognize as clearly as Schleiermacher that our moral behavior is imperfect. In Part II of the second *Critique*, called the "Methodology of Pure Practical Reason," Kant turns his attention from the universal moral law to "the method of founding and cultivating genuine moral dispositions" that can regulate our lives. By the term *methodology*, he writes,

> we understand the way in which we can secure to the laws of pure practical reason access to the human mind and an influence on its maxims. That is to say, it is the way we can make the objectively practical reason also subjectively practical.[8]

In other words, in the final pages of his *Critique* Kant turns his attention to the question that is central to Schleiermacher's ethical analysis, the relation of general moral laws to the actual maxims of our behavior.

We can illustrate the difference in emphasis between the two philosophers, however, by observing that, whereas the question of practical application is Schleiermacher's central concern, Kant devotes to

---

[6]"Denkmale," 9.

[7]Some thirty years later, in his 1821 "Explanations" to his *Speeches on Religion*, Schleiermacher was to write, "It has never seriously been my opinion that ethical doctrine should everywhere be one and the same. . . . Namely, it appears to me that morality could not be everywhere the same, and all ages prove that it never has been everywhere the same. For its form is essentially speculative, and it can never be everywhere the same until speculation in general has become everywhere the same; but of this achievement even the last centuries, with their great fruitfulness in philosophy of universal validity, give no semblance. Nor can its content be everywhere the same; for even if everyone who dealt with ethics proceeded from pure human nature, still each sees the latter only through the medium of his own age and nationality. Thus any universally valid ethical doctrine can contain only the broadest generalities, and even these in formulas of varying worth, so that the universal validity will always be more apparent than real." *Über die Religion: Reden an die Gebildeten unter ihren Verächtern*, ed. Pünjer, 297.

[8]Second *Kritik*, 153, 151.

the place of Kant's moral incentive of *respect*, which mediates "directly" between the absolute obligation of pure practical reason and our intentions, Schleiermacher uses the traditional and less rigoristic terms *esteem* and *moral sense*. It is through moral sense "alone that reason is joined with the faculty of desire," he writes in *On Human Freedom* (above, p. 44). Like the Earl of Shaftesbury and other moral sense philosophers before him,[23] Schleiermacher understands moral sense to be an incentive in which the *a priori* and the *a posteriori* thoroughly interpenetrate. He conceives ethics to be the never-ending art of cultivating our moral sense under the guidance of the principles of practical reason, themselves gleaned from life's experiences. Kant's second *Critique* derives a "Fundamental Law of Pure Practical Reason" that is *a priori*, universal, and necessary, freed from the "pathology"[24] of any one individual's subjective experience. Schleiermacher's essay pursues a more illusive ideal, spurred on by practical reason's unsatisfied yearning for consistency among its maxims, which grow only under the subjective conditions of an individual's history. In concentrating here upon Schleiermacher's debate with Kant in *On Human Freedom* and his other writings from around 1792, we are still five years away from Berlin and Schleiermacher's introduction into the romantic salon of Henriette Herz, but already in these early treatises we come across seeds of the emphasis on individuality that we shall find as a hallmark of his romanticism in the years following 1797.

In fairness to Kant we must add that the geometrical form of his exposition in the second *Critique* does not by itself establish the truth of Schleiermacher's suspicion that Kant's philosophy was distorted by certain systematic compulsions. Even Spinoza may well have chosen the *more geometrico* of his *Ethics*, not because by ending each Proposition with the geometrician's *Q.E.D.*[25] he really meant that he had demonstrated a philosophical truth with geometrical certainty, but rather because he simply found the *more geometrico* the clearest and most coherent form of philosophical exposition. Evidence to support this view is found in the fact that in 1663 Spinoza had written an exposition of the philosophy of Descartes in exactly the same form, and Spinoza was certainly enough of a rationalist to realize that geometric method could not deduce two different philosophies—his own and that of Descartes— with equal certainty. Be that as it may with Spinoza, it seems to be true

---

[23]It appears to be impossible to specify just when Schleiermacher first became acquainted with the writings of Shaftesbury (1671–1713) and the other moral sense philosophers, or to what extent his early writings were influenced by Shaftesbury directly. The earliest reference to Shaftesbury I have found is in Schleiermacher's *Grundlinien einer Kritik der bisherigen Sittenlehre*, 43, begun as early as 1798 but not published until 1803. See Dilthey, *Leben Schleiermachers*, ed. Redeker, I/1, 166–74.

[24]Second *Kritik*, 25.

[25]*Quod erat demonstrandum*: "that which was to have been demonstrated."

that, despite the undeniable architectural urge of his system building, Kant remained basically faithful to his insight that philosophy must begin not as a deduction from first principles but rather as an investigation into given human experiences—particularly, into the discoveries of natural science (the first *Critique*) and into the experience of moral obligation (the second *Critique*). Philosophic principles will be the result of this "critical" investigation or "transcendental" deduction, but they cannot be its beginning point—though Kant did appear to believe that these principles could be established in the end with *a priori* or geometric certainty.[26]

Kant's insight that philosophy is finally not deduction but rather investigation was from Schleiermacher's perspective a redeeming feature of his philosophy. From the perspective of Schleiermacher's later colleague and sometime antagonist Fichte, however, the same insight appeared to be Kant's greatest weakness. In Fichte's philosophy, *a priori* deduction was a matter not merely of expository form but of essential method and substance. In Fichte's writings Schleiermacher's almost boundless distrust of philosophical system building, directed first against Kant, was to find its consummate object.

Fichte was Kant's disciple. During the time in which Schleiermacher was engaged in writing *On Human Freedom*, Fichte was writing his first publication, the *Critique of All Possible Revelation*, applying Kantian principles to the philosophy of religion. Published anonymously, Fichte's treatise was in fact widely taken to be a work by Kant himself. In 1794, Fichte was called to succeed Kant's great apologist Reinhold at the University of Jena. In the same year he presented his fundamental philosophical outlook in his *Foundation of the Entire Doctrine of Science*. Fichte considered it his mission to establish the Kantian philosophy upon a more solid foundation than the Königsberg master's own transcendental investigations had yet uncovered. "I have always said," Fichte writes in his important *First Introduction to the Doctrine of Science* of 1797, "and I say it once again here, that my system is none other

---

[26]Descartes himself writes of the deductive form of philosophical exposition, "It seems to me that the arguments follow one another in such a way that, just as the last principles are demonstrated by the first ones which are their causes, so these first ones are reciprocally demonstrated by the last which are their effects. And one must not suppose that I have here committed the fallacy which logicians call circular reasoning; for as experience makes most of the effects very certain, the causes from which I deduce them serve not so much to prove as to explain them. On the contrary, the truth of the hypotheses is proved by the actuality of the effects. And I have called them hypotheses only to let it be known that although I think I can deduce them from the first truths which I have previously explained, I expressly desired not to make the deduction. For there are certain people who imagine that they can learn in one day all that another has thought in twenty years, as soon as he has only spoken two or three words. . . ." *Discourse on Method*, tr. Laurence J. Lafleur, 55.

than the Kantian," only in an "entirely independent presentation."[27] By 1797, Fichte was aware of Kant's rumored opinion that the younger philosopher's system was in fact "wholly other than Kantian."[28] Nevertheless Fichte persevered in his essentially Kantian mission.

Fichte's goal was to discover a single, indubitable, universal and necessary principle from which all philosophic truth could be deduced. "In just this deduction," he writes, "philosophy consists," and thus the "only possible philosophy" must be his own.[29] Fichte called his philosophy "critical idealism," to distinguish it from Kant's "transcendental idealism," which had stopped short of the philosophic deduction Fichte now intended to supply.

The single, indubitable principle of Fichte's early philosophy was what he called "the absolute self-activity of the self," or "intellectual intuition":

> This intellectual intuition is the only firm standpoint for all philosophy. From it, all that presents itself to consciousness can be clarified, and from it only.[30]

Our interest here is not so much in Fichte's fundamental principle *per se* as in the claim he makes concerning the possibility of systematically deducing all philosophy, and indeed all experience, from it, completely *a priori*. With the fundamental principle once discovered, Fichte writes, "my philosophy becomes completely independent of all choice [*Willkühr*], and a product of iron necessity, insofar as necessity applies to free reason."[31]

> If the principle of idealism is correct, and if the deduction is correctly carried out, then it will have as its final result . . . the system of all necessary representations, or experience in general. Comparisons with experience will not be made as a part of philosophy itself, but only afterwards. For philosophy does not even have experience in its eye as a goal, known to it beforehand, and at which it must arrive. In the course of its operations, idealism knows nothing of experience, and pays it no heed. It proceeds from its beginning point according to its rules, unconcerned with what will result in the end. The correct angle, from which its straight line is to be projected, is given to it. Does it then need any other point toward which to be protracted? I say that the points of its line are given to it all at once.[32]

---

[27]Johann Gottlieb Fichte, *Erste Einleitung in die Wissenschaftslehre*, 419–20. Available in the English translation by Peter Heath and John Lachs, *Science of Knowledge, with the First and Second Introductions*, which gives in the margin the pagination of the German edition cited here.

[28]Fichte, *Zweite Einleitung in die Wissenschaftslehre*, 469n.

[29]*Erste Einleitung*, 438.

[30]*Zweite Einleitung*, 466.

[31]Ibid., 467.

[32]*Erste Einleitung*, 446.

From Schleiermacher's point of view the most astonishing thing about Fichte's vision of a completely *a priori* deduction of all human experience is that Fichte really believed in its possibility.[33] It is clear from what we have seen of Schleiermacher that he disagreed with almost every conviction expressed in these citations from Fichte. For Fichte, the highest ideal of philosophy is represented by a straight line, given to the mind *a priori* and "all at once." For Schleiermacher the highest good of ethics is a curve, to which our experience allows us only limited and approximate access (above, p. 50). Fichte's projected idealism "knows nothing of experience and pays it no heed." Schleiermacher's incipient romanticism seeks its ethical vision wholly within our experiences in space and time (above, p. 37). In Fichte's outlook philosophy "becomes completely free of all choice." In Schleiermacher's moral philosophy "choice is in every moment called not only into life, but into superabundant, multifarious, and active life" (above, p. 45).

Let us summarize by means of a metaphor. Our discussion of Schleiermacher's conception of moral law has brought us to a point of crucial difference between Schleiermacher and the two greatest moral philosophers of the early 1790s, Immanuel Kant and Johann Gottlieb Fichte. The contrast is vividly expressed in a single metaphor used distinctively, and apparently independently, by each of the three philosophers. It is the metaphor of the moral philosopher as chemist.

The admirable success of scientific method, Kant writes at the close of the second *Critique*,

> recommends to us the same method in treating the moral capacities of our nature, and gives hope of a similarly good result. We have at hand examples of morally judging reason. We may now analyze them into their elementary concepts, following, in the absence of mathematics, a process similar to that of chemistry. That is, we may, in repeated experiments on common human understanding, separate the empirical from the rational, exhibit each in its pure state, and make known with certainty what each by itself can accomplish.[34]

Every element of Kant's metaphor deserves emphasis. Moral philosophy begins with common moral understanding. It then succeeds in separating the rational from the empirical. Finally, it discovers "with certainty" what each element may accomplish "in its pure state" — in particular, what the rational may accomplish in isolation from the empirical.

Fichte goes farther. In his use of the metaphor, the deductive certainty of philosophy exceeds even the analytic certainty of chemistry:

---

[33]Georg Gurwitsch argues that such was in fact never Fichte's belief or intention. See his *Die Einheit des Fichteschen Philosophie*, 4. I do not find Gurwitsch's evidence quite accurate or convincing.

[34]Second *Kritik*, 163.

The chemist compounds a body, let us say a certain metal, out of its elements. The common man sees the metal familiar to him; the chemist sees the bonding of the body and its particular elements. Do they see different things then? I would think not. They see the same thing, only in different ways. The way of the chemist is the *a priori*; he sees the particulars. The way of the common man is the *a posteriori*; he sees the whole. But there is this difference: the chemist must first analyze the whole before he can compound it, because he has to do with an object whose law of combination he cannot know before the analysis. But the philosopher can compound without prior analysis, because he already knows his object's law, namely, reason.[35]

We should notice in Fichte's metaphor not only the Kantian separation of the *a priori* from the *a posteriori*, but also Fichte's separation of the common person's experience from that of the philosopher—a separation we shall later find Schleiermacher criticizing. But for our present purpose, the final sentence of Fichte's metaphor deserves emphasis, dramatizing as it does his absolute faith in the deductive powers of *a priori* reason: "The philosopher can compound *without prior analysis*." Schleiermacher found such rationalistic faith astonishing.

Schleiermacher's own chemical metaphor applies, typically, to the philosopher's method of characterizing a person's individuality:

Such a characterization should analyze the individual chemically, separating the inwardly different constituents from each other, and presenting them in their quantitative relation, but then should seek out the inner principle of their combination, the deepest secret of individuality, thus reconstituting the individual in an artistic way. But of course that can occur only if one combines the various appearances of the individual, and only if one has to some extent reflected ahead of time on the idea of how appearances must in general be combined in a human being.[36]

In the imagery of this metaphor we may say that the treatise *On Human Freedom* is Schleiermacher's "chemical analysis" of the constituents of an individual's power of choosing. But unlike Fichte, Schleiermacher regards the analysis solely as a means to the end of individual reconstitution. The *a priori* analysis must combine with the *a posteriori* of appearances; the general must be rejoined with the individual. And unlike Fichte again, Schleiermacher does not believe that philosophy can begin its work "without prior analysis." Philosophy has no possible beginning point apart from reflection upon common human experience.

Schleiermacher's chemical metaphor dates from 1799, Fichte's from 1794. We have thus jumped a bit ahead of ourselves. But the metaphor

---

[35] *Erste Einleitung*, 449.
[36] Schleiermacher, "Garve's letzte noch von ihm selbst herausgegebene Schriften," a review appearing in *Athenaeum*, III/1 (1800), 134. Also in *Sämmtliche Werke*, III/1, 512–13.

illustrates an attitude of which Schleiermacher was already fully conscious in 1791–92, namely, his suspicion of philosophical system building. Just how early and self-consciously this suspicion manifested itself we may learn from Schleiermacher's correspondence. In a letter of 1789, Schleiermacher's father wrote to his son cautioning him against the enticements of both petty social influences and tidy philosophical systems. As this letter reveals Schleiermacher's father at one of his finest moments, it deserves quoting at length:

> May your heart abhor all petty sentimental aestheticism and your understanding all equally petty system-mania and system-making. You will make no progress in your course of life if this early you make a system of some kind for yourself, or want to adopt that of anyone else as the only true one. Consider it rather it your calling, which it is, to seek truth and wisdom with an unprepossessed mind and with an upright and humble heart that trusts in God. Make a wise apportionment of your time, and in addition to the Bible—which I recommend now and always as your daily devotional book for the early morning hours, and of course in the original languages—let your other reading be guided by the advice of your dear uncle [Stubenrauch]. Beware of the writings of authors who quickly betray themselves to be petty, self-seeking, and exceedingly intolerant creatures, who, under the honorable name of enlightenment, concern themselves only with spreading their fame and imposing their systems upon others. The truly wise have never thought and acted so. On the contrary, along with their greatest progress in the investigation of truth, the truly wise have always become more modest and more distrustful of themselves, ever mindful of the deeply rooted self-conceit and pride of the heart that nourish prejudice and thereby blind the understanding. Such wholesome distrust, however, combined with unceasing and ardent inquiry and with a constant watchfulness of oneself, leads them at last to that noble freedom of spirit which lets itself be bound by nothing except the truth.[37]

From Drossen, Schleiermacher replied to his father's letter:

> I have always been far removed from system-mania. My thinking began in doubt; and for all that I have since read and thought for myself, for all my accustomed association with the stoutest adherents of this or that system, still I have remained at more or less the same stage, in theology as well as in philosophy. I do not believe that I shall ever bring things to a fully developed system, so that every question one can raise can be answered decisively and in connection with all the rest of my knowledge. Rather I have always believed that testing and investigation and the patient listening to all witnesses and parties are the only means by which we may at last arrive at an adequate [*hinlänglich*] sphere of certainty, and, above all, at a firm boundary between those matters, on the one hand, regarding which we must necessarily choose a party and for which we must be able to account to ourselves and others, and those matters, on the other hand, which we may, without detriment to our tranquillity and happiness, leave undecided. Thus I look with tranquillity upon the

[37]Dec. 10, 1789. *Br*. I, 74–75.

joustings of the philosophical and theological athletes, without declaring
myself for either side or wagering my freedom on one or the other. Yet I
never fail to learn something from both.[38]

We see in this exchange between father and son an early
manifestation of the antipathy to closed systems of thought that was to
shape Schleiermacher's attitude throughout his career. When later he
wrote and lectured on systems of his own, they were strictly limited in
the scope of their claims. *The Christian Faith* of 1821, for example, has
as its formal subject matter not God and the world, but rather
traditional Christian propositions about God and the world[39] — certainly a
vast, and yet a carefully circumscribed subject. Schleiermacher's
systematic thinking was consistently of a peculiarly dynamic and open-
ended kind, as in his lectures on "dialectics," or the foundations of
knowledge, from 1811 through 1831. Those lectures proceed on a most
un-Fichtean assumption:

> All science [*Wissenschaft*] wishes to become art, and all art, science; and
> indeed the more so, the higher the stage of each. Thus the highest
> science must also be art.[40]

From the exchange of letters we see also that Schleiermacher's
antipathy to closed systems is rooted in the pietism of his father — "ever
mindful of the deeply rooted self-conceit and pride of the heart"; ever
mindful of the modesty and wholesome distrust of self required of the
person "with an upright and humble heart that trusts in God." Schleiermacher did not retain the orthodoxy of the pietism in which he was
nurtured. But we shall find that when Schleiermacher becomes mature
and independent enough to begin using the word "piety" in his own
way, one focus of its meaning will be "the beautiful modesty, the
friendly, attractive forebearance that spring from the essence of
religion."[41] We shall learn that Schleiermacher regarded religious piety,
understood in this sense, as the absolutely essential equipoise to all
philosophical claims of systematic virtuosity.

---

[38]Dec. 23, 1789, *Br.* I, 78.

[39]See *The Christian Faith*, Proposition 19.

[40]*Dialektik*, ed. Jonas, 9.

[41]Schleiermacher, *Über die Religion: Reden an die Gebildeten unter ihren Verächtern*, ed.
Pünjer, 66–67. In English, *On Religion: Speeches to Its Cultured Despisers*, tr. Oman, 54.
Also available in the translation by Terrence N. Tice, *On Religion: Addresses in Response to
Its Cultured Critics*. I often follow Oman's English translation. Whenever I omit references
to the *Speeches* in English, it is because the third edition of the *Reden*, from which
Oman's translation was made, does not contain the passage in question.

Chapter 5. Responsibility, Determinism, and Accountability

The author is happy with the name of determinist, but only if the reader will promise that he does not want to attribute to this author a single sentence of any other determinist not contained in what the author has himself said or is about to say.

In a letter to his friend Brinkmann, written from Drossen, Schleiermacher mentions his three "dialogues on freedom" (above, p. 9), but then corrects himself: "or, as I prefer to say, dialogues on the nature of moral actions."[1] He prefers, in other words, the designation suggesting a practical rather than a theoretical content. It will be well for us to follow Schleiermacher's clue and return our discussion now to the specific practical question that motivates the treatise *On Human Freedom*: How is the human experience of moral responsibility to be accounted for? Our discussion of moral law and the issue of philosophical certainty in the preceding chapter is fundamental to an understanding of Schleiermacher's philosophical outlook. The ethical question central to *On Human Freedom*, however, is more particular. Even if the moral law is clear to us, even if the specific maxims of our behavior are sometimes congruent with universal requirements of moral law, how are we supposed to be able to determine our intentions accordingly?

Schleiermacher does not believe that an impulse of practical reason can, as Kant writes, determine our intentions "regardless of what inclination [*Neigung*] may say to the contrary."[2] This kind of absolutistic assertion leads Kant to postulate transcendental freedom, and it is with Kant's concept of transcendental freedom more than with Kant's definition of moral law that Schleiermacher's treatise *On Human Freedom* takes issue. Kant maintains vigorously that unless we suppose ourselves free "in every case"[3] to follow the command of moral law, regardless of what our inclinations urge us to do, then we cannot account for moral responsibility. Schleiermacher just as vigorously disagrees.

Schleiermacher argues that we can account for moral responsibility simply by observing two characteristics of the faculty of desire as his

[1]June 10, 1789. *Br*. IV, 8.
[2]Second *Kritik*, 32.
[3]Ibid.

treatise has described it. (1) Maxims of practical reason may in principle govern our choosing; that is, our faculty of desire is a *will* (above, p. 41). (2) Our will in itself is "neither good nor evil"; that is, neither moral nor immoral maxims are in principle denied the possibility of serving as incentives in our choosing.

Let us explore the implications of these two characteristics. The first is perhaps as easily clarified by what it denies as by what it asserts. It denies that we are animals ruled by instinct and palpable stimulation alone. Kant and Schleiermacher agree that creatures responsible to moral principles must be reasoning beings. Schleiermacher puts it this way:

> Since reason has given us the idea of law and responsibility, therefore the faculty of desire, if it is to realize this idea, must not be instinct. For if it were an instinct of sense, then the faculty of desire would be absolutely determined prior to the law; and if it were an instinct of reason, then the law of reason would in fact be a law of nature.[4]

The clause here about an "instinct of sense" seems clear enough. It reiterates Schleiermacher's agreement with Kant about our nature as rational, or at least potentially rational, creatures (above, pp. 47–48).

The clause about an "instinct of reason," however, is directed against Kant's doctrine of transcendental freedom and requires more explanation. It relates to the second characteristic that Schleiermacher specifies as a condition of moral responsibility: the will is in itself neither good nor evil. There are places in Kant's moral philosophy suggesting that he contradicts this second characteristic. Kant sometimes seems to suggest that the term *will* designates a faculty of desire determined by pure practical reason alone—that is, determined solely by the incentive of "respect" for the moral law. In that case, it is not true that the will is in itself neither good nor evil. Rather the will is good by definition. But if the will is good by definition, what then becomes of the will's "freedom"? To put this another way, there are places in Kant suggesting that the will is not free to choose between good and evil. Rather "transcendental freedom" *is* the will, determining our intentions in accordance with the moral law:

> *Will* is a kind of causality belonging to living beings so far as they are rational. *Freedom* would then be the property this causality has of being able to work independently of *determination* by alien causes. . . . A free will and a will under moral laws are one and the same.[5]

---

[4]MS 15.

[5]Kant, *Grundlegung zur Metaphysik der Sitten*, 446–47. Kant's emphases. I follow the translation of H. J. Paton: Kant, *Groundwork of the Metaphysic of Morals*. Paton's English translation gives in the margin the pagination of the standard German edition I cite here (*Königlich Preussischen Akademie der Wissenschaften*, vol. 4, 1911).

This passage is taken from Kant's work of 1785, *Groundwork of the Metaphysic of Morals*, but it expresses what appears to be the point of view of the second *Critique* of 1788 as well. Furthermore, in both works Kant seems at times to suggest that the incentive of pure reason in our will is uniquely privileged and can win any competition it enters, regardless of the strength of its competitors among our sensible incentives:

> To subordinate everything else to the holiness of duty, and to become conscious that we *can* do our duty because our own reason acknowledges it as its law and says that we *ought* to do it—that is to elevate ourselves, as it were, altogether out of the world of sense [*über die Sinnenwelt selbst gänzlich erheben*].[6]

If the passage ended here, Kant would appear to mean by free will what Schleiermacher has called an "instinct of reason." Mere consciousness of the moral law would inevitably produce moral intentions, without struggle, even without decision. "The law of reason would in fact be a law of nature," as Schleiermacher puts it. But Kant's passage continues:

> This elevation is inseparably present in our consciousness of the law as an incentive of a faculty that rules over sensibility, *though not always effectively*.[7]

The final phrase expresses Kant's recognition that dutiful action does not follow inevitably from a person's consciousness of the moral law.

The question arising out of this ambiguity in Kant is this: What decides whether a person who is aware of the moral law will also have moral intentions? It seems that for Kant the deciding factor is always and only transcendental freedom. Knowing our duty, we can do it if we exercise our transcendental freedom, and we are morally responsible to do our duty since we can always exercise our transcendental freedom, regardless of what our sensible inclinations urge to the contrary. The apparent conflict here "between natural necessity and transcendental freedom" can be resolved, Kant writes:

> This is because one and the same acting being as appearance (even to his own inner sense) has a causality in the sensuous world always in accord with the mechanism of nature; but with regard to the same event, so far as the acting person regards himself as noumenon (as pure intelligence, existing without temporal determination), he can contain a determining ground of that causality according to natural laws, and this determining ground of natural causality is itself free from every natural law.[8]

[6]Second *Kritik*, 159. Kant's emphases.
[7]Ibid. Emphasis added.
[8]Ibid., 114.

There are two difficulties with Kant's resolution of what he calls the antinomy of freedom. The first we have already seen. It is the difficulty of understanding how Kant's world of the noumenal can ever break into the necessary and all-inclusive causal connections of the world of phenomena (see above, p. 28). The second difficulty is new. For Kant, as we have just seen, the determination of our intentions in accordance with duty *is* transcendental freedom. Therefore to say that we can do our duty if we exercise our transcendental freedom is to say that we can exercise our transcendental freedom if we exercise our transcendental freedom. Kant seems in fact to accept this consequence of his moral philosophy. It becomes clear in Kant's work of 1792–93, *Religion within the Limits of Reason Alone*, that his doctrine of freedom sweeps us into a reflexive spiral: the exercise of freedom must itself be "grounded" in freedom, and so on. This grounding, Kant writes, is therefore "inscrutable to us."[9] Thus in trying to escape the infinite regress of a causal series without any "causality that is entirely self-determining" (above, p. 22), Kant must finally admit an infinite regress of his own: "We are directed back endlessly in the series of subjective determining grounds, without ever being able to reach the ultimate ground."[10] In the opening section of *Religion within the Limits of Reason Alone*, entitled "Concerning the Indwelling of the Evil Principle with the Good," Kant writes the following crucial passage:

> The source of evil cannot lie in an object determining choice through inclination, nor yet in a natural impulse; it can lie only in a rule made by choice itself for the use of its freedom, that is, in a maxim. *But now it must not be permissible to inquire into a person's subjective ground for the adoption of this maxim rather than its opposite.* . . . When we say, then, Man is by nature good, or, Man is by nature evil, this means only that there is in him an ultimate ground (inscrutable to us) of the adoption of good maxims or of evil maxims (i.e., those contrary to law), and this he has by virtue of being human, and hence he thereby expresses the character of his species.
>
> We shall say, therefore, of this character (which distinguishes man from other possible rational beings) that it is innate in him. Yet in doing so we shall ever take the position that nature is not to bear the blame (if it is evil) or take the credit (if it is good), but that the man himself is its author.[11]

This is of course Kant's treatment in philosophical guise of the Christian doctrines of the Fall and Original Sin. John Milton writes in *Paradise Lost*:

> But God left free the Will, for what obeyes
> Reason, is free, and Reason he made right. . . .
> (9.351–352)

[9] *Die Religion*, 7. English tr., 17.
[10] Ibid., 7n. English tr., 17n.
[11] Ibid., 7–8. English tr., 17. Emphasis added.

Kant agrees. Kant's difficulties lie in Milton's succeeding quatrain:

> . . . Reason he made right
> But bid her well beware, and still erect,
> Least by some faire appearing good surprised
> She dictate false, and missinforme the Will
> To do what God expressly hath forbid.
> (9.352–356)

For Kant it is impossible to say how reason can possibly "dictate false, and missinforme the Will." Thus the grounds for human responsibility for evil must remain inscrutable.

We have seen that in Schleiermacher's opinion, practical reason is never "pure." Human incentives are always and inevitably a mixture of the rational and the sensible. Schiller was to express this opinion well in 1795:

> In order to avoid all misunderstanding, I note that whenever freedom is spoken of here, that freedom is not intended which comes necessarily to a person, regarded as intelligence, and can neither be given him nor taken away, but rather that freedom which is grounded in our mixed nature [*gemischte Natur*].[12]

From the perspective Schiller shared with Schleiermacher, there is no risk of freedom's appearing to be an "instinct of reason." It is understood that incentives of reason must always compete with incentives of sense. There is nothing in the dynamics of choosing to guarantee the outcome of this competition. It is in principle thinkable that reason may carry the day, though in particular contests of deliberation the outcome may in fact be determined to be otherwise.

This, then, is Schleiermacher's second characteristic of the faculty of desire necessary to account for moral responsibility. The will is in itself neither good nor evil. It is possible, Schleiermacher writes, but not necessary that the influence of reason "can be great enough in every conceivable particular instance of choice to actualize that which conforms to reason's law, regardless of all other inclinations."[13] Schleiermacher's final phrase here seems to echo Kant's claim that practical reason can determine our intentions "regardless of what inclination may say to the contrary" (above, p. 63). We realize by now, however, that the two are not the same. Kant means that we can in fact always act morally and therefore should always do so. Our moral responsibility consists in the *a priori* obligation to act morally in every instance of choice. Schleiermacher means that we should always act morally, but that in fact we cannot always do so. Our moral responsibility consists in the *a posteriori* obligation to use our moral successes and failures to

[12] *Über die ästhetische Erziehung des Menschen*, Twentieth Letter.
[13] *Über die Freiheit*, "Denkmale," 24.

the *a posteriori* obligation to use our moral successes and failures to improve our character, our "mixed nature." In this cultivation of character, Schleiermacher writes, we have reason to hope for good, albeit gradual, success:

> For since no determinate boundary to impulses is decreed by the nature of the mind [*Seele*],[14] one may not think there is some level of impulse so high that no still higher level of another impulse could oppose it. Thanks to this boundlessness of impulses, their complete subordination to a moral impulse is quite easily thinkable.[15]

In other words, it is in general possible that a moral impulse, in competition with other impulses, may predominate; but whether or not this happens in any actual instance of choosing depends upon the training of moral character that has gone before. This training of moral character will be a subject of our succeeding discussion.

Wilhelm Dilthey, whose opinion always commands notice, maintains that Schleiermacher's account of the second condition of moral responsibility is the weakest point of his moral philosophy. Dilthey finds such phrases as the final phrase of the citation displayed just above, "quite easily thinkable," ambiguous:

> In this ambiguous "can be thought" . . . lies the whole problem. . . . Thus at this decisive point the question of whether determinism satisfies our moral consciousness remains unresolved, and Schleiermacher never supplied this lack.[16]

But in fact Schleiermacher not only supplies this lack, but supplies it in the treatise *On Human Freedom*.

Dilthey's objection goes like this: It may well be that the subordination of all other impulses to a moral impulse is in general "quite easily thinkable." But if in some particular instance I am simply incapable of subduing my immoral impulses, how can I be called morally responsible? The question is not what is "thinkable," Dilthey insists, but rather what intention I am actually able to form.

Schleiermacher's answer to such an objection is something like this: Yes, I was in this instance unable to subdue my immoral impulses. I should act morally, but my character is such that in this instance I did not. The term *morally responsible*, then, implies two things. First, my immoral action issues from my character, and thus I am responsible for it. It is *my* action, and it reveals that my character is morally blameworthy. Second, I am obligated to alter my character so that in the future it will issue not in immoral but in moral actions. I am responsible for cultivating a more moral character than my recent action has

[14]See footnote 14 of Chapter 2.
[15]"Denkmale," 27.
[16]Dilthey, *Leben Schleiermachers*, ed. Redeker, I/1, 139.

disclosed. But this latter responsibility would be impossible, Schleier-macher insists—or at least would be without any clear goal—if it were not possible to recognize that in my recent situation a moral course of action, different from my actual course, was at least thinkable:

> If in such an instance some sensible feeling was excessively elevated in my representations, still, despite all outer objects (whose influence after all is not absolute), another series of representations was possible. Namely, a series of representations by which the feeling that represents practical reason might have been affected with greater relative strength.[17]

I am responsible, then, for cultivating the representations of practical reason, or in traditional terms, for developing my "moral sense," so that in the future I shall be better prepared to act morally.

In summary, Schleiermacher's treatise anticipates Dilthey's criticism explicitly. Dilthey suggests that if the conditions for moral action are thinkable in general but are not actual in particular cases, then moral responsibility loses all meaning. Schleiermacher points out that in fact the opposite is true. If the conditions for moral action were actual both in general and in all particular cases, then moral action would at all times be *necessary* action, and moral responsibility would be under-mined:

> If those who contest our view demand that in order to show the possibility of moral action the grounds for the actuality of every particular instance must be given, then they do not consider that the idea of responsibility would thereby be much more nearly destroyed than rescued; for then the correspondence of the action to the law would be in every instance necessary.[18]

Schleiermacher's argument here hinges upon his assumption of determinism, and we must now turn our attention upon this assumption. For although we have followed Schleiermacher's analysis of the faculty of desire at length, we have not yet come to the question most crucial to his understanding of determinism and freedom in human choice. Even if we accept for the moment Schleiermacher's contention that our willful intentions always involve a contest among various incentives—of which none is pure, *a priori*, "direct," or otherwise uniquely privileged—one question still remains. How are we to explain why one incentive prevails over others in determining any particular intention? Schleiermacher's phrasing is clumsy, but he puts the question this way: "Wherein must the origin of a predominance of one part of the determining ground of choice over other parts itself be grounded?"[19]

[17]MS 23.
[18]"Denkmale," 29–30.
[19]Ibid., 25.

Schleiermacher's answer is that choice is always causally grounded in the condition of a person's character. Every intention, moral and immoral alike, is a necessary result of a person's state—mental, physical, and circumstantial—at the moment of the person's intending. We should recall again that by character Schleiermacher always means what Schiller calls a person's "mixed nature," our rational impulses and our sensible impulses, which together constitute what Schleiermacher calls our faculty of representation:

> Here nothing is to be further separated, and this grounding of the activities of the faculty of desire in the condition of the faculty of representation cannot at all surprise us if we consider the following points: that through the association of ideas, it always depends upon the state of the faculty of representation what sort of inner objects of impulse will arise upon the occasion of an outer object and, together with the outer, affect the faculty of desire; that it depends upon the state of the faculty of representation whether and how in each instance we formulate the maxims under which we believe individual cases to be included; that it rests upon the state of the faculty of representation whether or not certain outer objects of impulse appear to us as such; and that upon this same state depends the degree to which the syllogism applying moral law to the maxim in question will be formally and materially correct or not.

On the basis of these general observations Schleiermacher then states the fundamental principle of his determinism:

> Thus the proposition appears to be established that the predominance in which every comparison of choice must end, if it is to pass over into a full-scale action of the faculty of desire, must in every instance be grounded in the totality of present representations, and in the state of all the faculties of the mind [*Seelenvermögen*] and their relations among themselves, which are brought forth by the flow of representations in our mind [*Seele*].[20]

Schleiermacher's deterministic principle means that if a person decides to do this thing instead of that, it is because in the person's present state of mind the incentive to do this is stronger than the incentive to do that. What I am determines what I do. Or to put this a little less bluntly, at the moment of choosing, all the incentives in my state of mind are combined, and the vector sum of that combination is my effective intention. The dynamics of combination and counterpoise we call *deliberation*. The resulting vector sum we call *resolution* or *intention*. *Choice* as Schleiermacher defines it consists of these two taken together.

Schleiermacher realizes that there is no possibility of proof here. It is not important that an inductive proof of his deterministic hypothesis is

---

[20]Ibid., 26–27.

impossible, he writes, for an inductive proof of an hypothesis to the contrary would be equally impossible. Just as Kant had realized that the science of psychology might never complete its work since its subject matter is unlimited (see above, pp. 29–30), so too "it would be unending to show that among all perceived appearances, none could lie at the basis of a given appearance as its cause." As for a deductive proof, Kant's first *Critique* has taught that "the proof that something has a cause lies by its very nature outside the sphere of experience."[21] In other words, Kant has argued to Schleiermacher's satisfaction that to experience any event means to experience it as caused, and we have noted the ironic fact that Schleiermacher's deterministic outlook probably owes as much to this argument from Kant's first *Critique* as to any other single factor (above, p. 34).

What Schleiermacher presents here, then, is an ethical hypothesis — not a theoretical one, such as the hypotheses of the natural sciences, and not a transcendental postulate, such as Kant's idea of transcendental freedom. His claims for his hypothesis are relatively modest. It is his description of the operations of choosing as they appear to him. Like any hypothesis it does not contain its own proof or means of validation. It may be considered confirmed only if its compliance with and its ability to illumine our actual moral experience can be shown. Schleiermacher argues that his hypothesis of determinism is superior to other ethical hypotheses in this respect. But his appeal is not to theoretical proof or transcendental deduction; it is rather to common moral sense:

> It appears not only that no other possible answer could be in accord with those [moral] conditions which we have accepted as established, but also that this would be the natural opinion of every person who is not misdirected either by misunderstood feelings or by metaphysical sophistries, but rather follows the judgment of common human understanding — which at all times has as its basis, not indeed the purely moral, but some sort of practical interest.[22]

Of course having made the claim he makes here about the consonance of his views with "natural opinion," Schleiermacher faces the difficulty of having to explain why the doctrine of determinism "has as yet never universally overcome the illusions" that obscure it.[23] He devotes the third of the four subdivisions of his treatise *On Human Freedom* to an historical investigation of factors accounting for the failure of the necessitarian world view to win universal consent. At no time in the history of philosophy, he writes, have the factors congenial to such a world view all coexisted. Only in the modern period, for example, has the Greek idea of final causality been set aside in favor of

[21]Ibid., 41.
[22]MS 23.
[23]"Denkmale," 39.

efficient causality, the explanatory power of which has been demonstrated in the natural sciences. Or again, in earlier ages of the Christian
era an acceptance of arbitrariness in the course of events was encouraged by naive concepts of divine punishment and reward—concepts now
widely set aside.[24] Like most historical arguments, Schleiermacher's
arguments in this third section are far from conclusive, though they
may claim some cogency. He was later to develop these historical
arguments more fully in his *Groundwork to a Critique of Previous Ethical
Doctrine* of 1803, and in his lectures on the *History of Philosophy* of
1812–1823.

It will be our business in the remaining chapters of Part I to follow
further the non-historical, moral arguments Schleiermacher marshals in
support of his deterministic position. But first we need to emphasize the
uncompromising character of his hypothesis. There is no mistaking its
thorough necessitarianism. "We are convinced that nothing will happen
except that which is grounded in our state and thus in the whole series
of preceding states," Schleiermacher writes.[25] Even our very ability to
recognize the necessity of our intentions is grounded in our state of
mind; and the recognition of necessity becomes itself a part of our state
of mind; and so on. We shall see that Schleiermacher takes great
pleasure in the reflexive quality of such psychological analysis. But no
amount of emphasis upon reflexive subtlety, when we come back to it
shortly, should be allowed to detract from Schleiermacher's insistence
that a succession of phenomena "never arises from subjects, but only
from modifications of subjects."[26]

This language of "modification" recalls again the terminology of
Spinoza's philosophy. In his private notes on Spinoza of 1793–94 (see
above, p. 45), Schleiermacher remarks on the fact that Spinoza grounds
his philosophy in two principles. The first is the widely quoted *ex nihilo
nihil fit*, "out of nothing, nothing is made." The second is less
frequently noted: *nihil ex nihilo fit*, "nothing is made out of nothing."[27]
The attempt to paraphrase these principles makes one appreciate the
conciseness of Latin, but we might do so as follows. Spinoza believed
that "once given a state of nothingness, nothing could ever have come
to be." That is the basis of his theology: God must exist eternally.
Spinoza believed also that "of all the things that are, none of them has
come to be out of nothingness." That is the basis of his determinism:
everything temporal is produced by causal antecedents. Schleiermacher's
notes point out that the second of these principles, in Spinoza's view,

[24]Ibid., 39–43.
[25]"Denkmale," 38.
[26]Ibid., 45.
[27]*Spinozismus*, ed. Mulert, 302.

pertains to thought as well as to extension or matter. In other words, our reasoning is as fully determined as our perceiving, and both are as fully determined as the course of events in the order of nature—which is to say, fully determined.

Schleiermacher agrees with Spinoza in all of this. The philosopher Jacobi, in his 1785 book on Spinoza's philosophy that occasioned Schleiermacher's notes on Spinoza,[28] had argued against Spinoza's determinism, insisting among other things that if efficient causality rules in the sphere of human consciousness, then the faculty of thought is a mere "spectator" of events in which, since they are determined, it has no substantial role. Schleiermacher comments in his notes:

> Here is the real point at which I believe Jacobi may not have understood
> Spinoza. And since this is exactly the point from which Jacobi's refutation
> proceeds, it thus appears as if Spinoza is correct and not Jacobi. [Jacobi
> has claimed that] if there are nothing but efficient causes then the faculty
> of thought is a mere spectator. But I do not comprehend why the faculty
> of thought cannot be included under efficient causes. A judgment, indeed
> even a judgment concerning what should happen, can certainly follow
> from a representation completely mechanically, in the sense that a purely
> logical consequence is completely mechanical.[29]

Schleiermacher uses similar mechanical imagery in *On Human Freedom* of 1792–93:

> We look upon all impulses [*Triebe*] as forces, the effects of which
> circumscribe each other as completely as if by mechanical laws. We look
> upon all actions as one whole which indissolubly coheres [*unauflöslich in
> sich zusammenhängt*], the as yet unknown parts of which one may already
> judge in advance according to the law of those already known. Through-
> out, therefore, we are pursued as it were by genial necessity; throughout
> we recognize its sign.[30]

These are very direct statements of a necessitarian position. There is something wry, therefore, in Schleiermacher's saying that he supposes his ethical theory will meet with the name of determinism.[31] Determin-ism of a kind is most certainly what it is. Schleiermacher freely acknowledges this fact, but on one condition:

> The author is happy with the name of determinist, but only if the reader
> will promise that he does not want to attribute to this author a single
> sentence of any other determinist not contained in what the author has
> himself said or is about to say.[32]

[28]Friedrich Heinrich Jacobi, *Über die Lehre des Spinoza in Briefen an Herrn Moses Mendelssohn.*
[29]*Spinozismus*, ed. Mulert, 301.
[30]"Denkmale," 31.
[31]Ibid., 28.
[32]MS 26.

Probably Schleiermacher is trying in this sentence to ward off any attempts at identifying his deterministic outlook with that of the seventeenth-century determinist Leibniz, who was frequently on Schleiermacher's mind during the 1790s but, as we have already seen (above, p. 36), never very near his heart. Schleiermacher wants his treatise to be judged on its merits, without preconceptions about its deterministic outlook. On the second page he observes that, as he takes up his pen to write on the question of human freedom, moral philosophy is more or less evenly divided between two opposing forces: the deterministic camp on the one side, commanded by Leibniz, and the Kantian camp of transcendental libertarians on the other.[33] Schleiermacher is convinced there is ethical ground to be gained by a third party to this philosophical struggle.

He never lost that conviction. His determinism remains a permanent feature in his philosophy. In his lectures on *Dialectics* of 1811–1831, for example, we find a passage on the theme, "All in the realm of being is equally free and necessary":

> Free and necessary are not mutually contradictory. . . . Indeed, one can say that freedom and necessity are each the measure of the other. The freedom of something is that thing entire, and the necessity of something is also that thing entire, only regarded from another side. Everything is thus the image of the whole, only in various measures. . . . Choice itself is in fact a product of the meeting of the person with all that is outward.[34]

Similarly in his great theological system, *The Christian Faith* of 1821–22, as revised in 1830, we find Schleiermacher making the following assertions in connection with his discussion of "the one and undivided divine causality":

> In the divine causality there is no division or opposition throughout. . . . True, we cannot avoid affirming the existence of the particular in itself as a part of this whole; but we immediately stray from the right path if we assume for this particular a special divine causality in any way separate from connection with the whole, and thus regard the particular in question as a special goal or result of divine governance, to which other things are therefore subordinated as means. Rather, as a necessary correction, we must immediately subordinate it to the other things, so that each particular appears as an intersection, equally conditioned and conditioning.

The divine rule of the world, he writes in the same place, is "an inwardly coherent order."[35]

It is striking to realize that, uncompromising as it is, there is nothing in Schleiermacher's hypothesis of an inwardly coherent world order that

---

[33]MS 2.

[34]*Dialektik*, ed. Halpern, 197–98. Cf. the Jonas ed., 132.

[35]*Der christliche Glaube*, ed. Redeker, Propositions 164.3 and 165.

jeopardizes his understanding of the moral responsibility we examined at the beginning of this chapter. The two characteristics of the faculty of desire presented by Schleiermacher as prerequisites for moral responsibility (above, pp. 63–64) led us directly to Schleiermacher's deterministic analysis of human choosing and are fully compatible with it. This is not to say that his understanding of moral responsibility is above criticism, however. We might imagine a Kantian arguing with Schleiermacher in the following way: "You may define the term *responsibility* as you want, I suppose. But if you couple your definition of responsibility with your hypothesis of determinism, then something essential is left out of your account of moral experience. You say that I am responsible for my actions insofar as what I *am* results in what I *do*. But might we not in the same sense hold the earth morally responsible for the loss of innocent lives in the Lisbon earthquake of 1755? It may be that what I am causes what I do. But ultimately, according to your deterministic view, I am *not* myself the cause of what I am. Thus I am ultimately not accountable for my moral character."

The word "accountable" is the heart of the issue here. From a Kantian point of view, the essential element left out of Schleiermacher's discussion of moral experience is what Kant terms moral *accountability* (*Zurechnung*). Kant believes that the concept of accountability is essential to an analysis of our moral experience, and he is convinced that it is impossible to reconcile accountability with a deterministic ethical scheme. "Without transcendental freedom," Kant writes, ". . . no moral law and no accountability to it are possible."[36] If we are not, in some moment of our choosing, free from the chains of causality that bind us, how can we possibly be held morally accountable for the actions we are caused to do? Kant's *Religion within the Limits of Reason Alone* of 1792–93 turns on precisely this point: that if we are not the cause of what we are—not the transcendentally free cause of our own character—then we cannot be held morally accountable for our intentions.

We have already glimpsed some of Kant's difficulties with this issue (above, pp. 66–67). Schleiermacher is fully aware of these difficulties as well. He calls the question of accountability the "most important" his own ethical analysis has to face.[37] Taking the point of view of a hypothetical Kantian critic at one place in his treatise, Schleiermacher asks rhetorically:

> If every action is the completely determined effect of previous actions and conditions, and if every condition in turn is grounded in a previous one, then we come finally to a condition in the childhood of a person in which no morality, indeed scarcely even any choice as to his actions, is present.

[36]Second *Kritik*, 97.
[37]MS 26. Cf. "Denkmale," 28.

No one, therefore, is the cause of what he is, and so how is it possible for
me to praise this person and blame that one?[38]

What is Schleiermacher to say in answer to this Kantian objection?
It is true that in Schleiermacher's point of view we are not ultimately
the cause of what we are. What is more, far from ever denying this
contention, Schleiermacher later broadens and deepens it. In *The Christian Faith* of 1821, he makes it the very foundation upon which his
understanding of religious piety rests. Piety, as anyone familiar with *The
Christian Faith* will recall, is grounded in what Schleiermacher calls the
feeling of absolute dependence—the feeling that "negates absolute
freedom," the feeling that "the whole of our existence is from
elsewhere,"[39] or in other words, our feeling that ultimately we are not
the cause of what we are.

In *On Human Freedom*, however, Schleiermacher is dealing with
ethical experience, not religious piety. What he does in response to the
Kantian objection is to deny that the concept of accountability, as Kant
uses it, has any place in the analysis of moral experience. "The question
of accountability," he writes in his Journal some years later, "does not
belong in ethics at all."[40] As early as 1789, while working on his three
dialogues on freedom, Schleiermacher was criticizing "incorrect and
murky" notions of moral accountability.[41] His teacher Eberhard had
given his Halle students the following definition: "Accountability is the
judgment that someone is the free cause of the morality of an action."[42]
But Schleiermacher points out that by its use of the phrase "free
cause," such a definition prejudices an investigation into moral
obligation from the outset; the question of "free cause" ought
"conscientiously to be avoided" until it, or its opposite, forms part of
the investigation's conclusion.[43]

Besides this methodological objection, Schleiermacher has two substantive quarrels with Eberhard's definition of accountability, and with
Kant's. First, as a concept, accountability is theoretically promiscuous
when judged by the epistemological standards of Kant's own first
Critique. Second, the notion of accountability is in any case without
ethical usefulness. The first of these quarrels grows from what we have
called Schleiermacher's "strict construction" of Kant's first *Critique*
(above, p. 34). Schleiermacher feels that in insisting on such notions as
the *a priori* feeling of respect, the postulate of transcendental freedom,
and moral accountability defined so as to entail transcendental freedom,

[38]MS 26. Cf. "Denkmale," 28.
[39]*Der christliche Glaube*, Proposition 4.3.
[40]"Denkmale," 133.
[41]Letter to Brinkmann, July 22, 1789. *Br.* IV, 19.
[42]Johann August Eberhard, *Sittenlehre der Vernunft*, 69.
[43]MS 28.

Kant in his second *Critique* has led reason back into the "metaphysical wastelands" from which he had rescued it in his first *Critique* (above, p. 11). Like an analysis of the transcendental freedom it presupposes, an analysis of the notion of accountability loses its way at the boundary between Kant's "two worlds" of phenomena and noumena. Schleiermacher's theoretical quarrel with accountability as a concept is therefore essentially the same as his quarrel with transcendental freedom (see above, pp. 37–38). His treatise at one place calls the latter concept *eine Dichtung*, "a fiction."[44]

As always in his treatise, however, Schleiermacher's primary objection is not theoretical but practical. Kant believes that we are "immediately conscious" of accountability to an unconditionally obligating moral law "as soon as we construct maxims for the will."[45] Schleiermacher agrees that we are conscious of an experience of moral obligation, but he cannot agree that our moral experience must be thought of as Kant conceptualizes it in his notion of accountability. He disagrees with Kant's observations concerning the nature of our moral experience, with Kant's moral phenomenology. He feels that Kant's analysis of our moral experience has not only strayed back into the wastelands of metaphysics, but has done so unnecessarily. Schleiermacher himself speaks of moral accountability, but not in Kant's sense. He includes accountability under what he has already defined as moral responsibility, letting "accountability" settle into a more particular and individual connotation,[46] while the conditions for "responsibility" are more abstract and general, as we have seen (above, pp. 63–64). Schleiermacher's definition of accountability, then, reads as follows:

> Accountability is the judgment by which we assign the morality of an action to the one who has performed it, in such a way that the judgment concerning the action constitutes a part of our judgment of the agent's worth. I believe that if one makes allowance for all that experience contributes here, no judgment of accountability will contain more than this, not even the strongest and most severe.[47]

To clarify his definition of accountability Schleiermacher draws the first of what will be many analogies from the aesthetic sphere of experience. The judgment by which we assign the morality of an action to the person who is accountable for it is analogous to the judgment by which we assign the greatness of a work of art to the artist who conceived and executed it.[48] A woman is an artist. Our judgment of any

---

[44]"Denkmale," 37.

[45]Second *Kritik*, 29.

[46]MS 31. See Dilthey's discussion of Schleiermacher's use of these terms in *Leben Schleiermachers*, ed. Redeker, I/1, 138–40.

[47]MS 28–29. Cf. "Denkmale," 28.

[48]"Denkmale," 31.

single work of her art "constitutes a part of our judgment" of her worth
as an artist—but only a part. It is only one work, whereas her artistic
output comprises many. We praise her for her work, or we fault her if it
fails to satisfy our canons of taste. But we do not deify the artist,
however great her work may be. We recognize how much her greatness
owes to earlier masters, or to the ferment of the age in which she lives,
or to what we refer to as her God-given talent, and so on. We recognize
that the artist is not autonomously the cause of what she is. Nor do we
damn the artist for her failures. We are probably even more prone to
attribute the artist's failures to the necessities of her personal history
and circumstances than we are her successes. No artist, then, and no
ethical agent, enjoys absolute autonomy. Both are supported and hin-
dered by an organic system of necessity, now genial, now intractable.
Yet both agents are able to produce individual expressions of themselves, to create and act characteristically and uniquely. We fault or
praise not only the work but also the person accountable for it, though
always in proportion to the work's relative importance in the context of
its creator's whole productivity.

Accountability understood in the light of this analogy is compatible
with Schleiermacher's determinism. In fact, like the broader concept of
responsibility, it presupposes determinism. Schleiermacher believes that
such an understanding of accountability is sufficient to account for our
experience of moral obligation. We praise or blame a person's *actions*
insofar as they satisfy or offend our rational standards of moral judgment. We praise or blame the *person* insofar as the actions express the
person's character. And the difference between persons and the earth
under Lisbon in 1755 is that persons, under the influence of reason and
sense, can alter their moral character—a theme we shall return to
presently when we discuss the practical issues of regret, punishment,
self-improvement, and the like.

Chapter 6. Freedom and the Goal of Ethical Life

> *By freedom of the will we convey the denial of all outward constraint and express the essence of conscious life—namely, that no outer influence so determines our whole state that the reaction is also already determined and given.*

If the principle according to which one incentive of the will prevails over others is determinism, as Schleiermacher maintains; if moral responsibility depends upon the principle that our choices are causally grounded in our character and circumstance at the moment of choosing; then one must ask what possible meaning is left for Schleiermacher's use of the term *freedom*.

Schleiermacher states the most general criterion of freedom as follows: "At the basis of every concept of freedom there always lies *the absence of a constraint*."[1] This criterion—the *absence* of a constraint—is a negative condition of freedom, or what Schleiermacher calls "the indeterminate mark of freedom." We need to understand this negative criterion before we proceed to Schleiermacher's positive characterizations of freedom. Schleiermacher's treatise does not define the term *constraint* (*Nöthigung*). In general, however, the German word may convey what we might call an active sense, as in the English "coercion" and "compulsion"; or it may convey a passive sense, as in "impediment" and "restraint." The word "constraint" seems best suited to bear this dipolar implication, being defined by the *Oxford English Dictionary* as "the exercise of force to *determine or confine* action."

How Schleiermacher uses this term is more difficult to decide. We already know that the absence of constraint is not equivalent in Schleiermacher's mind to the absence of necessity (*Nothwendigkeit*). We have seen his fundamental belief that we are immersed, body and mind, in what he calls "amiable" or "genial" (*liebreich*) necessity. An entire world view is contained in that adjective "amiable." To appreciate this, one need only compare Schleiermacher's language with Kant's. Both men speak metaphorically of necessity as *ein feines Spiel*, "a subtle play." But the modifiers they use indicate their utterly disparate attitudes toward the issue of human freedom. For Kant, the play of

---

[1] *Über die Freiheit des Menschen*, "Denkmale," 44. Editor Dilthey's emphasis.

necessity is *bloss ein mechanisches*, "merely a mechanical" play. For Schleiermacher it is *ein äusserst feines*, "a most exceedingly subtle" play.[2] Schleiermacher does not mislead his reader by avoiding the word "mechanical." His determinism is strict enough to justify that adjective, and he uses it occasionally, as we have already seen.[3] But Schleiermacher took pleasure in the fact that the causality presupposed by his ethical hypothesis is a most exceedingly subtle mechanism.

One might think it obvious—although the history of controversy over determinism shows it is not—that if someone hypothesizes necessary causality as the explanation for certain phenomena, then even the critics of that hypothesis must suppose the causality to be at least as subtle and intricate as the phenomena to be explained. In the case of ethical analysis, this would mean at least as subtle and intricate as the play of thoughts and inclinations in human consciousness. If human intentions are to be accounted for on the mechanical analogy of a myriad different inclinations of various intensities, uniting as a sort of vector sum to determine choice (see above, p. 70), then the emphasis must be on *myriad* and *different* and *various*.[4] We shall see in the *Speeches* of 1799 and its later editions the growing importance of the term *living*, which Schleiermacher uses to express the intricacy of the determinism he presupposes.

Schleiermacher had to emphasize that intricacy in the face of critics who tried to reduce deterministic philosophies to a position of absurd crudity. Even the great Reinhold invokes against determinism the tired philosopher's cliché of Buridan's Ass: "Between two haystacks that tempt him equally, he must starve"[5]—as if even in a donkey sheer impatience would not sooner or later prompt a move in one direction or

[2]Kant, second *Kritik*, 39. Schleiermacher, *Kurze Darstellung des Spinozistischen Systems*, 310.

[3]Above, p. 73. A few years before Schleiermacher's treatise, Schiller had used mechanical imagery in his *An die Freude* to express the motive power of joy:

> *Freude heisst die starke Feder*
> *In der ewigen Natur.*
> *Freude, Freude treibt die Räder*
> *In der grossen Weltenuhr.*

[4]Ernest Lee Tuveson puts this observation nicely in relation to the psychology of John Locke: "Experience for Locke is not a mere automatic connection of impressions, as if an adding machine were being set up. He always has the sense of a living being, with inclinations of its own, responding in a myriad of ways to a world which affects it in as many ways. In the center is an autonomous organizing power; but its area is not sharply defined, and its boundaries expand and contract with the exigencies of the creature's total response to its ever-changing environment. The personality is potentially the whole of its experience, existing in a state of constantly shifting tensions." *The Imagination as a Means of Grace*, 40.

[5]Karl Leonhard Reinhold, *Briefe über die Kantische Philosophie*, II, 280. The example takes its name from the medieval French philosopher Jean Buridan, against whose qualified moral determinism it was apparently first directed.

the other, depending, we may suppose, upon which way the unfortunate beast happened to be looking when its hunger finally outweighed its indecision. Apparently oblivious to the possibility of so obvious a rejoinder to his example, Reinhold proceeds to the conclusion that human freedom

> is denied by determinists insofar as they seek the determining grounds of all a person's actions *outside him*. . . . Thereby they actually place human beings in the same class with Buridan's Ass, in that they allow in *both* a faculty for action only insofar as they are both constrained [*genöthiget*] to act by a predominance of outer grounds, completely independent of themselves. There is only this difference: that the human is constrained *with*, the ass *without*, consciousness of those grounds.[6]

Again it is assumed that our consciousness of causal grounds could not itself become a determining factor in our choosing. Even Fichte was not above caricaturing the determinist's position as "materialism," ignoring in the process Spinoza's specific assertion that in his philosophy intellectual determination is not to be reduced to materialistic determination.[7] Spinoza taught that a modification of ideas is caused by prior ideas, and that a modification of matter or "extension" is caused by prior material conditions—the two modes of causality occurring always together.

In fairness to Fichte it must be pointed out that in 1797 he may have known Spinoza's philosophy only at second hand. Editions of Spinoza's works were rare. Many German philosophers knew Spinoza only from Jacobi's book of 1785, *On the Doctrine of Spinoza, in Letters to Moses Mendelssohn*, and Jacobi is misleading on the issue of Spinoza's materialism. In 1791–92, Schleiermacher, too, was familiar with Spinoza only from the same source. And yet, with his greater affinity for Spinoza's determinism, Schleiermacher was able to see through Jacobi's misrepresentation:

> Now I feel confident that I can prove the opposite from the Spinozistic propositions Jacobi himself has drawn up. . . . According to Spinoza it is certain that every modification in thought, regarded as an effect, relates to previous thought; though it is equally certain that this modification cannot exist alone, but rather can constitute the modification of the thing in question only together with a modification of extension. . . . So how then can Jacobi say that an activity such as conversation is an activity of the body alone? How can he say that the inventor of the clock has not really invented it? The idea of the clock developed as the consequence of other ideas. That the bodily correlative to that idea is a consequence of bodily forces makes no difference.[8]

---

[6]Ibid., 280–81. Reinhold's emphases.
[7]Fichte, *Erste Einleitung*, 436–37. Cf. Spinoza, *Ethics*, Part I, Proposition 10, and Part II, Proposition 6.
[8]Schleiermacher, *Spinozismus*, ed. Mulert, 301–3.

In the face of such misunderstandings it is no wonder that Schleiermacher insisted that his philosophy not be identified with any preconceived notion of determinism (above, p. 73). His own determinism, whatever its ethical value may prove to be, is not to be ruled out because it is reductionistic in the way that critics such as Reinhold and Fichte would like to suggest. "Our faculty of desire is not to be thought of as absolutely determined by any one object," Schleiermacher writes in *On Human Freedom*:

> We do not wish to be aware of a liberation from all necessity, for this cannot be exhibited in any example whatsoever . . . , but rather of a freeing from the constraint [*Nöthigung*] of the object, and this is exhibited whenever we determine our faculty of desire through a representation that relates solely to self-consciousness.[9]

One senses that Schleiermacher would have had no difficulty incorporating later theories of genetic, subconscious, and unconscious motivations in human life, had such theories been available to him in the 1790s. He stresses the reflexive character of his hypothesis: the theory of determinism affects our feelings, thoughts, and intentions; the theory must account for its own influence; and so on. His determinism thus involves a subtlety that amounts to an infinite regress, the complete specification of which no amount of motivational vector analysis can ever exhaust.

It was this infinite regress that Kant was unable to tolerate in the midst of ethical analysis. To think that we can include *a posteriori* analysis of human motivations in ethical judgments, Kant insists, will not do. Without the absolute guidance of purely *a priori* moral law, "the occasional exceptions one is permitted to make are endless and cannot be definitely comprehended in a universal rule."[10] Kant therefore chooses a philosophical course that encounters its infinite regress elsewhere (see above, p. 66). In contrast, Schleiermacher enjoys relating ethical obligation to each individual's unique position in the infinite causality of nature, which, as he writes in 1798, "always works rather like La Fontaine."[11] The sophistication and delicacy of Jean de La Fontaine's *Fables* cannot "be definitely comprehended in a universal rule," it is true. But from Schleiermacher's point of view, La Fontaine's idiosyncratic insights can be as ethically illuminating as the formal universality of Kant's categorical imperative. The two belong in ethics side by side.

To recapitulate, by "the absence of a constraint" Schleiermacher does not mean that freedom involves the absence of necessity—unless one pictures necessity in a crude way that makes us into jerky mechanical robots, which we obviously are not. Schleiermacher does not mean

[9]MS 64. Cf. "Denkmale," 36.
[10]Second *Kritik*, 28.
[11]Letter to Herz, Sep. 9, 1798. *Br.* I, 192.

merely the absence of external physical constraints either. Kant had already insisted that moral obligation is a matter of a person's intentions, and not necessarily of the person's consequent activity also. Our moral judgments are based upon what we intend to do and not upon what our physical abilities permit us to accomplish in actuality. Papageno in Mozart's *Magic Flute* of 1791 gets a padlock installed on his mouth, but only until he intends to become truthful. Papageno is still free in the sense required by moral responsibility, which Kant and Schleiermacher—and apparently Wolfgang Amadeus Mozart as well—held to be a matter of intention and not of physical action as such.

It can happen, of course, that our physical or psychological condition constrains our intentions to such a severe degree that we speak of a loss of freedom and thus a loss of moral responsibility, as in cases of persons under conditions of extreme danger or blinding pain. In such cases we find ourselves saying, "She simply was not in possession of herself," or "He did not intend to do it, but he could not help himself." Short of such extremes, however, Schleiermacher speaks of degrees of constraint and degrees of freedom.

We began this chapter with Schleiermacher's negative criterion of freedom, and we have discovered what freedom is not: it is not the absence of necessity, and it is not merely the absence of physical constraint. To advance beyond this double negative to Schleiermacher's positive definition of freedom we must now consider the notion of *inner* constraints upon our intentions. The distinction between inner and outer constraints usually become nebulous upon careful examination, but still the distinction is an ethically useful one. An unsettling dream, a burst of sensual stimuli, the sudden recurrence of some long dormant memory, an unaccustomed synthesis of ideas—any of these internal factors can throw us off balance and constrain our intentions. We suffer a loss of freedom to the extent that we merely react to such internal constraints, to the extent that we are caught off guard by some state of mind we have not previously entertained and integrated into the dispositions and habits of our personality.

These considerations bring us to Schleiermacher's positive definition of freedom. Freedom is self-expression. I am free, according to Schleiermacher's definition, insofar as my intentions express myself. The emphasis here must be on the *self*. I am free to the extent that my intentions express not merely some fleeting state of my mind, created for example by some surprising combination of circumstances to which I must react in unaccustomed ways, but rather the characteristic state of mind—more or less permanent, though never unchanging—that I may refer to as myself. We should notice that according to this definition, if my intentions express myself, then I am free, regardless of how I have arrived at the state of mind that is characteristically my own. This property is the key to the compatibility between Schleiermacher's definition of freedom and his hypothesis of determinism. By defining freedom as unconstrained expression of characteristic individuality, Schleiermacher is left at liberty to think of our character as having developed necessarily from our personal history. Freedom is not the absence of necessity. Freedom is necessity incorporated, necessity understood. "With the feeling of necessity," Schleiermacher writes in *On Human Freedom*, "consciousness of personality makes ethical progress."[12]

Freedom defined in this way is inversely proportional to foreign constraints upon a person's characteristic state of mind. It is therefore directly proportional to my ability to incorporate the foreign, to come to terms with the new, to make it my own, to include it as a part of my nature. I am free in proportion to my ability to accept necessity as "genial" and appropriate its conditions as my own, incorporating them in memory, rationality, and disposition—even in my physical constitution—in order to express them again at appropriate moments as my own intentions and actions.

Such is the understanding of freedom that will sustain the development of Schleiermacher's thought to the end of his career. In an address delivered before the Berlin Academy of Sciences in 1825, we find Schleiermacher still assigning the highest degree of moral freedom to the person who is immersed in the causality of nature, "appropriating and cultivating, and thus manifesting himself in creation that is his own and self-contained."[13] These three aspects of freedom distinguished in Schleiermacher's address of 1825—freedom as appropriating (*aneignend*), cultivating (*bildend*), and manifesting (*offenbarend*)—may serve as valuable guides to Schleiermacher's thinking about freedom. In his lectures on psychology, delivered four times between 1818 and 1834, Schleiermacher describes these three aspects of freedom as the "three forms of self-activity."[14] They are basic categories of freedom for Schleiermacher, and we shall employ them here in the same way. We shall deal with freedom under its third aspect, self-manifestation, in Chapter 3 of Part II, where we shall see how the *Speeches* of 1799 and the *Soliloquies* of 1800 provide illustrations of Schleiermacher's free expression of himself "in creation that is his own and self-contained." This third aspect of freedom, however, presupposes the other two— freedom as cultivation and freedom as appropriation—upon which we must dwell a moment here.

---

[12]"Denkmale," 39.

[13] *Über den Unterschied zwischen Naturgesetz und Sittengesetz*, 416.

[14]*Psychologie*, 243–61. Here Schleiermacher designates the three aspects of freedom as the impulse to self-preservation (*Selbsterhaltungstrieb*), self-acquisition (*Besizergreifen*), and self-manifestation (*Selbstmanifestation*).

Self-cultivation was a principal theme of German romanticism, reaching an early climax in Johann Wolfgang Goethe's "cultivation novel," *Wilhelm Meister's Apprenticeship*. The preoccupation with self-cultivation, the broadening and deepening of one's experience, was an element of the atmosphere of the age. Schleiermacher was breathing that atmosphere well before his entry into the romantic world of Berlin in 1796, the year of *Wilhelm Meister*'s completion. The ethical ideal presented in Schleiermacher's treatise *On Human Freedom* is the personality whose cultivation is so complete, whose comprehension of the causal world order so broad, that he "appears to act in accordance with circumstances but not to be altered by them."[15] The ideal freedom is "activity," in the sense that persons are free who do not have to react to circumstances, but rather find in them a catalytic stimulation for intentions they have already cultivated. Persons are free who do not find themselves passive in a given situation, but rather active, prepared to meet events with a creative response that arises from within them. Schleiermacher speaks of this ideal freedom in his *Soliloquies* of 1800 as the "cultivated force" that propels the "free motion of the ethical person about his own axis."[16] He speaks of it in his *Groundwork* of 1803 as the "soul that is just the same in its inner and enduring manifestations as in its outward and changing, one and the same force in all its various expressions."[17] And in the theological work of his maturity, *The Christian Faith* of 1821, we find Schleiermacher employing the same concept of freedom in his discussion of human responsibility for sin:

> By freedom of the will we convey the denial of all outward constraint [*Nötigung*] and express the essence of conscious life—namely, that no outer influence so determines our whole state that the reaction is also already determined and given. Rather, every stimulation first receives its determination from the innermost focus of life, from which the reaction also then proceeds. Thus the sin proceeding from this focus is always the sinner's own act and not that of any other.[18]

Freedom in this sense involves not only the cultivation or broadening of a person's experience but also an appropriation of experience of a particularly thorough kind, and this is freedom in the third of its aspects, the aspect that will prove most central to Schleiermacher's moral philosophy. To *appropriate* (*aneignen*) means to make something a part of one's integrity or *proprium* (*Eigentum*). Schleiermacher will write in 1798 that he considers it an "eternal law" of ethics "that everyone

---

[15]MS 73. Cf. "Denkmale," 39.

[16]Quoted in Dilthey, *Leben Schleiermachers*, ed. Redeker, I/1, 161.

[17]*Grundlinien einer Kritik der bisherigen Sittenlehre*, 68.

[18]*Der christliche Glaube*, ed. Redeker, Proposition 81.2. I am indebted to Richard Brandt, *The Philosophy of Schleiermacher*, 135n, for calling this passage to my attention.

deserves all that he understands how to appropriate."[19] Schleiermacher regards ethics as the art of forming a *proprium*, of molding what the early romantics call a person's *Gemüth*[20]—an integral, harmonious sphere of knowledge and desire. In his treatise *On the Worth of Life*, Schleiermacher writes that ethics is a person's search for a principle that will shape an "aggregate" of experiences into a "whole."[21]

Schleiermacher believed that his ethical investigations had discovered such a principle, which we may call his formula for the goal of ethical life. In order to share this discovery we may begin by asking the question, What is it that makes a *free* action a *moral* one? We have seen that it is possible to interpret Kant's philosophy in such a way that a free act and a moral act are one and the same (above, p. 64). In Schleiermacher's philosophy the two are clearly not identical. Schleiermacher speaks of freedom as self-expression, for example. But an act can express either a moral or an immoral character and still be free in this sense, as Schleiermacher's use of sin to exemplify freedom in *The Christian Faith* has just indicated. Some of the early romantics, such as Schleiermacher's Berlin roommate Friedrich Schlegel, may be suspected of advocating a morality (or amorality) of sheer expressionism, but the suspicion does not apply to Schleiermacher.

Under its second aspect freedom is the cultivation or broadening of one's character. Schleiermacher recognizes freedom in this aspect also to be an element but no sufficient guarantee of morality. Thus he writes in his treatise *On the Worth of Life* that there must be some other measure of the moral worth of people "than the vigor with which they are affected and effect in return."[22] This other measure has to do with freedom in its third aspect, with the way in which we are able to appropriate our experiences. In the remainder of this chapter we shall see that by a moral action Schleiermacher means an action that is free, but only if freedom is thought of under the aspects of cultivation and appropriation understood in a particular way. That particular way of understanding moral freedom we are referring to as Schleiermacher's formula for the goal of ethical life.

If Schleiermacher's definition of freedom amounts essentially to the proposition that we are free insofar as we are able to resolve to do what we want, regardless of how we have come to want it, the question still remains, But what *should* we want to do? We have seen that in answer to that question Schleiermacher does not accept without qualification Kant's idea of guidance of an *a priori* moral law. Kant, for his part, condemns the opposite alternative—the elevation of *a posteriori* principles

---

[19]Letter to Herz, Sep. 9, 1798. *Werden*, 122.

[20]See footnote 14 of Chapter 2. The best simple translation of *Gemüth* might be "mind and heart."

[21]"Denkmale," 50.

[22]"Denkmale," 52.

to the rank of practical laws. We cannot learn morality merely from our life's experiences, Kant writes. "It would be better to maintain that there are no practical laws at all, but merely counsels for the service of our desires."[23] We are about to see that Schleiermacher follows Kant's advice here. He does not elevate *a posteriori* principles to the rank of practical laws, if practical laws are understood in Kant's sense to be immutably fixed and absolutely obligating moral principles. Instead, Schleiermacher suggests a formula for the goal of ethical life for which Kant's phrase, "counsel for the service of our desires," is not an unfair characterization.

This formula is presented in Schleiermacher's treatise *On the Worth of Life*, the composition of which Dilthey places in Schlobitten during the winter of 1792–93,[24] immediately following the treatise *On Human Freedom*. The goal of ethical life is to appropriate knowledge and desire in perfect harmony. As counsel for the service of our desires Schleiermacher recommends that "knowing and desiring should not be two in me, but one."

> Complete, invariable consonance of the two, in the fullest degree to which both are possible in me; unity of both in purpose and object; that is humanity, that is the beautiful goal [*das schöne Ziel*] established in human nature. And the first condition I make upon life is to furnish objects which not only occupy each of these powers individually, but also can exhibit this consonance of both, and through which it can be promoted.[25]

The phrase in the first sentence here, "in the fullest degree to which both are possible in me," represents freedom under the aspect of self-cultivation. An essential component of the goal of ethical life is the expansion of our capacities for knowledge and desire. Schleiermacher's ethical ideal consists not of this one component alone, however, but of two. It entails not only the obligation to push back the constraining limits of ignorance and narrow passions and so to extend the range of our concern, but also the further obligation to keep our comprehending and our desiring in congruence as we expand them. The moral ideal counsels us not to surrender ourselves to desires for things we do not comprehend, and counsels us to desire or love whatever we are able to embrace in comprehension. The broadening and expressing of our powers of comprehension are components of Schleiermacher's ethical goal, but he believes that we must at the same time try to keep our love apace. We should not analyze beyond our capacity to cherish. We should not give in to desires to create beyond our capacity to love our

[23]Second *Kritik*, 26.
[24]"Denkmale," 47.
[25]"Denkmale," 53.

creations, and this presupposes the ability to comprehend their potential for destruction or for cure. "Wisdom," Schleiermacher writes in his Journal around 1796, "consists in this: that one *wants* not what he *can* not; prudence in this: that one *does* not what he *wants* not."[26]

This is the goal of Schleiermacher's ethics: an expanding, integral sphere of knowledge and desire. It is far removed from the outcome of Kant's ethical analysis in the second *Critique*, where Kant speaks of persons as "belonging to two worlds" (above, p. 30), the natural "world of sense" and the "intelligible world" of morality.[27] According to Kant's ethics, it is only in an eternal "kingdom of God" that the two worlds of "nature and morality can come into a harmony, *which is foreign to each as such*."[28] But Schleiermacher finds his ethical goal of harmony "established [*gesteckt*] in human nature." It serves no ethical purpose "to divide man. All is joined in him; all is one."[29] Schleiermacher's ethical ideal is to foster the harmony intrinsic to morality and nature, intrinsic to *ought* and *is*, in the realm of space and time. Unity of being, not some dualism, was Schleiermacher's lifelong presupposition—the wholeness of humanity and nature, of human morality and human desire. Kant's ethics seeks to "elevate man above himself as a part of the world of sense."[30] Schleiermacher's seeks to attune us to an intrinsic harmony of human reason and sense.

Schleiermacher's most graphic statement of disagreement with Kant's separation of human life into two spheres appears in his Journal around 1800: "The human being is an ellipse; one focus is the brain and the other the genitals." He adds by way of elaboration, "The further the two foci are removed from each other, the greater is the difference between the lines that together are proportional to the axis."[31] By itself, this is a rather cryptic Journal entry. Its mathematical imagery suggests another approach to Schleiermacher's formula for the goal of ethical life, however. Beginning with its assertion of what a human being is, we may make our way by another route to Schleiermacher's ideal of what a human being ought to be.

First we need to realize that the mathematical imagery of this Journal entry is not merely incidental. Mathematics was an important enthusiasm of Schleiermacher's intellectual life. His mother reports Schleiermacher's facility in mathematics as a child,[32] and a letter from Stubenrauch inquires of his seventeen-year-old nephew "whether you

[26] "*Weisheit besteht darin, dass man nichts wolle was man nicht kann; Klugheit darin, dass man nichts thue als was man will.*" "Denkmale," 93.

[27] Second *Kritik*, 87, 105, et passim.

[28] Ibid., 128. Emphasis added.

[29] *Über die Freiheit*, "Denkmale," 27.

[30] Second *Kritik*, 86.

[31] "Denkmale," 140.

[32] Letter to Stubenrauch, 1780. *Br.* I, 20.

still take as much pleasure in mathematics as before?"[33] The answer
was yes. While living with his uncle Stubenrauch and family in Drossen
in 1789, Schleiermacher completed the first of his dialogues on freedom
(above, p. 9). He wrote to ask his friend Brinkmann, still in Halle, to
discuss its ideas with their teacher Eberhard. But he instructs Brinkmann not to show Eberhard the text. He feels his writing is too
"crude," and he tells his friend that the difficulty he is having with his
writing, together with a spell of foul autumn weather, has put him in a
state of depression. Nothing, he writes, can elevate his mood at such
moments except "games or algebra":

> Nothing else helps. The best society or the best book—I have no sense
> for any of that. Strange! I would not understand two lines of Aristotle,
> but yet I look forward to the most difficult calculations in Euler. They are
> but a trifle to me. And if the function of some curve does not give me
> back my cheerfulness, then it is lost for the day.[34]

During his period as tutor in the Dohna household in Schlobitten, at
the time he was writing his treatise *On Human Freedom*, Schleiermacher
sent a lengthy letter on mathematics to a brother of his young pupils,
Count Alexander Dohna (Fig. F), recently departed for Berlin to seek
his career. The letter is a lucid presentation of certain elementary
fundamentals of mathematics: definitions of the sciences of arithmetic,
algebra, and geometry; basic properties of number systems, with a
mention of the binary system of Leibniz; defining properties of arithmetic and geometric progressions, with examples.[35] Later, as an instructor in Gedike's Berlin seminar for teachers in 1793–94 (above, p. 18),
Schleiermacher lectured in mathematics.[36]

We have already seen Schleiermacher putting the mathematical
image of function and curve to ethical use (above, pp. 49–50). His
enthusiasm for this "most sublime science," as he calls mathematics in
his letter to Brinkmann, is often reflected in his writings. But of all the
instances of his use of mathematical imagery, the most striking by far is
Schleiermacher's plan to represent his ideal of the goal of ethical life
schematically in a geometric diagram.

We learn of this plan from two letters Schleiermacher wrote in 1803
to his Berlin publisher and close friend, Georg Reimer. In January of
that year, when Reimer was preparing Schleiermacher's *Groundwork to a
Critique of Previous Ethical Doctrine* for publication, Schleiermacher wrote
that he would like to have "a symbolic vignette that very nicely

---

[33]Dec. 10, 1785. *Br*. I, 36.

[34]Aug. 8, 1789. *Br*. IV, 25–26. A few pages of Schleiermacher's mathematical exercises
are still to be found among his papers. *Schleiermacher Nachlass*, Item #514.

[35]Dec. 16, 1791. The text of the letter is given in H. Borkowski, "Schleiermacher als
Mathematiker," *Archiv der Mathematik und Physik*, 2nd Series, 16/4 (1898), 337–46.

[36]Heinrich Meisner, *Schleiermachers Lehrjahre*, 65.

expresses my moral principles" carefully printed on the title page.[37] Six months later, as the date of publication drew near, Schleiermacher changed his mind about including his "vignette" in a book presenting not his own moral philosophy but rather his critical evaluation of the ethical theories of others: "I would rather save the vignette for my own Ethics (if it ever appears), where it will be more suitable and understandable. Here it seems to me almost too mystical, really."[38]

Schleiermacher's own Ethics did not appear in published form during his lifetime,[39] and thus the vignette never came to print. Schleiermacher's description of it, however, is preserved in his first letter to Reimer:

> It is only a mathematical figure, namely, two ellipses enclosed in each other, of the same axis but not the same foci, with the characteristic lines for both.[40]

"Sketched very poorly freehand," the letter goes on, "it looks like so . . ."; but then, where the figure once was, there is a hole in the manuscript of Schleiermacher's letter. Someone, quite possibly Reimer himself, has cut the sketch out.

Schleiermacher's sketch must have looked something like this:

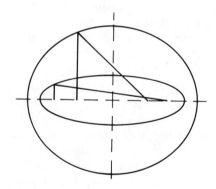

---

[37]Jan. 22, 1803. *Br*. III, 333.

[38]Letter to Reimer, June, 1803. *Br*. III, 349.

[39]Because of the time and energy Schleiermacher always devoted to his friends, according to one friend's opinion. See Henriette Herz, *Henriette Herz. Ihr Leben und ihre Erinnerungen*, 161.

[40]"*Es ist nur eine mathematische Figur, nämlich zwei ineinander geschlungene Ellipsen von gleicher Achse aber ungleichen Brennpunkten mit den charakteristischen Linien für beide.*" *Br*. III, 333.

"It makes not much of a figure, it is true," Schleiermacher's letter concludes, "but yet it signifies a great deal."

What does Schleiermacher's figure signify? As we know from Schleiermacher's Journal entry, the figure of an ellipse represents the human being. Its two focal points represent reason and sense. The lengths of the "characteristic lines," or rays emanating from the two foci, would represent the extent of cultivation of a person's rationality and sensibilities, respectively. The ratio of these lengths would represent the proportion of rationality and sensibility in a person's character.

In Schleiermacher's geometric vignette, therefore, the two ellipses stand for two different stages of moral development. The smaller, more flattened ellipse represents a person at a less advanced stage. Its smaller area signifies less fully developed capacities for knowledge and passion. The greater disproportion between its characteristic rays indicates the possibility of greater ethical imbalance in a person's life, in the form of either excessive rationality or overweaning desire. The larger, more nearly circular ellipse, on the other hand, represents a person at a more mature stage of moral development. Its larger area signifies a greater cultivation of reason and passion. Its greater symmetry indicates reason and desire in a more harmonious appropriation. Its characteristic rays are more nearly equal in length and more nearly congruent, emanating as they do from focal points that have more nearly come together at the center of a circle. That circle symbolizes Schleiermacher's goal of ethical life. In the *Speeches* of 1799 he will speak of it as "the circle that is the emblem of eternity and completeness."[41] The asymptotic approach to that ever expanding, ideal circle represents ethical growth under the impulse of moral virtue and the guidance of moral sense.

Thus, beginning with Schleiermacher's description of what we are — ellipsoidal natures with two points of focus, rational creatures occupied with desire — we have arrived at Schleiermacher's ideal of what we ought to be. Perhaps we may now see more clearly what it means to say that Schleiermacher's ethics fosters the harmony intrinsic to *ought* and *is*. His moral philosophy begins by describing what we are and evolves, without transcendental postulate or leap of faith, into a description of what we should, that is, what we most rationally desire to be.

Here again Schleiermacher's outlook is close to that of Spinoza. Like Spinoza in the *Ethics*, Schleiermacher recognizes that we are beings whose first desire after sheer survival is for the pleasure we gain by extending the scope of our powers — in particular, our powers of comprehending or knowing, and of desiring or loving. But we are able to recognize, if we take the pains to try, situations in which particular desires outstrip our comprehension, or our knowledge outdistances our

[41] *Reden*, 7. *Speeches*, 5.

capacity to love. Schleiermacher believes that as rational beings we are able to see that these situations are in a fundamental sense undesirable. The concern of our practical reasoning, then, is to minimize the possibility of such undesirable situations. Schleiermacher's moral ideal, symbolized in his geometric vignette, unifies the maxims of our behavior to accomplish this end. This is the sense in which Schleiermacher's goal of ethical life is not unfairly named by Kant's pejorative phrase, a "counsel for the service of our desires."

Chapter 7. Practical Applications of the Ethics of Schleiermacher and Kant

Without the supposition that our representations are the sufficient grounds of our actions, we could not justify our endeavors to alter our will; the production of representations could not be regarded as a means to this end, and in fact there would be no means to this end at all. If we maintain the idea of the necessary causal connection of representations and actions, however, then while it is indeed true that we can only judge in terms of probability whether or not a particular means we have adopted to a certain end is the correct one, still our end is at least possible, and our method is appropriate to its achievement.

Several practical ethical issues appeared in connection with our mention of Schleiermacher's early dialogues on freedom (above, p. 10) to which we are now prepared to return: the validity of a person's feeling of radical freedom, the attractiveness of a moral philosophy of quietism, and the dynamics of the feeling of regret. In addition to these, the isses of blame and punishment arise in Schleiermacher's treatise *On Human Freedom*. These issues invite a comparison of the practical applicability of Schleiermacher's ethical outlook with that of Kant, to which Schleiermacher was reacting.

First, the question of our feeling of freedom. We have seen that Schleiermacher counts "misunderstood feelings" as one of the chief obstacles to an acceptance of a philosophy of determinism (above, p. 71). The question is this: If we accept determinism as our ethical hypothesis, how are we to account for the fact that we feel ourselves radically free—free not only from foreign constraints upon our actions, but also from the yoke of causal necessity altogether? Schleiermacher seems to recognize the persuasiveness of such a feeling. But he argues that the degree to which we feel ourselves free in this sense is simply proportional to the extent to which we are ignorant of the determining factors that unite to form our intentions:

Now it is of course true that experience can never instruct us that from *this* totality of representations *such and such* an action must necessarily follow. Further, experience cannot even assure us that an action was grounded in such a whole of representations, because we can never

observe the condition of the soul precisely enough to know a totality of
representations in all its details.[1]

Thus we feel ourselves radically free. At a moment of decision we are
never fully aware of even those determining influences we can often
identify in retrospect. Still less are we aware of all determining influences, which no amount of motivational analysis could ever exhaust
(see above, p. 82).

This seems an obvious enough explanation for our feeling of freedom. It was Spinoza's explanation earlier when the same question was
put to him.[2] And it was soon to be Schiller's explanation of what he
calls "aesthetic freedom":

> The mind [*Gemüt*] in its aesthetic state is indeed free, and free in the
> highest degree from all coercion [*Zwang*]. But in no way does it act free
> from laws, and this aesthetic freedom distinguishes itself from the logical
> necessity of thinking and from the moral necessity of willing, only in that
> the laws according to which the mind operates are in this case *not repre-
> sented*, and, because they encounter no opposition, do not appear as a
> constraint [*Nötigung*].[3]

Thus the feeling of radical freedom may grip us at times, and when it
does, the feeling may influence our intentions. On the other hand, an
understanding of this feeling of freedom in terms of determinism can
also influence our intentions. Schleiermacher insists that it is a false interpretation to take the feeling of radical freedom as evidence in support
of Kant's postulate of transcendental freedom. And Kant would have
agreed. Transcendental freedom is a postulate of *a priori* reason in
Kant's moral philosophy, not a conclusion drawn *a posteriori* from our
feelings.

But if, in spite of our feelings, we assume that we are not endowed
with radical freedom, Schleiermacher asks in his treatise, "What happens then to plans for the future, to resolutions concerning future
improvement?"[4] How, in short, can we plan to change our ways, if our
ways are thought to be determined? Schleiermacher believes that if we
think carefully about this question, we can see that it is not the feeling
of radical freedom that is essential to moral planning, but in fact the
very opposite—a sense of the causal connectedness of our lives. How is
planning for the future possible? It is possible only because we can
anticipate "with a high degree of conviction that what we undertake will
in fact happen, since when the time comes to carry it out, there will be

---

[1]MS 25.

[2]Spinoza, *Ethics*, Part II, "Note" to Proposition XXXV. Also Spinoza, Epistle 62; see
Frederick Pollock, *Spinoza*, 208.

[3]Schiller, *Über die ästhetische Erziehung des Menschen*, Twentieth Letter. Schiller's
emphasis.

[4]"Denkmale," 38.

no other ground to determine its actuality except this act of resolution."[5] Planning for the future is possible, in other words, because we can count on the intentions we conscientiously cultivate to persist in our character and to issue in actions. We do not have to reckon on some incomprehensible faculty of freedom that could at any moment override habits of character we have cultivated or contradict plans we have previously laid. We improve our character and form our intentions by cultivating moral representations, Schleiermacher writes; "but what good would this do us, if our actions were not grounded in representations?"[6] We presuppose determinism in this form, which we might call the continuity of our intentions, in every sequence of planning for the future.

We find Schleiermacher reiterating this basic theme of his moral philosophy many years after his treatise *On Human Freedom*. If we presuppose some kind of radical freedom in human actions, he writes in his lectures on psychology of 1818–1834,

> then we must presuppose it at every moment. As a person has today established his individual character, so tomorrow he can annul it; that is, regarded in the whole continuity of existence, the individual being appears to us as something absolutely fortuitous. What is pure choice for the individual is fortuitous for all others; that is, there is absolutely no basis for maintaining that a person will still be the same tomorrow as today, but no basis for denying it either. Now it is perfectly clear that no one really acts upon this presupposition, for we always act as if we believe that in a certain sense we are able to count on people.[7]

Similarly, in the theological context of *The Christian Faith* of 1821 Schleiermacher writes:

> This leads us to consider . . . whether the divine knowledge about the free actions of human beings can coexist with their freedom. . . . If the temptation to answer this question in the negative, and even the need to pose such a question, are grounded in the interest of protecting human freedom, then we must consider the fact that our own foreknowledge of free actions and the foreknowledge of others must annul freedom even more than divine foreknowledge does; and yet we regard those people as *least* free who in general cannot know their actions beforehand, that is, who are not conscious of any determinate pattern in their actions. But where this is the case, particular foreknowledge is lacking only because [knowledge of] the particular outer conditions, and inner conditions produced from without, is lacking. We measure the intimacy of relationship between two persons by the foreknowledge one has of the actions of

---

[5]"Denkmale," 38.
[6]MS 24.
[7]Schleiermacher, *Psychologie*, 268–69.

the other, without believing that the freedom of the one or the other has been endangered. So even divine foreknowledge cannot endanger freedom.[8]

In summary, Schleiermacher believes that a philosophy of determinism does not lead to moral quietism. That is, it does not lead to moral quietism in the sense of our ceasing to plan for the future or to work for our moral improvement—though in Part III we shall discover quietism of another sort in Schleiermacher's outlook. Schleiermacher's ethical hypothesis is determinism, not fatalism. It does not view us as paralyzed nor as awash in the stream of history. But it does not leave our planning for the future untouched either. An awareness of the causal connectedness of our lives contributes a sense of "discretion" to our judgments, Schleiermacher writes. We realize that we cannot look forward to the future complacently, as if endowed with "the infallibility of a miracle worker."[9] We cannot escape having to lay plans for the future with foresight and thoughtful preparation of character. At the same time, we may rely on our preparation, if it is adequate, to sustain our intentions when moments of action arrive.

At this point it is appropriate to note a fact about Schleiermacher's early career that we have neglected till now. From the time of his first series of theological examinations in 1790 at the age of twenty-one until his death in 1834 at the age of sixty-five, Schleiermacher was almost continuously engaged in his calling as a preacher. We know of fifteen sermons he delivered in Schlobitten during the period in which he produced his treatise *On Human Freedom*, for example[10]—most of which have not survived, owing to Schleiermacher's habit, unusual for the time, of not writing out his sermons in full.[11] From the early sermons that survive, one thing is clear. Whatever Schleiermacher's difficulties with theological orthodoxy in his early sermons, whatever his difficulties in matching the tone of his sermons to the less erudite capacities of his congregations—and at first these difficulties were considerable—Schleiermacher's transmutation of his deterministic outlook into the pastoral idiom of his sermons at no time takes the form of fatalism. The determinism is frequently undisguised. The opening sermon of Schleiermacher's first published collection of sermons, "On the Similarity of the Future and the Past," is on the text from Ecclesiastes:

> What has been is what will be,
> and what has been done is what will be done;
> and there is nothing new under the sun.

[8] *Der christliche Glaube*, ed. Redeker, Proposition 55.3. Emphasis added.
[9] "Denkmale," 38.
[10] Heinrich Meisner, *Schleiermachers Lehrjahre*, 58.
[11] Schleiermacher explains his reasons for this irregularity in his letters to his father of Feb. 10 and May 5, 1793. *Br.* I, 104–5, 112–13. See also the Preface to Schleiermacher's first collection of sermons, published in 1801: *Predigten. Erste Sammlung*, 5, 13.

In it Schleiermacher asks:

> Of what importance is the position that the heavenly bodies occupy just
> now? Every one has evolved from the positions that have preceded,
> according to the same laws God has prescribed for their movement from
> the beginning. Of what importance is it whether this or some other small
> portion of inanimate matter belongs to my body? My body is the
> workshop of the same forces whose conjunction constitutes its character-
> istic nature, and just those portions as are necessary will always be
> produced in it.

So it is also, Schleiermacher goes on, in the world of the spirit.
Whatever happens, the person of religious sensibility will recognize
every event as "only that which has already happened, and which he
already knows; and he can patiently observe the way in which it
evolves." But Schleiermacher makes it clear that the determinism he
expresses here is not the same as fatalism: "Certainly it *would* be the
newest thing under the sun if people ever stood still and ceased to
improve themselves." Christian men and women are called to cooperate
in the daily work of human betterment. Schleiermacher amplifies this
theme in another sermon of the first collection, "The Limits of
Forbearance":

> I challenge you in the name of righteousness . . . to endure nothing and
> to tolerate nothing that hinders or holds back goodness and perfection,
> the advancement of which is our highest calling—no opinion, no disposi-
> tion, no action. *Regard the origins of these with as much forbearance as you
> wish*, only count it as your duty to oppose them with all your might.[12]

Thus Schleiermacher's sermons employ his philosophy of determinism in the service of the "chief effect of Christianity" that he tried to
advance among his early congregations, first in Schlobitten, later in
Drossen, Landsberg, and Berlin—"namely, true alteration and improvement of character."[13] He felt that his supposition of the causal connectedness of our lives is essential in accounting for repentance and the
improvement of life that Christianity recognizes as the fruit of true
repentance. "Without the supposition that our representations are the
sufficient grounds of our actions," he writes in *On Human Freedom*,

> we could not justify our endeavors to alter our will; the production of
> representations could not be regarded as a means to this end, and in fact
> there would be no means to this end at all. If we maintain the idea of the
> necessary causal connection of representations and actions, however, then

---

[12] *Predigten. Erste Sammlung*, 19–23, 150. Emphasis added. These two sermons were
delivered in 1797 and 1800, respectively.

[13] "*Die hauptsächliche Wirkung des Christenthums, nämlich wahre Sinnesänderung und
Besserung. . . .*" *Predigten in den Jahren 1789 bis 1810 gehalten*, in *Sämmtliche Werke*, II/7,
45.

> while it is indeed true that we can only judge in terms of probability
> whether or not a particular means we have adopted to a certain end is the
> correct one, still our end is at least possible, and our method is
> appropriate to its achievement.[14]

Let us assume for a moment a sort of *dis*connection in the causal chain of our representations and intentions—a disconnection of the kind Kant assumes in his doctrine of freedom, or at least appears to assume when he speaks of the causality of transcendental freedom as a determination of the will to which "nothing is antecedent."[15] Under such an assumption, Schleiermacher writes, a past action

> which I regret is connected only incidentally with my present self; . . . it
> was only a peculiar aberration of some power determinable apart from all
> causal connection. To be sure, it may distastefully affect my moral feeling.
> But since all expressions of this power together are not a continuous path
> but only discrete steps, then this past step is of no influence on the
> direction of those that follow.[16]

To apply this directly to Kant's doctrine of freedom, the "peculiar aberration of some power" of which Schleiermacher speaks here would take the form of a person's failure to exercise transcendental freedom when, according to the obligations imposed by the moral law, the person should have done so. One might, as Schleiermacher rather derisively suggests, experience a sense of "distaste" for such a failure. Why should one feel more than distaste, however, when the failure was not really an expression of character, but was only. . . . Only what? A careless oversight? A whimsical omission? A chance neglect? Or in Schleiermacher's words, "a sheer bestowal of chance, an accidental coincidence"?[17]

Kant would certainly not admit any of these alternatives. We have already seen Kant's view that the failure to exercise transcendental freedom can only be itself an act of transcendental freedom. We have seen also that Kant's claim sweeps ethical analysis into a reflexive spiral: an act of transcendental freedom must itself be "grounded" in an act of transcendental freedom, and so on without end. This grounding is therefore "inscrutable to us" (above, p. 66). But Schleiermacher is pointing out that in this case, there is absolutely no reason to assume that the moral failure cannot be avoided should an identical occasion present itself to a person a second time. If a person is free in Kant's sense, then the second time, *without any particular alteration of his character in the meantime*, the person might surely choose better. At least there is no ground for assuming that the person will not.

---

[14]MS 25.
[15]Kant, second *Kritik*, 97.
[16]MS 65. Cf. "Denkmale," 38.
[17]MS 25.

Kant's *Religion within the Limits of Reason Alone* includes a profound, even heroic, struggle with the issue that Schleiermacher is on to here. Schleiermacher can find no place for genuine moral regret or Christian repentance in Kant's moral philosophy—that is, no place for regret that is directed inward and made to lead to tangible improvement in a person's moral character, no place for repentance that bears true fruit. Part of Kant's point, when he amplifies it in his complicated book of 1792–93, appears to be that there is in the human soul a subjective ground of action that is in fact *not* susceptible of tangible improvement, a seed of "radical evil." In the first major division of his book, "Concerning the Indwelling of the Evil Principle with the Good, or, On the Radical Evil in Human Nature," Kant calls this seed our "natural propensity to evil; and as indeed we must always hold man himself guilty for it, we can further call it a *radical*, inborn *evil* in human nature (yet nonetheless brought upon us by ourselves)."[18] Once again, this is Kant's philosophical translation of the Christian doctrines of the Fall and Original Sin (see above, p. 66).

It has been a perennial criticism of Schleiermacher that he had little capacity for a sense of radical human guilt and sin such as we find in Kant's philosophy and in the strand of Protestant Christian tradition to which Kant belongs. The criticism is accurate. There is little evidence that Schleiermacher was ever able to share Kant's sense of radical evil. In *On Human Freedom* Schleiermacher writes:

> If we must seek the ground of particular actions of the faculty of desire elsewhere than in the condition and other activities of the soul, then the inquiry into the state of the soul, so natural to every person—into the laws of its various faculties, into the path it ascertains by means of these laws, into exceptional appearances in particular cases, into the premises that would be required for a certain result, and into the result that certain premises would have produced—all this inquiry is *cut off at the root*.[19]

This is of course precisely what Kant accomplishes by his portrayal of "radical" human evil.

The radicality of Kant's sense for original sin is nowhere more clearly exposed than in his discussion of moral blame. In *Religion within the Limits of Reason Alone* he writes:

> In the search for the rational origin of evil actions, every such action must be regarded as though the person had fallen into it directly from a state of innocence. For whatever his previous deportment may have been, whatever natural causes may have been influencing him, and whether these causes were to be found within him or outside him, his action is yet free and determined by none of these causes; hence it can and must always be judged as an *original* use of his choice. He should have

---

[18] *Die Religion*, 27. English tr., 28. Kant's emphases.
[19] MS 23. Emphasis added.

refrained from that action, whatever his temporal circumstances and connections may have been; for through no cause in the world can he cease to be a freely acting being.[20]

In his first *Critique* Kant had illustrated this argument in the more vivid terms of a criminal offender. The illustration merits quotation here at length, in the interest of both clarity and fairness to Kant:

> In order to illustrate this regulative principle of reason [transcendental freedom] by an example of its empirical employment—not, however, to confirm it, for it is useless to endeavour to prove transcendental propositions by examples—let us take a voluntary action; for example, a malicious lie by which a certain confusion has been caused in society. First of all, we endeavour to discover the motives to which it has been due, and then, secondly, in the light of these, we proceed to determine how far the action and its consequences can be imputed [*zugerechnet*] to the offender. As regards the first question, we trace the empirical character of the action to its sources, finding these in defective education, bad company, in part also in the viciousness of a natural disposition insensitive to shame, in levity and thoughtlessness—not neglecting to take into account also the occasional causes that may have intervened. We proceed in this enquiry just as we should in ascertaining for a given natural effect the series of its determining causes. But although we believe that the action is thus determined, we none the less blame the agent, not indeed on account of his unhappy disposition, nor on account of the circumstances that have influenced him, nor even on account of his previous way of life; for we presuppose that we can leave out of consideration what this way of life may have been, that we can regard the past series of conditions as not having occurred and the act as being completely unconditioned by any preceding state, just as if the agent in and by himself began in this action an entirely new series of consequences. Our blame is based on a law of reason, whereby we regard reason as a cause which, irrespective of all the above-mentioned empirical conditions, could have determined, and ought to have determined, the agent to act otherwise. This causality of reason we do not regard as only cooperating, but as complete in itself, even when the sensuous impulses do not favour but are directly opposed to it. The action is ascribed to the intelligible character. In the moment when he utters the lie, the guilt is entirely his. Reason, irrespective of all empirical conditions of the act, is completely free, and the lie is entirely due to its default.[21]

"In spite of his whole previous course of life," Kant writes a page later, "the agent could have refrained from lying."[22]

One thing we see in these extraordinary sentences is that when Schleiermacher disagrees with Kant over the causal connectedness of our lives, he is not attacking a straw man. Schleiermacher considers Kant's portrayal of human accountability to be inaccurate and thus a misleading basis for moral action. If the offender in Kant's example

---

[20] *Die Religion*, 42. English tr., 36. Kant's emphasis.
[21] Kant, first *Kritik*, A554–55.
[22] Kant reiterates this position in the second *Kritik*, 98.

thinks of himself as Kant thinks of him, how is he possibly to feel constructive regret? Or to pose a more pragmatic question, How is society to think of "correcting" Kant's transcendentally free offender? "The action," we read in Kant's long paragraph, "is ascribed to the agent's intelligible character. In the moment when he utters the lie, the guilt is entirely his." It is at some later moment, however, that society must decide whether and how to punish the offender. What is more, it is not the agent's "intelligible character" but rather his empirical or sensible character upon which society's punishments will be inflicted. "Punishment is indubitably a sensible evil," Schleiermacher writes, "an act of deliberate choice following upon some previous moral evil."[23]

In contrast to the sensible character, an offender's "intelligible" character is "inscrutable" to us. Thus in the ethics of Kant, with his profound sense for the underground of human perversity, it is far from clear that punishment can ever make contact with, and still less that it can ever correct or redeem, the source of offense in a criminal offender. We find ourselves asking once more, What in fact is the source of the criminal's offense? We read in the paragraph from Kant's first *Critique* that "reason, irrespective of all empirical conditions of the act, is completely free, and the lie is entirely due to its default." But to what is reason's default due? It cannot be due to reason itself, because according to Kant the incentives of reason are by definition moral. Not, then, to "the agent's intelligible character," since the intelligible character consists in reason alone. But not to the agent's empirical character either, as Kant insists in his phrase, "irrespective of all empirical conditions." Is there no way we can rid ourselves of this question?

One is forced to admire Kant's candor at this point, and to suspect him of profundity. The question of "why reason has not determined *itself* differently," he writes, is a question "one may not ask." We may ask only "why reason has not through its causality determined the *appearances* differently. But to this question no answer is possible."[24] The great Reinhold, in his re-presentation of Kant's moral philosophy, recognized that no revision or concession can be allowed at this crucial point. The absurd inquiry after the "ground" of a free act, he writes,

> amounts to asking, "What is the objective ground by which the faculty of acting independently of objective grounds is determined?" No objective ground of the will can be conceived that is not included in this circle of freedom. A free act is therefore nothing other than *groundless*. Its ground is freedom itself. . . . To ask why the free will has determined itself in this or that way is to ask why it is free.[25]

[23]MS 48.

[24]Kant, first *Kritik*, A556. Kant's emphases.

[25]Karl Leonard Reinhold, *Briefe über die Kantische Philosophie*, II, 282. Reinhold's emphasis. In my opinion, when in the works of his old age, such as *The Metaphysics of*

So once again, this time in the context of a pragmatic application, we have tracked Kant's doctrine of freedom up to its point of incomprehensibility, and again we must suppose that our understanding of Kant's doctrine of transcendental freedom has gone as far as it may be expected to go (see above, p. 32). Taking Schleiermacher's perspective, however, we may ask how a judge with ethical fairness at heart, let us say, is supposed to proceed from this point where Kant's doctrine of freedom passes off into inscrutability, carrying the source of the offender's blame with it. Schleiermacher feels strongly that, in connection with a theory of penal justice, the Kantian notions of transcendental freedom and moral accountability all too easily "authorize us to blame without sympathizing with the one who has acted wrongly."[26] In light of some of Kant's language, Schleiermacher's fear appears to be justified. There is the passage in the second *Critique*, for example, in which Kant recommends the concept of punishment as "mere harm in itself":

> Becoming a partaker in happiness cannot be united with the concept of punishment as such. For even though he who punishes can do so with the benevolent intention of directing punishment to this end, it must nevertheless be justified as punishment, i.e., as mere harm in itself, so that even the punished person, if it stopped there and he could see no glimpse of kindness behind the harshness, would yet have to admit that justice had been done and that his reward perfectly fitted his behavior.[27]

In the strongest contrast to Kant, Schleiermacher thinks of punishment as essentially an extreme application of his theory of moral cultivation: criminals "deserve" only the punishment they understand how to appropriate (above, pp. 85–86). Kant's ethics seems to endorse a sort of legalistic calculus that arbitrarily matches seriousness of offense with severity of punishment. Schleiermacher remarks in his Journal that Kant appears to promote "the idea of a punishment that is not correction but merely *convenance*."[28] Schleiermacher's own ethics supports the theory that the severity and nature of punishment should match the offender's capacity to internalize it and turn it to the improvement of his character. It is a theory that might be accused of idealistic naivete. Schleiermacher recognized that harsh social realities may make the application of such a theory of rehabilitative punishment impractical. He insists, however, that a theory of justice must not confuse "the principle from which punishment itself proceeds with the principle by which the

---

Morals, Kant begins to make certain revisions and concessions at this problematic point, the effect, as Reinhold anticipated, is to weaken his moral philosophy.

[26]MS 28.

[27]Second *Kritik*, 37.

[28]"Denkmale," 74. *Convenance*: "convenience" or "expediency."

measure of punishment must be determined."[29] If practical social realities necessitate strict uniform sentences without regard to individual circumstances and without reference to the possibility of rehabilitation, then so it must be. But a society must recognize such practices as a compromise of principle; society must admit failure in its penal system and try to overcome it. Schleiermacher believes that even in the midst of harsh practical realities, the principle of punishment he advocates can guide a society toward reducing the malicious vindictiveness in a penal system, encouraging punishments to fit the criminal instead of the crime, and tempering a people's irrational scorn for criminal offenders.

Like a court of justice, Schleiermacher's own ethics has to do, and argues that it should have to do, with a person's empirical character. Kant's ethics no less self-consciously disagrees. Just how explicitly Kant disagreed was something Schleiermacher could not have known in 1791–92 as he worked on his treatise *On Human Freedom*. It is in *Religion within the Limits of Reason Alone*, published in 1792–93, that Kant specifies a clear distinction between *legal* judgments, made "by an empirical standard (before a human judge)," and *moral* judgments, made "according to the standard of pure reason (at a divine tribunal)." The latter, Kant writes, are judgments of a person according to whether he is pleasing "to God, that is, virtuous according to the intelligible character."[30] Kant appears to be suggesting that his moral philosophy has all along been concerned only with "moral" judgment of a person "at a divine tribunal." Schleiermacher would seem to be correct in perceiving that Kant's doctrines of transcendental freedom and radical evil cannot illumine empirical questions of individual and social ethics, as Schleiermacher would like to see them illumined. Writing in 1791–92, however, Schleiermacher fails to note that Kant does not seem to intend such illumination. At least this appears to be true of Kant's intentions in 1792–93, and he had intimated as much in his second *Critique* of 1788, where already he had separated legal from moral duty (above, p. 29), and spoken of the latter as "inexorable duty, transgression against which violates the moral law, *in itself and without respect to human welfare*, and tramples as it were on its holiness (the kind of duties one usually calls duties to God . . .)."[31]

In Part II we shall find Schleiermacher distinguishing morality from religion as carefully as Kant here identifies the two. Kant's ethics has to do with the "intelligible" character of the human being before God, Schleiermacher's with the empirical character of individuals in human

[29]Ibid.
[30]*Die Religion*, 13n and 54. English tr., 20n and 43.
[31]Second *Kritik*, 158. Emphasis added.

society. In Kant's outlook, immorality is sin. It is "*inextirpable* by human powers," and thus moral improvement "cannot be brought about through gradual *reformation* . . . but must be effected through a *revolution* in the man's disposition . . . , only by a kind of rebirth, a new creation, as it were, and a change of heart."[32] In Schleiermacher's outlook, immorality is traceable to limitation or disharmony in a person's character, and improvement comes by way of gradual moral cultivation, not inscrutable conversion. The effect of Kant's philosophy of transcendental freedom is to bring a person to accountability before "the moral law, in itself and without respect to human welfare." The effect of a moral philosophy of determinism as Schleiermacher sees it is to strengthen the sympathetic "solidarity of human society."[33]

Both Schleiermacher's language here and the deterministic philosophy underlying it anticipate his first independent publication, which was to appear in 1798. Almost no notice of this first publication has ever been taken in Schleiermacher scholarship. By remedying this inattention, we may summarize and conclude this part of our study and prepare the way for Part II.

In 1797, at the age of twenty-eight, Schleiermacher chose to translate and publish two volumes of addresses originally delivered in London in 1795 by the English clergyman Joseph Fawcett — "a product of an original mind and a masterpiece of a certain kind of eloquence," he called them.[34] Fawcett (1758?–1804) was a dissenting minister of Baptist persuasion, a popular lecturer, and an anti-war poet. At the time Schleiermacher set to work in Berlin translating Fawcett's addresses, Fawcett in London was eliciting the admiration of another incipient romantic, the young William Wordsworth. In his introductory note to *The Excursion*, Wordsworth describes Fawcett as "an able and eloquent man." Of Fawcett's pacifist poem of 1795, *The Art of War*, Wordsworth writes: "He published a poem on war, which had a good deal of merit, and made me think more about him than I should otherwise have done."[35] The essayist William Hazlitt, Wordsworth's friend in later years, wrote of Fawcett:

> The conversations I had with him on taste and philosophy (for his taste was as refined as his powers of reasoning were profound and subtle), gave me a delight such as I can never feel again. . . . Of all the persons I have ever known, he was the most perfectly free from every taint of jealousy or narrowness. Never did a mean or sinister motive come near his heart. He was one of the most enthusiastic admirers of the French Revolution; and I believe that the disappointment of the hopes he had cherished of

---

[32] *Die Religion*, 54. English tr., 43. Kant's emphases.
[33] "Denkmale," 32.
[34] Letter to his sister Charlotte, June 16, 1798. *Br.* I, 177.
[35] Quoted in Arthur Beatty, "Joseph Fawcett: The Art of War," *University of Wisconsin Studies in Language and Literature*, No. 2 (Sep., 1918), 233–34.

the freedom and happiness of mankind, preyed upon his mind, and hastened his death.[36]

In addition to his other characteristics, Fawcett, like Schleiermacher, was what we might call a free-lance determinist. For Schleiermacher this was an attractive affinity. It worked, however, to the distinct discomfort of Schleiermacher's ecclesiastical overseer, Friedrich Samuel Gottfried Sack. In a preface to Schleiermacher's translation of Fawcett, Sack felt obliged to apologize for his young colleague's intellectual taste. "Whatever reception these sermons, published three years ago in London, may find among us . . . ," Sack begins, and then goes on in the obvious hope of shifting the reader's attention from the substance of Fawcett's thought to the stylistic mastery of Schleiermacher's translating skills.[37]

One of the central manifestations of Fawcett's determinism in these addresses is an emphasis upon that "solidarity of human society," to return to Schleiermacher's phrase, that a deterministic world view implies. "We are none of us complete in ourselves," Fawcett writes. "We are parts of a whole; we are members of a body," joined by the "perfectly uninterrupted, and the infinitely extended" causal activity of divine power. In such a nexus there is no place for radical extremes of pride and contempt in our judgments:

> With as much propriety might we ascribe eloquence to the quill, rather than to the writer; or ingenuity to the machine, rather than to the inventor; as take to ourselves the praise of any personal superiority, with which our Maker may have distinguished us. . . . As the consideration that God is our creator renders it impossible for us to be proud of any personal excellence which we have inherited from nature, so the reflection that God is the maker of *others*, should lead us to pay a proper respect to all mankind, and prevent us from despising any because they are poor. The respect arising from this reflection is intimately connected with the practice of justice, in our intercourse with those, who are our inferiors in situation. Contempt is the parent of injury and of oppression, both in public and in private life.

As it rules out absolutism in our judgments, so determinism rules out moral absolutism in the standards we set:

> We may rest assured, that he who hath made us all, and who knoweth the nature he has given us, does not expect from any of us such a perfectly faultless character, such an entire freedom from all flaw and imperfection, such a sleepless vigilance of mind and superiority to all moral surprises, such an unflagging flight and effort of virtuous fortitude, as is utterly out of the reach of the faculties he has bestowed upon us, in the present state of human cultivation.[38]

[36]Quoted in ibid., 232–33.

[37]Quoted in Dilthey, *Leben Schleiermachers*, ed. Redeker, I/1, 73n.

[38]Joseph Fawcett, "Sermon II. Reflections Drawn from the Consideration that God Is Our Creator," *Sermons Delivered at the Sunday-Evening Lecture, for the Winter Season, at the Old Jewry*, 2nd ed., I, 51, 32, 40, 44, 52. Fawcett's emphasis.

It cannot surprise us that Schleiermacher chose these addresses as his first publishing project. The religious language in which Fawcett's addresses are cast is foreign to Schleiermacher's early essays of 1789–93, and we have not yet come across much of Fawcett's pantheism in Schleiermacher's earliest writings on moral philosophy. But Fawcett's language of divine omnificence is not foreign to Schleiermacher's 1797 sermon, "On the Similarity of the Future and the Past" (see above, p. 96):

> For those who seek the Lord everywhere in the world there is no dis-
> tinction between the great and the small. As it is the Lord who does all,
> and in all is efficacious, therefore all must be worthy, all great and
> excellent. Nothing may predominate over some other. . . . All are only
> developments of the same divine thoughts, approaches to the same goal
> of his grace, according to the same design of his wisdom.[39]

In non-religious language Schleiermacher's treatise *On Human Freedom* anticipates Fawcett's philosophy of "perfectly uninterrupted" determinism, his theme of social solidarity, his concern to exclude from judgments of moral accountability the presupposition of radical "freedom from all flaw and imperfection," and his accommodation of ethics to "the present state of human cultivation." Furthermore, Schleiermacher was impressed by the fact that Fawcett's addresses were not sermons delivered before a parish congregation, but rather evening addresses to a cultured, voluntary London audience. Schleiermacher wrote to his sister that he considered Fawcett's addresses

> a proof of how much one can accomplish, and how much more pene-
> tratingly and forcibly one can speak, when one addresses a homogeneous
> and not too greatly diverse gathering, and knows with surety that each is
> there because—and only because—he finds the subject to his taste and is
> convinced of the personal excellence of the speaker.[40]

We shall soon find Schleiermacher, in his *On Religion: Speeches to Its Cultured Despisers* of 1799, addressing a sophisticated audience of friends in language often remarkably similar to that of Fawcett:

> All that is human is holy, for all is divine. . . . The more each draws near
> the universe, the more each communicates with the other, the more
> completely all become one. None has a consciousness for himself, each
> has also that of the other. They are no longer only human beings but also
> humankind.[41]

The question of Fawcett's influence on Schleiermacher, though that influence seems to have been appreciable, is not of the greatest

---

[39] *Predigten. Erste Sammlung*, 20.
[40] June 16, 1798. *Br.* I, 177.
[41] *Reden*, 216. *Speeches*, 180.

importance to us here. Suffice it to say that Fawcett in 1795 expressed a philosophy of life to which Schleiermacher was already strongly attracted, and that his addresses influenced Schleiermacher's later expressions of that philosophy. Fawcett is worth our attention as we now leave Part I and move to Part II of our study because Schleiermacher's similarities to him, both in the treatises before 1795 and in the later writings to which we are about to turn, bind together two stages of Schleiermacher's early career that might easily be taken to be more discrete than in fact they are. Schleiermacher's agreement with Fawcett on both sides of the year 1795 testifies to a continuity in Schleiermacher's outlook, from the all but anti-religious phenomenalism of his early treatises, to the cultural romanticism, philosophical idealism, and tendency toward religious pantheism that we shall find enlivening his thinking after his 1796 entry into the Berlin romantic circle. Both the ground and the consequence of that continuity of outlook are to be found in Schleiermacher's deterministic world view.

Part II. Freedom (1796–1799)

Chapter 1. The Environment of the Speeches

I have always lacked a companion with whom I could freely communicate my philosophical ideas, and who would enter with me into the deepest abstractions. This great void he [Friedrich Schlegel] now fills most gloriously. Not only can I pour out to him what is already in me, but also by the inexhaustible stream of new views and ideas that flows into him without ceasing, much is set into motion in me that had lain dormant. In short, since my closer acquaintance with him a new period in my existence in the philosophical and literary world has begun.

We now leave the analytic treatise in which Schleiermacher worked out his early commitment to a deterministic world view. Schleiermacher's determinism will be evident at many points in what follows, and one object of this study is to illustrate the thesis that even where determinism is not explicitly evident in Schleiermacher's early philosophy of life, it is consistently presupposed. A second object is to appreciate Schleiermacher's understanding of freedom, and to this we turn now in Part II.

In Part I we discovered Schleiermacher's fundamental concept of freedom as "the absence of a constraint" (above, p. 79), arrived at in the course of his analysis of Kant's doctrine of transcendental freedom. In this second Part we shall take that concept and, by means somewhat less closely analytic than those employed in dealing with the treatise *On Human Freedom*, illustrate it under its three positive aspects (above, p. 84): freedom as self-expression, freedom as appropriation, and freedom as self-cultivation. Finally we shall come to the religious, mystical meaning of freedom that Schleiermacher contrasts with the ethical. We shall take our illustrative materials from Schleiermacher's writings, correspondence, and course of life around the time of his book of 1799, *On Religion: Speeches to Its Cultured Despisers*.

In the autumn of 1796, Schleiermacher left his ministerial post in Landsberg for the position of chaplain at the Charité Hospital in Berlin. He was to serve the Charité for six years, but his chaplaincy there was not the focus of his Berlin life. Then Berlin's hospital for the indigent, the Charité was under the administration of the Berlin Directory of the Poor. Its location beside a school of veterinary medicine prompted the satirist Johannes Daniel Falk's acerbic comment that, in the one, dogs were treated like humans, while in the other, humans like dogs.[1] Malicious exaggeration aside, it is true that Schleiermacher's congregation of hospital patients and neighborhood residents was such as to profit from simpler preaching than that Schleiermacher was accustomed to prepare. In 1801, while still at the Charité, Schleiermacher published his first collection of sermons. In the Dedication of that volume to his uncle Stubenrauch, Schleiermacher explains the omission of sermons preached at the Charité:

> You are aware that not a single one of these sermons was delivered to my present congregation. You know the congregation well enough to realize that the subjects treated here, and the whole design of this collection, even if the style had originally been as popular as possible, would have constituted in that context an unpardonable sin against my beloved calling.[2]

Schleiermacher's inaugural sermon at the Charité on September 28, 1796, has been preserved. The aptness of its text reflects Schleiermacher's characteristic pastoral familiarity with the Bible:

> Blessed be the God and Father of our Lord Jesus Christ, the Father of mercies and God of all comfort, who comforts us in all our affliction, so that we may be able to comfort those who are in any affliction, with the comfort with which we ourselves are comforted by God.
>
> (2 Cor 1:3–4)

The sermon reveals Schleiermacher's sincere effort to identify with the needs of his congregation:

> Here, where so much apparently undeserved suffering is heaped up and so many plaintive voices of distress are raised, and where on the other hand even suffering that is unavoidable is greeted with such dull indifference, such shameless indolence—here the question can easily arise whether the Lord in heaven looks down upon the children of men.

Yet the intellectual and social discrepancies between the Charité congregation and their new minister were clearly weighing on Schleiermacher's mind:

> It is true that I do not see here many who are much regarded and honored by the world, or who have enjoyed a great portion of the world's joys and possessions; most are poor and humble. But I know also that the Lord is no respecter of persons. If only I am able to direct your hearts to the good, to hold you back from the wrong turns that lead so many away from the path of righteousness, then it matters not to me whether I have been of service to you or to the mighty of the world; for I know that my honor will be no less in the eyes of that One before whom every soul that turns away from evil and walks in righteousness is of equal worth . . . .

---

[1] Cited in Wilhelm Dilthey, *Leben Schleiermachers*, ed. Redeker, I/1, 220.
[2] *Predigten. Erste Sammlung*, 9.

> Do not let me ask you in vain for that good will, that brotherly love, which one must give to every Christian, and which I require so much more as your fellow resident. As such I ask you all . . . to accept me in love as your friend.[3]

As for Schleiermacher's attention to his non-preaching duties at the hospital, an official of the Prussian cabinet, writing two years after the termination of Schleiermacher's chaplaincy, recalled his young subordinate's tenure with dissatisfaction:

> Schleiermacher is a good preacher, and as a theological scholar he distinguishes himself favorably. At the Charité . . . I was sometimes annoyed with him. He was smug [*kommode*], indifferent to the patients' needs for consolation, and did not want to submit to authority.[4]

Thus one official's opinion. Whatever its accuracy, the evidence from these years indicates that Schleiermacher's chief enthusiasms were focused elsewhere than upon the Charité, which is rarely mentioned in his letters.

Now twenty-eight years old, Schleiermacher was first welcomed into Berlin by his friend from Schlobitten days, Count Alexander Dohna. Though three years younger than Schleiermacher, Dohna was already advancing swiftly in Prussian government service. During Schleiermacher's previous residency in Berlin in 1793–94 (see above, p. 18), Dohna had introduced Schleiermacher into the household of Markus and Henriette Herz. That social contact was now to prove a factor of determining importance for the course of Schleiermacher's life.

Markus Herz was a prominent Berlin physician, Jewish, and a former student and now confidant of Immanuel Kant. Henriette, thirty-two, was seventeen years younger than her husband, to whom she had been engaged at the age of twelve and, with little regard for her own wishes, married at the age of fifteen. The childless marriage appears to have been one of mutual respect and trust. At the same time, a degree of emotional distance was perhaps inevitable in such a match. By all accounts Henriette Herz was a woman of exceptional intellect and beauty (Fig. C). Alexander Dohna was in love with her. After the death of Markus, Dohna went counter to both the social and racial predilections of his aristocratic class and proposed marriage to Henriette. Kindly but firmly she refused him, and Dohna never married.

The Herz household was one of the gathering places for Berlin's intellectual society. Schleiermacher describes these Berlin salons in a letter to his sister, who by 1798 was having doubts about her ministerial brother's social contacts:

---

[3]Schleiermacher, *Sämmtliche Werke*, II/7, 373–74, 370, 380.
[4]Letter from Minister von Massow to Minister Beyme, Apr. 17, 1804. Dilthey, *Leben Schleiermachers*, ed. Redeker, I/2, 214.

> That young *savants* and *elegants* frequently visit the great Jewish houses here is very natural, for they are by far the richest non-noble families, and almost the only ones that hold an open house and in which, owing to their extended connections in all countries, one meets foreigners of all ranks. Therefore whoever wishes to enjoy good society in a rather unceremonious way gets introduced into such households, where everyone of talent, even if it is only social talent, is well received—and also well entertained, since Jewish women (the men are too early plunged into business) are highly cultivated, know how to converse on all subjects, and have usually mastered one or another of the fine arts.[5]

Henriette Herz was such a woman. Schleiermacher soon became her closest companion, and we shall see in Part III that more influential persons than his sister were to have their doubts about the young minister's associations, both with women and with Jews.

At the Herz's home in 1797 Schleiermacher first met Friedrich Schlegel, one of Germany's best known young literary figures. Schleiermacher wrote of him:

> He is a young man of twenty-five, of such comprehensive knowledge that one cannot conceive how it is possible for one to know so much at so early an age. He possesses an original intellect [*Geist*] that far surpasses all, even here where there is a great deal of intellect and talent, and in his manner there is a naturalness, openness, and childlike youthfulness, the combination of which with his other qualities is perhaps the most remarkable thing of all. Wherever he goes, his wit as well as his openness makes him the most agreeable companion. But for me he is more than that; he is of very great and essential usefulness. . . . I have always lacked a companion with whom I could freely communicate my philosophical ideas, and who would enter with me into the deepest abstractions. This great void he now fills most gloriously. Not only can I pour out to him what is already in me, but also by the inexhaustible stream of new views and ideas that flows into him without ceasing, much is set into motion in me that had lain dormant. In short, since my closer acquaintance with him a new period in my existence in the philosophical and literary world has begun.[6]

On December 21, 1797, Schlegel moved in with Schleiermacher, and for the better part of a year the two were constant companions. In time, their differences of temperament—Schlegel, brilliant and impulsive; Schleiermacher, pensive and restrained—were to drive the two young men apart. But in 1797, Schleiermacher was broadened and stimulated by the idiosyncrasies of Schlegel, whom he lightheartedly described to his sister as his "better half,"[7] knowing that she would be relieved to learn that his domestic partner was a Gentile and a man.

[5] Aug. 4, 1798. *Br.* I, 186.
[6] Letter to his sister Charlotte, Oct. 22, 1797. *Br.* I, 161.
[7] Letter to Charlotte, Dec. 31, 1797. *Br.* I, 170.

Under the influence of this prototypical young romantic Schleiermacher was prompted to publish his first original work. "He is always picking at me to write something: there are a thousand things that must be said, he claims, and which I alone can say. . . . He leaves me no peace."[8] At a surprise party in celebration of Schleiermacher's twenty-ninth birthday, November 21, 1797, Schlegel had extracted a promise of authorship from his friend. Schleiermacher reports the moment as follows:

> Twenty-nine years and still nothing produced! He would not desist, and I had solemnly to give him my hand that in this very year I would write something of my own—a promise that weighs heavily upon me, as I have no inclination at all to authorship.[9]

True to his word, by the time of his thirtieth birthday Schleiermacher had set to work, and despite his disclaimer of inclination, five months later he had completed *On Religion: Speeches to Its Cultured Despisers*.

The "cultured" or "cultivated despisers" (*gebildete Verächter*) of religion whom Schleiermacher addressed in these *Speeches* were these same friends who had urged him to write, and whose association with Schleiermacher was arousing the suspicions of his sister and others. The substance of his *Speeches* to these cultured despisers was to give rise to deeper suspicions still, many of them justified. Schleiermacher anticipated as much. He chose to write his *Speeches* "in the strictest incognito,"[10] and availed himself of the era's widespred custom of anonymous publication (see above, p. 56). There was nothing unusual about this mode of authorship. In Schleiermacher's instance, however, it had one bizarre consequence. In order to come to print, Schleiermacher's manuscript had to receive the imprimatur of the Prussian board of censors. It fell to the lot of Schleiermacher's immediate church superior, Sack, to censor the *Speeches*. As they arrived anonymously, section by section, Sack was in the habit of discussing his opinion of them with Schleiermacher. Sack appears to have had an inkling that Schleiermacher was the author, but at first he did not know this with surety. For a time Schleiermacher managed to equivocate successfully, but with the second of five *Speeches* the tension of the situation approached a climax. "If only S[ack] would finish censoring the end of the second *Speech*," Schleiermacher wrote to Henriette Herz,

> and I could know how he has taken it, then I could adjust myself accordingly. If he lets it pass, then I see no reason to disavow to him any longer, and he seems to be so firmly convinced that he might take a disavowal amiss. But if the end has been a thorn in the flesh for him,

[8]Schleiermacher to Charlotte, Dec. 31, 1797. *Br.* I, 162.
[9]To Charlotte, Nov. 21, 1797. *Br.* I, 165–66.
[10]Letter to Brinkmann, July 6, 1799. *Br.* IV, 51.

> then I must continue incognito, come what may. In the meantime I can
> remain *entre deux* in writing, but face to face? I confess to you, my
> shrewdness is getting a little wobbly.[11]

The reasons for Schleiermacher's anxiety about Sack's reception of
the end of his second *Speech* are not difficult to understand. Schleiermacher had audaciously reinterpreted the traditional Christian doctrine
of miracle, revelation, prophecy, and grace, devoting a few terse
sentences to each. Then he had reinterpreted the doctrines of God and
immortality, no less audaciously, and at greater length.[12] These passages
were not lost on Sack. In his office as censor, he passed the *Speeches*.
But in his role as ecclesiastical overseer, when Schleiermacher's authorship became known to him with certainty,[13] Sack felt that he had to call
his young ministerial colleague to task. In the winter of 1800–1801, Sack
expressed his concern over both Schleiermacher's social connections
and the content of his *Speeches* in a letter of such bluntness that for five
months he hesitated to deliver it. In the spring of 1801, as a step toward
overcoming their estrangement (the two had avoided seeing each other
for some eighteen months), Schleiermacher sent Sack a copy of his first
collection of *Sermons*.[14] This initiative broke the ice, and in early
summer Sack finally delivered his letter, together with an introductory
note including a word of thanks for the *Sermons*.

Sack's criticism focused especially upon a passage in the second
Speech that Hermann Mulert has aptly called Schleiermacher's "canonization of Spinoza":[15]

> Offer up reverently with me a lock to the manes of the holy, rejected
> Spinoza. The high world-spirit pervaded him; the infinite was his begin-
> ning and his end, the universe his only and eternal love. . . . Full of
> religion was he, and full of holy spirit.[16]

Following some opening expressions of fatherly concern and regret,
Sack comes directly to the point:

> When I read a portion of the first *Speech* in manuscript, I formed the
> pleasant representation that the writing of a man of spirit would win for
> religion admirers and friends from among those who simply misunder-
> stood it, and that it was written for no other purpose than this. No doubt
> you remember with what enthusiasm I let you know of my delight and
> my hope. Meanwhile the sequel has quickly taught me how grossly I had
> deceived myself. Unfortunately, I can acknowledge the book, now that I

---

[11]Mar. 1, 1799. *Br.* I, 201. *Entre deux*: "in between."

[12]*Reden*, 115–33. *Speeches*, 88–101.

[13]Just when this happened cannot be ascertained, but it appears to have been during the
month of March, 1799. See *Br.*III, 107.

[14]Letter to Charlotte, July 1, 1801. *Br.* I, 270.

[15]*Spinozismus*, ed. Mulert, 313.

[16]*Reden*, 52. *Speeches*, 40.

have read it through with deliberation, as nothing more than a spirited apology for pantheism, a rhetorical presentation of the Spinozistic system. I now confess to you quite frankly that this appears to put an end to all that religion has heretofore signified and meant to me, and that I hold the theory lying at its basis to be the most desolate as well as the most pernicious, and do not know any way or means to bring it into any kind of union with either a sound understanding or the needs of the moral nature of man. No more can I comprehend how a man who is an adherent of such a system could be a preaching teacher of Christianity; for no art of sophistry and rhetoric will ever be able to convince a reasonable person that Spinozism and Christian religion can coexist.

In an outright accusation of hypocrisy, Sack goes on to compare Schleiermacher unfavorably with his philosophical mentor, Spinoza:

I can imagine that a Spinoza could be at peace with himself, and perhaps even happy; but that he could have been so as a constituted teacher of the Christian religion, even though he had to teach publicly the opposite of his philosophy—that I doubt.[17]

Twenty years later, Sack's son, Karl Heinrich, was to pronounce Schleiermacher's absolution from the elder Sack's charge of homiletical hypocrisy. In a generally critical review of Schleiermacher's second revision of the *Speeches* in 1821—by which time Schleiermacher had altered a great deal in this second *Speech*, but not a syllable of his canonization of Spinoza—the theologian Sack spoke of the book's "pantheistic appearance" (*pantheistischer Schein*). "I say *appearance*," Sack writes, "because the author's theological writings as well as his efficacy in the church clear him of this reproach."[18] In 1801, however, Schleiermacher had to come to his own defense. His letter of reply is no less candid than Sack's original. "I must most earnestly protest against your view of the book," Schleiermacher writes. Sack has failed to appreciate the central purpose of the *Speeches*, which is to establish the independence of religion from every metaphysics. The metaphysics of Spinoza's system is no exception. "I am as little a Spinozist as anyone. I have appealed to Spinoza as an example, simply because throughout his *Ethics* there prevails a disposition that one can only call piety."[19] Schleiermacher insists that his adherence is to this pious "disposition" (*Gesinnung*) of Spinoza's philosophy, not to its metaphysical system. In the "Explanations" which Schleiermacher appended to each of the *Speeches* in his revision of 1821, he was to describe his debt to Spinoza in similar terms:

[17]No date (summer, 1801). *Br.* III, 276–78.
[18]*Heidelbergische Jahrbücher der Literatur*, XV (1822), 834.
[19]No date (summer, 1801). *Br.* III, 282–84. For the complete texts of these letters see my article, "The Antagonistic Correspondence of 1801 between Chaplain Sack and his Protégé Schleiermacher," *Harvard Theological Review* 74 (1981) 101–121.

How was I to expect that because I ascribed piety to Spinoza, I myself
would be taken for a Spinozist? This, despite the fact that I had never
defended his system, and that whatever philosophy there was in my book
was manifestly inconsistent with the characteristics of his views, and had
a basis quite different from the unity of Substance.[20]

To understand Schleiermacher's wish to dissociate himself from
Spinoza's metaphysical system, we may first recall Schleiermacher's
innate distrust of philosophical systems in general (see above, p. 60).
We must also recall that the critical philosophy of Kant rises like a
continental divide between the philosophies of Spinoza and Schleiermacher. In 1786, Kant had written that his *Critique of Pure Reason*
"clips the wings of dogmatism with respect to knowledge of supersensu-
ous objects, and here Spinozism is so dogmatic that it even competes
with the mathematician in rigor of proof." Metaphysics such as that of
Spinoza's *Ethics* is prone to "fanaticism," Kant continues, and "there is
no sure means of uprooting fanaticism except to determine the limits of
the pure faculty of reason."[21] No sure means, that is to say, except
Kant's own critical philosophy.

We have seen Schleiermacher's suspicion that Kant himself was
inclined to compete with the mathematician in rigor of proof (above,
p. 54). There is no need to belabor that issue. For we have also seen
Schleiermacher's great admiration for Kant, and how strictly Schleiermacher construed Kant's critical survey of reason's limits in the first
Critique (above, pp. 34 and 76). It is no wonder then that Schleiermacher bristled when Sack labeled his *Speeches* as nothing more than "a
rhetorical presentation of the Spinozistic system." Had not Schleiermacher been explicitly negative on that point when he wrote in the
second *Speech* that the metaphysical ambition to "penetrate into the
nature and substance of the whole is no longer religion, and will, if it is
nevertheless regarded as religion, unavoidably sink back into empty
mythology"?[22]

But despite all this, Sack was perceptive in sensing the pervasiveness
of Spinoza's influence in Schleiermacher's *Speeches*. At points in
Schleiermacher's reply to Sack's letter, one senses that he protests too
loudly. "You take something spoken of only in passing, on only a few
pages, for the principal part?" Schleiermacher objects.[23] But his complaint oversimplifies the issue. It is true that Schleiermacher does not
advocate Spinoza's metaphysics in his *Speeches*. It is also true that

[20] *Reden*, 136. *Speeches*, 104.
[21] Kant, *Was heisst: Sich im Denken orientiren?*, 143. English tr.: *What is Orientation in Thinking?*, 302. For a definition of rationalistic dogmatism, see above, p. 14.
[22] *Reden*, 58–59.
[23] *Br.* I, 282.

Spinoza's name is mentioned on only two pages. Yet the mood of the entire second *Speech*—considerably the longest of the five speeches that comprise the book—corresponds closely to the tone of Spinoza's philosophy: "Religion lives its whole life in nature, in the infinite nature of the whole, of the one and all."[24] This same mood colors the first *Speech* as well. And had Schleiermacher perhaps forgotten that in March of 1799, he had assured Sack that he "would find nothing" in the final three speeches that was not to be found "more or less" in these first two?[25] Sack was mistaken in accusing his young colleague of adopting Spinoza's metaphysical system. But his displeasure over Schleiermacher's marriage of Spinozism with Christian religion was not without basis in fact, if by Spinozism we understand the mood of Spinoza's philosophy, and not the details of his metaphysical system.

For over a hundred years, the chief objection to Spinoza had been what Sack refers to as his "pantheism," that is, Spinoza's identification of God with the creative and created "Substance" of nature, and Spinoza's consequent refusal to speak of God as a transcendent being, distinct from Creation. In the minds of many this was equivalent to atheism, and in 1799, atheism was an especially sensitive issue. During the months in which Schleiermacher was completing his *Speeches*, Fichte was being hounded from his professorship at Jena for his refusal to speak of God in transcendent terms. The Fichte affair became known as *der Atheismusstreit*, "the atheism controversy."

In an excellent article of 1904, Emil Fuchs describes Schleiermacher's *Speeches* as a "document from the atheism controversy," written in defense of the beleaguered Fichte.[26] Fuchs overstates his case somewhat. There is no evidence in the *Speeches* that Schleiermacher intended any defense of Fichte. In fact, as Fuchs points out, the passages in which Schleiermacher criticizes the presumptuousness of what he calls "speculative philosophy" or "speculative idealism" are directed against Fichte.[27] The passage of the *Speeches* in praise of Spinoza is in immediate juxtaposition to one of these passages critical of Fichte. Nevertheless, Fuchs is correct in saying that Schleiermacher's *Speeches* opposed the same orthodox defenders of religion as were opposing Fichte. Furthermore, it is certain that in 1799 the German ecclesiastical establishment, including Schleiermacher's superior, Sack, was highly sensitized to the issues of divine transcendence and philosophical atheism.

---

[24] *Reden*, 48. Cf. *Speeches*, 36.

[25] Letter to Herz. *Br*. III, 107.

[26] Emil Fuchs, *Von Schleiermacher zu Marx*, 31–34. The essay appeared originally as Part III of Fuchs' *Vom Werden dreier Denker*.

[27] See for example *Reden*, 9 and *Reden* 52 (cf. *Speeches*, 40). Fichte is not named in these passages, but for similar terminology connected explicitly with Fichte see Schleiermacher's letter to Brinkmann, July 19, 1800. *Br*. IV, 75.

Sack was by no means the first to be incensed by Spinoza's "desolate" and "pernicious" theory. Even the skeptical Scotsman David Hume had at mid-century referred to Spinoza's philosophy as "a monstrous hypothesis."[28] In German thought the most influential reaction to Spinoza had been that of Jacobi, some twenty years before the Sack-Schleiermacher exchange. In 1780, Jacobi had been jolted when Gotthold Ephriam Lessing, the German philosopher of Enlightenment whom he greatly admired, asserted that "there is no other philosophy than the philosophy of Spinoza." The fascinating account of Lessing's disclosure is given in Jacobi's book of 1785, *On the Doctrine of Spinoza, in Letters to Moses Mendelssohn*. Mendelssohn was the grandfather of composer Felix; the father of Dorothea, who, as the wife of banker Simon Veit, was Friedrich Schlegel's illicit companion and who later became Schlegel's wife; and the prototype of the Jewish sage Nathan in Lessing's dramatic poem of 1779, *Nathan the Wise*. He was also Lessing's close friend. Jacobi addressed his *Letters* to Mendelssohn to inform him of Lessing's endorsement of Spinozism. Mendelssohn had never heard Lessing speak of Spinozism, and he was inclined to doubt the testimony of Jacobi. The conversation between Lessing and Jacobi had occurred only shortly before Lessing's death, and so there was no longer any possibility of confirming Jacobi's account directly.[29]

As Jacobi reports the conversation, he had handed Lessing a copy of Goethe's still unpublished poem "Prometheus," with the remark that Lessing, having so often given offense to others, should at least once experience the feeling himself. Lessing read the poem, and the following conversation ensued:

> Lessing: I take no offence; I have long had that at first hand.
>
> I [Jacobi]: You know the poem?
>
> Lessing: That is not what I mean. The viewpoint of the poem is my own viewpoint. The orthodox concepts of the deity are no longer for me; I can no longer enjoy [*geniessen*] them. ἐν καὶ πᾶν! I know nothing else.
>
> I: Then you would be rather in agreement with Spinoza.
>
> Lessing: If I should have to name someone, I know no other.
>
> I: I find Spinoza good enough; yet it is a poor salvation [*ein schlechter Heil*] we find in his name.
>
> Lessing: Yes! If you will. And yet do you know anything better?

---

[28]For sources tracing Spinoza's fortunes in German thought see Frederick H. Burkhardt's note in the Introduction to his translation of Johann Gottfried Herder, *God: Some Conversations*, 14n.

[29]For a more complete account of the Jacobi-Mendelssohn *Pantheismusstreit*, see Lewis White Beck, *Early German Philosophy*, 356–60. For reflections on the theological differences between Jacobi and Lessing, see Søren Kierkegaard, *Concluding Unscientific Postscript*, tr. Swenson and Lowrie, 91–97.

On the morning following this conversation, Lessing showed up while Jacobi was still at breakfast to reengage him on the same topic and to needle him a little:

> Lessing: You were terrified yesterday.
> Jacobi: You surprised me, and I did feel perplexed. It was not terror.[30]

Jacobi's book makes it plain that the persuasive powers of Lessing and Spinoza together were never able to shake Jacobi, any more than Schleiermacher was able to shake Sack, from the conviction that "Spinozism is atheism."[31]

Schleiermacher's attempt to reassure Sack may well have made matters worse, in fact, instead of better. By insisting that he could not accept Spinoza's metaphysical claims, Schleiermacher was at the same time betraying the fact that he could not agree with Spinoza's metaphysical concept of God, but only with Spinoza's pious temperament. This means that while Sack, like Jacobi, felt that Spinoza's concept of God was so meager as to amount to sheer atheism, Schleiermacher was betraying his belief that Spinoza's concept of God asserted not too little but in fact too much. He believed that Spinoza's concept of God as "Substance" is not too empty and vague, as Jacobi and Sack maintained, but rather too metaphysically detailed and specific to allow post-Kantian acceptance. Spinoza's concept asserts more about God's nature than Kant's first *Critique*, having "clipped the wings of dogmatism," any longer allows one to assert. Already in his unpublished *Short Presentation of the Spinozistic System*, written in 1794, Schleiermacher had been convinced that when Spinoza speaks of the divine attributes of "positive unity and infinity," or of "the essence and characteristics of that which exists of itself," he is claiming "more knowledge than he should." Spinoza would not have made such claims, Schleiermacher adds, if Kant's "idea of critical idealism had come to him."[32] In other words, Schleiermacher believes that Spinoza would not have continued to assert his metaphysical concept of God as such if he had been able to anticipate the way in which Kant's first *Critique* ascertains the scope and limits of human reason.

Thus Kant's critical philosophy, if it is construed as strictly as Schleiermacher construed it, reveals not only the overextension of orthodox Christian claims concerning human knowledge of God, but an overextension of the theological claims of the heretic Spinoza as well. Kant has both chastened the orthodox claims made in the name of

---

[30]Jacobi, *Über die Lehre des Spinoza*, 53–55. ἐν καὶ πᾶν: "one and all." I discuss Goethe's poem *Prometheus* further in Chapter 6 of this Part.

[31]Ibid., 216.

[32]*Kurze Darstellung des Spinozistischen Systems*, 300. Schleiermacher goes on to say that Spinoza "appears to have been quite close" to this Kantian point of view.

Christian revelation and deflated the pretensions of dogmatic metaphysics. That is why Schleiermacher feels that he can retain only the "disposition" of both the Christian and the Spinozistic visions of God. He is akin to Lessing here. To use Lessing's word, he is able to "enjoy" both Christianity and Spinoza, not metaphysically, but ethically and religiously, in accordance with the metaphysical modesty demanded by Kant's *Critique of Pure Reason*. The clarification of exactly what the adjectives "ethical" and "religious" here signify for Schleiermacher will occupy us in the remaining chapters of this Part.

Chapter 2. Schleiermacher's Debt to Spinoza and Plato

How little I understood of Plato on the whole when first I read him at the University . . . , and yet even then how I loved and admired him.

Metaphysics, ethics, and religion, Schleiermacher writes at the opening of the second of the *Speeches*, all have the same object: "the universe and man's relation to it."[1] But again and again Schleiermacher tries to make it clear that his *Speeches* are not concerned with metaphysical or ethical approaches to that "object." These are *Speeches on Religion*. They are addressed to those cultured despisers of religion whose negative attitude results precisely from a confusion of piety with some "instinct that craves for a mess of metaphysical and ethical crumbs":[2]

> You always think only of metaphysics and ethics. This mixture of opinions about the highest being or the world, and of imperatives for a human life (or indeed for two) you call religion! And the instinct that seeks those opinions, together with the obscure presentiments of what the real final sanction of the imperatives will be, you call religiosity![3]

Schleiermacher intends to present religion in its own characteristic form, which he calls "intuition of the universe."[4] His hope is that his cultured audience, far from despising religion in this form, will recognize it as a component of human life they already cherish, but without knowing its true name. In the light of this intention, Friedrich Schlegel judged Schleiermacher's *Speeches* a success. A few months after their publication he wrote, "Whoever senses something of the Highest deep within himself and does not know by what name he should call it, let such a one read the *Speeches on Religion*, and what he has felt will become clear to him."[5]

As a matter of fact, however, there is a great deal of ethics in the *Speeches* of 1799, and more metaphysics than Schleiermacher could later

[1] *Reden*, 35.
[2] *Reden*, 41, 2nd ed. *Speeches*, 31.
[3] *Reden*, 39.
[4] *Reden*, 46.
[5] Schlegel, "Ideen," in *Athenaeum*, III/1 (1800), 26.

be comfortable with. It has often been remarked that in his first and second revisions of the *Speeches* in 1806 and 1821, Schleiermacher largely replaces the term *universe* with other terms, such as *whole* or *world*, and many reasons have been put forward to account for such changes.[6] In part, Schleiermacher seems to have set aside the term *universe* for "critical," Kantian reasons. That is, the term *universe* suggests that same "positive unity" which, under the influence of Kant's first *Critique*, Schleiermacher had been discrediting in Spinoza's metaphysics since his *Short Presentation of the Spinozistic System* of 1794. Yet at the same time, it is with a degree of metaphysical nostalgia that Schleiermacher praises Spinoza in the *Speeches* and in the same paragraph calls for the critical idealism of Kant and Fichte to make way for some "higher realism" than that which Kantian idealism "has so boldly and with such legitimacy subordinated."[7] To trace Schleiermacher's attempt to arrive at this "higher," post-Kantian, metaphysical realism would take us far beyond the bounds of this study.[8] Our concern here is with a concept of freedom that persists through all stages of Schleiermacher's metaphysical outlook, and insofar as we can, we shall do well to take Schleiermacher at his word when he says that the reader of the *Speeches* should not look there for metaphysical insight.

Postponing for yet a little while the religious insight that is the principal theme of the *Speeches*, we must, however, look at the ethical perspective they offer. The passage displayed just above, with its reference to "imperatives for a human life (or indeed for two)," is clearly directed against Kant's ethics, and as we have earlier observed, Schleiermacher writes his *Speeches* to distinguish religion from Kant's kind of transcendental moralizing (see above, p. 103). Furthermore, there is a high degree of correspondence between Schleiermacher's *Speeches* and the ethical themes of his treatise *On Human Freedom*. In particular, nothing in the *Speeches* brings into question the moral determinism hypothesized by that earlier treatise. If anything, the hypothesis of determinism has become broader and deeper—more comprehensively social and (we must already say) more nearly metaphysical in its function. The first *Speech*, for example, speaks of the ethical goal of solidarity among persons, in which "a common band of consciousness embraces them all; so that *although no individual can be other than what he must be*, yet each knows every other as clearly as himself, and comprehends completely all particular manifestations of

[6]See Emil Fuchs, "Wandlungen in Schleiermachers Denken zwischen der ersten und zweiten Ausgabe der Reden," *Theologische Studien und Kritiken*, LXXVI (1903), 71–99.
[7]*Reden*, 52.
[8]In this connection see Arthur von Ungern-Sternberg, *Freiheit und Wirklichkeit. Schleiermachers philosophischer Reiseweg durch den deutschen Idealismus.* Also Theodor Camerer, *Spinoza und Schleiermacher: die kritische Lösung des von Spinoza hinterlassenen Problems*, esp. 152–78, and Gerhard Spiegler, *The Eternal Covenant*, esp. Ch. V.

humanity."[9] Earlier we saw how the determinism implicit in such a passage reflects the influence of Kant and of Fawcett (above, pp. 34 and 105), and we have seen in the preceding chapter that Schleiermacher's advisor Sack points an accusing finger at Spinoza as the source of Schleiermacher's deterministic heresy.

There has been confusion about Schleiermacher's indebtedness to Spinoza, some of which we need to clear away. Dilthey asserts that Schleiermacher wrote his treatise *On Human Freedom* of 1791–92 without any knowledge of Spinoza.[10] This is not correct, unless, contrary to appearances, Dilthey means that Schleiermacher wrote *On Human Freedom* without direct familiarity with Spinoza's own texts. In 1787, Schleiermacher's father recommended to his son a little book, published anonymously the year before by Thomas Wizenmann, entitled *The Results of the Jacobian and Mendelssohnian Philosophy, Critically Investigated by a Freewiller*.[11] Wizenmann was a young friend of Jacobi. Though similarly offended by Goethe's poem "Prometheus," he was more cordial to Spinoza's philosophy than Jacobi was, and Wizenmann's book on the Jacobi-Mendelssohn debate would have served Schleiermacher as a thirdhand introduction to Spinoza's ideas.

There is no evidence that Schleiermacher read Wizenmann's book; but it seems to be in answer to his father's recommendation that he writes in August, 1787:

> The Jacobian philosophy I still do not understand correctly, due to the great confusion and indeterminacy in his philosophical language. I will have to read *once again* all the writings exchanged between him and Mendelssohn.[12]

Schleiermacher's reference here must be to the Jacobi-Mendelssohn letters in Jacobi's *On the Doctrine of Spinoza*, which had appeared in 1785. Thus he appears to know Jacobi's secondhand presentation of Spinoza's philosophy as early as 1787. We may therefore conclude that Schleiermacher knew the general outlines of Spinoza's philosophy by the time of his 1791–92 treatise *On Human Freedom*. He would have known at least something of Spinoza from Kant's *Critique of Practical Reason* itself, in fact, where Kant praises Spinoza's philosophy for its "cogency" even while criticizing "the absurdity of its basic idea."[13]

It is clear from Schleiermacher's *Short Presentation of the Spinozistic System*, however, that, when he wrote that essay in 1793–94,[14] he had

[9] *Reden*, 6. *Speeches*, 4. Emphasis added.
[10] *Leben Schleiermachers*, ed. Redeker, I/1, 132 and 140.
[11] Letter of May 17, 1787. *Br.* I, 61. Wizenmann, *Die Resultate der Jacobischen und Mendelssohnschen Philosophie: kritisch untersucht von einem Freywilligen*.
[12] Letter to his father, Aug. 14, 1787. *Br.* I, 66. Emphasis added.
[13] Kant, second *Kritik*, 102.
[14] Dilthey discusses the dating in "Denkmale," 64–65.

not yet had direct access to Spinoza's own texts. "Here Spinoza, to judge from Jacobi's propositions, is particularly difficult":[15] such sentences from the *Short Presentation* indicate that what Schleiermacher knew of Spinoza in 1794 he had learned indirectly from Jacobi's *On the Doctrine of Spinoza*. Schleiermacher's only citations of Spinoza's ideas are from the second edition of Jacobi's work, published in 1789.[16] Thus it appears to be an ironic fact that Schleiermacher, like many German philosophers in the 1780s and 1790s, was attracted to Spinozism by means of the book Jacobi had written to oppose it.

Schleiermacher probably did not possess Spinoza's complete works before 1802–03, when Heinrich Eberhard Gottlob Paulus issued his edition of Spinoza's *Opera* in Jena. Until Paulus's edition there had been no new publication of Spinoza's works since the original Amsterdam edition of 1677,[17] and copies of Spinoza were rare. By 1800, however, Schleiermacher had obtained at least the portion of the 1677 edition that contains Spinoza's posthumously published works, including the great *Ethics*. In an undated letter to Schleiermacher, his friend Friedrich Schlegel writes, "Send me by post as soon as possible your whole Spinoza," to which on September 20, 1800, Schleiermacher replies: "Here, dear friend, is the Spinoza — but not the whole, for I do not have the whole. I lack all that appeared during his lifetime."[18] Schlegel's letter goes on to state that both Henriette Herz and Fichte have copies of Spinoza's works in Berlin — quipping, not very kindly, that "neither, certainly, will be having any use for them." Schleiermacher might well have made use of these friends' copies of Spinoza by the time he wrote his *Speeches* in 1799.

But whatever the precise sequence and details of Schleiermacher's acquaintance with Spinoza, Dilthey is certainly correct when he observes that Schleiermacher discovered in Spinoza's philosophy ideas to which he was already by nature inclined. In the same sense, Sack was correct in observing that Schleiermacher's *Speeches* are steeped in Spinozism. Schleiermacher's longstanding disagreement with Kant's idea of transcendental freedom allied him naturally with Spinoza's belief that moral virtue is proportional, not to the isolation, but to the immersion of a person's will in the causal relations of space and time. Schleiermacher also shares Spinoza's ideal of rising above mere opinion to the rule of

---

[15]Schleiermacher, *Kurze Darstellung des Spinozistischen Systems*, 305.

[16]Rudolph Haym in *Die romantische Schule*, 410n, argues that Schleiermacher had read Spinoza by 1792, since in a letter of Jan. 2, 1827, Schleiermacher writes to a friend, "Ever since I first read Spinoza — and that is now thirty-five years ago — I have sincerely admired and loved him" (*Br.* IV, 375). But to derive the date 1792 from this passage seems to me too precise a deduction from a merely casual reference. In any case, "read Spinoza" here does not necessarily mean "read Spinoza directly from his own writings."

[17]Adolph S. Oko, *The Spinoza Bibliography*, 9–11.

[18]*Br.* III, 231, 232.

reason in moral life. We shall presently see that he shares the religious intuition that Spinoza calls the "intellectual love of God" as well.[19] But what is most pertinent here, Schleiermacher, in the *Speeches* as elsewhere, shares the deterministic outlook that Spinoza's *Ethics* joins with the rule of reason in human life:

> Proposition XLIV. It is not in the nature of reason to regard things as contingent, but as necessary.
>
> *   *   *   *   *   *
>
> Proposition XLVIII. In the mind there is no absolute or free will; but the mind is determined to wish this or that by a cause, which has also been determined by another cause, and this last by another cause, and so on to infinity.[20]

In the treatise *On Human Freedom*, written under the influence of Spinoza as mediated by Jacobi, Schleiermacher's determinism takes the form of an ethical hypothesis. In the *Speeches*, however, written under Spinoza's more immediate influence, determinism takes on metaphysical depth and scope. To repeat our earlier conclusion (above, p. 119), then, Schleiermacher's objections to Sack's accusation of Spinozism are valid only in the strict sense that Schleiermacher nowhere endorses the details of Spinoza's metaphysical system, with its terminology of "Substance," "Attributes," "Modes," and the like.

Insofar as Schleiermacher may be said to have had a "metaphysics" at all in the years around his *Speeches*, it was not that of Spinoza, but in fact that of Plato. It is an index of Schleiermacher's philosophical loyalties that in the course of his early career he speaks of only two philosophers in terms of veneration: the "holy, rejected Spinoza" (above, p. 116), and the "divine" Plato.[21] The growth of Schleiermacher's veneration for Plato had begun with his student days at Halle, where his enthusiasm for classical learning—already awakened during his youthful studies at the Moravian *Gymnasium* at Niesky from 1783 till 1785—flourished under the direction of his teacher Eberhard. "How little I understood Plato on the whole when first I read him at the University . . . ," Schleiermacher was to recall a dozen years later, "and yet even then how I loved and admired him."[22] At the time of the *Speeches* Schleiermacher's love was beginning to develop into a near identification with Plato's point of view. It was at the moment of the *Speeches'* completion, in fact—mid-April, 1799—that Friedrich Schlegel invited his roommate Schleiermacher to collaborate with him on an

---

[19]On Spinoza's "three kinds of knowledge"—opinion, reason, and intuition—see the *Ethics*, Part II, Proposition XXXIX, Note II. On the intellectual love of God see Part V, Propositions XXXII–XXXVII.

[20]Spinoza, *Ethics*, Part II, tr. Elwes.

[21]Letter to Brinkmann, June 9, 1800. *Br.* IV, 72.

[22]Letter to Herz, Aug. 10, 1802. *Br.* I, 312.

edition and German translation of Plato's works. Schleiermacher accepted Schlegel's offer both with enthusiasm and with some trepidation. "The project excites me," he wrote to Brinkmann, "for I have been inexpressibly deeply penetrated by reverence for Plato for as long as I have known him. Yet I feel also a holy awe before it and almost fear that I have gone beyond the limits of my powers. May heaven help us."[23]

A life with Plato thus began for Schleiermacher. By September, 1802, his immersion in the project was such that he could write, "Plato is incontestably the author whom I know best, and with whom I have almost coalesced."[24] This immersion in Plato separates the first edition of the *Speeches* from the second edition of 1806, and because of this, alterations in the latter provide a particularly sensitive index of Plato's influence on Schleiermacher's thinking, as we shall shortly see. But let us first trace the history of the Schleiermacher-Schlegel collaboration, which, like the exact sequence of Schleiermacher's acquaintance with Spinoza, has been frequently misunderstood.

Schlegel had first pointed out the need for a Plato translation in conversations with Schleiermacher in August, 1798. Upon their formal agreement in 1799 to undertake the project, Schleiermacher conceived it as a long term collaboration. He wrote to Henriette Herz:

> O! it is a divine idea, and I can well believe that few would be able to do it as well as we. But I shall not be able to undertake it for several years, and then it must be undertaken as free from outer dependence as ever a work was, with no regard for the passage of years. Indeed it is a secret, and still lies a long way off.[25]

But Schlegel's plans were different. Here we first encounter the differences of character that were in time to prove so damaging to this famous early romantic friendship. In March, 1800, pressed by both natural impetuosity and financial need, Schlegel released a public announcement of his Plato project:

> I have resolved to edit a precise and complete translation of the collected works of Plato, of which the first volume will appear by Easter, 1801.[26]

Schlegel took this step without the consent of his collaborator. In fact, Schleiermacher scarcely had prior knowledge of the announcement,[27] and his collaboration with Schlegel was nowhere mentioned in the

---

[23]Letter to Brinkmann, Apr. 22, 1800. *Br.* IV, 65.

[24]Letter to Eleonore Grunow, Sep. 3, 1802. *Br.* I, 327.

[25]Apr. 29, 1799. *Br.* I, 220–21.

[26]*Intelligenzblatt der Allgemeinen Literatur-Zeitung,* 1800. No. 43, Col. 349. Partial text given in Dilthey, *Leben Schleiermachers,* ed. Redeker, I/2, 62–63.

[27]See Schlegel's letter to Schleiermacher, Mar. 10, 1800. Before Schleiermacher had a chance to reply, Schlegel's announcement of the Plato project had already appeared.

announcement's text. Schleiermacher was dismayed. He had believed
that months of pioneer scholarly effort would be required to determine
the order in which Plato had written his dialogues before the translation
of their texts could even be begun. Now Schlegel had pledged the first
fruits of this effort to both the publisher and the public within twelve
months' time. Schleiermacher felt he had no choice but to leave the
work of dating the dialogues to Schlegel, restricting his own efforts to
translating those dialogues which the two of them had already agreed
upon as early.

Schlegel's activities during the first two years of the Plato project
were characteristically brilliant and erratic. He produced a chronology of
the dialogues. He also completed introductions to the *Parmenides*, which
he had judged to be Plato's earliest dialogue, and to the *Phaedo*—
though not until the fall of 1802, and thus far behind schedule.
Meanwhile, in March, 1801, Schleiermacher had completed his translation of the *Phaedrus*, which he, in disagreement with Schlegel, judged to
be Plato's earliest dialogue.

This disagreement, along with many others, was never to be resolved. In the fall of 1800, Schlegel—together with Dorothea Mendelssohn Veit, who the year before had separated from her husband to live
with Schlegel—left Berlin for Jena, where his brother, A. W. Schlegel,
was teaching alongside the most impressive assemblage of young talent
in Germany. The resolution of scholarly issues by letter was tedious and
ultimately unsatisfactory. In December, 1801, Schlegel once again
moved into Schleiermacher's quarters in Berlin for a time. But according
to Schleiermacher's later report, Schlegel was "very distracted, and I
recall only a single orderly conversation about Plato."[28] In January,
Schlegel was off again. During 1802 he had addresses in Dresden,
Leipzig, and Paris—a moving target for Schleiermacher's attempts at
correspondence. By August of 1802, Schleiermacher was frustrated to
the point of asking the publisher Friedrich Frommann "whether, in case
Schlegel leaves us in the lurch and decides to retire from this undertaking, he [Frommann] would venture the Plato with me alone.
. . . Otherwise I am firmly determined to seek another publisher; for I
cannot set Plato aside after so much work."[29] In September he wrote,
"With fear and trembling I await a letter from Frommann. If Friedrich
[Schlegel] has sent no manuscript—actually, unless he has sent all—
then our Plato collaboration, to my great sorrow, is at an end."[30]
Schlegel defaulted. Within six months the Plato project was Schleiermacher's alone.

[28]Letter to August Boeckh, June 18, 1808. Quoted in Dilthey, *Leben Schleiermachers*,
ed. Redeker, I/2, 72.
[29]Letter to Herz, Aug. 24, 1802. *Br*. I, 321.
[30]Letter to Herz, Sep. 6, 1802. *Br*. I, 329.

Discussions of the Plato collaboration, especially discussions in the Schleiermacher literature, usually emphasize the remarkable degree of patience in Schleiermacher's dealings with Schlegel. This emphasis is justified. Schleiermacher stood by his friend through storms of emotional, literary, matrimonial, and fiscal crisis and controversy. Yet it must be said that there was pique and even provocation on both sides. In December of 1802, Schleiermacher wrote to his friend Georg Reimer, the Berlin publisher who had accepted Schleiermacher's *Groundwork to a Critique of Previous Ethical Doctrine* for publication and who was having difficulties of his own with Schlegel: "I am sorry that you are having trouble with Schlegel — the more so, since he solemnly promised me that you would never have occasion to complain about him. Meanwhile he is treating Frommann and me no better with respect to the Plato. I wish we were already satisfactorily separated in this matter, since a happy outcome is unthinkable."[31] Schleiermacher then learned that Schlegel, sensing Schleiermacher's attitude, had expressed injured feelings to Henriette Herz. He wrote to Schlegel:

> What you said about the Plato, that I have more *desire* to translate him alone and that you only *wish* the matter were decided, causes me concern that you have completely misunderstood me on this point. My *desire* is but the surrogate of your own, and a decision in this matter is not something you need to *wish*, since it rests entirely upon you. For if only you do not give it up, then there is no necessity for me to think of translating alone; and if Frommann has your manuscript — of which he has still not given me any knowledge, however — then you have already decided the matter. This wish is thus for me alone to express, and I herewith present it to you against the time when you shall again have the tranquility for friendly reflection.[32]

A taunting irony plays between these lines. Was Schlegel, the connoisseur of romantic irony, to take them as conciliation or rebuke?

The ambiguity was intensified by Schlegel's attitude toward the intermediary in this exchange, Henriette Herz. Schleiermacher felt that Schlegel harbored a "jealousy" of Henriette Herz, dating from the Berlin days when she had competed with Schlegel for Schleiermacher's intimacy.[33] "I have yet another worry, deeper and more important," Schlegel had written in a letter to his sister-in-law, Caroline Michaelis Böhmer Schlegel, cataloguing his current complaints:

> Schleiermacher, by his association with Herz, is ruining our friendship, for himself and for me as well. The feminine wiles of this woman are actually so common that she must possess this fifth-man-on-the-totem-pole alone, if it suits her pleasure. They render each other vain — no grand

---

[31]Dec. 29, 1802. *Br.* III, 332.
[32]Mar. 15, 1803. *Br.* III, 339. Schleiermacher's emphases.
[33]Schleiermacher to Charlotte, May 30, 1798. *Br.* I, 175.

pride, but rather a foolish humor, such as one gets from drinking some barbaric punch. Every little exercise of virtue, however lousy, they highly credit to themselves. Schleiermacher's spirit fawns; he loses his sense for the great. In short, I could go mad over their damned trifling cosiness.[34]

Already in his novel *Lucinde* of 1799, in a clear reference to Schleiermacher under the guise of the novel's character Antonio, Schlegel had written:

You have changed so since before! Be careful, friend, that before you know it you do not lose your sense for the great.[35]

By mid-1803 personal separation had followed the dissolution of the Plato project. Schlegel and Schleiermacher were never to meet again, though until 1817 they continued an infrequent but friendly correspondence.

In 1804 a new Plato announcement appeared in Jena's *Allgemeine Literatur-Zeitung*, this one signed by Schleiermacher:

Three years ago by now, Fr. Schlegel promised the friends of philosophy a complete and richly appointed translation of the writings of Plato. Although not then publicly named, and, at a distance, not aware of his announcement, which was rushed into print by circumstances, I was to have been his assistant, according to both an old agreement and my own wish. The causes that have held back the appearance of this work need not be mentioned here, except only this: on the one hand the publisher withdrew, wearied (and not unjustly so) by perpetual delay; and on the other hand, at almost the same time, Fr. Schlegel became convinced that in the next few years he could not pursue the business of the translation as zealously and persistently as the continuation of the undertaking would demand. Thus abandoned by my confederates, I am nevertheless not able to abandon the work, but rather find myself in every way urged to venture upon it alone.[36]

In the Easter season of 1804, the first volume of Schleiermacher's Plato appeared. It contained a General Introduction and the four dialogues that Schleiermacher's scholarship had established as the earliest, together with critical annotations, but included no mention of Schlegel. Schlegel's complaint to the new publisher, Georg Reimer, drew this reply from Schleiermacher:

Let me answer the part of your letter to Reimer that concerns me, which for my part I find astonishing. How much you communicated your ideas

[34]Quoted in Henriette Herz, *Henriette Herz. Ihr Leben und ihre Zeit*, ed. Landsberg, 63–64. No date is given.

[35]Schlegel, *Lucinde*, "Julius an Antonio, I," 99. *Lucinde* is available in English in Peter Firchow, *Friedrich Schlegel's "Lucinde" and the Fragments*.

[36]*Intelligenzblatt der Jenaischen Allgemeinen Literatur-Zeitung*, 1804, No. 2, Col. 13. Text given in Dilthey, *Leben Schleiermachers*, ed. Redeker, I/2, 63–64.

> about Plato to me you yourself must know. I know that it was little, and
> what you did communicate was only bare results without grounds, so that
> either to oppose them or to arrogate them for myself was equally
> impossible. My entire arrangement rests upon the grouping of the
> Platonic works, and this is grounded in their [inner] construction. I never
> heard anything of this sort from you. Thus if we agree in certain
> particulars, that is accidental. . . . I have not named you in the work
> because I have not seen how to; but of course I named you in the
> announcement, and I think you can be quite satisfied with the consider-
> ate, friendly way in which I did so. . . . Instead of this astonishing kind of
> sensitivity, suitable neither to the matter at hand nor to us, I would
> rather have heard from you something about the translation that could
> have been instructive to me, and I invite you once again to grant me
> this—if this work, which only through your fault cannot be called your
> own, is still dear to you. But enough of this. . . . Live well, and do not
> again let yourself be seized by such petty agitations. They are not worthy
> of you and only obstruct the truth.[37]

Schleiermacher's publisher Reimer could not of course have known
it at the time, but in accepting Schleiermacher's edition of Plato after
Frommann's withdrawal, he was accepting what would in time be
judged as Germany's greatest work of Plato scholarship. Between 1804
and 1828, Schleiermacher introduced, translated, and annotated all of
Plato's dialogues except three. Schleiermacher's death in 1834 left the
Timaeus, the *Critias*, and the *Laws* unfinished. Schleiermacher pio-
neered in the scholarly reconstruction of the order in which the
dialogues were written. But what is more, his scholarship is itself
embued with the spirit of Plato's philosophy. In a review of 1808, the
classical philologist August Boeckh—Schleiermacher's former student at
Halle and later Professor at Heidelberg and Berlin—recognized these
qualities in Schleiermacher's edition of Plato, by then in its second
volume:

> No one yet has understood Plato and taught others to understand so
> completely as this man, who, with a rare comprehension of the highest,
> yet treats with no less care the smallest detail as well—a talent perfected
> in but few scholars.

Boeckh goes on to commend Schleiermacher's Platonic sense of balance
between "imprudent exaggeration" and "prosaic restriction," his sense
of proportion between attention to the whole of Plato's philosophy and
to the particular dialogues that comprise it.[38]

Boeckh's opinions have stood to our own day. Allan Bloom writes in
the Preface to his 1968 translation of Plato's *Republic*, "Schleiermacher's old German version was the most useful translation I found.

---

[37]Letter of Oct. 10, 1804. *Br.* III, 405–6.

[38]*Heidelbergische Jahrbücher der Literatur*, I (1808), 83. Excerpt quoted in Dilthey, *Leben
Schleiermachers*, ed. Redeker, I/2, 74n. Boeckh goes on to say that Schleiermacher is also
like Plato in being difficult to understand.

Although his text was inferior to ours, he seems to have had the best grasp of the character and meaning of the dialogues."[39] Werner Jaeger, in the second volume of his *Paideia* (1943), provides a summary of Schleiermacher's pioneering "endeavour to apprehend the miracle of Plato's philosophical achievement, both through the philologist's attention to detail and through the aesthete's sympathetic perception of the organic whole." At the end of the eighteenth century, Jaeger writes,

> the true Plato was discovered; and it was Schleiermacher—himself a theologian, but in active contact with the newly awakened spirit of German philosophy and poetry—who initiated the movement that led to his discovery. . . . The trend of this approach was towards seeing Plato, who had become a mighty figure detached from time and history, within his own social background, and making him a real, solid, historical character. . . . Schleiermacher had the romanticist's keen perception that form is the expression of intellectual and spiritual individuality; and it was he who recognized the special property of Plato's philosophy—that it was intended not to take the form of a closed and orderly system, but to look like a continuous philosophical discussion aimed at discovering the truth. . . . He held that the essential characteristic of Plato was to set forth philosophy in the life and movement of dialectic rather than in the form of a finished system of dogma.[40]

Like Schleiermacher's Greek text, mentioned in the citation from Allan Bloom's Preface, Schleiermacher's chronology of the Platonic dialogues is today out of date, due to philological discoveries made since Schleiermacher's time.[41] But this in no way lessens the influence of Plato's philosophy upon Schleiermacher's outlook. We have seen in Part I the reverence Schleiermacher felt for Plato's ideal of the rational governance of life (above, p. 47). We have seen also how his agreement with the Socratic principle of Plato's *Apology*—that wisdom consists in the acknowledgement of ignorance—contributes to Schleiermacher's suspicion of philosophical systems claiming completeness and finality (above, p. 54). The *Speeches* are imbued with two further aspects of Schleiermacher's Platonism. The first is Plato's influence upon Schleiermacher's moral philosophy of determinism. Increasingly Schleiermacher tends away from a mechanistic and toward a more organic vocabulary of determinism. This tendency is expressed, for example, by his frequent replacement of the term *bewegen*, "to move," by the term *beleben*, "to enliven," in the second edition of the *Speeches*. The same tendency is already to be seen in the extraordinary proliferation of the adjective *lebendig*, "living," in the language of the first edition of the *Speeches* in 1799, as compared with Schleiermacher's earlier, more analytic treatises. The second aspect of Schleiermacher's

[39]Bloom, tr., *The Republic of Plato*, xix.
[40]Werner Jaeger, *Paideia: the Ideals of Greek Culture*, tr. Gilbert Highet, II, 78–79.
[41]Ibid., 80.

Platonism provides a principal religious theme of the *Speeches*. It is Schleiermacher's sense for the infinite. Both these Platonic aspects can be seen in a characteristic passage from the *Speeches*:

> The contemplation of the pious is solely the immediate perception of the universal being of all finite things in the infinite and through the infinite, and of all temporal things in the eternal and through the eternal. To seek and find this in all that lives and moves, in all becoming and change, in all activity and passivity, and to have and to know life in immediate feeling only as this being—that is religion.[42]

Schleiermacher's sense for the infinite will occupy us in Chapters 6 and 7 of this Part. In this chapter we shall take the Platonic emphasis upon life and motion, becoming and change, in Schleiermacher's *Speeches* as our concluding theme.

Plato's sense for "the organic whole," his preference for setting forth philosophy "in the life and movement of dialectic rather than in the form of a finished system of dogma"—these Platonic qualities which Jaeger summarizes and to which Schleiermacher was by nature inclined affected Schleiermacher intimately during the period of his writing of the *Speeches* in 1798–99 and his preparation of their revision in 1806. Increasingly in those years Schleiermacher came to prize the complex wholeness and inward delicacy of life. Everywhere in his writings we find him expressing the opinion that narrow attempts to analyze the inward and vital in terms of the outward and inorganic alone are bound to lose the living person "in the general mechanism."[43] In a philosophical fragment he contributed in 1798 to the romantic journal *Athenaeum*, edited by the Schlegel brothers, Schleiermacher calls this loss of life "the most wretched of suicides."[44] It is suicide by reductionism (above, p. 82), suicide by the chemical analysis of life into isolated elements (above, p. 59), by limiting one's ethical or religious attention to less than the wholeness of a person's life (above, p. 88). "One can analyze the juices of an organic body into its elemental ingredients," Schleiermacher writes in the *Speeches*:

> But take these separated elements now, mix them in every proportion, treat them in every proportion, treat them in every way; will you be able again to make heart's blood out of them? Will that which is once dead ever again be able to move in a living body and unite with it? The reconstitution of the offspring of living nature from their separate ingredients frustrates every human art—and just as little will you succeed with religion, however completely you have assembled its elements from without. It must come forth from within.[45]

---

[42] *Reden*, 47, 2nd ed. *Speeches*, 36.
[43] Letter to Herz, Sep. 6, 1798. *Br.* I, 191.
[44] *Athenäum*, I/2 (1798), 272.
[45] *Reden*, 82. Cf. *Speeches*, 48.

Schleiermacher despised all reductionism, undeceived by its many guises. That of the schools of orthodox theology, for example, he pins with the epithet "nurseries of the dead letter."[46] In a passage of the *Speeches* as characteristic of early romanticism as it was influential upon it, Schleiermacher ridicules the "calculating understanding" of certain utilitarian philosophers of the eighteenth century who, wanting to "enlighten" us, "would gladly do so to the point of fatal transparency if they had their way."[47]

In Plato—with his philosophical medium of the dialogue, "fashioned like a living being, with parts in proportion and body appropriate to mind";[48] with his use of myth and poetic symbol to entice a pupil's thinking beyond the limits of dialectic rationalism; with his modest claims of certainty in any sphere of experience, and especially the sphere of transcendence—in this Plato, Schleiermacher found the teacher for whom he felt "inexpressibly" deep reverence (above, p. 128). He knew at first hand the struggle to preserve epistemological modesty, as recommended in Plato's day by Socrates and in Schleiermacher's day by Kant's first *Critique*, a modesty that warded off the reductionistic tug of rationalism in its many prosaic forms. As he entered into the sensibilities of romanticism, in fact, Schleiermacher sensed in his own early writings the poetic deficiency that results when critical philosophy not only limits ethical analysis to the phenomenal sphere of experience, but also allows its tone to be attuned to the palpably sensible and nothing else.

In his Journal at one point Schleiermacher proposes the composition of a new Platonic dialogue, "a new *Phaedo*, in which Spinoza is the principal figure."[49] The idea must have delighted him, for several reasons. First of all, the form of dialogue attracted him as "the form that truly living instruction must necessarily have":[50]

> What method has from of old been more gloriously or more satisfactorily employed to reveal the higher nature of knowledge and of inner feeling?[51]

Second, Plato complements Spinoza in exactly the manner Schleiermacher's post-Kantian romantic sensibilities require. That is, Schleiermacher felt that Spinoza, for all his ethical genius and religious spirit, "lacked the intuition of a poetic nature."[52] But the first lesson of Plato,

---

[46] *Reden*, 22.

[47] *Reden*, 163. *Speeches*, 132.

[48] Schleiermacher, "Einleitung zum *Phaidros*," *Platons Werke*, I/1, 3rd ed., 40. In English: *Schleiermacher's Introductions to the Dialogues of Plato*, tr. Dobson, 49.

[49] "Denkmale," 140.

[50] Schleiermacher, "Einleitung," *Platons Werke*, I/1, 15. Dobson's English tr., 15.

[51] *Reden*, 45, 2nd ed. *Speeches*, 34.

[52] "Denkmale," 140.

whom Schleiermacher repeatedly refers to as "a philosophical artist,"[53] is the insight that "the best in human beings proceeds from intuitions."[54] Finally, Schleiermacher is attracted to Plato's *Phaedo* as the model for his proposed dialogue "because in it human beings are held so fast to the earth."[55] That is, Socrates' modest refusal in the *Phaedo* to claim certainty in his speculations about life after death is a model for the epistemological modesty Schleiermacher felt necessary in our post-Kantian dealings with transcendence. Schleiermacher confided this proposed dialogue to his Journal some three years or so after the publication of his *Speeches*. That he never got around to realizing it has left students of ethics and religion immeasurably the poorer.

[53]Schleiermacher, *Platons Werke*, I/1, 7, 14, 28. English tr., 4, 14, 35.
[54]Letter to Herz, Aug. 10, 1802. *Br.* I, 312.
[55]"Denkmale," 140.

Chapter 3. Freedom as Self-Expression

Single actions must depend upon something quite different from momentary feeling. Only when each is in its own connection and its own place do they manifest in a free and characteristic way the whole inner unity of the spirit—not when they correspond in a dependent and slavish way to some particular stimulation.

In the context of a Spinozistic determinism mellowed by the Socratic spirit of Plato's dialogues we now return to Schleiermacher's concept of freedom under the three aspects we encountered in Part I. Freedom as self-expression, freedom as appropriation, freedom as self-cultivation—all are themes of Schleiermacher's *Speeches* of 1799. We find them stated explicitly in the book's content, and we may develop them further in terms of the book's form and the circumstances in which Schleiermacher wrote it.

Spinoza's *Ethics* gives the following definition of freedom:

> A thing is called free, which exists by the mere necessity of its own nature and is determined to action by itself alone; but necessary, or rather constrained [*coacta*], if it is determined by something else to exist and act in a certain determinate manner.[1]

According to Spinoza's explication of this definition, God alone is absolutely free, for no finite creature can be said to exist "by the mere necessity of its own nature." To use Schleiermacher's phrase, we are aware that "the whole of our existence is from elsewhere" (above, p. 76), that we are dependent upon the world around us and the power that posited it as the ultimate sources of our existence and our actions.

Schleiermacher's fundamental definition of freedom as "the absence of a constraint" (above, p. 79) is strikingly close to that of Spinoza's *Ethics*. In these terms, human beings are "absolutely dependent," never absolutely free. We can be no more than relatively free, free from

---

[1]Spinoza, *Ethics*, Part I, Definition 7. Spinoza's definition echoes that of the Stoics. Epictetus, for example, writes, "He is free who lives as he wishes to live; who is neither subject to compulsion nor to hindrance, nor to force; whose movements to action are not impeded, whose desires attain their purpose, and who does not fall into that which he would avoid." *The Discourses of Epictetus*, tr. Long, 295.

constraints only to a greater or lesser degree. Freedom of this relative kind is a principal theme of the *Speeches*, as when Schleiermacher speaks of a free person as "a part of the whole, active through his own power."[2] For by a phrase such as "his own power," Schleiermacher always means power appropriated (*angeeignet*) from the universe, never power originating with absolute spontaneity and self-sufficiency from the finite agents themselves.

An infinitive phrase from the *Speeches, das Eigenthümliche hervorzubringen*, "to bring forth the characteristic,"[3] epitomizes Schleiermacher's definition of freedom. To bring forth the *characteristic*, not the *original*. In Schleiermacher's understanding, our actions are never the "causality that is entirely self-determining" of which Kant speaks (see above, p. 22). They are rather the "bringing forth" of powers we have internalized from the world around us. Our actions are free to the extent that they express a characteristic internalizing of power, or in other words, to the extent that they are not the result of any reactive impulse but are rather the unconstrained expression of our character. Freedom is first to "enjoy that which is enlisted" from the universe,

> to absorb it into one's innermost spirit and fuse it into a unity; to strip it of the temporal, so that it does not dwell in one as something discrete and disturbing, but as something eternal, pure, and calm. Then, from this inner unity, action springs of its own accord. . . . Single actions must depend upon something quite different from momentary feeling. Only when each is in its own connection and its own place do they manifest in a free and characteristic way the whole inner unity of the spirit—not when they correspond in a dependent and slavish way to some particular stimulation.[4]

Freedom in all its three aspects is implied by this passage from the *Speeches*. In this chapter we shall concentrate on the first of the three, freedom as self-expression—the freedom of actions that "manifest in a free and characteristic way the whole inner unity of the spirit."

Schleiermacher's *Speeches* convey in their very form the freedom thus defined by their content. They spring immediately to their principal theme in a burst of expressive energy, without overture, without preface. Schleiermacher deliberately chose to omit a preface, in fact, as he wanted to avoid the formal constraints such an opening would have imposed on his freedom of expression.[5] Here as always in Schleiermacher, however, freedom does not imply the absence of necessity (see above, p. 79). He attributes his choice to write the *Speeches*, not to a faculty of radical spontaneity, but rather to the opposite: "I am urged

---

[2] *Reden*, 74.
[3] *Reden*, 270. Translated "characteristic production" in *Speeches*, 234.
[4] *Reden*, 2nd ed., 72–73. *Speeches*, 59.
[5] Letter to Herz, Apr. 14, 1799. *Br*. I, 218.

to speak by an inner and irresistible necessity that governs me, god-like."[6] In his reply to Sack's criticism of the *Speeches* Schleiermacher denies the charge that his writing is grounded in an irresponsible "search for the strange and uncommon": "In fact it has no other ground than my own character [*eigenthümlicher Charakter*], my inborn mysticism, my cultivation, proceeding outward from within."[7]

This grounding of outward expression in inner necessity is for Schleiermacher identical with freedom in its first aspect. In his treatise *On Human Freedom* of 1792 Schleiermacher had written that to act freely is to act "in accordance with circumstances but not to be altered by them" (above, p. 85). In the *Speeches* of 1799, caught up in the artistic ebullience of early romanticism, Schleiermacher goes even further. He suggests that expressive freedom may more nearly ignore outward circumstances altogether. The poet, seer, or artist ideally expresses himself, not in accordance with some outer goal or purpose, but instead freely from within: "For he would so act even if no one were there."[8] Schleiermacher sometimes calls freedom in this expressive aspect "inspiration." To recognize it one must be alert to the "feeling that action, in spite of or regardless of all outer occasion, goes forth from a person's inwardness."[9] What we are suggesting here is that Schleiermacher's production of the *Speeches* was "inspired" in just this sense.

Henriette Herz writes in her reminiscences that Schleiermacher often sought her opinion, as well as the opinions of Friedrich Schlegel and Schlegel's companion Dorothea Veit, on matters relating to the *Speeches*, but typically ignored their advice, "since he was already too much at one with himself before he went to work."[10] Thus Schleiermacher valued his *Speeches* not simply for their content, but also for the freedom with which he expressed himself in them. He valued them as characteristic expressions of his unique individuality, as free communications of the world view he had inwardly appropriated. Friedrich von Schelling's delayed but eventually enthusiastic reception of the *Speeches* must therefore have come to Schleiermacher as the most pertinent of the compliments paid his book, for Schelling singled out exactly these qualities—Schleiermacher's thorough appropriation of his subject and his expressive freedom in communicating it—for praise. "I honor the author," he wrote in 1801,

> as a spirit whom one can only regard as belonging to the first rank of original philosophers. Without this originality it would not be possible to have penetrated the most inner reaches of speculation to such a degree

[6] *Reden*, 2–3. *Speeches*, 2.
[7] *Br.* III, 285.
[8] *Reden*, 10.
[9] *Reden*, 2nd ed., 117. *Speeches*, 89.
[10] *Henriette Herz. Ihr Leben und ihre Erinnerungen*, ed. Fürst, 158.

without having left behind even a trace of the steps one must have gone through. As it is, the work appears to me to have sprung purely from itself, and is therefore not only the most beautiful presentation but at the same time itself an image of the universe. Yet for all that, whoever would produce something of this kind has to have made the deepest of philosophical studies—or else he has written under blind divine inspiration.[11]

This praise was all the more welcome to Schleiermacher because Schelling's initial reaction to the *Speeches* had been negative. Though seven years younger than Schleiermacher, Schelling was already a professor of philosophy at Jena when, in 1799, he wrote a philosophical poem in doggerel verse, characterizing the author of the *Speeches* as proud and presumptuous.[12] With the mercurial swiftness typical of the young Schelling, however, his attitude had by 1801 reversed itself. Friedrich Schlegel concurred with Schelling's later, positive judgment. "It is a highly cultivated and at the same time highly characteristic book," Schlegel writes in his *Anthenaeum* review of the *Speeches*; "the most characteristic book we have cannot be more characteristic."[13]

In writing his *Speeches*, then, Schleiermacher felt the exhilaration of free creativity for which, as he writes in his Journal, "the birth of Minerva is a lovely allegory."[14] At least he felt such freedom in writing the crucial first two *Speeches*. As he neared the completion of the second *Speech*, however, Schleiermacher's circumstances changed, and in his writing of the final three *Speeches* we can see a living embodiment of Schleiermacher's theory of the damaging effect of external constraints upon free expression.

In mid-February, 1799, Sack's son-in-law, a court chaplain in Potsdam by the name of Bamberger, died. Schleiermacher was called from

---

[11]Letter to A. W. Schlegel from Schelling, July 3, 1801. *Aus Schellings Leben in Briefen*, I, 345. Quoted in Dilthey, *Leben Schleiermachers*, ed. Redeker, I/1, 455. See Walter Grossmann, "Schelling's Copy of Schleiermacher's *Über die Religion*," *Harvard Library Bulletin*, XIII (Winter, 1959), 47–50.

[12]Entitled "Epikurisch Glaubensbekenntnis Heinz Widerporstens," Schelling's poem had this to say of the author of the *Speeches*:

> Deswegen mir nichts ist so sehr verhasst,
> Als so ein fremder fürnehmer Gast,
> Der auf der Welt herumstolziert
> Und schlechte Red' im Munde führt
> Von der Natur und ihrem Wesen;
> Dünkt sich besonders auserlesen.
> Ist eine eigene Menschenrasse.

Aus Schellings Leben in Briefen, I, 282. Quoted in Hermann Süskind, *Der Einfluss Schellings auf die Entwicklung von Schleiermachers System*, 61–62. Süskind maintains—correctly, I believe—that Schelling's influence on Schleiermacher was slight until after 1803. See pp. 57–99.

[13]Schlegel, "Reden über die Religion," *Athenaeum*, II/2 (1799), 289.

[14]"Denkmale," 109.

nearby Berlin to fill the interim preaching position in Bamberger's church, the *Hof- und Garnisonkirche* of Potsdam. It proved to be an exhausting ministry, owing not least to the fact that Schleiermacher's new congregation included the Prussian king, Friedrich Wilhelm III. During the same period Schleiermacher somehow became involved in an assortment of minor but time-consuming projects with the Berlin publisher Christian Sigismund Spener.[15] Suddenly Schleiermacher found his writing of the *Speeches*, formerly so free, under severe constraints.

As Schleiermacher's mood of exhilaration yielded to one of weariness under the pressures of his new situation, his writing suffered accordingly. Schlegel pointed this out to him: "I implore you not to hurry overmuch, always to begin and stop at your convenience. It will be good even for the outward appearance of the *Speeches*, for one can easily notice it in your style when you become anxious."[16] Schlegel was not telling Schleiermacher anything he did not already realize. "It is peculiar," he wrote to Henriette Herz,

> that in the first and second *Speeches* I would no longer know anything to improve or add (although Schlegel finds fault with some things in the second), but in the third and fourth there is still a great deal. Whether that is really a proof that the first two are finished I do not know; but it is a testimony against constrained production in general.[17]

"Constrained production" translates Schleiermacher's expression at the end of this passage with only the barest adequacy. The German is *das Machen*. In the correspondence of the Berlin romantic circle it seems to mean something like "make-work"—having to work, more for the sake of mere working than for the sake of one's genuine interests. In short, it seems to denote exactly the limitation upon freedom that Spinoza calls the "constraint" upon something "determined by something else to exist and operate in a certain determinate manner." It refers to the stifling necessity of having to contrive something out of phase with the flow of one's characteristic interests, to the dissatisfaction one feels with ideas that have been picked from the mind and marketed before they have ripened.

In Berlin, Schleiermacher had grown accustomed to the freedom he enjoyed working at the Charité and moving in the society of his

[15]These appear to have included the translation of some British travelogues, in collaboration with Henriette Herz, and the assembly of an historical almanac. See Heinrich Meisner, *Schleiermachers Lehrjahre*, 76–81.

[16]Letter to Schleiermacher, no date (Mar., 1799). *Br.* III, 108. By Schlegel, I always mean Friedrich Schlegel unless I specify his brother August Wilhelm. This, despite A. W. Schlegel's humorous complaint to Schleiermacher for employing the same practice: "I have a bone to pick with you. By calling my brother merely Schlegel you thereby declare me null and void." *Briefe Schleiermachers an August Wilhelm Schlegel*, ed. Elstner and Klingner, *Euphorion*, XXI/3 (1914), 589n.

[17]Mar. 28, 1799. *Br.* III, 110.

romantic circle of friends. From Potsdam his letters again and again complain of the new and unaccustomed constraints upon his expressive freedom. "Hm! Hm!" one letter begins, in which Schleiermacher whimsically blames the poor Potsdam tea for his recent lack of inspiration in the *Speeches*.[18] "Pfui," an angrier one begins, written at the close of a particularly unproductive Saturday. And on the following Sunday Schleiermacher writes:

> You see how right I am that constrained production is an unnatural condition for me. . . . It costs me too much life, and in the end that which results is not worth the trouble, neither to me nor to the world nor to my friends.[19]

A fortnight later, however, in a better mood, Schleiermacher suggests a highly significant exception to what he has said: while *das Machen* is a poor motivation for his writings, it is of "moral use" in his self-cultivation.[20] Unconstrained expression is but one component of freedom. Extending the reach of our comprehension is another, and an essential means of this self-cultivation is a disciplined encounter with the constraints that are unavoidable in all new experience. Schleiermacher values uninhibited self-expression. But even in these relatively indulgent years of early romanticism, he recognizes that persons must continually balance their purely expressive freedom in the short run over against the increase in freedom that comes with disciplined self-cultivation in the long run.

While Schleiermacher's *Speeches* illustrate his theory of freedom under the aspect of self-expression, therefore, they are not an ideal instance. According to a purely expressive criterion of freedom, their very title indicates a sacrifice of expressive freedom on their author's part. These *Speeches* on religion are addressed to "cultured despisers" and are tailored to fit the needs of the Schlegels and Brinkmanns and Herzes of Berlin whose point of view was not identical with that of Schleiermacher—who even had difficulty understanding how one with Schleiermacher's intellect could devote himself to the calling of a minister of religion. Thus the opening speech, for all the expressive freedom of its form, is entitled "Defense" (*Apologie*). In fact, Schlegel called the *Speeches* "a polemical work of art,"[21] and Schleiermacher was later to agree. In the Dedication to his companion from Moravian school days, Gustav Brinkmann, which Schleiermacher added to the second edition of the *Speeches* in 1806, he writes:

---

[18]Letter to Herz, Mar. 20, 1799. *Br.* I, 204.
[19]Letter to Herz, dated only "Sunday morning" (Mar. 17, 1799). *Br.* I, 203–4.
[20]Letter to Herz, Apr. 1, 1799. *Br.* I, 213–14.
[21]In his review of the *Speeches*, "Reden über die Religion," *Athenäum*, II/2 (1799), 297.

> The contents of this book are not unsuited to remind you of that time in which our way of thinking developed communally, and in which — unharnessed by our own spiritedness from the same yoke, and seeking the truth with free spirits unhindered by any consideration — we began to call forth from ourselves that harmony with the world which prophetically set our inner feeling as our goal, and which was to express life ever more fully from all sides. It was that same inner song, as you know, that was to have been communicated in these *Speeches*, as in other speeches I have delivered publicly. But not as in true works of art of a higher kind, *not in a wholly free way. Rather, theme and development were here wrung from me by the time and circumstances, and stand in the most intimate relation to those who were my immediate audience.*[22]

We must recall too that Schlegel's cajoling, and not Schleiermacher's own inclination, drew Schleiermacher into his first public authorship (see above, p. 115).

Once the ice was broken by the *Speeches*, however, Schleiermacher's second work of authorship, the *Soliloquies*, followed quickly. More completely than the *Speeches*, the *Soliloquies* illustrate Schleiermacher's ideal of free self-expression. "I am glad I have written the *Soliloquies*," Schleiermacher wrote to a friend around 1801:

> It was an invincible yearning to express myself, completely out of the blue, without purpose, without the least regard for effect. I have often told myself that this is foolish — but since I consider myself a fool, I must have become wise.[23]

In 1802, looking back over his early authorship, Schleiermacher felt more fully satisfied with the style of his *Soliloquies* than with that of his other works, with the one exception of his preaching.[24] The reason for this exception is clear. Some of Schleiermacher's sermons contain the most purely expressive writing he ever published, owing in part to his habit of delivering sermons freely from an outline and writing them out from recollection only afterwards, if at all (see above, p. 96). Of Schleiermacher's first collection of sermons, published in 1801, Schlegel wrote:

> I am inclined to consider them your best work, namely as a work not of reaction but of pure inclination. They are so full of calm, so free from every appearance of constraint [*Gezwungenheit*].[25]

"A work not of reaction but of pure inclination . . . full of calm . . . free from every appearance of constraint": Schlegel's characterization of Schleiermacher's sermons is a virtual definition of free action as

---

[22] *Reden*, ix. Emphasis added.
[23] To Ehrenfried von Willich, no date (1801?). *Br.* I, 277–78.
[24] Letter to Reimer, Dec., 1803. *Br.* I, 388.
[25] Letter to Schleiermacher, no date (1801). *Br.* III, 292.

Schleiermacher understands it under its first aspect. The *Soliloquies*, like the sermons, approach this ideal of expressive freedom. Schleiermacher wrote to Henriette Herz that his *Soliloquies* were born from an objective, polemical state of mind. But as he began to write, he explains, his purely expressive inclinations gained the ascendancy, so that in the final result "polemic remains only here and there as a mood."[26] Like the *Speeches*, the *Soliloquies* spring immediately to their principal theme:

> No costlier gift can one person give to another than the most inward converse of his spirit [*Gemüth*] with itself; for this affords the greatest thing there is, a clear and undistorted look into a free being.[27]

As this opening sentence and the book's title both indicate, the polemic of the *Soliloquies* is interior, not overt. Schleiermacher speaks to Henriette Herz of his practice of carrying on an "unquenchable and almost universal inner polemic," and attributes his sense of self-confidence, which as a rule was quite robust, to this inward process.[28] He considered inner polemic an essential part of self-cultivation. It contributed toward his ideal of freedom as "activity" (see above, p. 85) or inner preparedness for the outward contingencies that destiny might bring his way. But though he was in this sense a polemical thinker,[29] and believed that polemic is "the procedure of every system" of philosophy,[30] the ideal he pursued in his early writings was an expressive freedom that transcends the polemical. He wished his publications to express an appropriation of their subject matter so thorough that their polemical genesis remained "only here and there as a mood."

We can appreciate just how close Schleiermacher's *Soliloquies* came to that ideal of free expression by contrasting them with his *Groundwork to a Critique of Previous Ethical Theory*, published in 1803. It is not accidental that this rigorous work, on which Schleiermacher spent a formidable amount of energy, is one with which he was never pleased. It consists of sharply polemical evaluations of previous moral philosophies. Some of Schleiermacher's friends, A. W. Schlegel among them, found the book altogether too polemical in its treatment of Kant and Fichte.[31] Schleiermacher had the objectivity and good humor to compare reading his *Groundwork*, as he mercifully called his book for short, to hacking one's way through "an underbrush of West Indies cactus"[32]—a

---

[26]Sep. 16, 1802. *Br.* I, 338.

[27]Schleiermacher, *Monologen: Eine Neujahrsgabe*, ed. Schiele, 7. In English, *Schleiermacher's Soliloquies*, tr. Friess, 9. I sometimes follow Friess's English translation.

[28]Letter of Apr. 29, 1799. *Br.* I, 221.

[29]For a more detailed discussion of the role of polemics in Schleiermacher's early writings see Paul Seifert, *Die Theologie des jungen Schleiermacher*, 105–6.

[30]*Kurze Darstellung des Spinozistischen Systems*, 285.

[31]Letter to Herz, July 26, 1803. *Br.* I, 373. Letter to Reimer, Nov. 11, 1803. *Br.* III, 370.

[32]Letter to Brinkmann, De. 14, 1803. *Br.* IV, 93.

judgment in which readers and editors ever since have concurred. Georg Ludwig Spalding, a former classmate of Schleiermacher at Halle who in 1803 was a teacher in Berlin, wrote to Schleiermacher of the *Groundwork*:

> I have read it through without interruption. But how? Like a burrowing mole. Nothing, nothing at all have I understood in context. Do not be angry with me—as I am not angry with you.[33]

Naturally enough, Schleiermacher was discouraged with such a result of so much labor. To Brinkmann he wondered aloud whether an assortment of "thought-chips," such as his *Soliloquies* or even the "Fragments" he was contributing to the Schlegel's journal *Athenaeum* during this period, did not represent a greater accomplishment than his *Groundwork*.[34] Despite their incompleteness, the former are at least a free and active expression of their author's own views—far preferable in Schleiermacher's mind to an author's constrained reactions to opinions he does not share.

In fact, Schleiermacher was in this same period discovering in Plato the answer to his own query to Brinkmann. From Plato's "complete deviation from the usual forms of philosophical communicaton," Schleiermacher writes in 1803, he has learned that the ideal form of philosophical discourse is neither the "systematic" nor the "fragmentary,"[35] but rather the *dialogue*—"the form that truly living instruction must necessarily have" (above, p. 135). Schleiermacher finds in the Platonic dialogue a balanced dynamics of freedom in all its three aspects. The dialogue's substance is provided by the pupil's self-expression. Its Socratic form guarantees self-cultivation on the part of both teacher and pupil. Finally, the dialogue's ultimate reliance on poetic intuition ensures that if conclusions are reached, they will be the participants' own conclusions, inwardly appropriated, not constrained from without. What is more, the dialogue is essentially social. It is mutual, communal, transcending the individualism of both the soliloquy and the speech—individualism for which some of Schleiermacher's early writings may justly be criticized.

This brings us to a concluding question about the expressive freedom of Schleiermacher's early romantic style. The question is what ever happened to that expressive style in his writings after 1800. To compare the elevated, dithyrambic rhetoric of the *Speeches* and *Soliloquies* with the dense and didactic prose of *The Christian Faith* of 1821, for example, is to discover an astonishing contrast. After the *Soliloquies* of 1800, Schleiermacher never returned to his early romantic style, and we may wonder why not.

[33]Oct. 21, 1803. *Br*. III, 367.
[34]*Br*. IV, 93.
[35]Schleiermacher, "Einleitung," *Platons Werke*, I/1, 8. English tr., 5–6.

An adequate answer to this question would be as complicated as an answer to the question of why the early romantic movement as a whole faded so rapidly from the brilliance of its first decade. But a few factors that fall within the limits of our study seem clear. For one thing, while Schleiermacher's early literary style is unquestionably free and had considerable influence on the early romantic ideal of literary expression, it is sometimes excessive and obscure. Schleiermacher had friends, as well as some antagonists, who told him as much. We have seen that Schelling, who later came to praise the *Speeches*, at first found them presumptuous. In 1799, the great Schiller remarked of the *Speeches*, "For all their talk of warmth and inwardness, still they are on the whole very tedious [*trocken*] and often pretentiously written"[36]—though by 1804, Schiller too appears to have recognized in the *Speeches* much that was praiseworthy.[37] Brinkmann, while admiring the *Speeches* himself, reported to Schleiermacher that some "right clever" men were calling the book a "mystical Galimathias."[38] A little later Brinkmann wrote that Jacobi was finding Schleiermacher's *Soliloquies* "beautifully written— only, too beautifully," and Brinkmann further confessed that their style struck him, too, as "a little artsy."[39] The Weimar satirist Falk (see above, p. 111) was not so gentle. In 1800 he published his opinion of the *Speeches*: a "mystical, confused, and therewith very wordy book," without originality except in its "forging of every popular concept." The author's "pompous prattle," Falk concludes, "nauseates the reader."[40]

Schleiermacher accepted these criticisms in good humor, but he took them to heart. He did not think of himself for long as a creative writer, even though his friends, especially Schlegel, pressed him in that direction. His basic image of himself was as a teacher. "It is really my calling," he was to write to his new fiancée in 1808, "to present more clearly that which ordinary people already know, to bring it to their consciousness."[41]

This Socratic sense of "calling" helps to explain why Schleiermacher took to heart the opinion of Brinkmann, Falk, and others that the expressive style of his *Speeches* was sometimes hindering rather than furthering communication. It also helps to account for the fact that Schleiermacher several times tried his hand at writing Platonic dialogue,

[36]Quoted in Julius Burggraf, "Goethe, Schiller, Schleiermacher," *Christliche Welt*, XIX (Apr. 13, 1905), 367.
[37]See ibid., 368, 373.
[38]Letter to Schleiermacher, Mar. 14, 1800. *Briefe von Karl Gustav v. Brinckmann an Friedrich Schleiermacher*, 23. Of unknown French origin, *Galimathias* translates loosely "hodgepodge" or "spongy nonsense."
[39]Letters of July 4 and Apr. 29, 1800. Ibid., 33, 29.
[40]Johannes Daniel Falk, *Taschenbuch für Freunde des Scherzes und der Satire*, V (1801), 271–72.
[41]To Henriette von Willich, Sep. 11, 1808. *Br*. II, 134.

though his success was never great.[42] In time, Schleiermacher found that systematic presentation was after all the medium best suited to his pedagogical temperament and calling. This cannot surprise us. His intellectual heritage was the Teutonic rigorism of Kant and the systematic lucidity of Spinoza. His professional peers were systematizers such as Fichte, Schelling, and Hegel. As we have seen, however (above, p. 61), Schleiermacher always subjected his systematic efforts to Socratic strictures, more delimiting than his systematizing contemporaries would have found acceptable.[43]

The *Speeches* were Schleiermacher's first published experiment in educating. He was told by some that the experiment's success was limited by the expressive excesses of its style. Immediately after completing the *Soliloquies* in 1800, Schleiermacher wrote to Brinkmann that for all the ease with which he had written that conversational book, he felt his genuine talent would have to wait for other writings, employing other means of expression:

> Do not think they will all be in this style. Look upon the *Speeches* and the *Soliloquies* only as if someone planning to give a regular concert—before he began, and before the audience were fully assembled—were to fantasize something from his own hand.[44]

In these terms, Schleiermacher's *The Christian Faith* of 1821 is very much a "regular concert." It is a work of systematic pedagogy, and not by any means pure romantic expression, "completely out of the blue, without purpose, without the least regard for effect" (above, p. 143). In this sense it is not as free a production as the *Soliloquies*. Yet its motivation is the same as that of the *Speeches*, namely, a pedagogical concern over the lamentable fact that

> many not only claim to be but also think they are opponents of every belief in God, when in fact they are simply rebelling against the customary presentations of the subject, having by no means parted with all those conditions of the heart and mind [*Gemütszustände*] that rest on God-consciousness.[45]

---

[42]Schleiermacher's use of the dialogue is to be found in his three dialogues on freedom of 1789 (above, p. 9); in *Über die Anständige* (*On the Respectable*, 1801); and in *Die Weinachtsfeier* (*Christmas Eve Celebration*, 1806). Dialogue was to have been the form of Schleiermacher's projected "*Phaedo*, in which Spinoza is the principal figure" (above, p. 135). There is a short dialogue inserted in the middle of the treatise *Über die Freiheit des Menschen* (*On Human Freedom*, 1792–93) to which we shall return in Part III. Finally, a short satirical dialogue comprises Part II of Schleiermacher's review of Fichte's *Die Bestimmung des Menschen* which appeared in *Athenäum*, III/2 (1800).

[43]For Schleiermacher's discussion of his systematic form of presentation see the Introduction of *The Christian Faith*, Ch. II, Section 2, esp. Proposition 28.2. See also *Schleiermachers Sendschreiben über seine Glaubenslehre an Lücke*, ed. Mulert, 34.

[44]Mar. 22, 1800. *Br.* IV, 60.

[45]*Der christliche Glaube*, ed. Redeker, Proposition 172.2

Both works are interpretations of Christianity projected to a specific audience. In the *Speeches* the audience are the cultivated among religion's despisers. In *The Christian Faith* they are the cultivated among the ministers and teachers of Christian religion in the Evangelical Protestant churches of the Age of Enlightenment.[46] The expressive abandon appropriate to the former would be out of place in the latter. Yet Schleiermacher's comprehension of the Christian doctrine he presents is so broadly cultivated and intimately appropriated that *The Christian Faith* is no less his free creation than the *Speeches*. He has simply come to value freedom as cultivation and appropriation more highly than freedom as expression. As a minister and a teacher of ministers, he has come to place more value upon the sense of social responsibility already acknowledged in the *Speeches*:

> If there is religion at all, it must necessarily be social: this is intrinsic not only to human nature but also quite particularly to the nature of religion. . . . In the perpetual reciprocity in which a person stands with the rest of his species, he should express and communicate [*äussern und mittheilen*] all that is in him.[47]

In the *Speeches* the greater emphasis falls upon expression; in *The Christian Faith*, upon communication.

[46]"For in the congregation of our Church it is only those who are scientifically cultivated who can be expected to take their bearings in the realm of popular religious communications from Dogmatics, and to these the key will not be lacking." *Der christliche Glaube*, ed. Redeker, Proposition 28.1.

[47]*Reden*, 181. *Speeches*, 148.

PLATES

Fig. A. Friedrich Schleiermacher

Fig. B. Schleiermacher's signature

Fig. C. Henriette Herz, Schleiermacher's friend and confidante from soon after the time of his arrival in Berlin in 1796 throughout the period covered by this book.

Fig. D. Detail of an 1800 caricature including Schleiermacher and Henriette Herz. Behind them are the Schlegel brothers. In Schleiermacher's pocket, a copy of the *Speeches*; under Schlegel's arm, "Athenaeum Scraps" (a parody of the *Athenaeum* "Fragments"). In the caricature's caption Schleiermacher and Herz are labeled "Jew wives."

Fig. E. Town square of Drossen as it appears today. Here Schleiermacher spent the year 1789–90 preparing for his theological examinations and working at his earliest formulations of the concepts of determinism and freedom. Behind the City Hall may be seen the church where Schleiermacher's uncle Stubenrauch was pastor.

Fig. F. Alexander Dohna, Schleiermacher's close friend from his Schlobitten days.

Fig. G. Friederike Dohna. After her death in 1801 at twenty-seven, Schleiermacher wrote, "My sense for womanhood was first awakened in the Dohnas' domestic circle. The credit for this Friederike has carried with her into eternity. . . . Only through knowledge of the feminine mind and heart have I gained a knowledge of true human worth."

Figs. H and I. Two views of the Dohna palace in Schlobitten as it appeared in the 1930s. Here Schleiermacher was tutor, October, 1790 to May, 1793, and wrote his treatise *On Human Freedom*.

Fig. J. The Dohna palace after its destruction by Soviet forces in the closing days of World War II, March, 1945.

Fig. K. The Court Church in Stolp as it appears today. Here Schleiermacher was pastor during his Baltic "exile," May, 1802, to June, 1804.

Fig. L. The pulpit from which Schleiermacher preached in Stolp.

Fig. M. The first page of Schleiermacher's manuscript *On Human Freedom*, written at Schlobitten in 1791–92 (approximately 15 x 20 cm.).

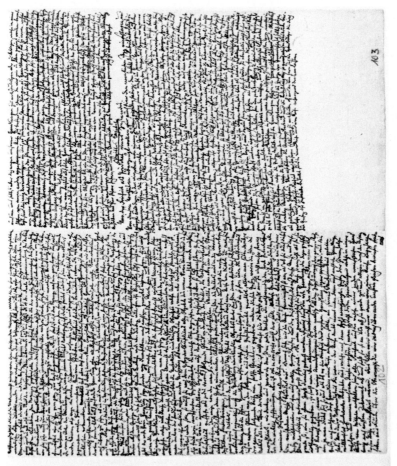

Fig. N. The final two pages of Schleiermacher's *On Human Freedom* (each only slightly larger than the first page), illustrating the virtual illegibility of the manuscript's concluding sections.

Chapter 4. Freedom as Appropriation

From living intuition all must proceed. And whoever lacks the longing to intuit the infinite has no touchstone by which to assay whether he has thought anything appropriate to that subject.

Throughout his career Schleiermacher devoted a great amount of attention to the art of communication which he regarded as his real "calling" (above, p. 146). As we have seen in connection with his translation of Fawcett in 1797–98, Schleiermacher recognized that formal means of presentation, such as Fawcett's Sunday evening *Sermons*, communicate best "when one addresses a homogeneous and not too greatly diverse gathering, and knows with surety that each is there because — and only because — he finds the subject to his taste" (above, p. 106).

The *Speeches* had as their audience the circle of cultivated young Berlin savants who were homogeneous in their inability to understand their friend Schleiermacher's devotion to religion and the Christian ministry, and in their even greater inability to appropriate religious consciousness because they were distracted by traditional forms of religious practice. These traditional forms seemed to them empty and unworthy of a thinking person's serious attention. Schleiermacher sympathized with his friends' attitude:

> From of old, faith has not been everyone's thing. Always but few have discerned religion itself, while millions have in various ways juggled with its trappings.[1]

Because he sympathized, he believed that he might be able to awaken dormant religious sensibilities in his audience of cultured despisers.

Yet even with their specialized audience the *Speeches* represent risk. As with every piece of authorship, communication is not guaranteed. Schleiermacher learned this hard lesson both from his experience with his own publications and from his ever deepening immersion in the thinking of Plato. In 1804 he observes that in the *Phaedrus*, Plato

---

[1] *Reden*, 1. *Speeches*, 1.

complains about how uncertain the written communication of thinking always remains. There is always the question of whether the mind [*Seele*] of the reader has actively reproduced the thinking for himself and thus truly appropriated it, or whether, with a merely apparent understanding of the words and letters, there comes to the mind an empty imagination that it has understood what in fact it does not understand. Therefore it is foolish to rely too much on written communication, and trust is more justifiably put in oral, living instruction. Still the risk of writing must be hazarded, though more for the writer and those who already share his knowledge than for what it might become for those who do not yet know.

These uncertainties associated with written communication, Schleiermacher goes on, account for Plato's "exalted preference for oral instruction," in which

the teacher, standing in a present and living reciprocity with the learner, can every moment know what he grasps and what he does not, and thus assist the activity of his understanding where it falters; but the actual attainment of this advantage rests, as everyone may see, upon the form of dialogue.[2]

Schleiermacher's most satisfactory emulation of Plato's ideal of oral instruction appears to have been not in his attempts at written dialogue, but rather in his confirmation classes for young people of the church. These classes were for Schleiermacher always a favorite part of his ministry. His stepson reports, in a tone not altogether approving, that Schleiermacher conducted his confirmation classes according to the Socratic method:

My father's confirmation instruction was famous, and indeed was powerfully stimulating to many. I can scarcely say the same for myself. Even though he appreciated the level of understanding of his youthful auditors quite well and sought to accommodate his remarks accordingly, still they were not very arresting or stimulating in the usual sense. He had the tendency less to present things in a finished form than to awaken and to unfold.[3]

How many students have set aside Plato's dialogues with exactly the same sense of anticlimax and disappointment. They too are "not very arresting or stimulating in the usual sense." In fact the essence of Plato's dialogues, as Schleiermacher perceives them, consists precisely in the Socratic genius for unfinished form. Repeatedly Plato's dialogues propel us toward some ultimate height or depth, but then either stop short, letting the dialectical momentum we have gathered carry us on as far as it naturally will, or change tone, introducing the poetic language of symbol or myth to carry us in immediate intuition

---

[2]Schleiermacher, "Einleitung," *Platons Werke*, I/1, 14–15. English tr., 15.

[3]Ehrenfried von Willich, *Aus Schleiermachers Hause*, 80. Otto von Bismark was a participant in Schleiermacher's confirmation class as a child. What conclusions, if any, may be drawn about the success of Schleiermacher's method the reader may decide.

further than dialectical thinking can go. Schleiermacher was a pioneer in appreciating this quality in Plato's philosophy. In the General Introduction to his translation of Plato's works Schleiermacher writes that it must have been Plato's

> chief object to conduct every investigation, from the beginning onwards, in such a way that he could count on the reader's either being brought to his own inward generation of the thought in view, or being driven to surrender himself decisively to the feeling of having discovered nothing and understood nothing. To this purpose, then, it is required that the end of the investigation not be directly enunciated and put down in words—a procedure that might prove to be a snare for many who are quite satisfied if only they obtain the end result.[4]

Schleiermacher's love for Plato is closely associated with this recognition that the aim of Plato's open-ended philosophical instruction is an inward, living appropriation of truth that cannot be accomplished at secondhand or by rote. This rationale of Plato's dialogical form, though not the form itself, Schleiermacher imitates in his *Speeches*. His goal in that book is the reader's inward appropriation of living religious consciousness. His means, as we have seen in the previous chapter, is the free expression of his own religious life:

> To this goal, religion knows no other means than its own free expression and communication. Only through natural expressions of its own life does religion wish to stimulate the same in others; and where this does not succeed, it proudly despises every foreign allurement, every exercise of force, quieted by the conviction that the hour is not yet come for anything kindred to be quickened.[5]

At this point in the *Speeches*, as at many others, Schleiermacher turns to musical imagery to convey a sense for his Platonic aim:

> Such failure of result is not new to me. How often have I intoned the music of my religion in order to stir those in my presence, commencing with single soft notes, and progressing with youthful impetuosity, full of yearning, to the fullest harmony of religious feelings—only to have nothing quicken and respond.[6]

The aim of Schleiermacher's *Speeches*, we might say, is communication by sympathetic resonance. Schleiermacher was to learn that such an ideal has both strengths and weaknesses. On the side of strengths, Schleiermacher's musical imagery is apt in evoking the intention of his *Speeches*. He is convinced that a person's inward appropriation of religion will never come by means of dialectic argumentation. It will never come by way of conceptual thought at all. It must come by way of what Schleiermacher calls *lebendige Anschauung*, "living intuition":

---

[4]Schleiermacher, *Platons Werke*, I/1, 16. English tr., 17.
[5]*Reden*, 147–48. *Speeches*, 119.
[6]*Reden*, 148. *Speeches*, 119.

From living intuition all must proceed. And whoever lacks the longing to
intuit the infinite has no touchstone by which to assay whether he has
thought anything appropriate to that subject.[7]

Schleiermacher is attempting in his *Speeches* to direct us deep into our
lives, below the level of willful activity, conceptual thinking, and
particular feelings, to "the most inner depths whence every such form
shapes itself."[8] He is trying to plunge deeply enough to surprise will,
thought, and feeling together in an original, living unity of immediate
consciousness from which religious consciousness, like all consciousness, arises.

Schleiermacher shared the widespread romantic realization that music sounds these depths of human consciousness: in music the will is at
one with itself (Arthur Schopenhauer); music is communication without
concepts, "song without words" (Felix Mendelssohn); in music we feel
our feelings (Wilhelm Heinrich Wackenroder). For Schleiermacher, as
for many others of his age, music and musical metaphor communicate
living intuition more intimately than any other means of expression.

In order to appreciate how this is so, we should realize that the
central term *intuition* here is ambiguous, both in German and in English
translations of German. In Kant's vocabulary, for example, the term
intuition designates immediate receptivity or perception — in particular,
immediate *sense* perception, since for Kant there is no other kind. And
yet in English the term commonly denotes some subtle kind of apprehension *apart* from sense perception, with overtones of the uncanny or
clairvoyant — a connotation conveyed by the common usage of the
German term as well. Musical expression is perhaps unique in being
adequate to both these meanings. As a phenomenon of sense perception, music offers our most intimate access to proportion, balance,
harmony, and even logical order and coherence. Music allows immediate access to these forms of beauty and truth. At the same time, we
apprehend beauty and truth in music with a subtlety that seems to defy
analysis in terms of the sensible phenomena of acoustics.[9] Such also is
the religious intuition Schleiermacher seeks to awaken by his *Speeches*.
Its object in the phenomenal universe of space and time, and yet the
sublety of our apprehension of the universe is such as can be represented only metaphorically.

The phrase "living intuition" reverberates throughout early romanticism, and Schleiermacher's evocation of that mode of apprehension in
the *Speeches* was one of the phrase's sources. In mid-September, 1799,
for example, the young Novalis was, according to Schlegel's report,

[7] *Reden*, 51.

[8] *Reden*, 2nd ed., 15. *Speeches*, 11.

[9] In this connection see Victor Zuckerkandl's discussion of musical tone as "dynamic
symbol" in *Sound and Symbol*, esp. Chapters V and VI.

"completely captivated, permeated, inspired, and inflamed" by Schleier-macher's *Speeches*: "he says he cannot fault you on anything, and so far is one with you."[10] Less than three months later, at the beginning of December, 1799, Novalis began his novel *Heinrich von Ofterdingen*. In it the protagonist Heinrich recommends "the way of inner contemplation" as the way to a true apprehension of our place in nature and history, a way in which "the nature of every occurrence and every thing alike is immediately intuited and contemplated in its living, manifold connec-tions."[11] In this language of immediate, living intuition Schleiermacher's influence is unmistakable.

Schleiermacher's influence on the mystical Novalis does not neces-sarily imply a compliment, however. It is in part to language such as this, in Schleiermacher, Novalis, and others, that the notoriety of early German romanticism for imprecision of vocabulary and vagueness of thought can be traced. This is one of the weaknesses of Schleier-macher's romantic ideal of communication by sympathetic resonance. To make matters worse, in spite of all the indefiniteness of the rhetoric of his *Speeches*, Schleiermacher has the mettle to exclaim to his reader, "Would that you knew how to read between the lines!"[12] One of Schleiermacher's letters to Brinkmann reiterates the same wish in connection with his even more grandiloquent and imprecise *Soliloquies*: "I ask you not to look so much at what is written there as at the *blanc de l'ouvrage*."[13]

In view of such vagaries, students of romanticism are sometimes tempted to despair, and critics of romanticism are quick to pounce. As if such a phrase as "living intuition of the universe" were not problematic enough in context, Schleiermacher asks us to seek its meaning "be-tween the lines." There is risk here of mistaking Schleiermacher, however. It is true that we must resist the scholar's insidious analytic compulsion for pinning down Schleiermacher's concept of "universe," let us say, or exhausting the particulars of his understanding of the structure of self-consciousness, in the belief that by such methods we shall arrive at a clear and distinct definition of his phrase "living intuition." This would be what Wordsworth in "The Tables Turned" calls murdering to dissect. But on the other hand we must not assume that Schleiermacher's language is simply occult mystification. For one thing, the Schleiermacher who spent the decade of the 1790s locked in analytical struggles with Kant (above, p. 11) and who was temperamen-tally and philosophically a stranger to mystical conversions (above,

[10]Letter to Schleiermacher from Schlegel, no date (Fall, 1799). *Br.* III, 125.
[11]Novalis (Friedrich von Hardenberg), *Heinrich von Ofterdingen*, ed. Tieck and Schlegel, Ch. 2, 28.
[12]*Reden*, 44. *Speeches*, 33.
[13]Mar. 22, 1800. *Br.* IV, 59. *Blanc de l'ouvrage*: lit. "white of the work."

p. 104) is an unlikely candidate for occult mysticism. For another, we must not judge Schleiermacher on the basis of Novalis's use of his ideas. Novalis was a more fragile and other-worldly spirit than either of his mentors, Schleiermacher or Plato.

By the "living intuition of the universe" that constitutes the essence of religion, Schleiermacher refers to our encounter with the infinite whole of our environment—conceive of it as we may—insofar as it affects the fundamental balance and disposition of our lives. We have seen that Schleiermacher values his *Speeches* as a free expression of his own innermost character. Now he is trying to elicit from his reader a similar order of values in return. He wants his reader's encounter with the universe, whatever its conceptual framework, to be a living, an appropriating encounter. It should be an encounter that touches and molds our life. Schleiermacher knows that his *Speeches* can be no more than catalytic in this process. Their means of influence must be Socratic, indirect. A living encounter with the universe has to be the result of our own contact with the universe, not our exposure to a piece of writing. In this sense, "instruction" in religion

> is a tasteless and meaningless word. Our opinions and doctrines we can indeed communicate to others; for that we require only words, and they require only the mind's comprehending and imitating power. But we know very well that this is only the shadow of our intuitions and our feelings. Without sharing these with us, our pupils will not understand what they say and what they think they believe. We cannot teach others to intuit.[14]

This passage brings us to the main theme of this chapter. We see here how freedom as appropriation takes precedence in Schleiermacher's thinking over freedom as expression. Without the former, the latter is mere "imitation, like the mimicking of someone else's physiognomy, which, because it is mimicry, becomes caricature."[15] Freedom must be *self*-expression. Expression that is genuinely free must "issue outwardly from within, in an original, characteristic form"; otherwise it represents not freedom but "slavish imitation."[16] In order for a person's expression to issue in an original, characteristic form, the subject matter of that expression must first have undergone a thorough appropriation in the person's mind and heart.

Because of his strong opinions about this issue, Schleiermacher was a vigorous opponent of those conceptual schemes of metaphysics, ethics, or theology which by their abstraction, formalism, or moribundity estrange us from the deep unity of our own life, a unity without which freedom may not originate. We encounter a strongly judgmental

[14] *Reden*, 151. *Speeches*, 122.
[15] *Reden*, 81–82.
[16] *Reden*, 2nd ed., 82. *Speeches*, 48.

side of Schleiermacher's nature here. His age was aswarm with concep-
tions of the universe put forward by the brilliant assortment of his
teachers, friends, and acquaintances. It was one of Western philosophy's
richest ages in this regard. We have seen in Part I something of
Schleiermacher's analytic mastery of these philosophical schemes. But of
each of them Schleiermacher asked questions that penetrate beneath
analytic understanding: Has its author *intuited* the universe he *conceives*?
Is the author's conceptual scheme a free expression of an inner unity of
life? Or, what is closely related to this latter question, Will the scheme
aid its student or disciple to apprehend the universe in a living intuition
of his or her own? Insofar as Schleiermacher judged the answer to these
questions to be no, he concluded that the conceptual scheme in
question was contrived or that its expression was somehow unnaturally
constrained, and the validity of the scheme was proportionately cast in
doubt. It is typical, therefore, that when Schleiermacher proposed his
new *Phaedo* in which Spinoza was to be the protagonist (above, p. 135),
he postponed the project until the appearance of Paulus's complete
edition of Spinoza (above, p. 126), "so that I can study his *life* as much
as possible."[17] In 1802, after direct acquaintance with Spinoza's works,
Schleiermacher would write, "In Spinoza I find inner life indeed."[18]

This evaluation of Spinoza dates from the period in which Schleiermacher was struggling with the writing of his *Groundwork*. It occurs in
immediate juxtaposition with an evaluation of Kant as critical as that of
Spinoza is favorable: "Just now I am especially afflicted with Kant, who
grows ever more burdensome to me."[19] In the *Groundwork* itself, where
Schleiermacher elaborates upon his complaint about Kant, he expresses
the judgment that Kant has constructed his philosophy *aus Mangel an
Begeisterung und Überfluss an Vernunft*, "out of a deficiency of animation
and a superfluity of reason."[20] The *Groundwork* here echoes Schleiermacher's suspicion from a decade earlier that Kant's philosophy is too
hypnotically under the influence of such constraints as architectonic
symmetry and mathematical rigor to invite free appropriation in a
unified, individual inner life (see above, p. 54). Already in 1794
Schleiermacher was aware that others besides himself were suspecting
Kant of philosophizing under the constraint of attempting to contrive a
correspondence between the philosophical results of his critical investigations and the moral pietism of his Lutheran upbringing.[21]

Nor was Schleiermacher alone in finding Kant's philosophy too
abstract and one-sided in its emphasis upon the rational side of life to

---

[17]"Denkmale," 140. Emphasis added.
[18]Letter to Eleonore Grunow, Sep. 3, 1802. *Br.* I, 327.
[19]Ibid.
[20]*Grundlinien einer Kritik der bisherigen Sittenlehre*, 20.
[21]Letter to his father, no date (1794). *Br.* I, 88.

the neglect of the second focus of the ellipse of human nature, the passions. Schiller, who on the whole was considerably more sympathetic to Kant's system than Schleiermacher, had in 1795 conceded:

> In a transcendental philosophy, where everything depends on freeing form from content and keeping that which is necessary pure from everything which is occasional, one too easily becomes accustomed to thinking of the material merely as a hindrance, and to representing sensuality as necessarily opposed to reason, simply because it stands in the way of this pursuit. Certainly such a way of representing things is by no means in the *spirit* of the Kantian system, but it may very well be in the *letter* of it.[22]

Schleiermacher shared Schiller's judgment. Schleiermacher's difficulty is not with the spirit of Kant's intentions. Still less is his judgment of Kant merely *ad hominem*, directed against the personality of the man. Schleiermacher's one meeting with Kant in Königsberg in 1791 was too brief, he felt, to convey any trustworthy impression of Kant's personality.[23] But that is not important here. We shall see in Part III the high degree to which Schleiermacher honored differences among individual personalities. He would not have criticized Kant simply because Kant's mode of life did not match his own tastes. His criticism was directed rather against Kant's philosophical system. Overall, Schleiermacher found it too abstract, too formal to quicken an integral mode of life. In particular, he found that it tended to upset the balance of reason and sense so fundamental to his own conception of the ethical ideal (see above, p. 91).

This is Schleiermacher's quintessentially romantic criticism of Kant, and it is crucial for us to appreciate the form it takes. Schleiermacher did not criticize Kant for his rationalism. He did not, according to the caricature of romanticism one encounters all too often, oppose a romantic emphasis upon feeling to Kant's emphasis upon reason. "Kant does well to say that he will have nothing to do with anyone who does not want to be reasonable [*vernünftig*]," Schleiermacher writes in his Journal. "*But what will Kant do when someone comes and says that he would like to be more than reasonable?*"[24] This is the question romanticism at its best asks of the Age of Reason. How are we to realize our potential as *more*-than-reasonable beings? Thus one sees the importance of realizing that Schleiermacher embraced romanticism, with its delight in sense and feeling, only after a decade of appropriating the best of Kantian rationality. Thus Part I of our study has preceded Parts II and III.

---

[22]Schiller, *Über die ästhetische Erziehung des Menschen*, note to the Thirteenth Letter. Schiller's emphases.

[23]Letter to his father, May 15, 1791. *Br.* I, 87–88. Königsberg is today Kaliningrad, U.S.S.R.

[24]"Denkmale," 132. Emphasis added.

The question Schleiermacher poses to Kant has a great deal to do also with the ambiguity that Schleiermacher, the philosophical romantic, felt toward Fichte, the philosophical idealist. The ambiguity was extremely deep. While wrestling with his *Groundwork* Schleiermacher wrote to Henriete Herz, "I am now on to Fichte, and could get a pretty tight hold on him if it were not such an exhausting maneuver to admire a person and in the same breath despise him."[25]

When dismissed from the University of Jena in 1799 on the charge of atheism (see above, p. 119), Fichte moved to Berlin. On July 4, Dorothea Mendelssohn Veit brought him to meet Schleiermacher and Schlegel, then still rooming together, and for a time the quartet regularly shared meals. The impression Schleiermacher and Fichte made upon each other appears to have been slight. On July 20, writing to his wife about his mealtime company, Fichte referred to Schleiermacher only as Schlegel's companion and "a Reformed preacher," not mentioning his name.[26] The lack of affinity appears to have been mutual. "He has not affected me much," Schleiermacher wrote to Brinkmann after six months' acquaintance with Fichte, explaining that he found Fichte "lacking in wit and fantasy."[27] At the end of a year's acquaintance with Fichte, Schleiermacher reported to A. W. Schlegel, "We are on the best of footings with each other—insofar as no footing is still a footing."[28]

Like his attitude toward Kant, Schleiermacher's ambiguous attitude toward Fichte was not merely *ad hominen*. It was again grounded in philosophical differences. Schleiermacher found in Fichte's philosophy much that excited his admiration. In the letter to Brinkmann criticizing Fichte's personal qualities, Schleiermacher praises Fichte's "completely masterful gift of making himself clear" and calls him "the greatest dialectician I know."[29] Schleiermacher regarded many of the presuppositions and intentions of Fichte's philosophy, such as his Platonic search for the eternal in the midst of the temporal and his "elevated spirit of genuine

[25]Sep. 16, 1802. *Br.* I, 339.

[26]Quoted in Dilthey, *Leben Schleiermachers*, ed. Redeker, I/1, 367.

[27]Jan. 4, 1800. *Br.* IV, 53. "Besides," Schleiermacher adds, "I have recently observed that he is an almost passionate Freemason, and even before this I was aware that he is possessed of a certain vanity, and indeed likes to form, support, and govern factions—and what impression such observations make upon me you more or less know." This is not a very generous judgment of Fichte's Freemasonry. In 1802, Fichte was to define the purpose of Freemasonry as a blending of the "one-sided cultivation" necessary for practical life with the "all-sided cultivation of the whole man as man." This purpose, he adds, must be pursued with a due sense of human limitations—with a "holy modesty." In the abstract, at least, Schleiermacher could hardly have found fault with such a purpose. See Fichte, *Philosophie der Mauerei*, 17–19. Available in the English tr. by Roscoe Pound: *Philosophy of Masonry*, 34–36.

[28]Aug. 29, 1800. *Briefe Friedrich Schleiermachers an August Wilhelm Schlegel*, 752.

[29]*Br.* IV, 53.

morality,"[30] with approval. But again as in the case of Kant, Schleiermacher believed that Fichte's philosophical system, by its abstractness
and formalism, was more likely to encourage dialectical mimicry in its
students than to foster the inward appropriation of truth that molds a
person's life.

In his review of Fichte's book of 1800, *The Vocation of Man*,
Schleiermacher praises Fichte's application of his expository genius in
such a way as "to make the ideas it wishes to communicate really
intuitive and living." He is able to do this, Schleiermacher observes,
precisely because in that book, written as it was for the layman, Fichte
sets aside for once the "unrelenting systematic spirit of his philosophy."[31] When the fearsome inexorability of Fichte's system goes un-
checked, however, "philosophy and life are completely separated."[32]
Four years of association did little to bring Schleiermacher's image of
Fichte into congruence with his ethical ideal of a "living personality"
that

> seeks to overcome every antithesis in itself, even if this never comes to
> completion. Now what can be great about one who separates philosophy
> and life as rigidly as Fichte does? A great, one-sided virtuosity, but little
> humanity.[33]

An attempt to ascertain the fairness of Schleiermacher's judgments
of Kant and Fichte would carry us beyond the capacities of this study.[34]
There is unquestionably room for disagreement. Kant, for example,
insists repeatedly and eloquently that no one deserves the name of
philosopher who cannot "show the infallible effect" of the moral law
"on his own person as an example."[35] If ever anyone deserved the
name of philosopher according to this criterion it was surely Immanuel
Kant, whether or not the appropriation of his philosophy in "his own
person" resulted in the balance of reason and sense which Schleiermacher considers ideal. Or again, Fichte wrote in 1797:

> The kind of philosophy one chooses depends on what kind of person one
> is: for a philosophical system is not a dead utensil that one can set aside
> or take up as it pleases us; rather it is enlivened by the life [*beseelt durch
> die Seele*] of the person whose philosophy it is.[36]

[30]Schleiermacher, review of Fichte's *Die Bestimmung des Menschen* in *Athenaeum*, III/2
(1800), 287.

[31]Ibid., 287, 286.

[32]Letter to Brinkmann, Jan. 4, 1800. *Br.* IV, 53.

[33]Letter to Brinkmann, Dec. 14, 1803. *Br.* IV, 94.

[34]See Emil Fuchs' discussion of how Schleiermacher's criticism of Fichte here is only
"in a certain sense correct," in *Von Schleiermacher zu Marx*, 39–42. See also Walter E.
Wright's defense of Fichte, "Existentialism, Idealism, and Fichte's Concept of Coherence," *Journal of the History of Philosophy*, XIII (Jan., 1975) 37–42.

[35]Kant, second *Kritik*, 109.

[36]Fichte, *Erste Einleitung in die Wissenschaftslehre*, 434.

Schleiermacher cites this passage in 1802 and praises it as a truly Platonic insight.[37] Yet taken in context, this famous passage is not used by Fichte to advance the position Schleiermacher so cherishes: that a philosophical system proves its worth by its capacity to touch and mold a person's mind and heart. Fichte's point is in fact the opposite: that a person's state of mind and heart commonly amounts to a prejudice rendering the person incapable of appropriating systematic philosophical truth. Thus Fichte goes on in the same passage to claim that even Spinoza, the great "Dogmatist," was blinded to philosophical truth by personal prejudice of this sort:

> One can show the Dogmatist the inadequacy and inconsequence of his system . . . ; one can confuse and alarm him from every side; but one cannot convince him, because he is not able calmly and coldly to hear and evaluate that which he absolutely cannot endure. To philosophy — if idealism should prove to be the only true philosophy — to philosophy one must be born; one must be bred to it, and bring oneself up in it. For by no human art can one be made a philosopher.[38]

This is of course the opposite of Schleiermacher's ideal. Schleiermacher would have philosophical systems meet a person's needs. Fichte seems to be saying that persons should be tailored to fit the demands of the philosophical system, and that for most persons this is impossible. In one place Fichte even gives a tortured argument leading to the conclusion that "Spinoza could not have been convinced; he could only *think* his philosophy, not *believe* it."[39]

So the issue of Schleiermacher's fairness to Fichte is complicated; perhaps no philosopher ever invited more misunderstanding than Fichte did. It must suffice us here to say that Schleiermacher was at least conscientious in arriving at his judgments of both Kant and Fichte. We have seen his determined pursuit of an accurate understanding of Kant's philosophy over the decade of the 1790s. As for Fichte, Schleiermacher did not stop at mere criticism of what he took to be the inexcusable separation of philosophy and life in Fichte's idealism. He wrote his *Soliloquies* of 1800 in order to portray his own vision of philosophical idealism as it would appear in a living embodiment:

> The book is an attempt to translate the philosophical standpoint, as the idealists call it, into life, and to portray the character that, according to my understanding, corresponds to this philosophy.[40]

In Part III we shall return to the idealism of Schleiermacher's *Soliloquies*.

---

[37]Schleiermacher, *De Platonis Phaedro*, in the *Erlanger Literatur-Zeitung*, Vol. I, No. 30 (1802), 235. Also in *Br.* IV, 575.

[38]*Erste Einleitung*, 434–35.

[39]*Zweite Einleitung*, 513. Fichte's emphases.

[40]Letter to Brinkmann, Jan. 4, 1800. *Br.* IV, 55.

The importance of these illustrations for our purposes consists less in the question of whether Schleiermacher's judgments of Spinoza, Kant, Fichte, and others were fully justified than in the terms in which he made those judgments. The terms were these: whatever the brilliance of a person's system of thought, the final evaluation of that system depends upon how well the thought lends itself to the unified appropriation in mind and heart that for Schleiermacher is the first condition of human freedom.

Chapter 5. Freedom as Self-Cultivation: Virtuosity and Integrity

Every human soul is but the product of two contrary impulses. The one is the striving to draw all that surrounds us to ourself, to include all things in our own life, and wherever possible to absorb all wholly into our innermost being. The other is the yearning to extend our own inner self indefinitely outward, to penetrate all with ourself, to communicate ourself to all, and never to be exhausted.

The philosopher Jacobi, despite his radical disagreement with Spinoza's philosophy, praised Spinoza for the very quality that we found Fichte denying to him (above, p. 159), namely the unity of his philosophy and his life:

> Be thou blessed by me, great, yes holy Benedictus! Though thou mayest have philosophized concerning the nature of the Highest Being and erred in words, yet His truth was in thy soul, and His love was thy life![1]

This passage from Jacobi is a striking antecedent to the benediction Schleiermacher pronounces upon Spinoza in the *Speeches* (above, p. 116). At the same time, Schleiermacher praises Jacobi for his own unity of philosophy and life. In fact he comes very close to ranking Jacobi in a class with Plato and Spinoza (see above, p. 127) when in one place he calls Jacobi's opinions "holy" to him.[2] Brinkmann, upon first meeting Jacobi in 1800, reported to Schleiermacher that he had indeed found him "a true Plato."[3]

Jacobi (1743–1819) was in his own day a widely influential philosopher, combining literary talent, personal warmth, and a keen instinct for spotting philosophical inconsistencies. He was especially attracted to the philosophy of Spinoza, and later to that of Fichte, because he found these two systems to offer the greatest consistency possible to philosophy. In an open letter to Fichte in 1799, Jacobi writes:

---

[1]Jacobi, *Über die Lehre des Spinoza*, 245. *Benedictus*: the Latin form of Spinoza's Hebrew given name, Baruch. Both forms mean "blessed." Spinoza adopted the Latin form after his expulsion from his Amsterdam synagogue in 1656.

[2]Quoted in Schleiermacher, *Spinozismus*, ed. Mulert, 316.

[3]Letter to Schleiermacher, July 4, 1800. *Briefe von Carl Gustav v. Brinckmann an Friedrich Schleiermacher*, ed. Meisner and Schmidt, 32.

> I say it at every opportunity, and am ready to acknowledge it publicly,
> that I regard you as the true messiah of speculative reason, the genuine
> son of the promise of a *thoroughly* pure philosophy, subsisting *in* and
> *through* itself.[4]

Yet Fichte's philosophical consistency did not satisfy Jacobi. Rather, the systems of both Spinoza and Fichte confirmed Jacobi's basic conviction that, even at its most consistent, philosophy can never satisfy our need for certainty. No philosophy can contain its own sufficient verification. Jacobi was not an opponent of the philosophical pursuit of certainty. He was rather a shrewd observer of what appeared to him the inescapable fact that ultimately "all human knowledge begins in revelation and belief."[5] Thus he contrasts Fichte's philosophy, consisting "alone in *knowing*," with his own "unphilosophy, which has its essence in *not-knowing*."[6]

Schleiermacher's relation to the great Jacobi was complex. To say that Schleiermacher revered Jacobi's opinions does not mean that he agreed with Jacobi's philosophy. We have seen already that Schleiermacher was unable to share Jacobi's recourse to a *salto mortale*, "leap of faith," in the face of philosophical finitude and incompleteness (above, p. 37). "How could the temporal be begotten by the eternal," Jacobi had asked in 1791;

> what possible relation of the two can be thought in human fashion? No
> philosophy fills this cleft. To pass over, there is required a bridge—or
> *wing*.[7]

Finding himself stranded between the rationalistic philosophy of the Age of Reason and the orthodox piety of his Christianity, Jacobi tried to pass over to the realm of eternal certainty on the wings of faith—though he never accomplished this with the security for which he wished. In 1817, nearing the end of his life, Jacobi wrote to Reinhold, "Gladly would I exchange my feeble philosophical Christianity for the positive historical Christianity, and I do not understand why this nevertheless has never happened to me."[8] The distress in Jacobi's tone is both evident and characteristic.

Schleiermacher did not share this sense of distress. To be sure, Schleiermacher did not have a philosophical bridge to eternity, still less the wings of orthodoxy to follow where Jacobi had attempted to lead. But Schleiermacher possessed one resource in greater abundance than

---

[4]*Sendschreiben an Fichte*, Mar. 3–21, 1799, 9–10. Jacobi's emphases.

[5]Jacobi, *David Hume über den Glauben*, 3.

[6]*Sendschreiben an Fichte*, 9. Jacobi's emphases.

[7]Jacobi, the "Zugabe an Erhard O**" appended in 1791 to his novel of 1776, *Eduard Allwills Briefsammlung*, 248–49. Jacobi's emphasis.

[8]Oct. 8, 1817. *Friedrich Heinrich Jacobi's Auserlesener Briefwechsel*, ed. Roth, II, 478. An excerpt is given in *Br.* II, 349.

Jacobi. It was Schleiermacher's romantic sense for the infinite, with its accompanying tolerance for the finitude of the human condition and for the incompleteness of human knowledge (see above, p. 53).

In Jacobi there was a struggle between philosophy on the one hand, which nowhere offers the mystical completeness and certainty of Christian belief, and mysticism on the other, which had everywhere been damaged by attacks of Enlightenment philosophical skepticism. Jacobi's career consisted in a dignified search for spiritual rest by means of uniting these two poles: philosophical understanding and mystical certainty. Schleiermacher's career, in contrast, consists in a spiritual dynamics of oscillation in the dipolar field of philosophy and mysticism. In a letter of 1801, Schleiermacher writes to Brinkmann that Jacobi is of the

> false opinion that there can be a struggle between philosophy and mysticism, whereas on the contrary, every philosophy in fact leads the person who can see far enough, and wants to go far enough, to a mysticism. If Jacobi were clear on this point, he would polemicize only against that philosophy which does not lead to *his* mysticism; but he polemicizes against all philosophy in general. Why? Because he postulates that his mysticism should be deducible from some philosophy, and with it form a whole—which appears to me to be impossible for every mysticism, and therefore for his. If only Jacobi would decree that philosophy and mysticism lie entirely outside one another, and that the appearance of their connection arises wholly because they touch tangentially.[9]

Unending oscillation in the pattern of this tangential contact between the ever enlarging spheres of philosophical understanding and mystical intuition—

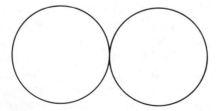

—constitutes the dynamics of Schleiermacher's lifelong search for truth, sustained by his romantic sense for the infinity of that undertaking.

In his 1817 letter to Reinhold, Jacobi writes:

> You see, dear R., that I am still the same as ever. Always a heathen with the understanding, but with my whole heart [*Gemüth*] a Christian, I swim between two currents that do not want to unite for me, so that jointly they are treacherous. For as the one perpetually buoys me up, so at the same time the other perpetually pulls me under.[10]

[9] Letter of July 19, 1800. *Br.* IV, 73.
[10] *Br.* II, 349.

At Jacobi's request, a mutual friend shared a copy of this letter to Reinhold with Schleiermacher. Heartened by this meager token of recognition from Jacobi, Schleiermacher addressed his first letter to the aging philosopher whom for three decades he had honored at a distance. In it he tries to explain his "own kind of equilibrium in the two currents":

> It is really nothing other than a reciprocity between being buoyed up by the one and pulled under by the other. But, my dear friend!—why should we not be satisfied with that? Oscillation is truly the general form of all finite existence, and it is a matter of immediate consciousness that this fluctuation proceeds from nothing other than the two foci of my one ellipse, and I have in this suspension the whole abundance of my earthly life. . . . Understanding and feeling remain for me alongside one another; but they act upon one another and form a galvanic pile. For me the innermost life of the spirit consists in this galvanic operation—in the feeling for understanding, and in the understanding of feeling—in which the two poles yet remain always removed from one another.

The fundamental difference between his own point of view and that of Jacobi, Schleiermacher concludes, consists in this:

> For you the "two currents" do not want to unite. Neither do they for me. But you wish for this unity and miss it painfully, while I remain satisfied with their separation.[11]

Schleiermacher traced the roots of his more particular disagreements with Jacobi to this fundamental difference between their presuppositions—between Schleiermacher's romanticism and what Schleiermacher called Jacobi's peculiar form of "rationalism."[12] Because Schleiermacher simply accepted the inevitable incompleteness of any metaphysical system, such as that of Spinoza, for example, he was more free than Jacobi to appropriate Spinoza's insights into his ethical and religious life. This "poetic" appropriation in turn gave Schleiermacher's *Speeches* the appearance of Spinozism in Jacobi's eyes. Schleiermacher realized this, and thus he very much regretted the tendency abroad to compare Schleiermacher with Jacobi, and to speak of Schleiermacher as the new bearer of the older philosopher's mantle. In 1802, with considerable insensitivity to what was actually involved, Georg Wilhelm Friedrich Hegel carried matters to an extreme by claiming that the *Speeches* represented "the Jacobian principle raised to its highest power."[13]

---

[11]Letter to Jacobi, Mar. 30, 1818. *Br.* II, 351, 353. A more complete text of the letter is given by Meisner in *Schleiermacher als Mensch. Sein Wirken*, ed. Meisner, 272–76.

[12]See Meisner's note #180 in *Wirken*, 394.

[13]Hegel, *Glauben und Wissen*, in *Kritisches Journal der Philosophie*, ed. Schelling and Hegel, II/1 (1802), 135. Readers may wonder at the infrequency of my references to Schleiermacher's great contemporary Hegel. Surprising though it seems, the mutual influence of these two during the period under consideration seems to have been negligible. Schleiermacher's letters, usually good indicators of his interests, do not

In fact, Jacobi had never broken his pointed silence regarding the *Speeches*, except for a few tentative first reactions when Brinkmann presented him with a copy in 1800. It belongs to Jacobi's "diplomatic system," Schleiermacher explained to Brinkmann in 1803, "neither to acknowledge me nor to engage in conflict with me."[14] But Schleiermacher feared that Jacobi's silence expressed "the most unlimited contempt" for his *Speeches*. He knew that Jacobi was "convinced" of his book's "atheism" and would consider Hegel's comment unjustified, to say the least. "This grieves me, I confess, since I love Jacobi greatly; all the more so, as this is almost the only example in my life in which my love is without any reciprocation."[15]

All the differences that separate these men do not obscure the sources of the affection for Jacobi which Schleiermacher expresses here, however. The two were similar in important ways — in part because from his early student days, Schleiermacher had looked to Jacobi as a mentor. For example, Schleiermacher followed Jacobi's evaluation of Kant as "a man whom all who have eyes call great,"[16] and yet followed him also in criticizing such transcendental assumptions as Kant's noumenal thing-in-itself (see above, pp. 34–35). Schleiermacher shared Jacobi's love of Plato, and his veneration of "the great, intuitive" Socrates, who "led uncertainty into the battle against insolence and falsehood, with truth positioned in ambush."[17] Both Schleiermacher and Jacobi understood human freedom as expression of the impulses [*Triebe*] of a centered, unified personality. Finally, Schleiermacher agreed wholeheartedly with Jacobi's evaluation of a philosopher who emphasizes the rational side of human nature and neglects the emotional: such a person, Jacobi writes is like someone trying to cut with only "one half of a pair of scissors."[18] In short, Schleiermacher's suspicion of reductionism in all its many forms (see above, p. 135) is consonant with the holistic presupposition that underlies the "unphilosophy" of Jacobi: "TOTUM PARTE PRIUS ESSE, NECESSE EST,"[19] "the whole is necessarily prior to the part."

The taproot of Schleiermacher's affection for Jacobi goes even deeper than these common philosophical foundations, however. "I love Jacobi greatly," Schleiermacher writes to Brinkmann. And why? Because Schleiermacher found in Jacobi nothing to suggest that philosophy

---

mention Hegel until 1803, and their tone toward Hegel is, in Dilthey's word, "cool." Mentions of Hegel in Schleiermacher's early manuscripts and publications are sparse. See *Werden*, 319, 322, and Dilthey, *Leben Schleiermachers*, ed. Redeker, I/1, 348n and I/2, 78. See also Richard Crouter, "Hegel and Schleiermacher at Berlin: A Many-Sided Debate," *Journal of the American Academy of Religion* XLVIII (1980) 19–43, esp. 21.

[14]Dec. 14, 1803. *Br*. IV, 93.

[15]Letter to Brinkmann, Oct. 19, 1803. *Br*. IV, 80.

[16]Jacobi, "Zugabe" to *Eduard Allwills Briefsammlung*, 252.

[17]Ibid., 245.

[18]Ibid., 236.

[19]Ibid., 239.

was for him a dialectical chess game. For Jacobi philosophy was a matter
of vital importance, an intellectual dialogue with the heart, and this
philosophical vitality in Jacobi repeatedly evokes from Schleiermacher
such terms of endearment as *liebenswürdig*, "worthy of love":

> I wish that in time the man, so worthy of love, will be able to love me
> somewhat also; he is the only one of our renowned philosphers of whom
> I wish this. Reinhold is highly indifferent to me. Fichte I must indeed
> respect, but he has never appeared to me as worthy of love. For that, as
> you know, I require something more than that one be a speculative
> philosopher, even if the greatest.[20]

In a word, Schleiermacher found Jacobi "convinced" of his philosophy,
in the sense that Fichte found Spinoza and Schleiermacher found Fichte
"unconvinced" (above, p. 159). "If only one person should ever be
completely and at every moment equally convinced of his philosophy,"
Fichte writes,

> if in his philosophy he is completely one with himself, if his free
> judgment in philosophizing and that pressed upon him by life are in
> complete harmony; then in this one person philosophy has reached its
> goal and completed its circuit. . . . To be convinced is this alone: to be
> independent of every time and every change of circumstance. This is not
> something incidental to the soul [*Gemüth*]; it is rather the soul itself.[21]

Fichte was of the opinion that no philosopher had ever attained to such
an ideal, that none had ever been fully "convinced" in this sense.
Schleiermacher would have agreed. But he felt that Socrates, Spinoza,
and, of living philosophers, Jacobi approached this ideal most closely.

Schleiermacher believed that Jacobi's chief hindrance to complete
"conviction" was his polemical tendency:

> If only Jacobi . . . would stop polemicizing unnecessarily against philoso-
> phy and begin to disclose his beautiful nature in a more positive and
> inward way than he has done till now.[22]

In this wish we see Schleiermacher's concern for the two aspects of
freedom we have been discussing in the preceding sections. First,
freedom as active self-disclosure, which Schleiermacher contrasts here
with reactive polemicizing. Second, the freedom that self-disclosure or
self-expression presupposes: the unified, living appropriation of experience Schleiermacher here designates by Jacobi's own phrase, "beautiful
nature" (*schönes Wesen*). Schleiermacher believed that once liberated

---

[20]Letter to Brinkmann, July 19, 1800. *Br*. IV, 75.
[21]Fichte, *Zweite Einleitung*, 512–13.
[22]Letter to Brinkmann, July 19, 1800. *Br*. IV, 73.

from the constraint of unnecessary polemicizing, Jacobi's nature would be well represented by the more nearly circular ellipse of Schleiermacher's ethical vignette (above, p. 91) — a nature in which knowledge and love approach congruence.

Jacobi himself uses a small constellation of terms to designate this ideal of a beautiful nature, "convinced" in its harmony of philosophy and life: *heart, character, soul, taste, temperament, affect,* and *disposition* (*Herz, Charakter, Gemüth, Geschmack, Sinnesart, Affect, Gesinnung*).[23] Schleiermacher shares a number of the same terms, especially *disposition* and *soul.* "I cannot philosophize with someone whose disposition [*Gesinnung*] does not please me," he admits in a letter to his sister.[24]

Schleiermacher did not "philosophize" with Jacobi face to face until the fall of 1818, when the two finally met in Munich. Their discussions on three or four consecutive days left Schleiermacher certain that whatever the differences that had separated the two, they had not been differences of disposition:

> The old Jacobi was quite stirred by joy. We tried to come to an understanding with one another. In this we did not in fact get much further than to discover wherein our difference really lies. He always listened with the greatest amiability when I told him that to me his fundamental error appears to be that he confuses this difference with some other, and seeks its ground in the disposition [*Gesinnung*].[25]

His 1818 meeting with Jacobi was a moment Schleiermacher had anticipated for over two decades. He planned to dedicate *The Christian Faith* to Jacobi — "as a little memorial to our relationship, and at the same time to shed light, as best I am able, on Jacobi's real relation to Christianity."[26] Jacobi's death in 1819, however, only a few months after their Munich meeting, canceled the plan. In his 1821 dedication of the third edition of the *Speeches* to Brinkmann, however, Schleiermacher wrote:

> As I . . . reworked this book, it pained me deeply that I could no longer send it to the one with whom I most recently discussed it at length. I mean F. H. Jacobi, to whom we both owe so much — more, certainly, than we know. In a few distracted days I could not make myself understandable to him in all respects . . . ; yet it belongs to the most beloved memories of my life that shortly before his departure I could perceive and appropriate his personal image, and make palpable to him my veneration and my love.[27]

---

[23]"Zugabe" to *Eduard Allwills Briefsammlung,* 237.
[24]Oct. 22, 1797. *Br.* I, 162.
[25]Letter to his wife, Oct. 2, 1818. *Wirken,* 285.
[26]Letter to Barthold G. Niebuhr, Mar. 28, 1819. *Wirken,* 297.
[27]*Reden,* xii.

Like the romantics' phrase "living intuition," Jacobi's terms *disposition* and *heart* elude precise definition. But what Schleiermacher means by these terms can be clarified by their opposites. We have already seen that Schleiermacher contrasts his phrase "living personality" with the "great, one-sided virtuosity" he observed in Fichte (above, p. 158). In a revealing description of his friend Schlegel, Schleiermacher sets "heart" (*Gemüth*) over against both "genius" (*Genie*) and "intellect" (*Geist*).[28]

The English word "integrity" might do to designate the ideal form of disposition that both Jacobi and Schleiermacher emphasize so strongly—the balance and harmony of reason and sense in a person's innermost life. Integrity, as this condition of balance and harmony, is distinct from the degree of a person's mental cultivation. Such is the usage of Charles Dickens, for example, when in *Hard Times* he introduces the simple, guileless millworker Stephen Blackpool:

> Old Stephen might have passed for a particularly intelligent man in his condition. Yet he was not. He took no place among those remarkable "Hands," who, piecing together their broken intervals of leisure through many years, had mastered difficult sciences, and acquired a knowledge of most unlikely things. He held no station among the Hands who could make speeches and carry on debates. Thousands of his compeers could talk much better than he, at any time. He was a good power-loom weaver, and a man of perfect integrity.[29]

It does not follow from Schleiermacher's emphasis upon integrity in this sense, however, that his moral philosophy supports the notion one sometimes hears that persons are morally justified in clinging to any set of beliefs, just as long as they believe them "with integrity." As we have seen in discussing the geometric vignette Schleiermacher associated with his ethical ideal, moral growth involves motion in two degrees of freedom, not just one. In the first, which we have called freedom as appropriation, we must try to shape our character so that our knowledge and our desires are integrated into a harmonious whole. This integral whole Schleiermacher symbolizes by that special case of an ellipse, the sphere. This unified form of moral character is a person's integrity. For some, the pursuit of this quality of character is a continual struggle; for others it seems to come as a natural tendency. But in any case, this one degree of freedom is not a sufficient account of Schleiermacher's ethical ideal. Schleiermacher recognizes that there are ethical problems that will not yield to this first degree of freedom alone. Moral

---

[28]Letter to his sister Charlotte, Dec. 31, 1797. *Br.* I, 170. Ten days earlier Schlegel had become Schleiermacher's roommate in Berlin. About a year later Schleiermacher was to find himself defending his friendship with Schlegel with the remark, "I have never said that Schlegel and I have the *same* heart and mind [*Gemüth*]; I simply had to quarrel with your opinion that he has *none*." Letter to Herz, Feb. 22, 1799. *Br.* I, 197. Schleiermacher's emphases.

[29]Charles Dickens, *Hard Times*, Book I, Ch. 10.

responsibility requires growth in a second degree of freedom: cultivation of our comprehension. This second degree of moral growth Schleiermacher symbolizes by having the ellipse of his geometric vignette expand as it becomes more nearly spherical. The form of our character, our integrity, must be expanded to comprehend a fuller content of knowledge and love. For everyone, the achievement of this second quality of moral character is a challenge calling for endless effort.

This degree of freedom is freedom under the aspects of self-cultivation. It is the aspect of freedom to which Schleiermacher refers in the *Speeches* when he writes, "In every action and work, be it ethical or philosophical or artistic, a person should strive for virtuosity."[30] There is an element of elitism in Schleiermacher's moral philosophy here—in comparison with that of Kant, for instance. Kant's moral philosophy is strongly egalitarian. He insists that the moral law as he defines it can be "distinguished, without instruction, by the most common understanding":

> Were the voice of reason with respect to the will not so distinct, so irrepressible, and so clearly audible to even the commonest person, it would drive morality to ruin.

Our duty to the moral law is thus "easily and without hesitation seen by the commonest understanding," Kant writes, whereas the virtue required by an ethics of moral sense "is hard to see, and requires knowledge of the world."

> That is to say, what *duty* is, plain of itself to everyone; but what will bring true, lasting advantage to our whole existence is veiled in impenetrable obscurity, and much prudent intelligence is required to adapt the corresponding practical rule even tolerably to the goals of life by making suitable exceptions to it. The moral law, however, commands the most unhesitating obedience from everyone. Thus the decision as to what is to be done in accordance with it must not be so difficult that even the commonest and most unpracticed understanding, without any worldly prudence, should go wrong in making it.[31]

Kantian duty is thus a thoroughly egalitarian moral requirement.

Schleiermacher, however, speaks more often of moral virtue, or even virtuosity, than of Kantian duty (*Pflicht*). *Virtue* (*Tugend*) is a term denoting strength or fitness—what Kant calls "worldly prudence"—and it is the product of intellectual cultivation. According to the nineteenth-century dictionary of the brothers Grimm, *Tugend* denotes "excellence in every kind." As persons cultivate moral virtue, they enter upon an "aristocratic" company, a company of "the best in strength." The morally virtuous, Schleiermacher believed, are cultivated

---

[30] *Reden*, 111–12. Cf. *Speeches*, 85.
[31] Kant, second *Kritik*, 27, 35, 36. Kant's emphasis.

persons. They enjoy privileged perspectives. In his *Soliloquies*—which his friend Brinkmann trenchantly labeled "a Freemason book," written for the "initiated" alone[32]—Schleiermacher even refers to those who pursue ethical self-cultivation as "the elect."[33] Schleiermacher developed his moral ideals from the noble ethical tradition extending from Socrates through the Stoics to Spinoza. "The whole philosophy of the Stoics," he writes in his Journal, "is really the doctrine of cultivation [*Bildungslehre*]."[34]

There are considerations, however, that moderate the suspicion that Schleiermacher's ethics is insufferably aristocratic, esoteric, or elitist. Just as Schleiermacher values freedom under the aspects of appropriation and self-cultivation more highly than freedom under the aspect of self-expression (above, p. 148), so in turn he values freedom as appropriation more highly than freedom as self-cultivation. He values what we have called moral integrity (*sittliche Gemüth*) more highly than intellectual cultivation (*geistige Bildung*). Or to consider the extremes, we may say that he values innocent goodness more highly than intellectual virtuosity.

On June 22, 1800, half a year after the publication of the *Soliloquies*, Schleiermacher preached a sermon with the title, "That Intellectual Excellence without Moral Disposition Has no Worth."[35] The text is from I Corinthians 13:

> Though I speak with the tongues of men and of angels, but have not love, I am become as a sounding brass and a tinkling cymbal.

The sermon's title and text establish its theme:

> We call our age Enlightened and speak much of great progress which all segments of society are supposed to have made in the cultivation of the mind [*Bildung des Geistes*] and in the correction and broadening of its insight. . . . All of this is no small honor. But unfortunately, this progress is quite generally accompanied by the great disadvantage that the understanding and its cultivation are prized even apart from the disposition [*Gesinnung*], and prized much too highly. . . . I am far from placing great value upon that which we commonly call "a good heart" [*ein gutes Herz*]. The willingness to experience with and for others, to let oneself be used by them as an instrument, and to attach oneself with wonderment to all

---

[32]Letter to Schleiermacher from Brinkmann, Apr. 29, 1800. *Briefe von Brinkmann an Schleiermacher*, 28. Schleiermacher deserved the remark, as he actually uses the terms "initiated" and "uninitiated" in *Monologen*, 65 and 71 (translated "consecrated" and "unconsecrated" in *Soliloquies*, 66, and "uninitiated" in *Soliloquies*, 74). But what Schleiermacher thought of Brinkmann's characterization we may gather from his comment about Fichte's Freemasonry (above, Part II, Ch. 4, Footnote 27).

[33]*Monologen*, 66. *Soliloquies*, 68.

[34]"Denkmale," 125.

[35]"Dass Vorzüge des Geistes ohne sittliche Gesinnungen keinen Werth haben," in *Predigten. Erste Sammlung*, 54–67.

that appears great and good in them, is something quite equivocal. Often it is nothing other than an emptiness of one's own sensibility, an incapacity to will for oneself, a need to be led and pushed by others. But without a really good will, without a genuinely ethical disposition [*eine ächt sittliche Gesinnung*], without the firm and ever active direction of all our powers toward a self-apprehended good, without true obedience to divine laws, all the excellencies of the mind [*Vorzüge des Geistes*] — even if they have been developed to the highest peak of perfection — are nothing, quite simply nothing.[36]

Schleiermacher felt that self-cultivation in itself — in the sense of extending one's powers without sufficient attention to their harmony and balance — invites the "one-sided virtuosity" of which he was so critical in Fichte or in those whom he refers to as "philosophical and theological athletes" (above, p. 61). He holds the opposite extreme to be a less undesirable condition. Moral integrity in itself, that is, a personality in which knowing and desiring are in harmony, even at a restricted stage of cultivation, results at worse in what we might call moral naiveté. Such is the condition of Dickens's guileless figure of "humility, and sorrow, and forgiveness,"[37] Stephen Blackpool. Such is the condition that Goethe's cultivated young hero so longs to regain in *The Sorrows of the Young Werther*: that moral innocence, once and for all lost to Werther, which

in happy composure courses the small circle of its being, succors itself along from day to day, sees the leaves fall and thinks of nothing of it except that winter is coming.[38]

Such also was the non-fictional condition that Schleiermacher so loved in Eleonore Crüger Grunow. He first met Eleonore in Berlin in the spring of 1799. Immediately Schleiermacher was distressed by what he perceived to be a distortion of Eleonore's inner harmony by the unhappy, even cruel, conditions of her childless marriage, contracted when she was only twelve. Her husband, a Lutheran minister in Berlin, appears to have treated her with cold insensitivity.[39] Schleiermacher's friends wondered at Schleiermacher's affection for Eleonore and at the prolonged frustration their relationship was able to endure, for Eleonore was neither intellectually impressive nor attractive in the manner of a Henriette Herz. Eleonore herself shared this wonder. "To be the object of such a love — I can scarcely grasp it," she writes in the only lines from

[36]Ibid., 54–55.

[37]*Hard Times*, Book III, Ch. 6.

[38]Johann Wolfgang Goethe, *Die Leiden des jungen Werthers*, letter dated "Am 27. Mai [1771]," 17.

[39]We must say "appears," since our only accounts of the Grunow marriage are from sources sympathetic to Schleiermacher's point of view. These accounts are unanimous, however, in their critical portrayal of minister Grunow. See Hugo Weizsäcker's discussion of the marriage in *Schleiermacher und das Eheproblem*, 27.

her hand that have ever come to light; "but I worshipfully accept it
from the hand of Providence, which wills my relief from the sufferings
of my youth."[40] Schleiermacher confesses his appreciation of Eleonore's
wonderment in a letter to her of 1802: "At the time when I once
thought, 'Something can be made of this woman,' I had still not
discovered your innermost being, for that *is*, and does not require that
anything more be made of it. I had discovered only your understanding
[*Verstand*], and you know that the understanding alone does not much
affect me personally."[41] And in response to a friend's wonderment
Schleiermacher writes:

> In my love I make nothing of the degree of cultivation or the sphere in
> which a person expresses his powers. That is why my love so often
> annoys people and why they cannot understand it. I love the heart
> [*Gemüth*] itself, its malleability and its powers. But with respect to both
> the person and the world, the important thing for me is that a person
> enjoy and is now becoming what he is, that he work it out in the most
> beautiful way, and thereby is active and grows. And now in my first love
> [for Eleonore] I shall not witness this, but rather, out of an infinite
> abundance of beautiful buds in which the fruit is already visible, shall see
> only a few unfold and the rest shrivel up before they have developed —
> and this not from intrinsic disease, but because this wretched worm eats
> at the beautiful growth. It is a waste, and because of it I too am wasting
> away.[42]

The risk of simple integrity by itself is moral complacency. Schleiermacher is more suspicious of the risk of cultivation by itself, however.
The latter results in sheer virtuosity, and "all virtuosity," he writes in
the *Speeches*, "limits, and makes cold, one-sided, and hard."[43] The goal
of ethical life is to combine integrity and virtuosity in such a way that
their strengths reinforce and their risks counteract. The "determinate
existence" of every life, Schleiermacher writes at the beginning of the
Speeches, consists in

> uniting and maintaining in a characteristic way the two primordial powers
> of nature: the absorption of what is needful into oneself, and the active
> and living broadening of oneself. . . . Every human soul [*Seele*] is but the
> product of two contrary impulses [*Triebe*]. The one is the striving to draw
> all that surrounds us to ourself, to include all things in our own life, and
> wherever possible to absorb all wholly into our innermost being. The
> other is the yearning to extend our own inner self indefinitely outward, to
> penetrate all with ourself, to communicate ourself to all, and never to be
> exhausted.

[40]Letter to Charlotte Schleiermacher, 1802. Quoted in Dilthey, *Leben Schleiermachers*,
ed. Redeker, I/1, 544.
[41]Dated only "Tuesday." *Br.* I, 303.
[42]Letter to Willich, Oct. 8, 1801. *Werden*, 230. Schleiermacher expresses the same order
of values in *Monologen*, 45 (*Soliloquies*, 46). We shall follow Schleiermacher's relation with
Eleonore Grunow further in Part III.
[43]*Reden*, 112. *Speeches*, 85, where *Virtuosität* is translated "mastery."

These two impulses constitute the *nature* of our existence. But the "perfection" of our existence, Schleiermacher writes, consists in an "equilibrium uniting both."[44]

At this early point in the *Speeches* the relation between individual and social consciousness, so peculiar to Schleiermacher's romantic ethical genius, first asserts itself. It is crucial that we appreciate this relation, since romanticism is often accused of excessive individualism (see above, p. 145). We can easily "overvalue" the equilibrium that represents the goal of ethical life, Schleiermacher writes, if we take it to mean that humanity will approach homogeneity as persons increase in ethical maturity. Whoever falls prey to this misunderstanding lacks a proper sense for the infinity of the yearning to harmonize and extend our powers. Infinity is such that, though we progress from more limited to less limited appropriation and cultivation of spirit, still we are no nearer the goal of completeness. Thus every individual's ethical progress maintains its own characteristic form. None need copy or compete with another. But the obverse is that each person must look to all others for the completeness of perspective that shall forever elude single individuals. Moral completeness is an essentially social concept:

> How may these most extreme distances be brought together, in order to shape the long line of alternatives into the closed circle that is the emblem of eternity and completeness?[45] There is indeed a certain point at which a virtually perfect equilibrium unites both extremes. . . . But if all should stand at this point, having abandoned the outermost limits, then no joining of these ends with the center would be possible, and the final goal of nature would be altogether missed. Only the most thoughtful of seers can penetrate the secret of such an aggregate brought into rest.[46]

The "secret" of Schleiermacher's ethical genius consists in his vision of the ideal goal of ethics, together with his insight into the relation between individual and society necessary for the maximum embodiment of that ideal in actual life.

A "Fragment" Schleiermacher contributed to the second issue of the Schlegels' journal *Athenaeum* in 1798 summarizes his ideal of the ethically mature "character":

> It combines the talent for easily finding its own limit and desiring nothing except what it can accomplish, with the talent for broadening its final goals along with its powers. It combines the wisdom and quiet resignation of a heart and mind [*Gemüth*] turned in upon itself with the energy of a most exceedingly elastic and expansible spirit [*Geist*], which through the least opening that presents itself escapes to fill in an instant a far larger

---

[44] *Reden*, 5–7. Cf. *Speeches*, 3–5.
[45] See above, p. 91.
[46] *Reden*, 6–7.

circle than before. It never makes a vain attempt to escape the acknowledged limits of the moment, and yet there glows in it the yearning to
extend itself farther. It never struggles against fate, but demands that fate
in every moment allot it a broadening of its existence. It has always in its
eye that which a person might become and may wish to become, but
never strives for something until the favorable moment is come. That
such a character would be a perfected practical genius — that in it would be
found all intention and all instinct, all choice and all nature — this we can
say. But we shall search in vain for a word to designate the essence of this
character.[47]

This is the ideal, a unity of the two degrees of freedom that constitute
ethical perfection. But we shall "search in vain" for a name by which to
designate this embodiment of "all intention and all instinct, all choice
and all nature" in any individual, for such comprehension is not granted
to mortals. The "way" of Schleiermacher's "Fragment," like the Way of
oriental Taoism which it could almost be thought to echo,[48] cannot be
named. The "perfected practical genius" never exists in reality.

Yet Schlegel, together with other friends, observed a living approach
to that ideal in Schleiermacher himself. In 1797, Schlegel sent his
brother a description of his new Berlin companion:

> Schleiermacher is a person in whom the human is cultivated, and
> accordingly, for me he really belongs in a higher caste. . . . He is only
> three years older than me, but in moral understanding he surpasses me
> infinitely. I hope to learn much more from him. His whole being is moral,
> and in comparison with all the excellent persons I know, in him morality
> surpasses all else.[49]

A year later, in a letter to Schleiermacher, Schlegel expresses his
assessment in terms of a ratio: what Goethe is to poetry, and Fichte is
to philosophy, Schleiermacher is to humanity.[50]

Later still, however, in connection with his suspicion that Schleiermacher's association with Henriette Herz was constricting his unique
"sense for the great" (see above, p. 131), Schlegel was forced to
exclaim in dismay: "Is this the famous many-sidedness?"[51] Schleiermacher was not of course the "perfected practical genius" his "Fragment" depicts as the moral ideal. Nevertheless, the romantic author
Bettina Brentano von Arnim, excessive though she sometimes was,
seems to have expressed a consensus of Schleiermacher's friends when,

---

[47]"Fragmente," *Athenaeum*, I/2 (1798), 314–15. For a determination of which of the
anonymous "Fragments" are attributable to Schleiermacher see Peter Firchow, tr. *Friedrich
Schlegel's "Lucinde" and the Fragments*, 16n.

[48]In his review of Schleiermacher's *Speeches* Schlegel calls that book "an unexpected
sign of the Orient, approaching from afar!" *Athenaeum*, II/2 (1799), 297.

[49]Dec., 1797. Quoted in Dilthey, *Leben Schleiermachers*, ed. Redeker, I/1, 260.

[50]No date (1798). *Br*. III, 81.

[51]Schlegel, *Lucinde*, "Julius an Antonio, I," 100.

referring probably to Schleiermacher's slight build and slight stoop due to a deformity of the upper back, she asserted that though Schleiermacher was not the greatest man (*Mann*) of his time, he was the greatest human being (*Mensch*).[52]

[52]Reported in Ehrenfried von Willich, *Aus Schleiermachers Hause*, 127.

Chapter 6. Moral Virtue and Religious Sense

Religion is infinite . . . not only by virtue of the fact that it is intrinsically imperfectible, like ethics. Religion is infinite from all sides, an infinity of matter and form— of being, and therefore of seeing and knowing. This feeling must accompany anyone who really has religion.

Readers acquainted with Schiller's essays *On the Aesthetic Education of Man* (1795) and *On Naive and Sentimental Poetry* (1795–96) will have recognized many similarities between Schleiermacher's ideal of the "perfected practical genius" and Schiller's concept of the "idea of humanity" or "humanity in its most complete possible expression."[1] There is also an illuminating contrast between Schleiermacher's ideal and Schiller's. In our brief look into these similarities and this contrast in this chapter, we shall have to set aside the attempt to specify the degree of direct influence of Schleiermacher and Schiller upon one another. Evidence is simply lacking. We have seen in Part I that Schleiermacher's ethical ideal of a harmonious appropriation of knowledge and desire dates from 1792–93 (above, p. 87), three years before Schiller's essays were to express their similar "aesthetic" ideal. Likewise, in an essay of 1789, "On the Naive," Schleiermacher formulated his definition, "The naive is the simple that we had not expected"—six years prior to Schiller's famous formulation, "The naive is childlikeness where it is no longer expected."[2] These early writings of Schleiermacher remained unpublished, however, and there can be no question of any direct influence upon Schiller.

On the other hand, by the time of the *Speeches* in 1799, Schleiermacher must have been acquainted with Schiller's philosophical essays. He would certainly have known *On Naive and Sentimental Poetry* through his friend Schlegel, who was involved in antagonisms with Schiller through the second half of the 1790s. In Schleiermacher's correspondence, journals, and publications of this period, however, references to

---

[1]Friedrich Schiller, *Über naive und sentimentalische Dichtung*, 139. Available in the English translation by Julius A. Elias, *Naive and Sentimental Poetry*, 111. I usually follow Elias's excellent translation.

[2]Schleiermacher, "Über das Naive," abridged in "Denkmale," 6. Schiller, *Über naive und sentimentalische Dichtung*, 123; English tr., 90.

Schiller are notable chiefly by their scarcity. And when Schleiermacher's *Speeches* appeared in 1799, Schiller was little impressed by them (see above, p. 146). "They are a Berlin product, out of *that* coterie," he wrote from Jena; ". . . for all their talk of warmth and inwardness, yet they are on the whole very dry and often pretentiously written; besides, they contain little that is new."[3] So there appears to have been little direct influence of either man upon the other.[4] The two never met. We may say simply that these two student's of Kant's writings follow parallel paths for some distance from that common ground of origin.

In view of this apparent independence, Schiller's idea of completed humanity is remarkably similar to the goal of ethical life represented in Schleiermacher's geometric vignette: an expanding, integral sphere of knowledge and desire. Aesthetic education, Schiller writes, "has as its aim the cultivation of the whole of our sensuous and intellectual powers, in the fullest possible harmony." Freedom "consists simply in the cooperation of these two natures"; freedom is thus "not lawlessness, but harmony of laws; not arbitrariness, but the higher inner necessity."[5] Such assertions could easily pass for Schleiermacher's own.

Like Schleiermacher, Schiller recognizes that his ideal of completed humanity and perfected freedom can never be fully actualized in any individual—though "a few rare individuals" in every age approach the ideal.[6] Like Schleiermacher he sees that the extremes of rationality and passion cannot be united by reducing them to some mid-point of equilibrium, since this would not be to unite extremes but rather to dissipate them in compromise and blandness:

> It appears . . . that between matter and form, between passivity and activity, there must be a *middle condition.* . . . But on the other hand, nothing is more inconsistent and contradictory than such a concept, since the separation between matter and form, between passivity and activity, between sensation and thought is *infinite* and absolutely cannot be mediated.[7]

Each individual's pursuit of completeness takes its own characteristic form, therefore, and each must look to all for the fullest possible realization of the ideal:

> One-sidedness in the exercise of powers, it is true, inevitably leads the individual into error, but it leads the race to truth. Only by concentrating the whole energy of our spirit in *one* focal point, and drawing together

---

[3]Letter to Christian Gottfried Körner, Sep. 1799. Quoted in Dilthey, *Leben Schleiermachers*, ed. Redeker, I/1, 456.

[4]For a synopsis of the connections between Schiller and Schleiermacher see Hans Heinrich Borcherdt, *Schiller und die Romantiker*, 62–67, 564–75.

[5]*Ästhetische Erziehung*, Twentieth, Seventeenth, and Eighteenth Letters.

[6]*Über naive und sentamentalische Dichtung*, 186. English tr., 176.

[7]*Ästhetische Erziehung*, Eighteenth Letter. Schiller's emphases.

our whole being into one single power, do we attach wings, as it were, to this individual power and lead it artifically far beyond the limits nature seems to have set for it. Just as surely as all human individuals, taken together, with the power of vision nature has apportioned to them, would never have succeeded in espying a satellite of Jupiter which the telescope reveals to the astronomer, so too it is certain that the human power of thought would never have achieved an analysis of the infinite, or a *Critique of Pure Reason*, if reason had not isolated itself in individuals called to such pursuits, wrenched itself loose from all matter, as it were, and armed itself by the most intense abstraction for its look into the unconditioned. But will such a one, dissolved as it were in pure understanding and pure intuition, in fact be capable of exchanging the rigid fetters of logic for the free course of the poetic imagination, and of grasping the individuality of things with true and chaste sensibility? Here nature sets even for the universal genius a boundary it cannot overstep. . . . Thus, however much may be gained for the world as a whole by this separated cultivation of human powers, it cannot be denied that the individuals whom it affects suffer under the curse of this universal aim. . . . The exertion of individual powers of the spirit certainly produces extraordinary human beings, but only the even tempering of these powers produces happy and completed human beings.[8]

This is Schiller's sensitive account of what Schleiermacher calls the "deficiency of animation and . . . superfluity of reason" in Kant's individual genius (see above, p. 155). Probably Schleiermacher could have shared its sympathetic tone. He recognized as keenly as anyone the value of Kant's extraordinary rationality, and he shared Schiller's sense for the dynamic interdependence between the welfare of the race and the genius of such eccentric individuals—between the whole and the part, the many and the one.

Nonetheless we begin to encounter here a crucial difference between Schleiermacher and Schiller. Both men longed to unite the two degrees of freedom in the exercise of our powers: appropriation and cultivation, balance and extension, harmony and range, integrity and virtuosity—or, in Schiller's terms, "relaxation" and "tension," "concord" and "energy."[9] For Schiller, the reconciling medium is aesthetic education. The means of restoring wholeness to "the separated cultivation of human powers" are artistic means:

Can man really be destined to neglect himself for any goal whatsoever? Should nature by its goal be able to rob us of a completeness that reason prescribes to us by its own? It must be false that the cultivation of individual powers makes necessary the sacrifice of their totality; or even if the law of nature did strive ever so strongly in this direction, yet we must be in a position to restore this totality in our nature, which art has destroyed, by means of a higher art. . . . If human perfection consists in the harmonious energy of our sensuous and intellectual powers, . . . we

---

[8]Ibid., Sixth Letter. Schiller's emphasis.
[9]Ibid., Seventeenth Letter.

shall find the actual, and accordingly limited, man either in a condition of tension or in a condition of relaxation, according to whether the one-sided activity of his individual powers is disturbing the harmony of his nature, or whether the unity of his nature is grounded in the homogenous relaxation of his sensuous and intellectual powers. Both of these opposite limits are, as I shall now show, *removed* [*gehoben*] *by means of beauty*, which restores harmony in the tense man, and energy in the relaxed. In this way, beauty, in accordance with its nature, brings the limited condition back to an absolute condition and makes of man a self-completed whole.[10]

Schiller occasionally speaks as if the ideal of wholeness he expresses here can actually be accomplished in art, if not in larger life; more usually he acknowledges that it cannot. He seems never to establish his point of view with finality.[11] But he does at one point reveal his opinion that, in the pursuit of this two-fold ideal of wholeness, he gives preference not to the condition of concord or appropriation (which Schiller calls the "naive"), but rather to the condition of energy or cultivation (the "sentimentive"). It is here that Schiller's path diverges from that of Schleiermacher.

In man's state of naive integrity, Schiller writes, "nature sets him at one with himself"; in the state of cultivation, "art divides and cleaves him in two"; finally, through the ideal of completeness, "he returns to unity." These are the stages in what Schiller calls the "aesthetic education" of the human race:

> Because the ideal of the cultivated man is an infinitude to which he never attains, the cultivated man can never become perfect in *his* own way, but the natural man *can* in his. The former must therefore fall infinitely short of the latter in perfection, if one heeds only the relation in which each stands to his own way and to its maximum perfection. But if one compares the two ways with one another, it becomes evident that the goal to which man *strives* through culture is infinitely preferable to that which he *attains* in nature. For the one obtains its value by the absolute achievement of a finite greatness, the other by approximation to an infinite greatness. . . . Insofar as the ultimate goal of mankind is not to be attained except by . . . progress, and man cannot progress except by cultivating himself and hence passing again into the first condition, thus there cannot be any question as to which of the two is more advantageous with reference to that ultimate goal.[12]

---

[10]Ibid., Emphasis added.

[11]See the place in *On Naive and Sentimental Poetry* where Schiller raises the question of "a higher concept" under which both extremes can be "subsumed," and then drops it again: "This is not the place further to pursue these thoughts, which can only be expounded in full measure in a separate disquisition." This disquisition was never written. *Über naive und sentementalische Dichtung*, 139. English tr., 112.

[12]Ibid., 139–40. English tr., 112–13. Schiller's emphases.

In other words, of the two degrees of freedom comprising the ideal human wholeness, namely, appropriation and cultivation, Schiller calls the latter "infinitely preferable" to the former.

We have seen that Schleiermacher reverses Schiller's order of preference, valuing freedom as appropriation more highly than freedom as cultivation (above, p. 170). Reasons for this difference are not difficult to discover. Schleiermacher's romantic sense for the infinite is in this instance more finely tuned than that of the great classicist Schiller. We must recall that Schleiermacher's ethical ideal involves not only two degrees of freedom, but *motion* in two degrees of freedom. Cultivation entails the infinite expansion of reason and sense. Appropriation entails the asymptotic approach of the human ellipse to the ideal circle in which reason and sense are congruent and harmonious. In Schleiermacher's view, *both are infinite motions*—the asymptotic approach no less than the unlimited extension. When Schiller speaks of the first degree of freedom as "approximation to an infinite greatness," therefore, his view and Schleiermacher's are the same. But when Schiller speaks of the second as "the absolute achievement of a finite greatness," Schleiermacher disagrees. Schleiermacher believes that the molding of individual personality into a harmonious congruence of reason and sense is no less an infinite ideal than the expansion of reason and sense. Or to put this more exactly, while the ideal of a personal sphere of reason and sense in congruence and harmony is a finite ideal, as Schiller suggests, the asymptotic approach to that ideal is an infinite process. It is true that an asymptotic approach gets ever nearer to its ideal limit. Yet it always remains infinitely short of absolute completion.

From Schleiermacher's point of view, Schiller's talk of naive integrity as "the absolute achievement of a finite greatness" repeats the fallacy of the eighteenth century's idea of the noble savage. Schleiermacher believes that no perfected integrity is ever to be observed in actual life, civilized or uncivilized, ancient or modern. His romantic sense for the infinite serves him here—his recognition that, while there may be progress along the path toward infinity, any stage of that progress is yet infinitely short of its goal. Virtuosity involves the inifnte pursuit of an infinite goal; integrity involves the infinite approach to a finite goal. Both processes are infinite. In any actual individual, then, both integrity and virtuosity elude absolute and final achievement.

Dickens realizes something like this in portraying his character Stephen Blackpool (see above, pp. 168 & 171)—who therefore takes on real life and avoids the list of Dickensian melodramatic sterotypes:

> It is said that every life has its roses and thorns; there seemed, however, to have been a misadventure or mistake in Stephen's case, whereby somebody else had become possessed of his roses, and he had become

possessed of the same somebody else's thorns in addition to his own. He had known, to use his words, a peck of trouble.[13]

Stephen's "perfect integrity" is not a static or perfectly achieved condition; it is rather his characteristic tendency, which, in the midst of his troubles, suffers disequilibrium and distortion. Similarly, in the actual world, the naive integrity of Eleonore Grunow was an attribute for which Schleiermacher loved her (above, p. 171). But Eleonore's attempt to maintain her integrity in the conflict between her commitment to an unhappy marriage and her love for Schleiermacher was an unceasing struggle and a source of the vacillation that frustrated their relationship for close to a decade.

When Schiller, the classicist, looked to ancient Greece, he was struck by the naive perfection of the "art of finitude," represented in classical Greek statuary.[14] But when Schleiermacher, the romantic, looked to ancient Greece, he was struck by the artistry of Plato's dialogues (see above, p. 135), which, commencing always "indirectly" from "some individual instance," relate to the ideal only by way of "continual progression," never completed attainment.[15] Actually, Schleiermacher was more than either classicist or romantic; he was a moralist and theologian as well. So we might reformulate the contrast in the following way. Schiller is the classicist, for whom the means of reconciling the two aspects of human freedom is beauty. Schleiermacher's companion Friedrich Schlegel, the student and sometime antagonist of Schiller, is the romantic, for whom the means of reconciling the two aspects of human freedom is poetic irony.[16] Schleiermacher as a moralist combines the two degrees of freedom in his ideal of the goal of ethical life, but their reconciliation remains an infinite ideal. The "perfected practical genius" never exists in reality, however well cultivated in aesthetic beauty or thoroughly steeped in poetic irony. Unlike the writings of both Schiller and Schlegel, Schleiermacher's writings never for an instant betray a loss of this sense for the infinity of the human ideal.

[13]Charles Dickens, *Hard Times*, Book I, Ch. 10.

[14]Schiller, *Über naive und sentimentalische Dichtung*, 141. English tr., 114–15.

[15]Schleiermacher, "Einleitung," *Platons Werke*, I/1, 30. English tr., 37. Schleiermacher takes the qualities he describes here to be the characteristics distinguishing the genuine Platonic dialogues of antiquity from the counterfeit.

[16]For two good discussions of Schlegel's romantic reconciliation of Schiller's opposition between the naive and the sentimentive by means of the concept of irony, see Leonard P. Wessell, Jr., "Schiller and the Genesis of German Romanticism," *Studies in Romanticism*, X (Summer, 1971), 176–98, and H. Jackson Forstman, "The Understanding of Language by Friedrich Schlegel and Schleiermacher," *Soundings*, LI (Summer, 1968), 146–65. Wessell's article concludes: "Schiller had maintained that the infinite is mirrored in two different ways in simple and sentimental poetry. These two ways were not bridged by Schiller. But it was exactly in bridging them through irony that Schlegel was able to find a mediation to man of the 'infinite' and thereby German romanticism was born."

We may attribute this constant awareness to the "sense and taste for the infinite"[17] that for Schleiermacher is the essence of religion. In Schleiermacher's philosophy of life the ethical ideal of uniting the "two primordial powers" of our nature (above, p. 172) is always tempered by a religious sense for the infinity of that ideal. So it is time for us to recall that for all their ethical content, Schleiermacher's *Speeches* do not have ethics as their primary concern. They are speeches *On Religion*. While we have found a high degree of correspondence between the ethical content of the *Speeches* and that of Schleiermacher's early ethical treatises, their religious content is something new, and to this religious content we must now turn our attention.

Schleiermacher distinguishes ethics from religion as carefully as he can (see above, p. 103). At one point in the *Speeches* he states the distinction this way:

> Ethics proceeds from the consciousness of freedom, and wants to broaden its realm into the infinite and make all subject to it. Religion breathes where freedom itself is once again become nature. Beyond the play of his particular powers and his personality, religion lays hold on a person, and sees him from the point of view in which he must be what he is, whether he will or not.[18]

We may note in passing the determinism of the final sentence. Within this determinism, Schleiermacher regards the realm of ethics as the realm in which we try to enlarge the sphere of our freedom. We try to extend indefinitely the reach of our powers. As we become aware that our powers come up against inevitable limits, however, we enter religion's realm of consciousness. We become aware of our unavoidable "dependence"[19] upon the whole, concerning which we have no choice. When in the *Speeches* Schleiermacher calls religion a holy "instinct,"[20] he is using that word in precisely the sense he had established for it in his treatise *On Human Freedom*: immediate determination by a single object, concerning which we exercise no choice (above, p. 40). In the religious context of the *Speeches*, however, the "single object" is the infinite universe; and it is not an intention that is instinctively kindled, as in an ethical context, but rather a submission to the feeling of dependence upon the whole.

To put this another way, the ideal of ethics is a society of choosing, self-cultivating, appropriating, and self-expressing individual personalities—in short, a society of ethically mature "characters" (see above, p. 173). In the religious theme of the *Speeches*, however, there runs a

[17] *Reden*, 50–51, 2nd ed. *Speeches*, 39.
[18] *Reden*, 48–49.
[19] *Reden*, 110.
[20] *Reden* 14. In the second edition Schleiermacher changes *Instinkt* to *Trieb*, "impulse." See *Speeches*, 11.

powerful, mystical current in which individual character is lost in the whole:

> Seek then to give up your life out of love to the universe. Strive accordingly in this life to annihilate your individuality and to live in the one and all; strive to be more than yourself, so that if you lose yourself, you lose but little.[21]

The contrast between Schleiermacher's ethical vision and his religious sense could hardly be stronger. In ethics we set our eye upon virtue, and as we approach that goal we enter an aristocratic company (see above, p. 169). But we have seen that Schleiermacher fears this striving for virtue even as he recommends it. It can easily pass over into a kind of virtuosity, and ethical virtuosity, no less than virtuosity of every kind, ultimately "confines and makes cold, one-sided, and hard" (above, p. 172). Religious sensibility, as Schleiermacher recommends it, tempers this ethical striving to "broaden and isolate" our own character.[22] Our striving toward moral virtuosity should always be complemented by "the beautiful modesty, the friendly, attractive forebearance"[23] that flow from religious consciousness.

After this contrast between ethical virtuosity and religious sense, it grates on the nerves when later in the *Speeches* Schleiermacher makes reference to "virtuosos of religion."[24] Such was precisely the effect Schleiermacher sometimes intended. He uses this phrase to designate pretentious or hypocritical officials of ecclesiastical hierarchies. Nonetheless, even Schlegel found this phrase the "most offensive" in the *Speeches*,[25] and Schleiermacher removed it from the second edition, putting "those perfected in religion," or simply "the religious," in its place.[26]

In religious consciousness, even the distinction between "disposition" (*Gesinnung*) and "intellect" (*Geist*), so important for Schleiermacher's ethical analysis (see above, pp. 167–171), is dissolved in intuition for the whole and awareness of the interdependence of all:

> If we have intuited the universe, and then look back upon our self—upon how, in comparison to the universe, our self disappears into infinite smallness—what can lie nearer a mortal than genuine, unaffected humility? If in an intuition of the world we perceive our brothers also—and it is clear to us how each of them without distinction is in this sense his own manifestation of humanity, exactly the same as we are, and how without

---

[21] *Reden*, 132. Cf. *Speeches*, 100–101.

[22] *Reden*, 109.

[23] *Reden*, 66. *Speeches*, 54.

[24] *Reden*, 199, 200.

[25] Schlegel, "Reden über die Religion," *Athenaeum*, II/2 (1799), 298.

[26] See *Speeches*, 163 ("those who are perfect in religion") and 164 ("accomplished in religion" and "the religious").

the existence of others we would have to forego this intuition—what is more natural than to embrace them all, *without distinction even as to disposition [Gesinnung] and powers of intellect [Geisteskraft]*, with more intimate love and affection?[27]

Another passage in the *Speeches*—like the one just quoted, strongly recollective of Joseph Fawcett's sermons (see above, p. 105)—speaks of religion's quieting vision of "the eternal wheels of humanity in motion . . . , this unsurveyable meshing, where nothing is moved wholly by itself, and nothing moves itself alone. . . ."[28] These religious themes of egalitarianism and social solidarity in the *Speeches* cannot be emphasized too strongly. They provide another counterpoise to the component of elitism in Schleiermacher's ethical perspective (see above, p. 173). The ethical and the religious, while distinct from each other, must be held together in any adequate interpretation of Schleiermacher's world view.

Unlike moral virtue, though like what we have called moral integrity, religious piety in Schleiermacher's sense can accompany any stage of intellectual cultivation. In the *Athenaeum* of 1798, Schlegel had written, "The more cultivation, the less religion."[29] Schleiermacher did not agree with Schlegel's assertion about religion, and he wrote his *Speeches to Its Cultured Despisers* to make it clear that he did not. Nor did he agree with the view that the less a person's cultivation, the less his sense of religious piety. He alights in the *Speeches* with a sharp sting on those "theologians of the letter" who, forgetting the "beautiful modesty" and "attractive forbearance" of genuine religious sensibility, pride themselves on their supposed religious virtuosity. The truly religious, Schleiermacher writes, "do not let themselves be disturbed in the simplicity of their ways, and take little notice of all self-designated religious systems."[30]

Once again we see in Schleiermacher's position the influence of Plato, "who puts so high a value upon the consciousness of ignorance,"[31] and of Plato's Socrates, who so clearly understood what religious consciousness instinctively senses: that the really vicious enemy of truth is not ignorance, but rather presumption of knowledge.[32] Schleiermacher believes that in our pursuit of ethical virtue we run the risk of such presumption. The goal of moral growth is the balanced cultivation of adequate comprehension. The danger is that we tend to forget the infinity of that ethical task. But true religious consciousness,

[27] *Reden*, 109. Emphasis added.
[28] *Reden*, 99. *Speeches*, 77. Schleiermacher left the mechanical imagery of this passage unaltered through the successive revisions of the *Speeches*.
[29] *Athenaeum*, I/2 (1798), 239.
[30] *Reden*, 63, 2nd ed. *Speeches*, 52.
[31] Schleiermacher, *Platons Werke*, I/1, 7. English tr., 5.
[32] See *Reden*, 49–50, 2nd ed. Cf. *Speeches*, 38.

as sense and taste for this infinity, recalls our awareness of the infinite when it tends to disappear in the midst of our ethical ambitions.

It is often remarked how infinity was a preoccupation of the early German romantics. The notion surfaces repeatedly in the journals of such figures as Schleiermacher, Schlegel, and Schlegel's friend Novalis—whose relation with Schleiermacher around 1799 was one of mutual admiration, as we have seen (above, pp. 152–153). According to Karl Barth, Novalis writes in his literary fragments that "God is sometimes $1 \times \infty$, sometimes $1/\infty$, sometimes 0."[33] Never one to be out-romanticized, Schlegel goes even farther, writing in one of his literary notebooks:

$$\textit{Poetic Ideal} = \sqrt[\frac{1}{0}]{\frac{FSM^{\frac{1}{0}}}{0}} = \textit{God},$$

"F" standing for "fantasy," "S" for "sentiment," and "M" for "myth."[34]

Schleiermacher's romanticism was never as cryptic or flamboyant as that of these younger contemporaries. But in a passage that must have delighted Novalis and Schlegel, Schleiermacher describes the infinity of ethical striving and the infinity of religious intuition, and then insists that the latter infinity is *greater* than the former:

> Religion is infinite not only by virtue of the fact that activity and passivity oscillate endlessly between the same finite matter and the mind [*Gemüth*]—and you know that this is the only infinity of speculative knowledge—not only by virtue of the fact that it is intrinsically imperfectible, like ethics. Religion is infinite from all sides, an infinity of matter and form—of being, and therefore of seeing and knowing. This feeling must accompany anyone who really has religion.[35]

What does it mean to say that religion is "infinite from all sides"? Schleiermacher understands the ideal of moral virtue to involve comprehending all the world from a cultivated, privileged point of view. But even among persons whom we think of as most virtuous in this sense— perhaps we should say *especially* among such persons—points of view rarely coincide. Schleiermacher was Kantian enough to think that, in the ideal, "morality should everywhere be one."[36] But he was realistic enough to observe that this ideal universality is never realized. In fact it is impossible for any single point of view, however cultivated or privileged, to be fully comprehensive. Full comprehension would mean

[33] Barth, *Protestant Thought*, 247.

[34] Quoted in H. Jackson Forstman, "The Understanding of Language by Friedrich Schlegel and Schleiermacher," *Soundings*, LI (Summer, 1968), 165.

[35] *Reden*, 66. Cf. *Speeches*, 54.

[36] *Reden*, 274. *Speeches*, 237. See also above, Part I, Ch. 4, footnote 7.

the comprehension of all things from every point of view:

> To know one viewpoint for all is exactly the opposite of having all
> viewpoints for everything. It is the most direct way to leave the universe
> behind and, sunk in lamentable limitation, to become a true *glebae*
> *adscriptus* of the spot of earth on which one happens to stand.[37]

The goal of moral philosophy thus becomes the comprehension of all
points of view in one system. "But can you think of anything more
astonishing?" Schleiermacher exclaims:

> Do viewpoints, and especially viewpoints of the infinite, lend themselves
> to systematization? Can you say that because a person sees *this* in such
> and such a way, he must therefore see *that* in such and such a way?
> Someone may stand right behind you, or right beside you, and all appear
> different to him.[38]

Nothing is more important for an interpretation of Schleiermacher's
romanticism, and indeed of his philosophy of life, than an appreciation
of the sense of astonishment he expresses here—astonishment over the
presumptive notion of comprehending all truth systematically. Nothing
more fully recalls the most formative elements of Schleiermacher's
upbringing and education, more clearly explains Schleiermacher's attitudes toward his contemporaries in philosophy, ethics, and theology, or
more prophetically anticipates the best in the romantic movement that
the *Speeches* helped to inaugurate. Schleiermacher's astonishment over
philosophical attempts to systematize the infinite recalls his father's
letter of 1789, cautioning his son against "system-mania" and recommending the "wholesome distrust" of oneself that is commensurate
with "an upright and humble heart that trusts in God" (above, p. 60). It
echoes Schleiermacher's response to that letter, confessing to his father
that doubt is the generating impulse of his thinking, and discriminating
between the sphere of secure opinion and the sphere of "those
matters . . . which we may, without detriment to our tranquility and
happiness, leave undecided." And it explains Schleiermacher's reserve
in the midst of the general excitement of his age over the philosophical
systems of such contemporaries as Fichte and Schelling:

> Indeed Schelling's is an incomparably richer nature, and yet I almost fear
> that he is more similar to Fichte than people realize. To me it is always
> contemptible when someone has arrived at his system from some single
> starting point.[39]

---

[37] *Reden*, 161. *Speeches*, 130. *Glebae adscriptus*: lit. "attached to the soil." "Said of feudal
serfs, who were transferred along with the estate to which they hereditarily pertained"
(*Oxford English Dictionary*).

[38] *Reden*, 62.

[39] Letter to Brinkmann, Dec. 14, 1803. *Br.* IV, 94.

Schelling's early philosophy underwent rapid mutations, and with the passage of years, Schleiermacher found more and more in it to admire. In his 1804 review of Schelling's *Lectures on the Methods of Academic Study*, Schleiermacher praises Schelling for having perceived the inadequacy of narrow, exclusivistic deductive systems of philosophy:

> No less excellent is the Fifth Lecture's discussion of the pluralism of forms in philosophy. It is noteworthy, because it may be the first time that the certainty to which philosophy has attained since its renewal among us has revealed itself in such liberality.[40]

The "liberality" Schleiermacher appreciates in Schelling's book of 1803 traces back to Spinoza's recognition that there is truth in every point of view, though truth inevitably limited and obscured by our finite inadequacies.[41] This liberalism is at the very heart of Schleiermacher's philosophy of life. For him it traces even farther back, beyond Spinoza to Plato. In the 1804 Introduction to his editon of *Plato's Works*, Schleiermacher is gently sarcastic with those who investigate the dialogues in order to discover "in what person's mouth Plato presents his own opinion of this or that."[42] Such investigations, Schleiermacher insists, inevitably miss the essence of Plato, for whom truth is found in no single point of view. Truth is approached only asymptotically, by the dialectical examination of every point of view.

It was this liberal pulse that Schleiermacher had difficulty detecting in Fichte. He found Fichte's philosophy always constrained by its "relentless" deductive impulse, "every point on the periphery being spun out from the middle point, from which it emanates isomorphically on all sides."[43] Schleiermacher felt that Schelling, unlike Fichte, at least glimpsed the fundamental insight that "every philosophy in fact leads the person who can see far enough, and wants to go far enough, to a mysticism" (above, p. 163). Speaking in 1801 of his hopes concerning the future development of Schelling's philosophy, Schleiermacher writes:

> I think that there must finally be discussion of the limits of philosophy; and if nature is placed outside those limits, then room will be won on the other side, beyond philosophy, for mysticism. Fichte, with his facile virtuosity in idealism, will fare very poorly during this operation; but what does that matter?[44]

---

[40]Schleiermacher, "F. W. J. Schelling. Vorlesungen über die Methode des akademischen Studiums," *Br.* IV, 578. The review appeared originally in the *Jenaische Literatur-Zeitung*, I, Nos. 96 and 97 (1804), 137–51.

[41]See the *Ethics*, Part II, Propositions XXXIII–XLI.

[42]*Platons Werke*, I/1, 10. English tr., 8.

[43]Schleiermacher, review of Fichte's *Die Bestimmung des Menschen* in *Athenaeum*, III/2 (1800), 286.

[44]Letter to von Willich, June, 1801. *Br.* I, 282.

Schleiermacher's liberalism also traces back—not without a certain degree of irony—through the "upright and humble heart that trusts in God" of his father's Christian conservatism, to roots in the exclamation of the Psalmist:

> How precious to me are thy thoughts, O God!
> How vast is the sum of them!
> If I would count them, they are more than the sand.
> . . . Such knowledge is too wonderful for me;
> It is high, I cannot attain it.[45]

It has roots also in the words of Christ:

> I have other sheep, that are not of this fold . . . ,[46]

and in the astonished discovery by the earliest followers of Christ that the spirit of truth could be poured out "even on the Gentiles."[47]

In a sermon preached at about the time of the *Speeches*, Schleiermacher's Christian congregation heard their minister's liberalism expressed in the following terms:

> Each should learn to perceive how variously human life can be cultivated and conducted, and with what variety the right and good can be apprehended, according to the various kinds of human minds and hearts [*Gemüthsart der Menschen*]. This completion of our own imperfect experiences and insights, this mutual instruction, we who are brothers in Christ and citizens of the universal kingdom of God must acknowledge as the principal aim of our being joined together.[48]

To a young minister friend Schleiermacher writes in 1801 of his

> maxim, that every particular is only a part, and that one must have comprehended several parts before he can rightly understand the quiet waiting upon complete intuition, and the upright aversion from one-sided judgment and all too clever, premature human knowledge in isolated channels.[49]

Schleiermacher was fully aware that the liberal ethical ideal he expresses here is not the closed, deductive system of truth that some of

---

[45]Ps 139: 17–18, 6 (RSV). See also Isa 40:28 and 55:8.

[46]John 10:16.

[47]Acts 10:45. See Schleiermacher's liberal interpretaton of traditional Christian exclusivism in *The Christian Faith*, Propositions 118ff: "While Christian sympathy is not disquieted by the earlier or later adoption of one or another individual into the fellowship of redemption, yet, on the assumption of survival after death, there remains an irresolvable discord if we are to think of a part of the human race as entirely excluded from this fellowship."

[48]Schleiermacher, *Predigten. Erste Sammlung*, 86. Seifert, who gives a chronology of the sermons included in the first collection, dates this sermon from "1798/99 or 1800." *Die Theologie des jungen Schleiermacher*, 202.

[49]To Ehrenfried von Willich, June 11, 1801. *Br.* I, 280.

his contemporaries were seeking. It is on the contrary an "infinite chaos, in which every viewpoint in fact represents a world."[50] The ideal of moral philosophy is to comprehend an infinite number of perspectives. "Such a thinker," Søren Kierkegaard was later to observe in connection with his discussion of Hegel's philosophical system, "would have to be either God, or a fantastic *quodlibet*."[51]

Such is Schleiermacher's view precisely. No finite mortal can comprehend such a fantastic *quodlibet*. This doubly infinite comprehension — this infinity-squared, which rivals even the fanciful representations of God in the notebooks of Novalis and Schlegel — Schleiermacher regards as "in fact the highest and most suitable symbol of religion."[52] It is a symbol of the sense for the infinite that is the essence of religious consciousness.

Unlike the symbol of Schleiermacher's ethics, this symbol of religion defies the geometer's art. But this unrepresentable symbol of religion helps to clarify Schleiermacher's understanding of the relation between ethics and religion. To the extent that the religious sense for the infinite suggested by this symbol wanes in our self-consciousness at any moment, we suffer a proportional loss of ethical freedom. Schleiermacher defines freedom as the absence of constraint, and as religious sensibility wanes, we come under the constraint of presuming to know things with more certainty and finality than in fact we do. Schleiermacher agrees with Socrates that this presumption is the most insidious and binding of all constraints. Ignorance is a vacuum. It can be filled by direct education. But presumption of knowledge is not a vacuum. It is an illusion. It must be dispelled before education can begin, and this can be accomplished only by indirect, Socratic means.[53]

Religious "sense and taste for the infinite" offers protection from such presumption, such *hubris*, in science, ethics, and religiosity alike. "To want to have speculation and action without religion," Schleiermacher warns in the *Speeches*, "is impertinent presumption. It is impudent enmity against the gods." Without a counterbalancing religious sense, science and morality are expressions of "the profane sense of Prometheus,"[54] the pride that goes before a fall.

[50] *Reden*, 64.

[51] Søren Kierkegaard, *Concluding Unscientific Postscript*, tr. Swenson and Lowrie, 108. In musical terminology, a *quodlibet* is the simultaneous superimposition of any number of different melodies, as in the last of J. S. Bach's *Goldberg Variations*. In medieval philosophical terminology, a *quodlibet* is a dialogue in which every point of view may be expressed at will. Both meanings together provide Kierkegaard with a splendid satirical image.

[52] *Reden*, 64–65.

[53] This is another romantic theme that Søren Kierkegaard was to develop brilliantly some four decades later. See Kierkegaard, *The Point of View for my Work as an Author*, Part II, Chapter I, Section A.1: "That 'Christendom' Is a Prodigious Illusion."

[54] *Reden*, 49.

This passage from the *Speeches* recalls the epoch-making debate between Lessing and Jacobi over Spinoza's philosophy, triggered by Goethe's "Prometheus" (see above, p. 120). From Schleiermacher's perspective, the profane and the religious are to be seen in Goethe's poem side by side. In a profane sense of moral defiance against Zeus, Prometheus declares:

> Here I sit, form men
> After my own image,
> A race like unto me,
> To suffer, to weep,
> To enjoy and to be glad,
> And like me
> Thy race to despise.
>   (51–57)

Earlier in the poem, however, Prometheus asks of Zeus:

> Have I not been molded to a man
> By omnipotent time
> And eternal fate —
> My lords and thine?
>   (42–45)

Schleiermacher would see in this quatrain the sense of dependence that is the heart of genuine religious consciousness. The quatrain is a religious counterpoise to the Promethean moral defiance of the poem's other lines. The dynamic relation of the religious and the ethical in Goethe's poem is the same as that in Schleiermacher's philosophy of life. We have already seen, and shall presently see more clearly, that the poem's unorthodoxy could not have startled Schleiermacher in 1799 as it had startled Jacobi a decade and a half before.

Chapter 7. Mystical Freedom

Seek then to give up your life out of love to the universe. Strive accordingly in this life to annihilate your individuality and to live in the one and all; strive to be more than yourself, so that if you lose yourself, you lose but little.

We move now from Schleiermacher's understanding of religion as an essential counterpoise to ethics, to Schleiermacher's conception of freedom in this religious context. We have seen Schleiermacher's belief that the goal of ethical life is self-consciously to diminish our limitations, to liberate ourselves from the constraints of narrow or disproportionate knowledge or passion. We might say that religious sensibility, in contrast, heightens self-consciousness of our limitations. While ethics emphasizes activity and control, virtue and virtuosity, in religion there is awareness of receptivity and passive dependence. Repeatedly in the *Speeches* Schleiermacher maintains that religion is grounded in "intuition of the universe." As with Kant (see above, p. 152), Schleiermacher's use of *intuition* implies immediacy and receptivity:

> All intuition proceeds from an influence of the intuited upon the one who intuits—from an original and independent action of the former, which is taken up, collected, and comprehended by the latter in accordance with his nature. If rays of light did not stimulate your organ of sight, which happens wholly without your contrivance; if the smallest particles of matter did not mechanically or chemically affect the tips of your fingers; if the pressure of weight did not reveal an opposition and a limit to your strength—then you would intuit nothing and perceive nothing. What you intuit and perceive, therefore, is not the nature of things, but rather their action upon you. What you know or believe about the former lies far beyond the sphere of intuition. And thus religion: the universe is in uninterrupted activity and reveals itself to us in every moment. Every form that it brings forth; every being to which, according to the fullness of life, it gives a discrete existence; every occurrence that it yields from the richness of its ever fruitful womb—each of these is an action of the universe upon us. To receive all individual things as a part of the whole, all limited things as a manifestation of the infinite, that is religion.[1]

Our actions in the world, then, and our knowledge concerning the nature of things do not exhaust the sphere of religion and are not to be

---

[1] *Reden*, 52–57.

confused with it. Religion originates in immediate receptivity. The
essence of religion is "neither thinking nor acting, but intuition and
feeling. Religion wants to intuit the universe. Religion wants devoutly to
eavesdrop on its manifestations and actions, to let itself be grasped and
filled by its immediate influences, in childlike passivity."[2] Thus Schleiermacher distinguished religion, with its "childlike passivity," from ethics,
which "should strive for virtuosity" (above, p. 169). Unlike ethics,
religion give rise to no actions purely of itself. Rather it accompanies all
action, tempering virtue and moderating virtuosity in the ways we have
explored in the preceding chapter. "All action *per se* should and can be
moral, but religious feelings should accompany all human activity like a
holy music. A person should do all with religion, nothing from
religion."[3]

The reference to "a holy music" here is not merely incidental.
Whereas in Schleiermacher's analysis of ethical understanding his analogies are frequently mathematical (see above, p. 88), in his accounts of
religious consciousness he often turns to musical imagery (above, p.
151). Ethics is like mathematics insofar as both are rational and active
disciplines. But intuition of the universe is comparable to the attentive-
ness of a person absorbed in music: while neither static nor undiscern-
ing, yet both are essentially passive and appreciative; both involve a
pervasive, more than rational mood, never reducible to a conceptual
analysis of their sources. More particularly, Schleiermacher writes that
religion is like musical tonality and modulation,

> restoring the balance and harmony of a person's nature, which would be
> irretrievably lost if, without at the same time having religion, he aban-
> doned himself to some single pursuit. A person's virtuosity is only the
> melody of his life, as it were, and it is restricted to individual notes if not
> joined with religion. The latter, with an infinitely richer modulation,
> accompanies the former into every compatible tonality, and thus trans-
> forms the simple song of life into a full-voiced and glorious harmony.[4]

Musical harmony establishes the context and limits of musical form. It
restrains melodic virtuosity if the latter tends to become too presumptuous. At the same time, harmony is the enriching medium of melodic
development. So Schleiermacher's metaphor suggests that religious
consciousness is our sense for the universal context and ultimate limits
of our form as human beings. It is a restraint upon our tendencies to
presumption and pride. But Schleiermacher is also reminding us by his
image that religious consciousness is not awakened only at the outer
limits of our universe and the far extremes of our human condition. It
is also the medium in which we perceive the finest nuances and richest

[2] *Reden*, 46–47.
[3] *Reden*, 71. Cf. *Speeches*, 59.
[4] *Reden*, 113–14. Cf. *Speeches*, 87.

detail in the flow and development of our lives.

Religious consciousness, then, is the harmonic medium relating the infinite with the finite, joining the ultimate limits of our human nature with the immediate content of our individual lives. Religious consciousness is "immediate" intuition of the universe. That is, it is grounded in our instinctive, pre-rational sense of the ultimate *givenness* of our existence in the infinite environment of the universe. It is the worshipful sense of the Psalmist: "It is He that hath made us, and not we ourselves."[5] Schleiermacher believes that, in genuine religion, this fundamental sense precedes any distinct representation of the "He" of the Psalm. It precedes any knowledge or supposed knowledge of God's attributes, such as mercy or jealousy, love or wisdom. By his adjective "immediate" Schleiermacher means to say that this order of experience—from religious sense to theological representation—cannot be reversed. Religion is grounded in immediate experience, not theological abstraction, though the latter may serve to stimulate and refine the former.

This conviction is no manifestation of transcient, romantic mysticism for Schleiermacher. It is his fundamental conviction throughout his life. In 1829, in connection with his revision of *The Christian Faith*, we find Schleiermacher dismissing as vigorously as ever before the notion that

> one must first have grasped the idea of God before he can attain knowledge of this [religious] determinateness of being. Indeed I must deny this altogether. . . . What I understand by "pious feeling" does not follow from representation at all, but is rather the original expression of an immediate existential relation [*ein unmittelbares Existentialverhältnis*].[6]

Religious consciousness is not the product of philosophical deduction or theological abstraction. It is a pre-conceptual awareness. It is an instinctive sense for our "immediate existential relation" of ultimate dependence—a dependence which, to use a phrase of Samuel Taylor Coleridge, is "rationally insusceptible of all further question."[7]

At this point we may banish once and for all an inexcusable though common misunderstanding of Schleiermacher's philosophy of religion, perhaps the most common misunderstanding of all. It is the assertion that Schleiermacher reduces religion to mere subjectivity. Religion is subjective, it is true. What else may be said of any phenomenon of human consciousness? But according to Schleiermacher, religious consciousness is grounded in an immediate existential relation that is of all

[5]Ps 100:3 (KJV).

[6]Schleiermacher, *Schleiermachers Sendschreiben über seine Glaubenslehre an Lücke*, ed. Mulert, 13, 15. I am indebted to Robert Williams, "Schleiermacher and Feuerbach on the Intentionality of Religious Consciousness," *Journal of Religion*, LIII (Oct., 1973), 432, for calling this passage to my attention.

[7]Coleridge, *Essay on Faith*, 564.

relations most objective. Our ultimate dependence is insusceptible of question; it is an inescapable relation; it is absolute. It is, in brief, an objective fact. And subjective religious consciousness rests upon this most objective of facts.

So while religious consciousness is immediate and in this sense subjective, we may also say that it is mediated by the full content of our cosmic environment and is thus objective. Schleiermacher thinks of our religious sense of dependence as the most fully mediated of all our modes of awareness, in fact. Every experience may serve to reinforce it. No experience, perceived as a whole, can call it into question. For religious consciousness does not arise simply from our experience of this or that particular event or object, nor even from our feeling for the immeasurable infinity of events and objects as such. It arises primarily from our intuitive sense for the given interrelatedness of all events and objects in the universe. It arises from our sense that the source of the whole is not ourselves; from our awareness that an unfathomable structure not of our own design regulates the motion and development of all objects and events; from our feeling that a harmonic energy not of our own generation sustains the universe of objects and events and their exquisite interactions. Religious consciousness begins in an intuitive sense of universal dependence upon this absolute givenness of source, structure, and energy. At its most rudimentary level, religious consciousness is an instinctive sense of simple dependence. At its most developed, it may take the form of a trinitarian theology of praise for Creator, Word, and Spirit. But the origin of both extremes of theological sophistication is the same intuitive consciousness.

This is what Schleiermacher means when he writes in the *Speeches* that religion is not rooted in "little impressions" of natural beauty, or in "arithmetical amazement" over the sheer boundlessness of the universe ("easiest to awaken in adolescents and ignoramuses"), but rather in a sense for the "eternal laws . . . that embrace all things equally."[8]

> Space and mass do not comprise the world and are not the stuff of religion; therein to seek the infinite is a childish way of thinking. When not yet half of those worlds had been discovered, indeed when people still did not even know that those shining points were heavenly bodies, the universe was not any less glorious to intuit than now, and there was no more excuse for despisers of religion. Is not the most limited body in this respect fully as infinite as all that world? . . . That in the outer world which calls forth the religious sense is not its mass but in fact its laws. Lift yourselves up to see how these embrace all—the largest and smallest, world systems and specks of dust that float about restlessly in the air—and then say whether you do not intuit the divine unity and the eternal unchangeableness of the world.[9]

[8] *Reden*, 2nd ed., 85, 86, and 1st ed., 88. *Speeches*, 65, 66, 67.
[9] *Reden*, 88. Cf. *Speeches*, 67.

Schleiermacher echoes here the religious exclamation of the prophet Isaiah, struck not by the size or beauty of the heavens, merely, but by their sheer perfection:

> Lift up your eyes on high and see:
>   who created these?
> He who brings out their host by number,
>   calling them all by name;
> by the greatness of his might,
>   and because he is strong in power
>   *not one is missing.*
>   Isa 40:26 (RSV)

In his notes to the *Speeches* added at the time of their second revision in 1821, Schleiermacher explains his point further, and in such a way as to make explicit the Platonic mysticism intrinsic to his point of view:

> We do not feel ourselves dependent on the whole insofar as it is an aggregate of mutually conditioning parts of which we ourselves are one, but only insofar as underneath this coherence there is a unity conditioning all things, including our relation to all other parts of the whole. Only on this condition can the individual, as . . . a manifestation of the infinite, be so comprehended that its opposition to all else entirely vanishes.[10]

"The individual, as a manifestation of the infinite, so comprehended that its opposition to all else entirely vanishes": the mysticism Schleiermacher expresses in these words of 1821 is one of the most characteristic features of his *Speeches* of 1799. It is the immersion of individuality in the unity of the whole, the "giving up" of oneself "out of love to the universe," the "annihilation" of individuality in order "to live in the one and all" (above, p. 184). In the most sensuously mystical passage of his career, Schleiermacher writes:

> I lie on the bosom of the infinite world. I am in this moment its soul, for I feel its powers and its infinite life as I feel my own. In this moment it is my body, for I permeate its muscles and limbs as I do my own, and its innermost nerves, like my own, move in accordance with my sense and my presentiment.[11]

To appreciate fully the impact of this passage upon Schleiermacher's 1799 audience, especially upon his ecclesiastical elders, we must realize that in German the gender of "world" is feminine; thus the passage reads, "*she* is my body, for I permeate *her* muscles and limbs as I do my own," and so on.

Clearly this is no ascetic, world-denying mysticism. It is for Schleiermacher an emphatically positive aspect of religious consciousness. The mystical loss of oneself in the unity of the whole brings with it a new

---

[10] *Reden*, 137. *Speeches*, 106.
[11] *Reden*, 78–79. Cf. *Speeches*, 43.

and positive identity and strength. Mystical expansion of consciousness "alone gives a person universality," Schleiermacher writes—the universality for which ethics strives indefinitely and in vain.[12] In religious consciousness we take on identity with the universe. This "unlimited universality of sense," Schleiermacher writes, is "the first and original condition of religion."[13]

John Oman's English translation of the *Speeches* here renders the word "unlimited" (*unbeschränkt*) as "unconstrained." That is an appropriate translation. If religious consciousness is "unlimited universality of sense," then nothing lies outside its scope. Every event and object in the universe is dependent upon the trinitarian unity of origin, structure, and energy that is the object of religious consciousness. Nothing remains apart from this field of force that could determine intuitive religious consciousness to be other than what it is. There is nothing foreign that could constrain it. Recalling Schleiermacher's definition of freedom as the absence of foreign constraint, therefore, or Spinoza's definition of freedom as the absence of determination "by something else to exist and act in a certain determinate manner" (above, p. 137), we can understand what Schleiermacher means when he identifies religious consciousness with "unlimited freedom."[14]

Freedom in this religious context is an aspect of freedom we have not encountered before. Schleiermacher is saying that the highest degree of human freedom is not freedom in any of its ethical aspects of self-expression, appropriation, or self-cultivation, nor in all of these taken together as the goal of ethical life. The highest degree of human freedom is rather the mystical freedom of religious consciousness. This "unlimited freedom" is not a mode of acting, nor even of intending. It is rather a mode of expanded consciousness, in which a person identifies with the infinite dimensionality and fullness and unity of the universe.

Spinoza's *Ethics* suggests that God alone is comprehensively free in this sense, and that human freedom is always bound within the sphere of a person's opinions and desires. Yet Spinoza also glimpses a condition of "salvation, blessedness, or freedom" that he calls "the intellectual love of God."[15] Similarly Schleiermacher has in the *Speeches* a religious vision that bursts the sphere of individual knowledge and desire. He senses a state of consciousness expanded to mystical identification with the freedom of God. Seers of the eternal, he writes,

> with this wide vision and this feeling for the infinite, look also to that which lies outside their own sphere. They have the capacity for the most unlimited many-sidedness in judgment and contemplation, which is in

---

[12] *Reden*, 111. Cf. *Speeches*, 85.
[13] *Reden*, 188. *Speeches*, 154.
[14] *Reden*, 68. *Speeches*, 56.
[15] Spinoza, *Ethics*, Part V, Proposition XXXVI.

fact nowhere else to be found. Let anything else animate a person (I exclude neither ethics nor philosophy, and simply refer you to your own experience), and that to which his thinking and striving are directed draws a narrow circle around him. Inside it is enclosed all that is most important for him, and outside it everything appears common and unworthy. The person who thinks only systematically, who acts according to basic principle and aim and wishes to accomplish this or that in the world, unavoidably circumscribes himself and perpetually makes everything that does not further his activities an object of antipathy. Only the impulse to intuit—and this impulse, only when it is directed to the infinite—sets the mind and heart [*Gemüth*] in unlimited freedom; only religion rescues us from the ignoble fetters of opinion and desire.[16]

The sentence that follows this passage makes it clear that the mystical freedom of religion, no less than freedom in its ethical aspects, is not only compatible with determinism, but presupposes it: "All that is, is for religion necessary; and all that can be, is for religion a true and indispensable image of the infinite."[17] It is the paradox of Schleiermacher's mysticism that in "giving up" our ethical individuality and freedom to the deterministic unity of the universe, we gain the identity Schleiermacher describes here as the "unlimited freedom" of religious intuition—that in thus losing our life, we find it.

From at least the time of the *Speeches* onward, Schleiermacher never considers the issues of freedom and dependence separately. They are two sides of one issue. His way of speaking of this paradoxical inseparability of freedom and dependence, however, develops and undergoes modification after the first edition of the *Speeches*. We need to consider at least the direction of change that occurs in Schleiermacher's mystical notion of freedom, even though this will momentarily take us beyond the chronological limits of our study.

Not surprisingly, the general direction of change is toward greater moderation. Already in Schleiermacher's first revision of the *Speeches* of 1806, one sees that his romantic language of mystical surrender to the unity of the whole has begun to give way to language of reciprocal relation between the individual and the whole. In the *Speeches* of 1799, for example, we read, "In the infinite, all that is finite stands undisturbed beside each other; all is one, and all is true." In the *Speeches* of 1806, the same passage begins, "In *immediate relation to* the infinite. . . ." "Religion alone gives a person universality. . . ." in 1799, is changed to "religion alone *removes a person from one-sidedness and narrowness* . . ." in 1806. "Unlimited universality of sense" becomes "unlimited *generality* of sense."[18] And so on. Schleiermacher's concept of freedom as a mystical identification with the unity of the universe

[16] *Reden*, 68. *Speeches*, 56.
[17] Ibid.
[18] *Reden*, 67–68, 111, 188. *Speeches*, 56, 85, 154. In the final instance, Oman's English translation ignores the alteration.

gradually fades, along with the early romantic movement as a whole. His writings from later in his career still speak of losing oneself in the infinite, but they do so more and more in connection with the "devotional" feeling of absolute dependence, rather than with the "unlimited freedom" of mystical intuition. His lectures on *Psychology* of 1818–1834 are characteristic in this regard:

> What we mean by the term *devotion*, taken in its simplest and most general sense, is a . . . finding of oneself subordinated to another, a sinking, as it were, under the inexhaustibility of the object, and yet being absorbed by it again. It is a losing of self in the infinite, joined with the consciousness that here every reaction is completely inadmissible.[19]

The consciousness described here, the feeling of absolute dependence, is the central concept of *The Christian Faith* of 1821–22. At one moment of his existence, as a young romantic in 1799, Schleiermacher had a vision of mystical freedom as conscious identification with the unconstrained being of God. But the consciousness that persists through *every* moment of life, he writes in *The Christian Faith*, the consciousness that accompanies the *whole* of a person's existence, is "the consciousness that the whole of our self-activity is from elsewhere":

> The totality of our free inner movements, regarded as a unity, cannot be represented as an absolute feeling of freedom, because our whole existence does not present itself to our consciousness as having proceeded from our own activity. Therefore an absolute feeling of freedom has no place in any temporal being.[20]

This brings Schleiermacher to his definition of "the essence of piety: that we are conscious of ourselves as absolutely dependent, or, what is to say the same thing, as in relation to God."[21] Thus the positive mysticism of the *Speeches* and their vision of unlimited freedom appear by 1821 to be a thing of Schleiermacher's past, though the more general issue of freedom is not. His concept of freedom has brought Schleiermacher to the essence of his understanding of religious consciousness, albeit by the *via negativa*, the way of negation:

> The self-consciousness that accompanies our whole self-activity, and therefore, since the latter is never zero, accompanies our whole existence and negates absolute freedom, is itself precisely a consciousness of absolute dependence; for it is the consciousness that the whole of our own activity is from elsewhere, just as anything toward which we were to have a feeling of absolute freedom would have to proceed wholly from

---

[19]Schleiermacher, *Psychologie*, 211. Again I am indebted to Robert Williams' article of 1973 for calling this passage to my attention.
[20]*Der christliche Glaube*, Proposition 4.3.
[21]Ibid., Proposition 4.

ourselves. But without any feeling of freedom, a feeling of absolute dependence would not be possible.[22]

It would be incorrect to conclude from these modifications that Schleiermacher as an older man simply rejected the mysticism his *Speeches* of 1799 had expressed with such enthusiasm. We have seen Schleiermacher's assertion in *The Christian Faith* that unlimited freedom, such as that invoked by the mysticism of his *Speeches*, "has no place in any temporal being." But there remains the question of the moment at which a person's temporal life passes over into the eternal, the moment of death. In connection with the subject of death,[23] we find Schleiermacher's mysticism asserting itself at all stages of his career.

From the earliest days of his ministry, Schleiermacher was candid in confessing that death is a point beyond which he simply could not see, and he gently rejected orthodox images of life after death.[24] Christian belief, he writes in *The Christian Faith*,

> is naturally accompanied by an endeavor to form and hold fast an intuitive representation of the condidion of the personality after death. But we can make no claim that we shall succeed. . . . We are so generally aware of the connection of all our mental activities [*Geistestätigkeiten*], even our most inward and profound, with those of the body, that we cannot really attain to the representation of an individual, finite spiritual [*geistig*] life without that of an organic body. . . . Taking all these considerations together, we find that the various representations of the connection of the future life with the present cannot be pursued to any complete determination.[25]

In the absence of "any complete determination," Schleiermacher's mysticism comes to his service. Schleiermacher writes that, in the end, every philosophy "leads . . . to a mysticism" (above, p. 163), and death is such an end point, at which philosophy must fall silent and mystical vision may begin.

We see Schleiermacher's mysticism in connection with one of his close personal encounters with death, the death of his friend Ehrenfried von Willich. The young army chaplain von Willich and Schleiermacher first met in May of 1801, when Schleiermacher was accompanying Henriette Herz and her younger sister on a visit to the town of Prenzlau, a few miles outside Berlin. Markus Herz had stayed behind to care for some patients. The trio had come to visit another sister, Joanna, also married to a doctor Herz, no relation to Markus. When

[22]Ibid., Proposition 4.3.

[23]And the subject of birth as well: "Birth and death are points at which the perception is inescapable that our self is completely surrounded by the infinite" (*Reden*, 162. *Speeches*, 131).

[24]See my article, "Schleiermacher's Sermon at Nathanael's Grave," *The Journal of Religion*, LVII (January, 1977), 66, 74.

[25]*Der christliche Glaube*, Propositions 158.3, 161.1, 162.3.

Schleiermacher first met him, von Willich was very much in love with Joanna Herz. Schleiermacher, being older, having recently brought his own relation with Henriette Herz to a state of licit equilibrium, and being well schooled by the turmoil of his relation with Eleonore Grunow, assumed a role of counselor to von Willich in this relationship.[26] For his part, von Willich took the place of Friedrich Schlegel—who, with Dorothea Veit, had moved to Jena in the fall of 1800—as Schleiermacher's closest friend.[27] Von Willich was not Schlegel's intellectual equal. But he shared with Schleiermacher the finer inward sensibilities that had never resonated well with Schlegel. "In Willich," Schleiermacher wrote to his sister, "I have found a truly hearty friend, who loves me greatly, who both shares and understands all that goes on in me, and in whom I find so much that is beautiful and good that we are quite inwardly and mutually joined together."[28] Upon separating after their initial three days' acquaintance in Prenzlau, the two men became frequent and intimate correspondents.

In time von Willich and Joanna Herz loosened their attachment, and in September of 1804, von Willich married Henriette Sophie Charlotte von Mühlenfels. It was a marriage of warmth and mutuality. Schleiermacher assumed a fatherly relation toward his friend's young bride, only sixteen years old and an orphan since early in life. Henriette and Schleiermacher entered upon their own regular exchange of tender correspondence,[29] little realizing that in 1809 they were themselves to become husband and wife. For in February of 1807, during the Napoleonic seige of Stralsund where the von Willichs were living, Ehrenfried died in an epidemic of typhus, and in the succeeding two years, Henriette and Schleiermacher discovered their love outgrowing its former limits.

In the midst of her grief over Ehrenfried's death, Henriette—now eighteen, the mother of an infant daughter, and seven months pregnant with a son—implores her "Father Schleier" for solace and assurance:

> I shall endure this life as long as nature wills it, for I still have to manage for our children, his and mine. But, O God, with what yearning, with what foretaste of inexpressible bliss I look beyond to that world where he lives. What joy for me to die. Schleier! shall I not find him again? O my God, Schleier, I ask you by all that is dear and holy to you, give me if you can the certainty that I shall find him and recognize him again. Tell

[26]See Heinrich Meisner, ed., *Briefe Friedrich Schleiermachers an Ehrenfried und Henriette von Willich geb. von Mühlenfels, 1801–1806*, 16–23, 27, 29–30.

[27]Took Schlegel's place literally. For two weeks in February, 1802, von Willich lived in Schleiermacher's quarters in Berlin. "That I gain more enjoyment from him than from Schlegel you can well imagine," Schleiermacher wrote his sister. *Br.* I, 291.

[28]Letter to Charlotte, July 1, 1801. *Br.* I, 272.

[29]Collected by Heinrich Meisner in *Friedrich Schleiermachers Briefwechsel mit seiner Braut*.

me your innermost belief about this, dear Schleier—O, if this belief sinks, I am annihilated. For this I live; for this I endure with resignation and serenity. It is the only thing to which I look forward, which alone casts light upon my darkened life—again to find *him*, again to live for him, again to make him happy. O God, it is not possible, it cannot be destroyed; it is only interrupted. O Schleier, speak to my poor heart. Tell me what you believe. . . . Stand by me. Do you know when the pain grasps me most bitterly? It is when I think that in the future life there will remain nothing of the old . . . , when I think that his soul is dissolved, wholly merged in the great All—that the old will not again be recognized—that it is all over, our sweet life is all over—O Schleier, this I cannot bear—O speak to me, my Dear, my Dear.[30]

Schleiermacher responded to Henriette's anguished plea with the combination of sympathy and candor characteristic of all his correspondence:

My poor, dear, sweet child. Could I but press thee weeping to my heart! For I too am weeping bitter, scalding tears, and we would let them mingle. O, to see so sweet a happiness destroyed; you know how my heart participated in it. Yet you set me such a beautiful example. Your grief is so pure and holy that there is nothing in it your father could wish away. So let us count this grief among the most beautiful possessions of our lives, and love it as we love him who is dead, and submit serenely and sadly to the eternal and holy order of God. You appeal to me to destroy your doubts, as you say. Yet in truth you only wish me to confirm the unsettled images of your painfully suffering phantasy. Dear Jette, what can I say to you? Certainty with respect to what lies beyond this life is not granted us. Understand me rightly; I mean that there is no certainty for the phantasy, which wants to picture things in distinct images. But otherwise it is the greatest certainty—and nothing would be certain if this were not—that there is no death, no destruction for the spirit [*Geist*]. Personal life, however, is not the essence of the spirit; it is only an appearance. How this is repeated we do not know. We can know nothing about that; we can only poeticize. But in your grief let your pious, living phantasy poeticize on all sides, and do not restrain it. For it is pious; it can wish nothing that would be against the eternal order of God, and so all that it poeticizes will be true, if you tranquilly give it free rein.[31]

There can be no doubt that Schleiermacher tried to respond to Henriette's plea for assurance with all the support he could muster. Yet we see in his reply the departure of Schleiermacher's beliefs from traditional Christian dogma; we see the philosophy of resignation that fills the vacuums in his orthodoxy; we see his attribution of traditional religious consolations to what he calls the "poeticizing" of a "pious, living phantasy." These will all be themes for Part III of our study.

We also see in Schleiermacher's letter, however, that his ultimate

[30]Letter of Mar. 13, 1807. *Br*. II, 86–88. Henriette's emphasis.
[31]Letter of Mar. 25, 1807. *Br*. II, 88–89.

source of personal consolation in the face of death is the religious mysticism that has been our closing theme in Part II:

> If your phantasy presents you with the image of being merged in the great All, do not let yourself be seized by any harsh or bitter pain. Only think of it not as dead, but as living, and as the highest life. Indeed it is that to which we all aspire in this life, only never to reach it—to live in the whole alone, and to set aside the illusion that we are or could be something distinct and separate. If then Ehrenfried now lives in God and you love him eternally in God, as you knew and loved God in him, can you think of anything more glorious and beautiful? Is that not the highest goal of love, in comparison with which all that depends only on personal life, and proceeds from it alone, is as nothing?[32]

Schleiermacher's personal confession of belief to Henriette in 1807 is an echo of the mystical exhortation of his *Speeches* of 1799:

> Seek then to give up your life out of love to the universe. Strive accordingly in this life to annihilate your individuality and to live in the one and all; strive to be more than yourself, so that if you lose yourself, you lose but little. And when you have flowed together with the universe—as much of it as you find here—and a greater and more holy yearning has arisen in you, then we shall speak further of the hopes death gives us, and of the infinity to which, through death, we unfailingly soar.[33]

Schleiermacher reworked this passage in each subsequent edition of the *Speeches*. But even in the final edition of 1831, the only substantial alteration is the substitution of "God" for "universe." There is no diminution of the *Speeches'* fundamental sense and taste for the infinite, no attenuation of the mystical spirit of yearning for identification with the unlimited freedom of God.

[32]Ibid., 89.
[33]*Reden*, 132. Cf. *Speeches*, 100–101.

Part III. Phantasy (1800–1804)

Chapter 1. Religious Phantasy and Religious Orthodoxy

> *I hope you will not take it as blasphemy that belief in God depends upon the direction of phantasy. You know that phantasy is the highest and most original in a person, and that apart from phantasy all is only reflection upon it. You know that it is your phantasy that creates your world for you, and that you can have no God without a world.*

A major subject for Part III of our study will be Schleiermacher's conception of phantasy — its role in ethical life and its relation to the concepts of determinism and freedom we have explored in Parts I and II. Our principal source will be Schleiermacher's *Soliloquies* of 1800. That book together with the course of Schleiermacher's life during the years surrounding its publication reveals Schleiermacher's ethical character as perhaps no other work or period is able to do, and Schleiermacher's ethical character will be the second major subject of Part III. Before we take up these principal subjects, however, we must consider phantasy as Schleiermacher first puts the concept to use in the *Speeches*, where he introduces phantasy in a religious rather than an ethical context. Thus our subject for this first chapter of Part III is Schleiermacher's conception of the role of phantasy in religious life, examined in the light of Schleiermacher's attitude toward religious orthodoxy.

Schleiermacher's vision of mystical or "unlimited" freedom with which we ended Part II brings his *Speeches* near to both a Promethean deificaton of humankind and a Spinozistic deification of the universe. Neither, as we have seen from Sack's letter to Schleiermacher (above, pp. 116–119), was accepted by Schleiermacher's overseers as compatible with Christian orthodoxy. In a first reaction to the *Speeches*, which must have required considerable self-restraint, Sack called them "too original." Schleiermacher reacted to Sack's charge in a letter to Henriette Herz: "That is some theological dictum! My Christianity is in actuality very old."[1] This disagreement between Schleiermacher and Sack raises our first questions for this chapter: To what extent did Schleiermacher recognize that he was engaged in a reinterpretation of traditional doctrines? How self-conscious was his novel, epoch-making attitude toward Christian orthodoxy?

---

[1]Apr. 10, 1799. *Br.* I, 215.

We need to sketch a bit of background against which to place these questions. On the first page of the *Speeches* Schleiermacher writes that "from of old, faith has not been everyone's thing" (see above, p. 149). On the face of it, there is nothing particularly controversial in that observation. But in the succeeding sentences Schleiermacher reverses superficial expectations. The reader quickly discovers that Schleiermacher is not referring to the traditionally "irreligious"—to those who fail to subscribe to this or that formal religion—but on the contrary, to the very persons who "juggle the trappings" of traditional religion.[2] Those whose "thing" religion has not been, in other words, are in Schleiermacher's opinion the "virtuosos" of ecclesiasticism—the orthodox, preoccupied with the details of their religiosity.

It is little wonder, then, that these *Speeches* disquieted the ecclesiastical hierarchy. But it is no wonder either that Schleiermacher makes the assertion he does. We have seen already that skepticism with regard to religious orthodoxy was rooted deeply in his nature (see above, p. 15). His earliest letters abundantly show this, especially his letters to Brinkmann, who seems always to have drawn out irreverent tendencies in Schleiermacher's disposition. In 1789, while Schleiermacher was living with the family of his uncle Stubenrauch in Drossen (above, p. 9), he described his uncle's Christology to Brinkmann in these almost flippant terms:

> All the little matters concerning the substitutionary death and so forth he has of course long since rejected. Christ still appears to him in a certain supernatural light—but that too is now yielding little by little, and in reference to our age he considers the whole thing only as a means of representing to the people their duties in a more effective and persuasive way.[3]

The Berlin theological examinations for which Schleiermacher was preparing during his stay at Drossen suffer outright ridicule in his letters of the time:

> Of my activities here there is next to nothing to say; I vegetate more than I learn, and I forget more than I study. If I *do* study something it is theological rubbish, with which I am again becoming acquainted because, God willing, I will have myself examined in Berlin. A nauseating realization. And yet a lot depends on it. All I need is to have this examination come off unhappily, and I can see myself . . . compelled to sign up with the first bear dance troop that comes through Drossen—as bagpiper, since my lungs are still passable.[4]

---

[2] *Reden*, 1. *Speeches*, 1.
[3] Letter of July 22, 1789. *Br.* IV, 16.
[4] Letter to Brinkmann, Dec. 9, 1789. *Br.* IV, 42. The reference to his lungs reflects Schleiermacher's lifelong fear that he was developing tuberculosis.

Two months nearer his examination deadline, Schleiermacher writes that he is afraid he will simply lose his stage presence "if I am forced to preach and give answers concerning theological subtleties that in my heart I *mock* [*verlachen*]."[5]

While in Berlin for his first series of theological examinations in May, 1790, Schleiermacher was surprised by a letter from his father—who had so severely condemned Schleiermacher's doubts some three years before (above, p. 8)—confessing that he too shared the reservations toward orthodox doctrines that Schleiermacher had detected in his uncle Stubenrauch:

> I once preached for at least twelve years as an actual unbeliever. I was at that time fully convinced that Jesus had accommodated his speech to the notions and even to the biases of the Jews, and this opinion led me to believe that I ought to be *equally* modest toward popular doctrine. I could never have allowed myself to dispute the article concerning the divinity of Jesus and his atonement, because I knew from the history of the church and from my own experience with other people that since the beginning of Christianity this doctrine had brought comfort and improvement of life to millions, and I used to apply it to morality and love for God and man whenever the theme allowed it, even though I was not myself convinced of its truth. I wish that even if you cannot convince yourself of the rectitude of this manner of proceeding, you will at least never want to dispute that doctrine publicly.[6]

One cannot read many of these early letters and still theorize that Schleiermacher was naively unaware of the radical reinterpretation of Christian tradition in which he engaged throughout his career. The romantic poet Jean Paul Richter was perhaps the first to advance this mistaken theory, though not by any means the last. Jean Paul, as he was known, never took to Schleiermacher personally, nor Schleiermacher to him, though they came into contact in the Berlin circle. But Jean Paul admired Schleiermacher's *Speeches* and *Soliloquies*. In 1800 he wrote of the author of the "otherwise excellent" *Speeches*: "He gives the word 'religion' a new, imprecise, poetic significance. *Without his knowledge*, however, it is based upon the old theological significance."[7] Schleiermacher scoffed at Jean Paul's comment. The *Speeches* may have many faults, he wrote to Brinkmann. But anyone should be able to see that their relation to traditional theology is "quite precise." Nothing in the *Speeches*, Schleiermacher insists, "nothing has come to pass without my consciousness."[8]

---

[5]Letter to Brinkmann, Feb. 3, 1790. *Br.* IV, 47. Schleiermacher's emphasis.
[6]Letter to Schleiermacher from his father, May 7, 1790. *Br.* I, 84. The elder Schleiermacher's emphasis.
[7]Quoted in an editor's note, *Br.* IV, 70. Emphasis added.
[8]June 9, 1800. *Br.* IV, 70.

Jean Paul in 1800 suggested that Schleiermacher was unaware of how the new language of his *Speeches* corresponds with Christian tradition. H. G. Schenk, in a recent view of Schleiermacher that appears to be equally mistaken but in the opposite direction, writes that "*in spite of his contrary intentions*, Schleiermacher called into question the decisive presuppositions of Christian theology."[9] It was not Schleiermacher who called Christian tradition into question, however. He found Christian tradition already called into question by the criticism and skepticism that were predominant elements in the intellectual atmosphere of his age — the atmosphere breathed not only by Schleiermacher, but by his father and his uncle Stubenrauch as well. Schleiermacher's task in the *Speeches* is to reinterpret Christianity to cultured despisers who have been immunized against traditional religion by their immersion in this infectious atmosphere. Later, in *The Christian Faith*, his task will be to reinterpret Christianity to a church being permeated by that same atmosphere.

In 1799, it was natural that Sack, with his churchman's resistance to skeptical infection, had difficulty comprehending "how a man who adheres to such a system" as that of the *Speeches* could be "an honest teacher of Christianity."[10] Schleiermacher for his part could not comprehend how any conscientious teacher of Christianity could fail to attempt a reinterpretation of the letter of orthodox doctrine to the spirit of his own generation. In his epistle to Schleiermacher concerning the *Speeches* Sack writes:

> Perhaps without my knowing it you have formed a basic principle according to which you do not consider it improper to use words designating religious objects even though you consider the sense that common usage has attached to them to be nonsense. According to the cleverness of some of the new philosophers, it is allowable and expedient to grant the words "God," "religion," "providence," "future life" their place a while longer, and then to subordinate them little by little to other concepts, until one needs them no longer and, without any danger, can let them go.[11]

---

[9] *The Mind of the European Romantics*, 115. Emphasis added. Schenk is following the opinion of Karl Barth here. See for example Barth, *Protestant Thought: From Rousseau to Ritschl*, tr. Brian Cozens, 354: "The question as to how it was that Schleiermacher himself . . . could think—as he did in fact think—that he was not destroying Reformation theology, but taking up and continuing it in a way suited to his time; how he failed to notice that his result challenged the decisive premise of all Christian theology . . . —this question presents us with a mystery which cannot be solved." But this mystery is largely a phantom of Barth's own neo-orthodox assumptions that Schleiermacher's theology was in fact destructive, and that he was oblivious to the consequences of his theological reinterpretation. Expose these assumptions to the light of Schleiermacher's biography, it seems to me, and much of the "mystery" vanishes.

[10] Letter to Schleiermacher from Sack, *Br.* III, 277.

[11] Ibid., 278.

Schleiermacher does not consider religious terms "nonsense," and he does not intend to "let them go." But Sack is correct in identifying a basic principle of reinterpretation underlying Schleiermacher's work. In his 1821 "Explanations" to the *Speeches* Schleiermacher makes that principle explicit:

> It is evident that in the largest sense the ages are distinguished by the letter, and it is the masterwork of the highest human wisdom to assess correctly when human conditions require a new letter. For if it appears too early, then it is rejected by the still prevailing love for that which was to have been supplanted. If it formulates itself too late, then a fraudulence will have already set in which it can no longer exorcize.[12]

Schleiermacher's career was dedicated to the self-conscious pursuit of this "masterwork" of human wisdom, the reinterpretation of the letter of religion in the spirit of the age.

Among the first to appreciate both the need for this pursuit in his age and the degree of its success in Schleiermacher's *Speeches* was Schlegel. "There is nothing greater to be said in praise of Christianity," he wrote in 1800, "either in our age or in any other, than that the author of the *Speeches on Religion* is a Christian."[13] A year earlier he had written of the *Speeches*:

> *Religion*, in the sense that the author takes it . . . is one of those things of which our age has lost the very concept, and which must be *rediscovered* anew before one can understand *that* and *how*, in other forms, it was already present in ancient times as well.[14]

This is what Schleiermacher means when he writes in response to Jean Paul that the relation of his *Speeches* to traditional theology is "quite precise." Sack found Schleiermacher's "rediscovery" of traditional theology "too original," and from Sack's perspective no doubt it was. But Schleiermacher—younger than Sack, temperamentally more skeptical, and a member of a generation both more enlightened and more critical—was more concerned over the opposite extreme: that if theology waits too late to reformulate itself, "then a fraudulence will have already set in which it can no longer exorcise." Thus one sees the source of Schleiermacher's lifelong intolerance for theological literalism. The epithet *Buchstabentheologen*, "theologians of the letter," stands out repeatedly in his early writings. Intensified by such modifiers as *todt*, "dead,"[15] it sometimes takes on the force of an outright malediction—a blunt opposite to the "living" leitmotif that established the basic tonality of Schleiermacher's *Speeches* (above, p. 133).

[12] *Reden*, 177. *Speeches*, 144.
[13] Schlegel, "Ideen," *Athenaeum*, III/1 (1800), 24.
[14] Schlegel, "Reden über die Religion," *Athenaeum*, II/2 (1799), 289. Schlegel's emphases.
[15] *Reden*, 68. *Speeches*, 55.

In summary, just as it was not the literal system of Spinoza that Schleiermacher revitalized in the *Speeches* but rather the living spirit of Spinoza's philosophy, so it was not the letter of traditional theology but its living spirit that he hoped to reawaken in his generation's cultured despisers of religion. In what might stand as a motto for his lifework as an interpreter of Christian religion, Schleiermacher writes to Henriette and Ehrenfried von Willich:

> If in those spirits [*Gemüther*] who have been led astray by foolish disputes over the letter and by the dialectical impudence of empty ratiocination, one could only bring the idea home always to the heart, then it would be a miracle if one could not win friends for Christianity.[16]

Schleiermacher's efforts in this direction were rewarded with misunderstanding on many sides. Schleiermacher accepted this as in part unavoidable. "Some of the misunderstandings that have greeted this book in such wondrous variety," he writes to Brinkmann in the Dedication to the second edition of the *Speeches*,

> may have been occasioned by its imperfections, and these may now be remedied. But nothing would distress me more than to find that in the new judgments made of this book, the great misunderstanding no longer arose that has so often amused us: namely, that our way of thinking is always held by unbelievers to be enthusiasm, but by the superstitious and those who find themselves in servitude to the letter to be unbelief. For if my book should no longer bear this stamp, then I shall not have improved but rather wholly disfigured it.[17]

The hope Schleiermacher expresses here—that he had not refined away this central "great misunderstanding"—was not disappointed. In his 1821 Preface to the third edition of the *Speeches* we find him speaking still of his readers who "almost in one breath accuse me of Spinozism and Herrnhutianism, atheism and mysticism."[18]

Thus Sack asked in 1799, What right does Schleiermacher have to substitute "intuition of the universe" for adoration of the Deity worshiped in the congregations of Christendom? Some of Schleiermacher's friends among the cultured despisers of religion, on the other hand, put the question to him in reverse: Why does one need to speak of a Deity at all, since the notion of "sense and taste for the infinite" seems to exhaust the essence of religion?

Schleiermacher's answer to these questions—and essentially the same answer pertains to both extremes of the spectrum from belief to

---

[16]Letter of Oct. 30, 1804. *Br.* II, 10.

[17]*Reden*, x–xi.

[18]*Reden*, xiv. "Herrnhutianism": a synonym for "Moravian," from *Herrnhut* (lit. "the Lord's keeping"), the name of the Moravian settlement on the estate of Count Zinzendorf in Saxony, founded in 1722.

unbelief—contributes as much as any other factor toward explaining why the *Speeches* endeared Schleiermacher to the young romantic movement whom they addressed, and alienated him from the ecclesiastical colleagues to whom the author of the *Speeches* had found it necessary to remain "incognito" (above, p. 115). Schleiermacher concedes that a person who intuits the universe in the religious sense he has described may in fact do without a concept of God and yet be pious. For whether or not a person "joins God to his intuition," he writes, "depends upon the direction of his phantasy." Then, with more than a trace of condescension that to Sack may have seemed close to impudence, Schleiermacher adds:

> I hope that you will not take it as blasphemy that belief in God depends upon the direction of phantasy. You know that phantasy is the highest and most original in a person, and that apart from phantasy all is only reflection upon it. You know that it is your phantasy that creates your world for you, and that you can have no God without a world.[19]

Schlegel immediately picked up this romantic exaltation of phantasy in Schleiermacher's *Speeches* and called it to the attention of the readers of the *Athenaeum*: "The understanding, says the author of the *Speeches on Religion*, knows only of the universe; if fantasy rules, then you have a God. Quite so: fantasy is the human organ for divinity."[20] How seriously Schleiermacher himself took phantasy to be "the human organ for divinity" we have already seen in his letter of consolation to Henriette von Willich after the death of her husband Ehrenfried: "In your holy grief let your pious, living phantasy poeticize on all sides, and do not restrain it. For it *is* pious; it can wish nothing that would be against the eternal order of God, and so all that it poeticizes will be true, if you tranquilly give it free rein" (above, p. 203).

With this 1799 exaltation of phantasy[21] we are a long way from the

---

[19] *Reden*, 127–28. Cf. *Speeches*, 97–98.

[20] Schlegel, "Ideen," *Athenaeum*, III/1 (1800), 5. On the preceding page Schlegel had hinted strongly at Schleiermacher's identity as the author of the anonymous *Speeches* by a heavy-handed play on his name: "Already there is even speech about religion. It is time to rend the veil [*Schleier*] of Isis and reveal the secret."

[21] In the *Speeches* Schleiermacher spells the term *Phantasie*; in the *Soliloquies*, *Fantasie*. Possibly this change was a result of Schlegel's decision in the interim to use the latter spelling in the orthography of the journal *Athenaeum*. Schlegel explains: "*Fantastic, fantasy* I have written with an 'f,' because to me these words, as we use them, are not really Greek, but appear romantic and modern throughout" (quoted by Ernst Behler, *Athenäum: Die Geschichte einer Zeitschrift*, 21). Yet in the treatise *On Human Freedom* Schleiermacher had spelled the term with an "f," while in the 1807 letter of consolation to Henriette von Willich he spells it again with a "ph." Probably the spelling is of no significance; Schleiermacher wasted precious little of his time on orthographical details. When using the term myself I write *phantasy*, simply to avoid an unpleasant alliteration in my book's subtitle. When quoting Schleiermacher's words I use *fantasy* or *phantasy*, whichever corresponds to Schleiermacher's German.

Schleiermacher of 1792—the young rationalist who on his twenty-fourth birthday had declared, "The time of youth lies behind me; the dominion of phantasy comes to an end."[22] This birthday resolution is representative of Schleiermacher's use of the term *phantasy* before his move to Berlin in 1796. In the 1791–92 treatise *On Human Freedom* Schleiermacher uses *Fantasie* to designate the mental capacity "upon which every association of ideas depends."[23] This definition of phantasy persists in Schleiermacher's thinking throughout his career. To define phantasy in this way—as what philosophers had traditionally called the faculty of the association of ideas[24]—was of course to give it great potential importance. We shall presently see that the potential was fully realize in Schleiermacher's later writings.

As a younger man, however, Schleiermacher seems to have felt that in both religious experience and ethical analysis, phantasy deserved little attention. He associated phantasy with the mystical religious transports of Moravian piety, from which, in his skeptical decade from the mid-1780s to the mid-1790s, he discovered he was alienated. Writing in 1794 of his childhood among the Moravians, Schleiermacher diagnoses his religious doubts at age fourteen in the following terms:

> In vain I strove for supernatural feelings. I was convinced of their necessity by every look at myself in relation to the doctrine of a coming state of retribution, and I was persuaded of their reality *apart from me* by every utterance and every hymn, indeed by every expression of these people, so persuasive of such a mood. From *me alone* these feelings appeared to flee. For whenever I believed I had caught even a shadow of them, it soon revealed itself as my own work, as an unfruitful straining of my phantasy.[25]

The transcendent religious experiences that were so intimate a part of the Moravian inner life of the soul were an important influence upon Schleiermacher as a child. In later life he fully realized this. In 1802 he confesses to his friend Georg Reimer that he is again a Moravian, "only of a higher order."[26] But it appears that as a young person he realized the importance of such experiences scarcely at all. He discredited his early mystical strivings as simply misleading and "unfruitful" phantasies. He seems to have harbored some of the suspicion of phantasy that Blaise Pascal had expressed toward "imagination" in his seventeenth-century *Pensées*:

---

[22]Schleiermacher, *Über den Werth des Lebens*, "Denkmale," 51. Dilthey argues the probability of the birthday date in "Denkmale," 47.

[23]MS. 24

[24]See in this connection the discussion of Locke's theory of the association of ideas in Ernest Lee Tuveson, *The Imagination as a Means of Grace*, esp. 39–40.

[25]"Selbstbiographie," *Br.* I, 7–8. Schleiermacher's emphases.

[26]Letter of Apr. 30, 1802. *Br.* I, 294.

> It is that deceitful part in man, that mistress of error and falsity, the more deceptive in that she is not always so; for she would be an infallible rule of truth, if she were an infallible rule of falsehood. But being most generally false, she gives no sign of her nature, impressing the same character on the true and the false.[27]

In a letter of 1792, Schleiermacher's uncle Stubenrauch, with his characteristic sympathy, tries to reassure his nephew that he need not fear what Schleiermacher was calling the "wantonness" of his phantasy.[28] Five years earlier Stubenrauch had felt it necessary to caution his nephew against excessive rationalism and its consequent poetic deficiency: "I almost fear that with your good progress in mathematics, the doubts of which you complain may perhaps arise from the fact that you seek in the truths and propositions of theology the same certainty as obtains in the propositions of mathematics."[29] The positive role of phantasy, insofar as the young Schleiermacher thought it had any positive role, seems to have been simply to rescue him from the realities of the actual world. In 1789, for example, longing for escape from the pressures of his impending theological examinations, Schleiermacher wrote to Brinkmann of his losing struggle to picture a life after death: "My phantasy — which is usually quite obedient to me when I command it to make me a pleasant illusion outside the sphere of this life, often just as colorful as I wish — is like a balking horse and absolutely will not leap over this point."[30]

By the time of the third of his treatises of 1791–93, however, the rationalist in Schleiermacher was already beginning to yield to the romantic. We can see these two protagonists of his temperament contending in the treatise, *On the Worth of Life*, where Schleiermacher again discusses life after death. The idea of personal survival is at one moment knocked down by rational "understanding" (*Verstand*), he writes, only to be righted again by "the eternal vibrations of phantasy" (*die ewigen Schwingungen der Phantasie*).[31] It is in this treatise that Schleiermacher begins to use the term *phantasy* positively to refer to the associative, or creative and unifying, function of all thinking:

> Deep in me I feel the tender idea of the beautiful and all that is related to it. With respect to the regular organic forms of nature that in themselves comprise a whole, I first take delight in the consciousness of their laws and their gradual unfolding. But for me the highest pleasure lies in the irregular forms, in the gathering up of such things as *can be united in a whole only through phantasy and the association of ideas*.[32]

[27]Pascal, *Pensées*, tr. W. F. Trotter, #82, p. 186.
[28]Letter to Schleiermacher, July 20, 1792. *Br.* III, 48.
[29]Letter to Schleiermacher, Feb. 17, 1787. *Br.* I, 56.
[30]Dec. 9, 1789. *Br.* IV, 43.
[31]"Denkmale," 52.
[32]Ibid., 54. Emphasis added.

This passage is Schleiermacher's first step toward the romantic concept of creative phantasy. Wordsworth was to publish that concept in his *Lines Composed a Few Miles above Tintern Abbey* of 1798, where he observes that our world is a world we only half perceive and "half create" (1.106).[33] In 1799, Schleiermacher was to carry Wordsworth's observation one step further in his own, more extreme assertion in the *Speeches* that "it is your phantasy that creates your world for you" (above, p. 213). Later we shall follow this development in detail. Here we may simply observe that while Schleiermacher's companionship with the Berlin romantics provided the occasion for the flourishing of his positive conception of phantasy, it was not the occasion of its birth. The concept originates for Schleiermacher in his treatise of 1793. The early romantics learned from the appreciation of phantasy Schleiermacher brought with him to Berlin in 1796, even as they contributed to its further development.

The exaltation of poetic phantasy was the characteristic response of the Berlin romantic circle to the rhetorical question Schleiermacher asks of Kant: "What will Kant do when someone comes and says that he would like to be *more* than reasonable?" (above, p. 156). Novalis, for example, writes in his novel *Heinrich von Ofterdingen*:

> If I understand things rightly, it appears to me that an historian must necessarily be a poet as well, for only the poet may understand the art of combining occurrences appropriately. In their tales and fables I have noticed with quiet pleasure their tender feel for the mysterious spirit of life. There is more truth in their fairy tales than in scholarly chronicles.[34]

What Novalis says of poetry's place in the writing of history, Schleiermacher says of poetry's place in theology. Of Jacobi's theology, for example, Schleiermacher writes:

> Does Jacobi then want to get by without poetry? And does he not recognize that he always maintains poetic forms, even when the content of his philosophy does not poeticize? Then a great hope sinks in me. For I had concluded the contrary: that he knows full well that even with respect to content he poeticizes, and holds his God to be a poetic product, not a work of plastic metaphysics. He could be taken more seriously this way. What then does he understand by his *faith*, if it is not poetry?[35]

We have seen that in the *Speeches* Schleiermacher "enjoys" Spinoza's pantheism in this poetic sense (above, p. 122). He takes Spinoza's vision of God from the realm of "plastic metaphysics" and reassigns it to the realm of religious phantasy. This reassignment is in fact a

---

[33]See also Wordsworth's "The Recluse" of 1800, 11.819–24.

[34]Novalis, *Heinrich von Oftendingen*, Ch. 5, 115.

[35]Letter to Brinkmann, Dec. 14, 1803. *Br*. IV, 93–94. Schleiermacher's emphasis.

promotion, since the *Speeches* plainly assert that "phantasy is the highest and most original in a person" (above, p. 213). Schleiermacher appropriated orthodox concepts of God in this same poetic way. Around the time of the *Speeches* Schleiermacher came to believe that no concept of God, be it Spinoza's or that of one of the church fathers, is uninfluenced by the poetic phantasy of the individual whose concept it is. Schleiermacher's own notion of the "unlimited freedom" of God (above, p. 199) is no exception. Schleiermacher admits that not everyone's religious phantasy will be directed toward the same idea:

> In religion the universe is intuited; it is posited as originally active upon man. Now if your phantasy depends upon the consciousness of your freedom, so that what it thinks of as originally efficacious it cannot avoid thinking of in the form of a free being, then very well: your phantasy will therefore personify the spirit of the universe and you will have a God. If your phantasy depends upon the understanding [*Verstand*], so that it is always clear to you that freedom has a meaning only in individuals and for the individual, then very well: you will have a world and no God.[36]

Even in this latter case, however, there is no room for epistemological complacency. Suppose a person does not speak of "God" (Schleiermacher scarcely does so himself in the *Speeches*' first edition), but only of the "world." Still "world," or "universe," or the "one and all" of Lessing[37] all present conceptualizations in which creative phantasy has been at work. The concept Schleiermacher found to express religious intuition in his *Speeches* of 1799 is "unlimited freedom"—mystical identification in consciousness with the comprehensive freedom of the universe, understood very much as Spinoza understood God. Schleiermacher makes no claim of inevitability for his conceptualization, no claim that it represents definitive knowledge. Its justification is that it expresses the religious intuition Schleiermacher senses, in accordance with the direction of his phantasy. It is the free expression of the association of ideas stimulated by his own sense and taste for the infinite.

Let us summarize. Schleiermacher believed that religious consciousness is grounded in intuition that is ultimately passive. This fundamental intuition constitutes the objectivity of religious experience. But conceptual reflection can never catch this original religious intuition in its "pure" state (see above, pp. 152 and 199–200). In every conceptualization, phantasy, as a person's faculty of the association of ideas, has already been at work:

---

[36] *Reden*, 128.

[37] Above, p. 120. We learn from Jacobi that Moses Mendelssohn was fond of chiding suspected Spinozists by calling them *All Einern*, "all-one-ers." Jacobi, *Über die Lehre des Spinoza*, 99.

> Attempt with me to descend into the innermost sanctuary of life. . . .
> There alone you find the original relation of intuition and feeling. . . .
> You must learn how to listen to yourself, as it were, before conscious-
> ness. . . . It is the origination of your consciousness that you must notice,
> not a reflection upon something already there. For as soon as you have
> made any given definite activity of your soul an object of communication
> or of contemplation, you have already begun to divide, and your thinking
> can comprehend only that which is separated. Therefore my speech can
> lead you to no definite example. Precisely because this moment is a
> unity, that which my speech would adduce is already past.[38]

Yet Schleiermacher recognizes also that we cannot indefinitely supress
the need to articulate the religious intuition we sense. *Fühlt man es, so
muss man es sagen wollen*, Schlegel writes in his novel *Lucinde*: "If one
feels it, one shall want to say it."[39] Schleiermacher agrees: "A person
wants witnesses for that which enters into his senses; he wants participants in that which stirs his feelings. . . . Urged on by his nature, the
religious person necessarily speaks."[40]

Thus we arrive at a central and remarkable principle of Schleiermacher's theology. "Faith," he writes in his Journal, "is the unsatisfied
yearning of reason after phantasy."[41] This regulative principle of religious faith and theological knowledge, the seeds of which we first come
upon in the *Speeches* of 1799, will serve as a fundamental principle of
The Christian Faith. In the second revision of the *Speeches*, done as he
was working on *The Christian Faith* in 1821, Schleiermacher states his
theological principle in these terms:

> Recoil before the obscurity of indeterminate thought is the one direction
> of phantasy, and recoil before the appearance of contradiction when we
> lend the forms of the finite to the infinite is the other. Now should not
> the same inwardness of religion be joined with the one and with the
> other?[42]

Theology, then, is the art of saying neither too much of God nor too
little. The tension between these two "directions" of religious phantasy
provides the sustaining energy for Schleiermacher's great dogmatic
theology, *The Christian Faith*, which has secured his place in the history
of Christian thought.

[38] *Reden*, 2nd ed., 53.
[39] *Lucinde*, "Dithyrambische Fantasie über die schönste Situation," 15.
[40] *Reden*, 181–82. Cf. *Speeches*, 148–49.
[41] *Der Glaube ist die unbefriedigte Sehnsucht der Vernunft nach der Phantasie*. "Denkmale,"
138.
[42] *Reden*, 129. *Speeches*, 98.

Chapter 2. Religious Realism and Ethical Idealism

Oscillation is truly the general form of all finite existence. . . . We cannot ever escape the antithesis between the ideal and the real.

We transfer the focus of our attention now from Schleiermacher's *Speeches* to his *Soliloquies*. We shall begin in this chapter with a word about the contrasting fundamental philosophies underlying the two books. This is necessary background to what follows, and yet it is background. As with the *Speeches* (above, p. 123), Schleiermacher chose not to bring the metaphysical background of the *Soliloquies* to the fore, and for even better reasons.

The *Soliloquies* are hastily written and were described by Schleiermacher himself as "somewhat obscure."[1] He published the book anonymously, at the beginning of the new century in 1800. (The *Soliloquies* bear the subtitle *A New Year's Gift*.) Soon after receiving a copy, Brinkmann wrote to tell Schleiermacher of

> a judgment I am hearing these days: "Everyone can clearly see that a preacher has written it who cannot speak his opinion freely, lest it ruin him with his church party. He has thus cloaked himself in obscurity, in order that nothing may be held against him."[2]

We have seen enough of Schleiermacher's departures from orthodoxy to realize that there may have been truth in the judgment Brinkmann reports. At least the charge of obscurity is justified, for in a certain sense, the *Soliloquies* are deliberately imprecise.

We have already seen that Schleiermacher wrote his *Soliloquies* in order to portray a living embodiment of philosophical idealism (above, p. 159). He is not concerned in the *Soliloquies*, however, with the development of a philosophical system of idealism per se. At the time he sent Brinkmann a copy of the book, Schleiermacher wrote: "I predict that I shall be wholly misunderstood, because neither idealism nor the real world (which I will not allow to be taken away from me) has been

---

[1]Letter to Charlotte, Feb. 13, 1801. *Br.* I, 263.
[2]Apr. 8, 1800. *Briefe von Karl Gustav v. Brinckmann an Friedrich Schleiermacher*, 27.

expressly and formally deduced."[3] Schleiermacher was more than happy to leave such "deduction" to Fichte (see above, p. 58). These are soliloquies—dialogues with oneself. "So it was clear to me," Schleiermacher explains to Brinkmann, "that a development of principles could nowhere appear. For insofar as one *seeks after* fundamental principles, it is impossible for one to speak coherently with oneself."[4]

This is why one must look for Schleiermacher's philosophical principles not so much in the text of the *Soliloquies* as in the *blanc de l'ouvrage* (above, p. 153). Horace Leland Friess, the English translator of the *Soliloquies*, summarizes the situation accurately:

> The *Soliloquies* . . . aim to describe Schleiermacher's new experiences and insights, in this case particularly his insights into moral consciousness, without, however, striving for close definition, or for a dialectical treatment of concepts, in short, without determining precisely what these experiences might yield for a comprehensive system of philosophic thought.[5]

Friess goes on to contrast the "elan" of Schleiermacher's writings around 1800 with the "severely academic cast" of his earlier treatises.[6]

For us to attempt a conceptual analysis of phantasy as it figures in the *Soliloquies*, parallel to our analysis of freedom in Part I, therefore, would be a mistake. Schleiermacher intended his treatise *On Human Freedom* to invite and sustain analytic scrutiny, but his intentions in the *Soliloquies* are different. If we are to reflect those intentions without distortion, we must not simply analyze the concepts he employs, but also appreciate the human character shaped by the appropriation of those concepts. We must proceed less by means of conceptual analysis than by means of metaphorical appreciation and biography.

We have seen that the religious ideal of the *Speeches* is a mystical loss of oneself in the whole: "Strive . . . to annihilate your individuality and to live in the one and all" (above, p. 204). Yet in the same book we have found Schleiermacher maintaining that the world is a creation of a person's own phantasy (above, p. 213). The *Speeches* thus appear to be suggesting a loss of self in a whole that is the self's own creation—which is of course no loss of self at all. What is more, in the *Soliloquies* we find Schleiermacher exhorting his reader *not* to lose himself: "Take no care for what will come, weep not for that which goes, but take care that you do not lose yourself."[7]

---

[3]Letter to Brinkmann, Jan. 4, 1800. *Br.* IV, 55.
[4]Letter of May 27, 1800. *Br.* IV, 66–67. Schleiermacher's emphasis.
[5]Friess, "Appendix" to *Schleiermacher's Soliloquies: An English Translation of the Monologen*, 128.
[6]Ibid., 131.
[7]*Monologen*, 24. *Soliloquies*, 25.

The young Schelling had already remarked in 1795 on the paradox involved here:

> If the subject has its own . . . independent causality, then the demand "Lose yourself in the Absolute!" contains a contradiction.[8]

It was for this reason, Schelling goes on, that Spinoza's philosophy of the Absolute had to give up the concept of an "independent causality of the self." Schelling himself, being in 1795 in a Fichtean stage of his philosophical development, settles for the opposite extreme. He gives up the concept of an objective Absolute apart from the self. "In the self," Schelling writes, "philosophy has found its $\dot{\epsilon}\nu$ $\kappa\alpha\grave{\iota}$ $\pi\hat{\alpha}\nu$."[9]

Like many paradoxes, however, this one in Schleiermacher's thought between the *Speeches'* call for a loss of self and the *Soliloquies'* call for the opposite can be resolved by observing a distinction. It is a distinction that accounts for many of the contrasts between Schleiermacher's *Speeches* and his *Soliloquies*, namely, the distinction between his use of the term *universe* in a religious context, and his use of the term *world* in an ethical context. By distinguishing religion from ethics as carefully as he does, Schleiermacher is able to keep both extremes. He keeps the philosophical realism of Spinoza in the religious context of the *Speeches*, where the attitude is precisely that attributed by Schelling to Spinoza: "Accept yourself as absolutely passive with respect to the Absolute Causality."[10] He keeps the philosophical idealism of his contemporaries Fichte and the young Schelling, on the other hand, in the ethical context of the *Soliloquies*, where Schleiermacher can exclaim, "For me, the mind [*Geist*] is the first and only: for what I know as world is the mind's most beautiful work, its self-created mirror."[11]

Let us approach this contrast in another way. When Schleiermacher speaks of the whole that is the object of ethical activity, he uses the word "world," as in the sentence just quoted from the *Soliloquies*. When he speaks of the whole that is the object of religious devotion, however, he uses the word "universe." The universe is of course not an "object" in any usual meaning of the word (see above, p. 183). The object of religious intuition is an infinite environment. It cannot be exhausted by conceptual analysis. It is the given context of our experience. It cannot be deduced. Our contact with the universe is by means of our passive susceptibility to its pervasive presence in our immediate awareness. This is religious "sense"—an instinctive sense, pre-conceptual, more-than-rational. As our most immediate contact with reality,

---

[8]Friedrich Wilhelm Joseph von Schelling, *Philosophische Briefe über Dogmatismus und Kritizismus*. Quoted in Emil Fuchs, *Vom Werden dreier Denker*, 214.

[9]Ibid., 191. $\dot{\epsilon}\nu$ $\kappa\alpha\grave{\iota}$ $\pi\hat{\alpha}\nu$: see above, p. 120.

[10]Ibid., 214.

[11]*Monologen*, 15–16. *Soliloquies*, 16.

this sense is the foundation of the *Speeches'* metaphysical realism (see above, p. 124). In that realism, reality is held to be given objectively, apart from ourselves. We are inescapably passive with respect to that which is real.

When we are tempted to dismiss this religious realism of the *Speeches* as a nebulous romantic mysticism, we must ask ourselves whether we shall not also have to dismiss musical experience, let us say, on the same grounds. Schleiermacher insists repeatedly that the closest analogy to the intuitive, essentially religious sense his *Speeches* attempt to invoke is the evocation of mood by music, and it will help us clarify Schleiermacher's religious realism if we look into this analogy more closely.

Schleiermacher sometimes complained of a lack of musicality in himself—a deficiency he says he shared with Schlegel.[12] Yet he attained enough mastery of the keyboard to play chorales for his own enjoyment,[13] and for over twenty-five years, from 1809, soon after his move from Halle to Berlin in 1807, until the year of his death in 1834, Schleiermacher was to sing tenor in the Berlin civic chorus, the *Singaka-demie*. As minister of Berlin's Trinity Church he was the prime mover in the compilation of a new *Hymnbook for Worship in Evangelical Congregations*, published in 1829, for which Schleiermacher wrote the Foreword.[14] It appears that while Schleiermacher shared the poverty of visual sensibility that he describes as a general condition of Moravian pietism, he was an heir to the riches of the Moravian musical tradition. In particular, he was a child of Moravian marriage of religious piety and musical expression.

The most accessible manifestation of this musical legacy is found in Schleiermacher's little work of 1805 entitled *Christmas Eve: A Dialogue*. Eduard, host of the Christmas celebration that occasions the dialogue, is given this to say of the relation between religious piety and musical expression:

> Every beautiful feeling comes really completely to the fore only when we have found the tone for it. Not the word; this can always be only a mediate expression, only a plastic element, if I may put it that way. Rather, the tone, in the strict sense. And it is precisely to religious feeling that music is most closely related. There is so much discussion about how we might help restore the communcal expression of religious feeling; but almost no one considers that by far the best result might be achieved if we were once again to grant singing a more proper relation to

---

[12]Letter to Charlotte, Oct. 22, 1797. *Br*. I, 162.
[13]Letter to Henriette von Willich, Nov. 27–30, 1808. *Braut*, 229.
[14]For the text of this Foreword and an account of the musical activities of Schleiermacher's mature career, see Walter Sattler, "Vergessene Dokumente aus dem musickalischen Leben Schleiermachers." *Zeitschrift für Musikwissenschaft*, VII (1924–25), 535–44.

the word. What the word has made clear, tone must make alive [*lebendig*], conveying it immediately, as harmony, into the whole inner being, and there holding it fast.[15]

It is symbolically significant that Schleiermacher ends his dialogue with the appearance of Joseph, a friend of the assembled group, who promptly dismisses all their dialectical discussions of the meaning of Christmas with a call for laughter and music: "All speech is too tedious and cold. . . . Come then, . . . let us be glad and sing something religious and joyful."[16] This ending recollects Plato's dialogue *Phaedo*, in which Socrates ends an entire career of dialogical discussion with the admission to his astonished disciples that in his final days he has yielded to a lifelong urge to "make music" and has written a hymn to Apollo.[17] Like Schleiermacher, Socrates seems to be expressing symbolically his ironic recognition that dialogical argument encounters limits which only the arts of the Muses, in particular that of Polyhymnia, can transcend.

Schleiermacher nowhere offers particular musical illustrations to clarify the analogy between music and religious feeling that his character Eduard suggests. In their absence, perhaps we might approach Schleiermacher's meaning by giving attention to a song such as that of the Opus 105 of Johannes Brahms, *Wie Melodien zieht es mir leise durch den Sinn*, "Like melodies it steals softly through my sense." The "it" of the song's title and lyric is never given an antecedent; what "it" is, is never specified.[18] Furthermore, the music itself, like all of Brahms's music, is "pure" or nonrepresentational and offers no pictorial suggestions. The song's meaning is not conveyed conceptually or pictorially. It is conveyed harmonically and immediately, as the mood of the haunting song itself steals softly through one's sense. The sense of the music is

---

[15] *Friedrich Schleiermachers Weihnachtsfeier*, ed. Hermann Mulert, 22. Available in the English translation by Tice, which I follow here in part: *Christmas Eve: Dialogue on the Incarnation*, 46. Also translated by W. Hastie, *Christmas Eve Celebration*. For the dialogue's comment on the Moravian deficiency in the visual arts, see *Weihnachtsfeier*, p. 19, together with the addition from the second edition of 1827, p. 62. Tice, *Christmas Eve*, 44.

[16] *Weihnachtsfeier*, 55–56. *Christmas Eve*, 85–86.

[17] See Victor Zuckerkandl's discussion of this Socratic incident in *Man the Musician*, 1–3.

[18] This grammatical construction — a pronoun with unspecified antecedent — comparable to "it is raining" in English, has a wider range of application in German. Its use in the lyric of Brahms's song (by the nineteenth-century poet Klaus Groth) has parallels in Schleiermacher's usage. In a letter of 1802, Schleiermacher writes that the sight of a mountain citadel has inexplicably made him shudder. "It went through my marrow and bone as certain unpleasant tones do which otherwise have no significance" (letter to Eleonore Grunow, May 3, 1802, quoted in Dilthey, *Leben Schleiermachers*, ed. Redeker, I/1, 543). As in the song of Brahms, the "it" has no antecedent; its gender is wrong to refer to "shudder." Likewise in a letter of 1805: "In the mountains it came over me, and I simply had to hike on farther. . ." (to Henriette Herz, July 27, 1805. *Br*. II, 29).

evoked by the music. We cannot fail to recognize "it" when we thus sense it, and in it we can lose ourselves.

Schleiermacher seems to feel that religious sense for the universe is evoked by the universe in an analogous way. Thus he does not dwell in the *Speeches* upon the universe as an object of conceptual knowledge. To do so would be to risk smothering the sense he is seeking to awaken. The words Schleiermacher speaks about the universe of religious intuition are not components of a process of philosophical analysis or deduction. They are rather irrepressible expressions of an immediate evocation of feeling, and he hopes that his works may help to invoke the feeling in those who read them.[19]

Thus the language of religion is more closely related to poetic imagery than to conceptual analysis (see above, p. 216), and the religious sense that religious language expresses is more closely related to musical sense than to either analysis or poetry:

> A *miserere*, a *gloria*, a *requiem*—of what importance are their particular words? They are understandable enough through their character, and suffer no essential change if the words are exchanged with others of the same or another language, so long as they are singable and articulate suitably with the music. Indeed, no one will count it a loss if he fails to get the words at all.[20]

It would be a mistake to conclude from such a passage that Schleiermacher's romantic de-emphasis of the word betrays an underlying intellectual nebulosity, or even an anti-intellectualism. Such is not the case. Here again the Brahms song may be illustrative. Although its music is non-representational, the words of the song are nonetheless reflected with uncanny precision in its harmonic development.[21] The song's unobtrusive harmonic departures and returns will sustain intellectual analysis virtually to the limits of the theoretician's subtlety. Yet while the song's evocation of mood is illumined and reinforced by such

---

[19]In the words of Brahms's song:
> Doch kommt das Wort und fasst es
> und führt es vor das Aug',
> wie Nebelgrau erblasst es
> und schwindet wie ein Hauch.
> Und dennoch ruht im Reime
> verborgen wohl ein Duft,
> den mild aus stillem Keime
> ein feuchtes Auge ruft.

[20] *Weihnachtsfeier*, 22, including the 1827 addition, p. 63. *Christmas Eve*, 47.

[21]Notice for example the haunting upward tuning of a semitone to express "softly" (*leise*), and later "well hidden" (*verborgen wohl*); the poignant modulation to the subdominant, and then to the relative minor, to express "disappears like a breath" (*schwindet wie ein Hauch*) and its repetition; the mellow transition to the major on the diminished sixth to express "evokes a moistened eye" (*ein feuchtes Auge ruft*); and from there, the miraculously subtle return to an authentic cadence to resolve the song.

analysis, it does not depend upon it in the first instance. Too much attention to analysis, in fact, can smother the song's effect. Similarly, Schleiermacher feels that every experience and every analysis of experience (for "the person who can see far enough, and wants to go far enough") may serve to illumine and reinforce our religious sense of dependence (above, pp. 163 and 196). Religious sense for the universe is awakened immediately, however, and does not depend upon this or that particular experience or analysis.

It is in the context of Schleiermacher's assertion that his *Speeches* are "more musical than argumentative,"[22] then, that we may best understand their metaphysics of realism. Once this context is appreciated, certain passages that otherwise seem obscure may serve to summarize the *Speeches'* attempt to communicate their mystical realism. Describing the ideal preacher of religion, for example, Schleiermacher writes:

> He comes forward to present his own intuition as an object for the others, to lead them into the realm of religion where he is at home, to imbue them with his holy feelings. He expresses the universe, and in holy silence the congregation follows his inspired speech. . . . When he returns to himself from his wanderings through the universe, his heart and the hearts of all are the communal arena of the same feeling . . . , and holy mysteries—not merely meaningful emblems, but, rightly regarded, natural indications of a certain consciousness and certain sensibilities—are thus discovered and celebrated. It is like a higher choir that in its own sublime language answers the voice that calls. And this is no mere simile. As such speech, even without melody and tone, is music, so also there is a music among the saints that becomes speech without words—the most determinate and understandable expression of the most inward. The Muse of harmony, whose intimate relation to religion still belongs among the mysteries, has from of old offered the most splendid and perfect works of her most consecrated disciples upon the altars of religion. In sacred hymns and choruses, to which the words of the poet attach themselves only loosely and airily, things are breathed out that determinate speech can no longer grasp. Thus the tones of thought and sensibility mutually reinforce and interact, till all is permeated and full of the holy and the infinite.[23]

Thus the *Speeches* portray the interrelation of concept, word, and music in the service of religion's mystical intuition of the universe.

In the *Soliloquies*, however, where the metaphysical background is not religious realism but ethical idealism, musical figures virtually disappear. In their place, optical images predominate—images of light and reflection, of perspective, insight, and contemplation. *Universe*, the *Speeches'* term for the whole that is the object of religious intuition,

[22]Attributed to Schleiermacher by Karl Barth, *Protestant Thought: From Rousseau to Ritschl*, 326.
[23]*Reden*, 184–85. *Speeches*, 151–52.

disappears entirely. The *Soliloquies'* term for the comprehensive object of ethical consciousness is *world*, defined very nearly as Kant defines it in his first *Critique*: "By the term *world* we mean the sum of all appearances."[24] In relation to the universe of Schleiermacher's *Speeches* we are ultimately passive, absolutely dependent. But in the world, as the sum of Kantian "appearances," the mind is always an active contributor (see above, p. 216). The human organ for the apprehension of the universe is intuitive sense (*Sinn*), but in the apprehension of the world, sense is joined by active reason (*Vernunft*). The philosophical idealism of Schleiermacher's *Soliloquies* is based upon the assumption that in the world of appearances and concepts, including religious concepts such as the concept of God, the human mind is never purely passive. The world is half perceived by our senses and half created by our minds. A person cannot lose himself against this background, for there is no world apart from the person's mental activity. Lose the latter, and the former disappears along with it.

Schleiermacher's use of the term *world* is thus rooted in Kant's analysis of knowledge in the *Critique of Pure Reason*, where Kant argues his own form of idealism with extraordinary forcefulness. We have seen in Part I that Schleiermacher tried to restrict his early ethical analysis to the epistemological limits established by Kant's first *Critique*. We can therefore understand why Schleiermacher's *Soliloquies* observe those same limits, for that book is concerned solely with ethics. "Here self-reflection takes a purely ethical form," Schleiermacher writes in a Preface to the 1822 edition of the *Soliloquies*, "and nowhere does the religious in the more specific sense come forward."[25] The *Soliloquies* are not concerned with immediate intuition of the universe in the religious sense of the *Speeches*, but rather with ethical illumination of the phenomenal world of human events. "The stuff of ethics," Schleiermacher writes in 1801, is "human activities."[26]

In both metaphysical background and subject matter, therefore, the *Speeches* and the *Soliloquies* are very different books. At one point in the *Speeches* Schleiermacher declares, "And now I have said to you clearly enough that humanity is not my all, that my religion strives for a universe."[27] The ethical vision of the *Soliloquies*, in contrast, is in fact directed to humanity as its "all." By the world, Schleiermacher explains, he does not mean merely the material world:

> It I do not name with the name "world". What I deem worthy of the name world is only the eternal community of minds,[28] their influence

[24]Kant, *Critique of Pure Reason*, A419.
[25]*Monologen*, 4. *Soliloquies*, 6.
[26]Schleiermacher, *Über das Anständige. Zwei Gespräche*, 513.
[27]*Reden*, 122.
[28]Or "of spirits" or "intellects": *die ewige Gemeinschaft der Geister*.

upon each other, their mutual cultivation, the exalted harmony of freedom.[29]

To say this is not to remove the material world from consideration. It is only to say that the essence of idealism is the assumption that the material world is not "outside"[30] the "community of minds" of which Schleiermacher speaks here. Kantian idealism shows that we can speak of no world apart from unifying mental activity. Schleiermacher agrees. He believes that we are mistaken if we think of the world as a given order and connection of sensible objects and facts in relation to which we may orient ourselves with detachment and passive objectivity.

There are even places in the *Soliloquies* suggesting the extreme idealism of Fichte's early writings, where Fichte claimed that all reality is encompassed by the mind alone: "In all consciousness I intuit myself. . . . And the objective, that which is intuited and of which I am conscious, is likewise myself—the same self which intuits, only floating as objective before the subjective."[31] It is natural to ask what gave rise to the idealism of Schleiermacher's *Soliloquies*, and in light of certain extreme passages ("For me, the mind is the first and only . . ." and so forth, above, p. 221), it is tempting to answer: the philosophy of Fichte. Fichte's son, Immanuel Hermann Fichte, writing in 1846, claimed that Schleiermacher had taken certain fundamental notions from his father:

> In our opinion, from this source, namely from *The Vocation of Man*, Schleiermacher has taken his starting point—as a theologian, namely, in that which is most characteristic of him and most important: his doctrine of the origin of religion in *feeling*.[32]

But this is surely a mistaken opinion. Schleiermacher's *Speeches*, with their thesis that the "essence" of religion "is neither thinking nor acting, but rather intuition and feeling," preceded the appearance of Fichte's *The Vocation of Man* by a year.[33] Emil Fuchs even suggests that in the second edition of the *Speeches* Schleiermacher largely abandoned the term *intuition* in favor of *feeling*, precisely to avoid identification with Fichte's concept of "intellectual intuition."[34]

---

[29] *Monologen*, 16–17. *Soliloquies*, 17.

[30] *Monologen*, 44, 2nd ed.

[31] Johann Gottlieb Fichte, *Die Bestimmung des Menschen*, Zweites Buch, 81. *The Vocation of Man*, tr. William Smith, Book II, 70. For a discussion of the term *intuition* [*Anschauung*] see above, p. 152—though Fichte is not using the term here in any of its traditional senses but rather redefining it for his own purposes.

[32] Immanuel Hermann Fichte, *J. G. Fichte und Schleiermacher. Eine vergleichende Skizze*, 354. Fichte's emphasis.

[33] *Reden*, 46. Schleiermacher's *Speeches* were completed on Apr. 15, 1799. Fichte's *The Vocation of Man* was written during the summer and fall of 1799 and was published early in the year 1800.

[34] Fuchs, "Wandlungen in Schleiermachers Denken zwischen der ersten und zweiten Ausgabe der Reden," *Theologische Studien und Kritiken*, LXXVI (1903), 74–77.

Be that as it may, Schleiermacher's 1800 review of Fichte's *The Vocation of Man* leaves little room for doubt that Schleiermacher disagreed with Fichte's idealism. Indeed, from the tone of the review, which Friedrich Schlegel labeled with the English adjective "sprightly,"[35] and A. W. Schlegel called "a masterwork of finesse in irony, parody, and careful, respectable arch-devilment,"[36] it is obvious that Schleiermacher relished the differences between Fichte's idealism and his own. His review points out that, in its systematic form, Fichte's idealism is so extreme that it cannot even be convincingly voiced by a human being. Fichte is forced to adopt the device of having his metaphysical views spoken by a disembodied Spirit (*Geist*), "a peculiar Spirit, of which it is nowhere said who it is, and which goes about so utterly without costume."[37] Fichte's idealism is too extreme to have any pertinence to real people, "costumed" in flesh and blood.

Schleiermacher appreciated the fact that Fichte's book of 1800 represented an advance beyond his earlier, more rigidly systematic idealism. In Book III of *The Vocation of Man*, entitled "Faith," Fichte himself expresses reservations over pure idealism: "That there is nothing whatever besides my representations—this is to our natural sense a laughable and foolish thought, which no one can express in full seriousness, and which requires no refutation."[38] But Fichte's admission came too late. Schleiermacher's *Soliloquies* had appeared shortly before *The Vocation of Man*, with the purpose of portraying a living character embodying idealism according to Schleiermacher's own understanding (above, p. 159). We are shortly to see in the *Soliloquies* Schleiermacher's pleasure in the almost infinitely variable capacity of the human mind to conceive potential worlds and project them into reality. But from Schleiermacher's review of Fichte's "hopeless [*heillos*] book, which I cannot curse enough,"[39] we see that even at the high-water mark of Schleiermacher's idealism around 1800, his position is far from identical with that of Fichte.

After 1800, Schleiermacher's idealism receded. In his first revision of the *Soliloquies* of 1810, we no longer read, "For me the mind is the first and only." Rather we read, "for me the mind, the inner world, places itself boldly over against the outer world, the realm of matter, of things."[40] That is to say something considerably less extreme than

---

[35] Letter from Schleiermacher to Schlegel, Aug. 8, 1800. *Br.* III, 213.
[36] Letter to Schleiermacher from A. W. Schlegel, Aug. 20, 1800. *Br.* III, 218. Despite these compliments Schleiermacher realized that his review is in fact terribly obscure. He refers to it as "mustard" (letter to Willich, June 11, 1801. *Br.* I, 279).
[37] Schleiermacher, "Fichte's Bestimmung des Menschen," *Athenaeum*, III/2 (1800), 294.
[38] Fichte, *Bestimmung*, 105. English tr., 93.
[39] Letter to Henriette Herz, July 4, 1800. *Br.* III, 195.
[40] *Monologen*, 15, 2nd ed. *Soliloquies*, 105, note 21.

before. The mind is not magnified to infinity as in Fichte's early idealism, nor does the mind lose itself in the infinite as in the Spinozistic realism of Schleiermacher's *Speeches*. Rather, the infinite becomes for Schleiermacher "the only possible medium for our community and reciprocity with the remainder of the finite."[41] Ethics must deal with human beings as individuals among other individuals, each with his or her finite perspective. A virtual infinity of such perspectives interact with each other and with inanimate reality to constitute the ethical "world" (see above, p. 190).

In this way ethics and religion, which Schleiermacher has so carefully separated, come back together again. Religious sense for the infinite interpenetrates with ethical striving for completion. Just as Schleiermacher will not speak again in positive terms of a loss of self in the whole after the *Speeches* of 1799, so he will not speak of an utter reduction of the whole to the self, as a few passages of the 1800 *Soliloquies* suggest. Like the dipoles of mind and body, thought and passion, activity and receptivity, freedom and dependence, the individual and the social, and ethical elitism and religious egalitarianism— all of which we have encountered in Schleiermacher's outlook—his realism and his idealism must be considered side by side in an interpretation of his world view. His thinking oscillates from one pole to the other. Finding neither pole exclusively attractive, Schleiermacher eventually discovers his steady state in the oscillation itself. "Oscillation is truly the general form of all finite existence . . . ," Schleiermacher writes to Jacobi in 1818. "We cannot ever escape the antithesis between the ideal and the real."[42]

---

[41]Schleiermacher, "Fichte's Bestimmung des Menschen," *Athenaeum*, III/2 (1800), 296.

[42]Mar. 30, 1818. *Wirken*, 274 (see above, p. 164). For a thorough discussion of the concepts of oscillation and the polarity of the ideal and the real in Schleiermacher's mature thinking, see Gerhard Spiegler, *The Eternal Covenant*, pp. 93–95 et passim.

Chapter 3. The Whole and the Individual

So there dawned upon me what is now my highest intuition. It became clear to me that every person should manifest humanity in his own way, in his own mixture of its elements, so that humankind may reveal itself in every way and all that can come forth from its womb may become actual in the fullness of infinity.

In what we might take as a motto of the *Soliloquies*, Schleiermacher writes, "It is a clear consciousness of the contrast between world and man that is the ground upon which respect for myself and the feeling of freedom rest."[1] Schleiermacher's ethical genius, so highly assessed by Schlegel (above, p.174) and by many after him, derives in part from this clarity in his own consciousness. He possessed the peculiarly romantic facility for passing from a vision of the individual in the whole, to a vision of the whole in the individual, all the while holding the two in an irreducible complementarity. Friedrich Esselborn puts this point nicely: "The two poles about which Schleiermacher's thought revolves from the beginning are these: only in the whole can the particular come to life; only in the particular can the whole come to manifestation."[2]

The irreducible complementarity of individual and whole, the oscillation about the two, becomes a basic principle of Schleiermacher's writings after 1800, culminating in his lectures on dialectics from 1811 to 1831.[3] We have explored the dependence of the finite individual upon the infinite whole as a theme of the *Speeches*. A secondary them of the *Speeches*, Schleiermacher's consciousness of the whole as it is manifested in individuals, becomes a principal theme of the *Soliloquies*. Dilthey names this theme "the immanence or presence of the infinite and eternal in the finite," and he takes it to be the defining characteristic of Schleiermacher's ethical genius.[4] We shall take it as the subject of this chapter.

---

[1] *Monologen*, 44. *Soliloquies*, 45.

[2] Friedrich Wilhelm Esselborn, *Die philosophischen Voraussetzungen von Schleiermachers Determinismus*, 21. Cf. Schleiermacher's own formulation: "God knows each in the whole, as also the whole in each" (*Der christliche Glaube*, Proposition 55.3).

[3] See *Dialektik*, ed. Jonas, 62.

[4] Wilhelm Dilthey, *Leben Schleiermachers*, ed. Redeker, I/1, 322.

In developing their theme of consciousness of "immediate relation with the eternal and the infinite,"[5] the *Soliloquies* direct attention to the self. Their principal intuition is not the *Speeches' Anschauung des Universums*, "intuition of the universe,"[6] but rather *Selbstanschauung*, "intuition of self":

> Elevated self-contemplation, and it alone, puts me in a position to fulfill the sublime requirement that a person live not only as a mortal in the realm of time, but also immortal in the realm of eternity.[7]

Schleiermacher has passed beyond the *Speeches'* mystical consciousness of a loss of oneself in the infinite to an intensified, Platonic appreciation of individuality as a manifestation of the eternal. The *beyond* here must be emphasized. Schleiermacher did not arrive at his romantic love of individuality by stopping short of a mystical loss of self in the whole, but rather by passing through it.

Schleiermacher felt that there are no short cuts to the mature sense of individuality that he calls a person's "highest privilege":

> Only late and with difficulty does a person attain to full consciousness of his individuality [*Eigenthümlichkeit*]. Not always does he dare to look toward it, and would rather train his eye upon the common attributes of humankind, to which he clings so lovingly and gratefully. He often doubts whether he should again separate himself from humankind as an individual being, for fear of sinking back, in old, culpable limitation, into the narrow circle of the outward personality, confounding the sensible with the spiritual. Not until late does he learn to value and use correctly this highest privilege.[8]

The "often" in the middle of this passage (". . . he often doubts whether he should again separate himself from humankind as an individual being . . .") should not be overlooked. The discovery of individuality that is the subject of the *Soliloquies* must not be thought of simply as something that happens in a moment, once and for all, and is then a permanent possession of a person's consciousness. We are about to see that Schleiermacher renewed this discovery more than once, in various situations and different moments of his life. Both religious mysticism and ethical individuality were romantic yearnings as well as fervent loves of his life. It would be simplistic to suggest that Schleiermacher's mystical vision coincided with the period of the *Speeches* and then yielded to a new sense of individuality in the *Soliloquies*. We may say simply that these are the emphases of the two books. We must recall that already in the *Speeches* the concluding chapter is an apology

[5] *Monologen*, 11. *Soliloquies*, 12.
[6] *Reden*. 52.
[7] *Monologen*, 21. *Soliloquies*, 22.
[8] *Monologen*, 31–32. *Soliloquies*, 32.

for individuality, namely, the individuality of the "positive" or historical religions, and for Christianity in particular:

> You must give up your empty and futile wish that there were only one religion; you must lay aside your antipathy toward religion's multiplicity. . . . You will then find that the positive religions are simply the determinate forms in which infinite religion manifests itself in the finite — something to which natural religion is only an indeterminate, paltry, and impoverished idea that in itself can never really exist.[9]

Coming as it does after Schleiermacher's general account of religion in the second *Speech*, "The Essence of Religion," this impassioned defense of particular religions in the fifth *Speech*, "The Religions," surprised and re-alienated some of the enlightened despisers of religion to whom the book was addressed. One of these was the great Goethe. From Jena, Schlegel reported Goethe's reaction to the *Speeches*:

> Goethe had me give him my beautiful copy, and in his discussions with Wilhelm, after his first eager reading of two or three speeches, he could not praise the cultivation and many-sidedness of this publication highly enough. But then the more negligent the style became, *and the more Christian the religion*, the more this effect turned into its opposite. Finally the process ended in a wholesome and happy antipathy [*in einer gesunden und fröhlichen Abneigung*].[10]

Schleiermacher's response to such opinions was not to moderate his advocacy of particular religions, but in fact to intensify it. In the 1806 revision of the *Speeches*, for example, "natural religion" in the passage just quoted is altered to read "your so-called natural religion." In the Preface to the *Speeches'* third edition of 1821 he writes, "I have never set any other goal for myself than that of manifesting my own manner of thinking for the sole purpose of awakening and enlivening individuality."[11]

Thus the *Speeches* anticipate the *Soliloquies'* aspiration to pass through the loss of oneself in the whole to the full consciousness of individuality that is a person's "highest privilege." This yearning to achieve individuality by transcending the universal and the common is a hallmark of romanticism. We have seen it, for example, in Schleiermacher's philosophical struggle to go beyond Kantian respect for the "universal and necessary" to a new appreciation of practical reason's idiosyncratic embodiments in the lives of particular men and women (see above, p. 55).

---

[9] *Reden*, 243, 247. *Speeches*, 214, 217.
[10] Letter to Schleiermacher, no date (fall, 1799). *Br.* III, 125. "Wilhelm": A. W. Schlegel. Emphasis added.
[11] *Reden*. xi.

This hallmark is found widely distributed in the literature of romanticism as well as in its philosophy and ethics. Schleiermacher himself toyed during his early Berlin years with the idea of expressing his ethical outlook in the form of a novel—a possibility he alludes to at the close of Chapter 4 of his *Soliloquies*.[12] He regarded the novel as the medium best suited for "manifesting inward humanity," for communicating a "pure and determinate intuition" of individual character.[13] Never trusting his artistic talent sufficiently, however, Schleiermacher did not get his novel written. But in a sense he did not have to. Novalis did some of Schleiermacher's creative work for him.

Though Novalis and Schleiermacher never met, both were close friends of Schlegel, who cultivated and transmitted their mutual admiration.[14] When in March of 1801 Novalis died of tuberculosis, Schlegel was at his bedside. Schleiermacher, though at a distance, felt the loss keenly. "Without doubt," he wrote to Eleonore Grunow a little later, "Hardenberg would have become a great artist if he had been granted to us longer."[15] In the second edition of the *Speeches*, alongside the passage in praise of Spinoza, included unaltered from the first edition, Schleiermacher inserted a parallel memorial to Novalis,

> the divine youth, too early fallen asleep, who turned to art all that his spirit touched . . . , as deep of sense as lucid and living. See in him the power of inspiration and the circumspection of a pious heart [*Gemüth*], and acknowledge that when the philosophers shall become religious and seek God like Spinoza, and the artists shall become pious and love Christ like Novalis, then the great resurrection shall be celebrated for both worlds.[16]

We have seen how Novalis's *Heinrich von Ofterdingen* was strongly influenced by Schleiermacher's *Speeches* (above, pp. 152–153). Not surprisingly, Schleiermacher admired Novalis's novel in return. In the summer of 1800, Novalis's friend, the romantic author and folklorist Ludwig Tieck, asked Schleiermacher if he would take over the proofreading of *Heinrich von Ofterdingen*—a task the Schlegels had begun but set aside. Schleiermacher had to decline the offer: "I do not know the least thing about such work, and what is more, I do not have the time. I am very sorry that I cannot do Hardenberg this first favor."[17] But Schleiermacher read and loved the novel: "a book such as this, a memorial to so pure and

---

[12]See *Monologen*, 82. *Soliloquies*, 88.

[13]From Schleiermacher's Journal, "Denkmale," 116.

[14]For more detail concerning the relation among these three, see Wolfgang Sommer, *Schleiermacher und Novalis*, esp. Ch. II, Part B.3.b., "Friedrich Schlegels Mittlerolle," 41–44. See also the study by Jack Forstman, *A Romantic Triangle: Schleiermacher and Early German Romanticism*.

[15]July 29, 1802. *Br.* I, 309.

[16]*Reden*, 53, 2nd ed. *Speeches*, 41.

[17]Letter to Schlegel, July 11, 1800. *Br.* III, 205–6.

exalted a heart [*Gemüth*], which draws every kindred heart to itself and readily accommodates itself in turn to every worthy mood of such a heart, is a beautiful possession in any age."[18]

In the course of his novel, Novalis has a question put to the solitary, idiosyncratic sage he introduces in Chapter 5—a question that invokes our theme of the discovery of genuine individuality beyond the loss of oneself in the whole. "Do there not sometimes come hours in which you become anxious and your heart longs for a human voice?" the old prophet is asked. He replies to this question with a brief history of his lifelong search for the individual independence he has at last attained in old age:

> No longer, now. There was a time in my youth when a fervent enthusiasm prompted me to become a hermit. Dark presentiments occupied my youthful phantasy. I hoped to find in solitude adequate nourishment for my heart. The source of my inner life seemed to me inexhaustible. But I soon observed that one must bring with him an abundance of experiences, that a young heart cannot be alone; yes, that a person attains a certain independence of self [*Selbständigkeit*] only through manifold intercourse with his race.[19]

There is close agreement between this passage and Schleiermacher's emphasis in the *Soliloquies* upon the discovery of mature individuality. "I cannot cultivate myself in solitude," Schleiermacher writes:

> For me the juices of the heart [*Gemüth*] dry up, the flow of thought stops. I must go forth in variegated communion with other spirits to behold what there is to humanity and what of humanity remains foreign to me, what can become my own; and, through give and take, always to determine more surely my own nature.[20]

Both Novalis and Schleiermacher felt that there is no short path to the goal of individuality. A person finds it on the far, not the near, side of "manifold intercourse" (Novalis) or "variegated communion" (Schleiermacher) with the whole race.

The thumbnail autobiography Novalis invents for the hermit of his novel maps out not too roughly the course of Schleiermacher's own early development, in fact. We have seen that, as a student at Halle, Schleiermacher held himself apart from others: "I associated with almost no one . . . , a person turned inward upon himself" (above, p. 17). Schleiermacher's first year after leaving Halle was also spent in near solitude at Drossen (above, p. 7). During his two and a half years as tutor in the household of the Dohna family in Schlobitten, however, he "found humanity," as one of his interpreters puts it.[21] There he first learned to be at

[18]Letter to Eleonore Grunow, Dec. 10, 1802. *Br*. I, 353–4. See also his letter to Eleonore, July 29, 1802. *Br*. I, 309.

[19]Novalis, *Heinrich von Ofterdingen*, Ch. 5, 109–10.

[20]*Monologen*, 35–36. *Soliloquies*, 36. See also *Weihnachtsfeier*, 53 (*Christmas Eve*, 83).

[21]Friedrich Michael Schiele's Introduction to *Monologen* ("Die Entstehung der Monologen"), xxv.

ease, and then to thrive, in the company of creative individuals joined together socially. "In a strange house," he writes in the *Soliloquies*, meaning the Dohna manor, "my sense for beautiful social existence first arose. I saw how freedom ennobles and rightly proportions the delicate secrets of humankind."[22] Finally, it was after 1796, in the more informal association of romantic peers known as the Berlin Circle, that Schleiermacher "found individuality."[23] That is, in this social setting he grew into a mature sense of his own individual powers and into an appreciation for the rich variety of individuality among his Berlin friends and acquaintances.

Perhaps the most lyrical of all expressions of the romantic theme we are developing here— the rediscovery of the particular on the far side of the universal—occurs not in German but in the early English romanticism of William Wordsworth. Wordsworth was Schleiermacher's contemporary and in certain ways Schleiermacher's British counterpart,[24] though Schleiermacher of course had no poetic gift to compare with Wordsworth's, and the young Wordsworth was no minister of Christian religion. The two men never met, and there is no evidence from the period we are concerned with that either knew the work of the other. But there are substantial similarities between the two. We have seen that as young men both came under the influence of the determinist Joseph Fawcett (above, p. 104). Schleiermacher's *Speeches* of 1799 had an influence on the tone of early German romanticism comparable, though far from equal, to the influence on early English romanticism of the 1798 *Lyrical Ballads* of Coleridge and Wordsworth, with the famous discussion of poetry and feeling in Wordsworth's "Preface" to the second edition of that collection in 1800.

One of the *Lyrical Ballads* is the *Lines Composed a Few Miles above Tintern Abbey*, written one year before Schleiermacher's *Speeches* and two years before the *Soliloquies*. In it Wordsworth records the stages of his spiritual development. They parallel the romantic development of consciousness from naive solitude, through social universality, to mature individuality, that we have observed in the literature of Novalis and in the life and writings of Schleiermacher.

Wordsworth recalls first his innocent, positive enjoyment of the world when he was a lad:

> The coarser pleasures of my boyish years,
> And their glad animal movements. . . .

---

[22] *Monologen*, 71. *Soliloquies*, 74.

[23] Schiele, "Die Entstehung," xxv.

[24] For a more general comparison of Wordsworth and Schleiermacher than the one offered here, see J. Arundel Chapman, *An Introduction to Schleiermacher*, Ch. V, "A Comparison of Schleiermacher and Wordsworth," 100–125.

Wordsworth outgrew this innocence to enter a stage of enjoying nature, not positively, for itself, but rather comparatively, in contrast to "the fretful stir / Unprofitable, and the fever of the world,"

> ... more like a man
> Flying from something that he dreads than one
> Who sought the thing he loved.[25]

He then goes on to speak of the "dizzy raptures" of still a third stage of his growth, a superlative degree of mystical love for nature —

> For nature then . . .
> To me was all in all

—and within this ecstatic vision of universal nature there registers in the young poet's consciousness a social intuition of the "still sad music of humanity."

Then, attuned in this way to the universal "presence" that "rolls through all things," Wordsworth turns to his sister beside him. He addresses her first as "my dearest friend," but then catches and corrects himself:

> For thou art with me here upon the banks
> Of this fair river; thou my dearest friend,
> *My dear, dear friend.*

Why does Wordsworth change his salutation to his sister? Is it not because his mystical vision of the universal, in nature and in humanity, has already exhausted the superlative degree of comparison? "My dearest" no longer seems adequate to express Wordsworth's affection for his sister. Its grammer does not convey the intimacy he feels for the individual at his side, whom instinct has led him to address as "thou." But after the positive, comparative, and superlative degrees of comparison, what is left? All that remains is to intensify the positive degree, by repetition. This Wordsworth does, and then a second time, five lines later, as if to emphasize a lesson learned:

> Oh! yet a little while
> May I behold in thee what I was once,
> My dear, dear sister!

Schleiermacher shares Wordsworth's gift for appreciating particular individuals with the intensity of one who, having passed through a loss of his own individuality and that of others in a mystical sense for the whole, then rediscovers individuality with a new degree of poignancy.

---

[25]See Schiller's splended discussion of the loss of naiveté in one's love of nature in the opening pages of his essay *On Naive and Sentimental Poetry.*

We discern this gift in the language of the *Soliloquies*, where Schleiermacher traces the course of his own development from the "sensual
animal life" of childhood, through the ethical commitments of Kantian
universalism, to the rarer sense for individuality that distinguishes
human maturity:

> When a person disdains the unworthy individualism [*Einzelheit*] of sensual
> animal life and attains a consciousness of general humanity, submitting
> himself to duty, he is not immediately capable of rising to the higher
> particularity [*Eigenheit*] of cultivation and morality, or of perceiving and
> understanding the nature that freedom chooses for itself. Most persons
> remain hovering in an indeterminate middle condition, in actuality mani-
> festing humanity only in its raw elements, simply because they have not
> been grasped by the thought of their own higher existence. But it has
> grasped me. . . . So there dawned upon me what is now my highest
> intuition. It became clear to me that every person should manifest
> humanity in his own way, in his own mixture of its elements, so that
> humankind may reveal itself in every way and all that can come forth
> from its womb may become actual in the fullness of infinity.[26]

We may see this gift for appreciating individuality in Schleiermacher's life as well as in his writings. As with Wordsworth, Schleiermacher's relationship with his sister is particularly revealing in this
regard. Charlotte Schleiermacher lived a simple life. Throughout the
period covered by our study she was a "sister" in the Moravian
congregation in Gnadenfrei.[27] This Moravian center was in a geographical area in which Schleiermacher had been nurtured as a boy, and it
also represented the pietistic context from which he had broken in 1787
by going to the University of Halle against his father's wishes. With
Wordsworth, Schleiermacher could have said to his sister, "I behold in
thee what I was once." While visiting his sister in the spring of 1802,
Schleiermacher wrote from Gnadenfrei to his friend Reimer:

> I find myself very happy here, in the company of a dearly beloved sister,
> in lovely surroundings, and amid the wonderful impressions of an earlier
> period of my life. There is no other place that could better favor the
> living recollection of the entire course of my mind, from its first
> awakening to better things, to the point at which I now stand. Here it was
> that I first became conscious of the human relation to a higher world. . . .
> Here the mystical tendency first developed which is so essential to me,
> and which has rescued and sustained me amid all the storms of skepti-
> cism. Then it was only germinating; now it is cultivated; and I can say
> that after all, I am again a Herrnhuter, only of a higher order.[28]

Charlotte had not shared her brother's course of intellectual cultivation.
Like Eleonore Grunow, she was another of Schleiermacher's intimates

---

[26] *Monologen*, 29–30. *Soliloquies*, 30–31.
[27] Now Piława Gorna, Poland.
[28] Apr. 30, 1802. *Br.* I, 294–95.

whom he valued not for cultivation but for integrity (above p. 171). She frequently found it difficult to accept Schleiermacher's diverse circle of friends and new ways of life (see above, p. 113). Yet the two faithfully carried on what Schleiermacher accurately calls a "very candid and deeply engaging exchange of letters."[29] In 1799, Schleiermacher called his attempt to write Charlotte letters that would help render his life understandable to her a "very religious" act.[30]

Schleiermacher's visit to Gnadenfrei in 1802 reunited him with his sister after six years of separation. He wrote to Ehrenfried von Willich that he found her "quite perfected." Charlotte had not stirred from Gnadenfrei in the six intervening years, however. Schleiermacher's own development—his reaffirmation of the beauty of particular religions, such as his sister's Herrnhutianism; his extolling of distinctive individuality, such as that of his sister; his ranking of integrity over cultivation in the catalogue of human moral qualities—Schleiermacher's own development, more than his sister's, must account for how, despite all their differences of social and intellectual cultivation, the two found themselves able to enjoy one another "perfectly and more undisturbed than before."[31] Since their father's death in 1794, Charlotte had been Schleiermacher's closest relative.[32] He returned from his years in Berlin to discover that she had become doubly dear to him.

Still another letter dating from Schleiermacher's Gnadenfrei visit of 1802, this one to Eleonore Grunow,[33] is an extraordinary but neglected contribution to the documents of early romanticism. It expresses from yet another perspective the characteristically romantic discovery of individuality beyond universality. In it Schleiermacher describes a solitary climb he has made up the hill above Gnadenfrei to enjoy the view out over the rolling plain that surrounds that peaceful Moravian settlement:

> The sun was about to set . . . , and I sat down under a birch, rustled by
> the evening wind, to watch this beautiful spectacle. When the lower edge
> of the disk had almost touched the ridge of the mountains, all the glare
> disappeared, and unhindered I could see the splendid fireball clearly

[29]Ibid., 295. The Schleiermacher archives in the German Academy of Sciences in East Berlin contain 74 letters from Schleiermacher to Charlotte. (A fire in Charlotte's "Sisterhouse" destroyed all but three of Schleiermacher's letters from the Schlobitten period and earlier. *Leben Schleiermachers*, ed. Redeker, I/1, 52w.) From Charlotte to Schleiermacher there are 169 letters and 222 fragments of letters, only a few pages of which have ever been published. See Heinrich Meisner, "Schleiermachers Briefe," *Zentralblatt für Bibliothekswesen*, XXIX (1912), 545, 549.

[30]Letter to Henriette Herz, Mar. 24, 1799. *Br.* I, 211

[31]Letter to von Willich, May 19, 1802. *Werden*, 243.

[32]There was a younger brother, Karl. Schleiermacher's relation to him was close when the two were together, but after childhood that was the case only infrequently. Correspondence between the two was sparse, and it appears that none of it has survived.

[33]May 3, 1802. Quoted in Dilthey, *Leben Schleiermachers*, ed. Redeker, I/1, 542–44.

outlined. Thus it set, quietly and calmly. I thought about the illusion, and
then believed myself able to see the earth rotating and to hear the rush of
the mountains, which little by little darkened and flowed together, where
earlier I could have distinguished almost every range.

As soon as the sun had set, a nightingale sprang up here and there.
At first a thousand thoughts went through my head. The mountains
always remind me of the history of the world. I thought of the first
settlers in this paradise, of the barrenness of that time, of the present
splendor; the most varied centuries and ages hovered before me. . . .

Then suddenly it happened that everything condensed into two
feelings: I worshipped and I loved. I could have wished to die of devotion
and affection. I wished for you and my good Lotte by my side, all of us
with our piety in our hearts, each stirred alike, and all united and embraced in love. The worship and love persisted; but the history of the
world had made a place for the history of my soul, from my childhood
years to my sanctified and sanctifying love for you.

Thus Schleiermacher's letter unwittingly repeats the spiritual course of
Wordsworth's *Tintern Abbey*—the loss of self in nature's universal "all
in all," and the subsequent rediscovery of "the still sad music of
humanity." The focus of the intensified vision of humanity is also the
same in both, a sense of communion with a loved one:

Thus I arose and, beneath the song of the nightingales and the soft
luster of a pastoral afterglow, hurried through the thicket, without path or
trail, toward the peak of the hill, where several stone steps afford a
prospect out over the brush. There besides all that I have already
mentioned, I had serene, quiet Gnadenfrei at my feet, and behind me the
mountain citadel of Silberberg. I shuddered once at the sight of the latter.
It went through my marrow and bone as certain unpleasant tones do that
otherwise have no significance.

And in fact all worldly activity and stir had no significance for me in
this moment. I had only the one wish, to give you my whole being to
enjoy as I felt it in this moment, which permeated me so that I felt it was
eternal.

Finally, as Schleiermacher made his way back toward the village in
this mood, he came upon the Moravian burial ground:

The cemetery lay on the slope of a hill, enclosed by a hedgerow of
beeches and planted with several rows of trees, which have not the heart,
however, to thrive in the midst of the human remains. On the one side
lie the Sisters, on the other the Brothers, just as they sit in the chapel.
Every grave has a tombstone, bearing no legend, but only an inscription.
I had to smile at the larger, aristocratic stones. I do not idealize the
persons who have been brought here up to now—uncultivated, limited,
knowing little of the universe, and, in the search for the godly and the
ungodly, restricted to the smallest details of the human soul. Certainly
most of them have been so. But yet they bore the eternal in their heart;
they had that sense that holds the world together; and even if they did
not know much of the good, and had perhaps even timidly rejected it, yet
they would have loved no evil. Peace to them, I thought; they may know
more now, and be better off.

The mood of this letter—its sense for the intermingling of the universal and the particular, the eternal and the temporal—is like the state of consciousness Wordsworth expresses in his poem:

> While with an eye made quiet by the power
> Of harmony, and the deep power of joy,
> We see into the life of things.

Schleiermacher descended from his climb to appreciate the simple individuals of the Gnadenfrei community with a new sense of poignancy. He sensed in them Wordsworth's universal "presence" that "rolls through all things," which his own *Soliloquies* name "the equal measure of life" that "diffuses itself through all."[34]

These examples from Schleiermacher's correspondence are living manifestations of the romantic facility we defined abstractly at the beginning of this chapter: a sense for the irreducible complementarity of individual and whole. They parallel in Schleiermacher's life the progression in his philosophical thinking from the philosophy of Spinoza to the philosophy of Plato. In Spinoza, the individual is a mode of the whole, a lens gathering the flux of universal substance into a focal point we call individuality. But substance is prior. The stress of Spinozism is on the whole. The Spinozist is apt to lose sight of the individual in the divine One and All. "Individual things," Spinoza writes, "are nothing but modifications of the attributes of God."[35]

Schleiermacher never abandoned the pantheistic sense expressed here by Spinoza's assertion, but he found its statement excessively metaphysical, as we have seen (above, p. 121). In Plato Schleiermacher found the philosophical influence he required to moderate Spinoza's pantheism, specifically, Plato's consistent refusal to lose sight of the individual in the whole. The Platonic dialogues, by their "living apprehension of the goal of imitating oral instruction," Schleiermacher writes,

> have always to do with a determinate subject. But they take on a still further individuality that really fashions the Platonic dialogue: namely, that mimic and dramatic quality by means of which persons and circumstances become individualized—the quality that, by general acknowledgment, spreads so much beauty and charm over the dialogues of Plato. His great undisputed works show us plainly that he does not neglect this admixture even when he is most deeply absorbed in his subject.[36]

Plato's "admixture" of the individual and the general, the particular and the abstract, permeates the fundamental principle of Schleiermacher's romanticism: that only in the whole can the particular come to life, and only in the particular can the whole come to manifestation. In his

[34] *Monologen*, 51. Cf. *Soliloquies*, 52.
[35] *Ethics*, Part I, Proposition XXV, Corollary.
[36] Schleiermacher, "Einleitung," *Platons Werke*, I/1, 29. English tr., 36–37.

religious "feeling of absolute dependence" Schleiermacher retains Spinoza's holistic principle that "a thing that has been determined by God to act in a particular way cannot render itself undetermined."[37] But Schleiermacher infuses this holistic principle with Plato's complementary sense that an individual so determined is not thereby rendered any less an individual. Indeed, our sense of the whole heightens our love of individuals.

[37]Spinoza, *Ethics*, Part I, Proposition XXVII.

Chapter 4. Schleiermacher's Quietism

Those who would have everyone become a virtuoso and artist in science complain of me that I will not suffer myself to be limited, that it is deluded to hope that I shall ever seriously devote myself to something, since when I attain one perspective, then I rush on to other objects in the manner typical of a desultory mind. O that they would leave me in peace, and comprehend that my vocation is nothing else, that I cannot cultivate science, for I intend to cultivate myself.

From the reverie of his stroll above Gnadenfrei Schleiermacher writes to Eleonore, "And in fact, all worldly activity and stir had no significance for me in this moment." Here again Schleiermacher unwittingly echoes a sentiment of *Tintern Abbey*, where Wordsworth's "sylvan" reverie rescues him from "the fretful stir / Unprofitable, and the fever of the world." In both these young romantics there runs a distinctive vein of quietism.[1] We have encountered the issue of quietism in passing in the context of Schleiermacher's early dialogues on determinism and freedom (above, p. 10). Now this peculiar restraint upon freedom, so intrinsically related to Schleiermacher's philosophy of determinism, will be our subject for this chapter. It will return us, by way of the related concept of resignation in the following chapter, to Schleiermacher's concept of phantasy in the final two chapters of our study.

Like Schleiermacher's self-accusation of "innate laziness" (above, p. 16), quietism seems a paradoxical designation for a man as active as Schleiermacher. In the course of his career he was productive as a philologist and a classics scholar; as a philosopher and a lecturer in philosophy; as a theologian and a minister; as an educator and an educational, ecclesiastical, and social reformer; even as an amateurish spy in the resistance against the Napoleonic occupation of Prussia.[2] Nonetheless, through all these activities Schleiermacher's characteristic

---

[1]"A nonactivistic mysticism stressing passive contemplation, concentration on the interior life, and nonparticipation in affairs of the world" (*Webster's Third New International Dictionary, Unabridged*).

[2]See Richard C. Raack, "A New Schleiermacher Letter on the Conspiracy of 1808," *Zeitschrift für Religions- und Geistesgeschichte*, XVI (1964), 209–23.

strain of quietism is unmistakable, and this strain is expressed in an especially pure form in the *Soliloquies*.

The *Soliloquies*, as we have seen in the preceding chapter, recommend the active cultivation of personal individuality. At one point Schleiermacher equates the achievement of "freedom" with the attainment of an individual, characteristic point of view.[3] Thus the *Soliloquies* echo the definition from the *Speeches*: to act freely is "to bring forth the characteristic" (above, p. 138). They are written in praise of "the free act" that "has assembled around itself and inwardly combined the elements of human nature into a characteristic existence [*zu einem eigenthümlichen Dasein*]."[4] But the emphasis here must fall upon "inwardly." The freedom extolled by the *Soliloquies* is less a "bringing forth" in any external sense than an inward cultivation of oneself. It is freedom under the aspect of appropriation, which we have observed earlier as Schleiermacher's principal emphasis (above, p. 154).

Schleiermacher contrasts what he calls an "artistic" temperament, in which inward cultivation culminates in some form of outward expression, with an "ethical" temperament, in which the highest aspiration is the inward cultivation of a characteristic self. At the time of the *Soliloquies*, at least, Schleiermacher felt that the latter better described his own temperament: "The unquenched thirst constantly to cultivate my own nature does not permit the activity of giving outer perfection to the communication of the inner."[5] The *Soliloquies* themselves are a free expression of Schleiermacher's inner life, but hardly a perfected or "artistic" one. We should recall that he wrote them "out of the blue . . . without the least regard for effect," or so at least he told his friend von Willich (above, p. 143). Schleiermacher wrote to Brinkmann that the *Soliloquies* were completed in the short space of under four weeks, "virtually dictated to the printer." They are merely "a lyrical extract from a permanent journal," in which there are "a thousand ellipses to supply."[6] Like Schleiermacher's actual Journal, the *Soliloquies* were first of all a means of self-cultivation, a medium of that inner polemic which consists in "inward thinking, intuition, and appropriating the foreign," and which strives toward the "completion" of one's own nature.[7]

H. G. Schenk writes that Novalis "never regarded writing as a profession, but rather as a *Bildungsmittel* to help him develop and enrich his own mind. Altogether his social ambitions did not run very high."[8]

---

[3] *Monologen*, 40. *Soliloquies*, 41.

[4] *Monologen*, 31. *Soliloquies*, 31–32.

[5] *Monologen*, 34, 36. *Soliloquies*, 34, 36.

[6] Letters of Jan. 4, May 27, and Apr. 19, 1800. *Br.* IV, 55, 67, 64.

[7] *Monologen*, 36. *Soliloquies*, 36.

[8] Schenk, *The Mind of the European Romantics*, 89. *Bildungsmittel*: "means of cultivation."

What Schenk says of Novalis's artistic output relates equally well to Schleiermacher's writing of the *Soliloquies*. In making his book public, Schleiermacher writes,

> it does not concern me whether the sensibility of the beholders pene-
> trates through the rough crust, whether they successfully find the inner-
> most thoughts, the individual spirit, in the unperfected presentation.
> There remains to me no time, no desire to ask. I must go forward from
> the place where I stand to complete my individual nature, if in this short
> life, through new activity and thought, this be possible.[9]

Earlier we examined the incongruous fact that Schleiermacher's later works, in contrast to his earlier ones, are paradigms of thorough, orderly presentation (above, p. 145). Not long after 1800 one finds Schleiermacher repeatedly reworking his lectures on ethics, for example, when he had written in the *Soliloquies* only shortly before, "I hate to repeat even twice—a most unartistic temperament."[10] We concluded in Part II that there was more of the teacher—more of what he calls an "artistic" temperament—in Schleiermacher than he admits in the text of the *Soliloquies*. To our earlier attempt to understand Schleiermacher's understatement of his artistic nature in the *Soliloquies*, we may add that in 1800 Schleiermacher was comparing himself with prodigiously artistic contemporaries. In the context of the turn-of-the-century concentration of German genius in Berlin, Dresden, Weimar, and Jena, Schleier-macher was in fact relatively unartistic.

We must be careful, however, not to explain away the incongruity be-tween Schleiermacher's *Soliloquies* and the writings that followed. The incongruity runs too deep. What does it mean, for example, that Schleier-macher can write in the *Soliloquies*, "Free leisure is my dear goddess, where, in quiet contemplation a person learns to comprehend and deter-mine himself,"[11] while at the very same moment of his life he is de-scribing to his sister his comparatively active, even interfering, nature?[12] There almost seem to be two different personalities— Schleiermacher the quietist and Schleiermacher the activist—discernible in the one man. And in fact there are. Quietism and activism are yet one more dipole about which Schleiermacher's philosophy of life oscillates (see above, p. 229). Our challenge in this chapter is therefore not to explain away an apparent incongruity, but to understand an actual complementarity.

The question is this: How did Schleiermacher think of the relation between his ethical ideal of inward freedom and his tangible activity in the world? The nature of that relation seems to follow from Schleier-macher's determinism on the one hand, and from his idealism on the

---

[9]*Monologen*, 36. *Soliloquies*, 36–37.
[10]*Monologen*, 36. *Soliloquies*, 37.
[11]*Monologen*, 35. *Soliloquies*, 36.
[12]Letter to Charlotte, Dec. 27, 1799. *Br*. I, 239.

other. First, it follows from his determinism since Schleiermacher believed that there is no way to understand a person's outward activity except as the necessary consequence of his inner state. A person's outward activities need not concern us if we but "understand the inner person from whom they issue, and know that his outer activity must be so because he is as he is."[13] This fundamental understanding of the continuity between human character and actions seems no less thoroughly deterministic in Schleiermacher's *Soliloquies* than in his *Speeches* or his treatises around 1792 (see above, p. 70). Thus we see in still another context the compatibility between freedom and determinism in Schleiermacher's thinking. It would be no exaggeration to call the *Soliloquies* a hymn to freedom ("so thou, Freedom, art to me the primordial, the first and most inward in all"[14]), and it might at first seem improbable that such praise of freedom would issue from a deterministic world view. But in this connection a revealing alteration appears in the second edition of the *Soliloquies*. Where in 1800 Schleiermacher speaks of phantasy as "the clearest proof of *free choice* [*freie Wahl*]," in 1810 he calls phantasy "the clearest proof of *inner determinateness* [*innere Bestimmtheit*]."[15] We shall explore this connection between phantasy and determinism further in our concluding chapter.

Secondly, the nature of the relation between Schleiermacher's inner ethical ideal and his activity in the outer world follows from his idealism. According to the viewpoint of philosophical idealism, not only our actions, but also the context of our activity, the world itself, is created in part by our inner life (see above, p. 220):

> As often as I turn my gaze into the inner self . . . , I intuit the action of the mind [*Geist*], which no world can change and no time can dissipate — which itself first creates world and time.[16]

For these reasons it is scarcely possible to overstate Schleiermacher's emphasis upon what he calls a person's inner life. In a satirical letter to Henriette Herz, who had written, a little too ebulliently, about certain agricultural progress she had observed in the countryside around a town she was visiting, Schleiermacher tries to redirect her attention inward:

> I will for once turn a cold and unfeeling side of my character outward, and tell you that I do not in the least grasp *that* and *how* the country does this to you. Are *we* somehow not included in this great activity? In reality, there is no greater object of activity than the mind and heart [*Gemüth*] — indeed there is no other. Are you not active there also? O,

---

[13] *Monologen*, 43. *Soliloquies*, 44.
[14] *Monologen*, 18. *Soliloquies*, 18.
[15] *Monologen*, 32. Emphasis added. Cf. *Soliloquies*, 33, where editor Friess's notes do not take cognizance of this alteration.
[16] *Monologen*, 22. *Soliloquies*, 22.

you fertile, you ever active spirit, who are a veritable Ceres of the inner nature — you lay such a great stress upon the activity of the outer world. But it is so utterly a means only, where a person loses himself in the general mechanism, of which so little is advantageous to the true end and goal of all action, and where so much is always lost a thousand times along the way! And that activity and striving [*Thun und Treiben*] in which a person strains and sweats (something a person really ought never to do) — is it not loud and blustering in comparison with our quiet action? Who ever hears us? What does the world know of our inner nature and its movements? Is it not all a secret? Only look at what you have done and still are doing and will do: admit that this action and cultivation come to infinitely more than all man can accomplish over that great chaos he wishes to control.[17]

An element of social irresponsibility plays in the lines of this letter, recollective of the elitism we earlier detected in Schleiermacher's ethical outlook (above, pp. 169–170) and representative of romanticism at its least defensible. Schleiermacher had to eat, and there were hungry people in his day, as in ours, who stood to benefit from whatever agricultural progress it is that Schleiermacher satirizes here. At the close of his letter Schleiermacher admits that he has exaggerated his case "out of pure polemics. And yet," he adds, "it is correct!"

Polemics and exaggeration aside, it does not seem too much to say that with respect to his evaluation of outward activity per se, Schleiermacher was a quietist. Illustrations of this attitude are not limited to his whimsical letter to Henriette Herz. Genuine distress over "vain activity and striving" (*eitles Thun und Treiben*)[18] is a persistent sentiment in the *Soliloquies*. Early in the third chapter, "World View," Schleiermacher gets into a lengthy repudiation of the high value his age places upon its outward achievements and material progress:

How deeply do I despise the generation that boasts of itself more shamelessly than any has ever done before. . . . This feeling of life's general enhancement is in fact more vividly and satisfyingly present in me than in those who are so loud in its praise. . . . Yet even so, I value this whole feeling but little. It is not something still better of this kind that I wish for the world. It pains me to the point of annihilation to see that this is taken to be the entire work of humankind, an unholy squandering of its holy powers. My demands are not so modest as to be content with this better relation of humankind to the outer world. . . . For its whole striving is directed to this, and upon this it bases its unbounded pride. Only this high have they risen in their consciousness of humankind: that from caring for their own bodily life and well-being, they lift themselves to caring for the same well-being of all. For them, that is virtue, justice, and love.[19]

[17]Sep. 9, 1798. *Br.* I, 190–91. "Ceres"; the Roman goddess of agriculture.
[18]*Monologen*, 11. *Soliloquies*, 12 ("vain energetic bustle").
[19]*Monologen*, 50–52. *Soliloquies*, 50–53.

In the midst of this attack upon the materialism of his age, Schleiermacher's view comes to focus in the following passage:

> I am not disturbed and disillusioned by their dreary imagination [*Einbil-
> dung*] that all enjoy so unequally that which all help to produce and
> maintain. For by emptiness in thinking and indolence in reflection all of
> us lose as well, and from all, habitude takes its toll. Wherever I calculate
> the ratio of limitation and power, I find the same quotient, only variously
> expressed, and an equal measure of life spreads itself over all.[20]

The mathematical image of this final sentence contains Schleiermacher's conception of progress. Schleiermacher believed that human
progress is not accurately measured by any absolute index, or catalogue
of indices. It is measured rather in terms of a ratio: power over
limitation, or achievement over perplexity. Some in Schleiermacher's
"Enlightened" generation were claiming that its achievements outdid
those of any earlier age. In particular cases, of course, the claims were
true. Schleiermacher believed, however, that if one divides achievements by their accompanying perplexities, the resulting ratio remains
about the same in every age. There is in this sense no progress and no
retrogression. This is particularly true, Schleiermacher believed, if one
divides materialistic achievements by their accompanying perplexities for
spiritual or inner life. It is common, however, for the brilliance of the
former to blind us to the latter. "People do not know how to distinguish
the constant quantity in a ratio of coefficients," Schleiermacher writes to
Brinkmann, "because for them everything is merely coefficient."[21]

Schleiermacher's indifference toward outward achievements and
claims of achievement, together with an inseparable Socratic awareness
of the extent and limits of his own powers, is a constant and defining
feature of his ethical outlook. His walk above Gnadenfrei in 1802 was
not an isolated experience in his life, any more than Wordsworth's visit
to the banks of the Wye in 1798 was a merely transient experience for
him. "In this moment there is life and food / For future years,"
Wordsworth writes in *Tintern Abbey*. He carried his quieted mood with
him back into the world's "fretful stir unprofitable." It is in this sense,
and not because he was inactive in the stir of human affairs,[22] that we
may speak of quietism in Schleiermacher's life.

A remarkable thing about Schleiermacher's quietism, which we are
able to see both from his publications and from his letters, is that when

[20] *Monologen*, 51. *Soliloquies*, 52.
[21] Dec. 14, 1803. *Br*. IV, 86–87.
[22] For three studies in English of Schleiermacher's involvement in public affairs, see
Robert M. Bigler, *The Politics of German Protestantism*, esp. 29–32, Jerry F. Dawson,
Friedrich Schleiermacher: The Evolution of a Nationalist, and R. C. Raack, "Schleiermacher's
Political Thought and Activity, 1806–1813," *Church History*, XXVIII (Dec., 1959),
374–90.

he repudiates the world's "vain activity and striving," he is not merely criticizing supposed progress in fields of endeavor other than his own, such as the agricultural technology he satirizes in his letter to Henriette Herz. Nor is he merely repudiating the general reliance of his age upon materialistic accomplishment as a measure of the value of life—though this is clearly part of what he criticizes, as when he writes of British pragmatists, "They are never in earnest about anything that goes beyond palpable utility; for they have robbed all science of life, and use it only as dead wood to make masts and rudders for their life's voyage in pursuit of gain."[23] The arresting thing about Schleiermacher's repudiation of distorted notions of progress is that he includes activities upon which he himself placed high value, activities for which he is admired and has been remembered. Schleiermacher renounces scholarly research, for instance, insofar as it fails to touch the inner life of the knower. "There should be no meditation and no contemplation for the person who does not know the inner nature of the spirit," Schleiermacher writes near the beginning of the *Soliloquies*, and he goes on to satirize the scholar who "researches what he has learned . . . and steps proudly into the commodious and crowded hall of learning, delighted that so much knowledge has been concentrated in himself." For if we measure the scholar's advancement in terms of a ratio—quantity of learning divided by the price the scholar has paid to achieve it— it becomes clear that there is frequent tragedy in educational "progress":

> The old crowded out by the new; the thoughts lost in thinking; the representations lost in learning—these are not taken into account, and so the tally is never correct. And even if it were, how deeply it wounds me that people can think that this is self-contemplation, that this is called knowing oneself. How miserably this highly praised business ends![24]

Thus the opinion of the man who, fourteen years later, would become Secretary of the Royal Academy of Sciences in Berlin.

Schleiermacher did not confine his skepticism to the "business" of scholarly acquaintances. He evaluated his own professional life from the same point of view, as is evident in his personal correspondence. In a letter to his sister, written from Berlin in 1801, we find Schleiermacher reporting the growing esteem in which he is being held among his professional peers:

> My life is taking on worth from another side now, which it did not have before, and a certain brilliance, if I may say so. With the little I have been able to be and to do publicly up to now, I am in fact beginning to have an effect upon the manner of thinking of cultivated and prominent people. I am respected by those whom one calls philosophers, and from near and

---

[23] *Reden*, 13, 2nd ed. *Speeches*, 10.
[24] *Monologen*, 12–13. *Soliloquies*, 13–14.

far religious souls follow me with great affection. I can say that I am a
blessing to many. If I maintain the health and strength to complete
several significant works I have at hand, then it can be foreseen that in
this respect, as well as in several sciences, I shall soon gain even more
influence, and in a few years will belong to the knowledgeable men whose
word carries some weight. This is pleasing to me, not only insofar as it
flatters natural vanity, but also insofar as it guarantees that I will be able
to enjoy a certain effectiveness in the world.

But at this point in the letter, in an unsettling tack of mood, Schleiermacher expresses his still deeper longing for a quiet family life, where
relationships and influence are inward and need not be judged in terms
of public ambition and achievement:

> Yet all this would completely disappear to me and would be nothing
> beside the prospect of a quiet, joyful domestic life. If, in order to enjoy
> this latter, things could not be otherwise, then it would not be at all
> difficult for me to place myself in a situation wholly removed from the
> theater of a greater effectiveness, in a situation that was a great hindrance
> to my scientific progress. Indeed all in the world is vain and illusion [*eitel
> und Täuschung*]—what one can enjoy as well as what one can do—except
> domestic life alone. What one effects in this quiet way, that endures. For
> those few souls, one can really be something and mold something
> significant.[25]

In his treatise of 1793, *On the Worth of Life*, Schleiermacher had written
of family life:

> Your quiet joys of communal activity, of communal feeling, remain the
> crown of my life! . . . And when I consider all the manifold gifts of life,
> and analyze with all deliberateness the worth of each, the most beautiful
> always remains this: that human beings can make a home.[26]

The context of these 1793 reflections on family life was Schleiermacher's incorporation in the Dohna household during his tenure as
tutor in Schlobitten, at a time when he was secretly in love with the
daughter Friederika.[27] The immediate occasion of the reflections from
his letter of 1801 was Schleiermacher's indignation over the cruel lack of
sympathy Eleonore Grunow was suffering from her husband. At both of
these periods of his life Schleiermacher was lonely and frustrated in
love, and that condition certainly intensified his longing for a family life.
On the other hand, such reflections as these could not be of much
significance coming from a person not in love, and this high evaluation

---

[25]To Charlotte, Nov. 10, 1801. *Br.* I, 284–85.

[26]"Denkmale," 54.

[27]See above, p. 10. Henriette Herz reports that Schleiermacher's feeling for Friederika
Dohna had been "so deep that his sister actually marveled that anyone else could awaken
his love anew" (letter to von Willich, Aug. 30, 1804, in Henriette Herz, *Schleiermacher
und seine Lieben*, 77). For Schleiermacher's response to the news of Friederika's early
death, see his letter to Charlotte, Nov. 10, 1801. *Br.* I, 283–84.

of family life recurs in Schleiermacher's writings at all stages of his career.[28]

At one place in his correspondence Schleiermacher mentions Spinoza's refusal to accept the chair of philosophy offered him at Heidelberg.[29] Spinoza cherished the tranquility of his craftsman's life and feared being swept up in the learning "business" Schleiermacher laments in the *Soliloquies*. Schleiermacher's letter mentioning Spinoza implies that Fichte might do well to consider the same course of action, and in 1800, Schleiermacher actually advised Schlegel to lecture in Jena under his own auspices, thus sparing himself the "irksome bother" of submitting to the "chicaneries" of a doctoral examination, dissertation, and disputation at the University.[30]

It is with the devitalizing specialization of his own scholarly species in mind, therefore, that Schleiermacher writes in *Soliloquies*:

> Those who would have everyone become a virtuoso and artist in science complain of me that I will not suffer myself to be limited, that it is deluded to hope that I shall ever seriously devote myself to something, since when I attain one perspective, then I rush on to other objects in the manner typical of a desultory mind. O that they would leave me in peace, and comprehend that my vocation is nothing else, that I cannot cultivate science, for I intend to cultivate myself.[31]

Schleiermacher anticipated that in due course he would contribute his share to the advancement of the sciences. But believing that in scholarly knowledge, no less than in knowledge of other kinds, we only half perceive and half create, he felt that to cultivate himself inwardly *was* to contribute to scholarship. "My inner action," he writes,

> is indeed not empty. If only I have become in myself more determinate and individual, then through my development I have also cultivated the world, no matter how soon or late the activity of another meets with mine in a different and novel way and unites with it to establish a visible act.[32]

This external manifestation of internal cultivation in a "visible act" may well come late rather than soon. Appropriation of knowledge, as Schleiermacher values that process, requires composure and time:

---

[28]See Schleiermacher's series of sermons Christian family life, *Predigten über den christlichen Hausstand*, published in 1820 (consult Bibliography).

[29]Letter to Henriette Herz, May 2, 1799. *Br.* I, 222.

[30]Letter to Schlegel, July 11, 1800. *Br.* III, 206–7. In a letter to Reimer of Feb. 23, 1804, Schleiermacher refers to that "altogether too miserable folk, the university scholars" (*Br.* III, 381).

[31]*Monologen*, 38–39. *Soliloquies*, 39–40.

[32]*Monologen*, 19. *Soliloquies*, 20.

> When something new stirs my mind it is not possible for me to penetrate
> with fiery vehemence directly to the core, and to know it completely.
> Such a procedure is not appropriate to the equanimity that is the keynote
> of the harmony of my nature. Such specialization would throw me off my
> life's center. Burying myself in one thing, I would become alienated from
> another, yet without having even the former as part of my true character
> [*wahres Eigenthum*]. I must first store away every new acquisition in my
> inner heart and mind [*Gemüth*] and then carry on the usual play of life,
> with its manifold activity, so that the new may first mix with the old and
> establish points of contact with all that was already in me. Only by so
> acting am I able to prepare the way for a deeper and more inner
> intuition. . . . Thus my progress is slow.[33]

"Not in vain was the quiet activity which, from without, appears to
be a life of unoccupied leisure; for it has beautifully furthered the
inward work of cultivation."[34] Schleiermacher's thinking in such a
passage may have been influenced by the quietism of his friend
Schlegel's *Lucinde*. One chapter of that rambling novel, for example, is
called "Idyll on Idleness." In his early treatise *On Human Freedom*,
Schleiermacher had found his ideal of freedom in the person who
"appears to act in accordance with circumstances but not to be altered
by them" (above, p. 85). This ideal then took on a more inward
orientation in the *Speeches*, where free expression was said to be
prompted solely from within a person: "For he would so act even if no
one were there" (above, p. 139). Schlegel's *Lucinde* suggests still a third
degree of inwardness: "The apex of understanding is to keep silent of
one's own choice, to give the soul over to fantasy."[35] The greatest
freedom is to be in a position to choose not to act at all. The greatest
freedom is inward quietism, surrender to phantasy. A person is then
completely self-possessed and constrained by nothing.

Taken to its limit, Schleiermacher's quietism might entail this kind
of freedom. But we have seen that as a rule Schleiermacher lived a good
bit short of his friend Schlegel's extremes. He writes:

> I know that my outer life will never manifest and complete my inner
> nature from all sides. . . . Perhaps I will never enter into an open quarrel
> with the world and be able to show how little all that the world is able to
> give and take disturbs my inner peace and the quiet unity of my nature.
> Yet in myself I know how I would act even then, for my mind and heart
> [*Gemüth*] have long been prepared and cultivated.[36]

Easy to say, perhaps. In the next chapter we shall see Schleiermacher's response to outward events that were indeed to pick a quarrel
with the "inner peace and the quiet unity" of his nature. Let us close

---

[33] *Monologen*, 41. *Soliloquies*, 42.
[34] *Monologen*, 42. *Soliloquies*, 43.
[35] Schlegel, *Lucinde*, "Tändeleien der Fantasie," 107.
[36] *Monologen*, 78–79. *Soliloquies*, 83.

this chapter with the observation that the final clause of this passage from the *Soliloquies*—"for my mind and heart have long been prepared and cultivated"—expresses exactly what we have called Schleiermacher's idea of freedom as "activity": a person's preparedness to meet events with a creative response that arises self-contained from within (above, p. 85). Thus we might call Schleiermacher's quietism an active quietism, contradictory as that phrase appears on the surface. Freedom and quietism, like freedom and determinism, are compatible notions for Schleiermacher. Freedom, as a bringing forth of the characteristic, is first of all a quiet and inward process: the bringing forth of a characteristic self.

Chapter 5. Schleiermacher's Philosophy of Resignation

In the rules of the understanding, resignation *is everywhere life's governing* command.

Schleiermacher's tentative prophecy in the *Soliloquies* of 1800, "Perhaps I will never come into an open quarrel with the world," was soon to be proven incorrect. The years between 1802 and 1804, which Schleiermacher called the "unhappiest" period of his life,[1] were to test severely the "inner peace and quiet unity of my nature" of which he boasts in the *Soliloquies*. Our aim in this chapter will be to appreciate the philosophy of resignation, so closely related to the quietism discussed in the previous chapter and to the determinism that has been our theme throughout, that sustained Schleiermacher through this crisis in his life. Our method will be to compare the *Soliloquies'* idealized ethical point of view with the actual philosophy of life expressed in Schleiermacher's correspondence and manifested in his attitudes and actions. The treatment of Schleiermacher in this chapter will therefore be more biographical than usual. It will bring us in the next chapter to the roles of sympathy and phantasy in Schleiermacher's life and prepare us to relate phantasy to determinism and freedom more theoretically in the final chapter of our study.

A biographical approach to philosophical understanding is consonant with Schleiermacher's own methods. As we have seen, Schleiermacher wrote the *Soliloquies* as an attempt to translate abstract philosophical idealism "into life, and to portray the character that . . . corresponds to this philosophy" (above, p. 159). Yet the portrayal of character in the *Soliloquies* remains rather abstract and idealized. One reader in 1804 remarked skeptically that if Schleiermacher was portraying himself in the *Soliloquies*, then he "must be an extraordinarily perfect person." Upon learning of this reader's remark, Schleiermacher wrote to her "to protest the logic of your conclusion":

In the *Soliloquies* I have presented my ideas—and indeed not as dead thoughts, of which one calculates in his head that things must be approximately so and so, but as ideas that really live in me, as I live in

[1]Letter to Henriette Herz, Nov. 21, 1803. *Br*. I, 382.

them. But of course these ideas are not presented to me like some fairy gift. Rather, like every better thing that comes to a person, they have arisen in me only after many a mistake and much folly. Their manifestation in my life is therefore only progressive, in conflict with the influences and remnants of earlier ideas. If, notwithstanding this, there is in the *Soliloquies* no trace of any conflict with myself, then that is only because I am quite resigned to the fact that a person can *become* only progressively.[2]

It was because of his resignation to the inevitable abstractness of ethical discussion that Schleiermacher regarded the novel as the literary medium best suited for communicating a "determinate intuition" of "inward humanity" (above, p. 234). This preference, in turn, helps to account for Schleiermacher's controversial defense of Schlegel's novel, *Lucinde*. In the *Confidential Letters on Friedrich Schlegel's Lucinde*, which Schleiermacher published anonymously in 1800, he writes:

You know of course how inclined we are to abstraction—indeed, to speak more correctly, how we are true slaves to it—and how we are deprived of an object of sensibility and phantasy the moment someone asks us for a judgment of that object. Speak therefore, without restraint and in clear words, of love.[3]

Schleiermacher's defense of his friend Schlegel, and Schleiermacher's own speaking, "without restraint and in clear words, of love"—these were the precipitating causes of the crisis in his life between 1802 and 1804. In the 1801 letter to Schleiermacher from his ecclesiastical superior Sack, the blunt criticism of the *Speeches* of which we have already seen a part (above, p. 116) was not in fact the first complaint. Sack's first complaint related to a more personal issue:

There has been only one side of your manner of thinking and mode of living in opposition to my concepts and feelings of propriety. I could not bring your apparent taste for intimate associations with persons of questionable principles and morals into unity with my image of the responsibilities of a preacher, for himself and for his relationships.[4]

There was little question in Schleiermacher's mind as to whom Sack was referring. "Your letter," Schleiermacher writes in his reply, "speaks of persons of questionable principles and morals with whom I am supposed to be in intimate association. And wherever I look in the limited circle of my relations . . . , I find only Friedrich Schlegel to whom your remark can relate."[5]

---

[2]Letter to Charlotte Pistorius, July 28, 1804. *Br*. I, 401. Charlotte Pistorius was a friend of Ehrenfried von Willich whom Schleiermacher had met shortly before the date of this letter. The two became close friends.

[3]Schleiermacher, *Vertraute Briefe über Friedrich Schlegels Lucinde*, "Zweiter Brief," 105.

[4]Sack to Schleiermacher, no date (summer, 1801). *Br*. III, 276.

[5]No date (summer, 1801). *Br*. III, 281.

Schleiermacher had in fact anticipated Sack's criticism of his friend-ship with Schlegel. As Schlegel was working on his *Lucinde* in the spring of 1799, Schleiermacher wrote to Henriette Herz, "*Lucinde* will cause trouble for us both. That the intimate friend of a preacher should write such a book, and the preacher not break with him!"[6] Far from breaking with Schlegel when the publication of his sensual novel created its public sensation, Schleiermacher reviewed *Lucinde* for a Berlin literary journal in terms that seem deliberately calculated to intensify controversy:

> How could there fail to be poetry where there is so much love! It is precisely through love that this work becomes not only poetic, but also religious and moral. Religious, because love is always shown in a perspec-tive that looks beyond life to the infinite; moral, because love spreads from the beloved out over the whole world, and demands for all, as for itself, freedom from all unsuitable limitations and prejudices. We confess that we have scarcely found the relation of poetry to morality anywhere so pure as here, where neither serves the other, but rather each lives in the other and exalts it.[7]

This does seem, as many critics have charged, excessive praise for a flawed novel.[8] Yet from the first there has been misunderstanding of Schleiermacher's defense of *Lucinde*. Schleiermacher's agreement with the novel's joining of sensual love with spiritual, his closeness to Schlegel and Schlegel's companion Dorothea Veit, and his own increas-ingly intense relation with Eleonore Grunow certainly colored his view of *Lucinde*. But these factors did not blind Schleiermacher's critical insight. He recognized that Schlegel's novel was flawed. In his letter to Sack he writes that *Lucinde* is

> a book one could not defend fundamentally without writing a second book, and which I do not wish to defend completely, because alongside much that is beautiful and worthy of praise, it contains much that I cannot condone. But does it indicate pernicious principles and morals? When someone wants to express in an example a theory he has formed about the sphere of poetic presentation, this has nothing to do with his character. And immoral secondary aims, or arbitrary outbreaks of inner immorality, I for my part have not found in *Lucinde*—though I have found them in many German and French poets whom no one disparages and abuses. In comparison with these, my friend seems to me like an artist who paints a naked Venus, as contrasted with an oriental Sultan who allows the performance of voluptuous dances by living bodies in the presence of children.[9]

[6]Apr. 2, 1799. *Werden*, 143.

[7]Schleiermacher, "Lucinde. Ein Roman von Friedrich Schlegel," *Berlinisches Archiv der Zeit und ihres Geschmacks*, II (July, 1800), 43. Also in *Br*. IV, 540.

[8]See the good discussion of Schleiermacher's opinions of *Lucinde* in Rudolph Haym, *Die romantische Schule*, 518–31.

[9]*Br*. III, 281–82.

What Schleiermacher says to Sack here is borne out by an examination of his writings on *Lucinde*. He did not defend the novel indiscriminately or without qualification. This is especially clear from the *Confidential Letters on Friedrich Schlegel's Lucinde*, a work far more substantive than his journalistic review of *Lucinde* quoted above, and lengthy enough (it is four-fifths the length of *Lucinde* itself) virtually to constitute the "second book" Schleiermacher mentions in his letter to Sack. The work consists of an exchange of contrasting views in letters between the anonymous author and several fictional or semi-fictional characters. Its form thus resembles that of the Platonic dialogue, and Schleiermacher's insight into the dialogical form (above, p. 188) applies here: every point of view represents part, and only part, of the truth. When read in accordance with this principle, the text of Schleiermacher's *Confidential Letters* provides substantial criticism of Schlegel's novel. The third letter, for example, is entitled "Ernestine to Me" — a play on the name of Schlegel's older sister, Charlotte Schlegel Ernst,[10] who was one of her brother's best critics. The letter reflects Charlotte's criticism of *Lucinde* for its selfishly masculine and irresponsibly privileged point of view:

> Does not love in this book, for all the completeness of its presentation, retreat a bit too much into itself? I would have liked to see it extend also outward into the world, and there accomplish something excellent. The frivolous hero should have this much of the knight in him. . . . Yet what could he do, you will say, since he has such a decisive hatred for all middle-class arrangements? But that is exactly what I am saying: he should not feel such hatred once he has discovered love. At least not in a world such as ours, where middle-class circumstances stifle women so terribly. In such a world, anyone who has devoted himself to a woman must, if only out of self-defense, enter into middle-class life and try to accomplish something.[11]

The prose of these *Confidential Letters* is exceptionally difficult to follow, however, and their critical subtleties were lost on most of their readers. Schleiermacher wrote to Brinkmann that his *Confidential Letters* were "really more on the subject of love than on *Lucinde*."[12] But to Schleiermacher's critics the book appeared to be a public defense of Schlegel's novel. Thus it appeared to Sack, as we have seen. And thus it appeared to the irreverent satirist Falk, who published a heavy-handed parody of the *Confidential Letters* in 1801.[13]

---

[10]See Schleiermacher's indication to this effect in his letter to Henriette von Willich, Feb. 21, 1809. *Werden*, 346.

[11] *Vertraute Briefe*, "Dritter Brief. Ernestine an mich," 109–10.

[12]July 19, 1800. *Br.* IV, 74.

[13]Johannes Daniel Falk, "Vertraute Briefe über Friedrich Schlegels Lucinde," in *Taschenbuch für Freunde des Scherzes und der Satire*, V (1801), 273–306. Falk seems not to have been aware that Schleiermacher was the author of the original, anonymous *Confidential Letters*.

Schleiermacher's close association with Berlin's Jewish society was a further object of satire and source of suspicion in many quarters. In 1801, Schlegel was living with Dorothea Mendelssohn Veit — Jewish, recently divorced, and not yet married to Schlegel. Schleiermacher himself was the constant companion of Henriette Herz — Jewish and married to someone else. Sack was too large minded a person to be disturbed by Schleiermacher's Jewish associations per se. But he was distressed by the moral implications of his young friend's connections. Sack's concern for Schleiermacher's character and career reached a climax in 1798 upon the publication of a chatty account of Berlin social life by Friederike Helene Unger, whose husband, the Berlin publisher Johann Friedrich Unger, was to bring out Schleiermacher's *Speeches* a year later. Schleiermacher describes Madam Unger as "an old, sick, peevish woman" who writes in a spirit of "pique toward the Jews."[14] Whatever the accuracy of Schleiermacher's characterization, Madam Unger's account was not without its effect on Schleiermacher's reputation. Shortly after its appearance Schleiermacher wrote to his sister:

> Today I have had a heart-to-heart talk with Sack about my Jewish associations. . . . He said he is not pedantic enough to be opposed to association with Jews (as I knew, since both his father and his father-in-law associated a great deal with Mendelssohn). But for these *bureaux d'esprit*, for the association as Madam Unger describes it, he said, he has no taste [*Sinn*] at all, and if it were to become too well known that I live so entirely among these people, it would inevitably produce an unfavorable impression upon many. He himself is concerned, he said, that the tone a person little by little assumes in these societies will in time give rise in me to indifference and antagonism toward my profession.[15]

Sack's complaint that Schleiermacher was living "so entirely among these people" was hardly an exaggeration. "For the most part I live with Herz now," Schleiermacher had written to his sister Charlotte, who in 1798 was trying her best to understand her brother's behavior but finding it a struggle:

> She lives during the summer in a pretty little house on the *Tiergarten* where she sees few people and I can thus enjoy her properly. I make it a point to spend a whole day with her at least once every week. I could do this with few people. But with her, in an alternation between business and pleasure, the day passes very delightfully. She has taught me Italian, or rather is doing so; we read Shakespeare together; we busy ourselves with physics; I share with her some of my knowledge of nature; we read now this, now that from a good German book; and in between, in the most

---

[14]Letter to Charlotte, Aug. 4, 1798. *Br.* I, 186. Madam Unger's "Briefe einer reisenden Dame über Berlin" appeared in the *Jahrbücher der Preussischen Monarchie, 1797, 1798.*

[15]Aug. 4, 1798. *Br.* I, 187–88. *Bureaux d'esprit*: a disparaging reference to the Jewish intellectual open houses of Berlin (see above, pp. 113–114) as "bureaus of wit."

> beautiful hours, we go walking and speak with each other from the innermost heart [*Gemüth*] about the most important things. Thus we have done since the onset of spring, and no one has disturbed us.[16]

It is customary for commentators to describe Schleiermacher's relation with Henriette Herz as "Platonic," as if this were simply self-evident. Thus Martin Redeker writes that "mutual respect and understanding, free from erotic desire, was the basis of the friendship."[17] Friedrich Kantzenbach puts the matter even more simply: "The relation between Schleiermacher and Henriette had nothing to do with sensual love."[18] This seems a little too simple, however, for a person who preached the indissoluble unity of body and spirit as insistently as Schleiermacher did. More to the point, these accounts are not adequate to the historical record.

It is true that in Schleiermacher's attempt to render his relationship with Henriette Herz comprehensible to his sister Charlotte, he repeatedly reassures her that no passionate involvement has ever materialized between them.[19] There is no reason to doubt what Schleiermacher says. Close attention to the language of Schleiermacher's reassurances, however, reveals that his "Platonic" friendship with Henriette Herz was an achievement of self-discipline and not simply a matter of course:

> You fear my tender and intimate relations with persons of the other sex, and in this you are indeed completely correct; there is a certain danger in them, and viewed from a distance, where one sees things only in general, they appear more dangerous than when viewed from close by. In this connection I make it my constant business to watch over myself; I make myself accountable for the smallest detail; and as long as I do this, I do not think I am called upon to break off a relation which is otherwise essential and important to me, which contributes to my cultivation, and in which I am able to effect much good.

Then, specifically of Henriette Herz he writes:

> I belong . . . essentially to her existence; I can complete her insights, her views, her mind and heart [*Gemüth*] on many sides, and so she does for me as well. Something passionate will never arise between us, and in this relation to each other *we have in fact already passed the most decisive trials.*[20]

[16]May 30, 1798. *Br.* I, 174–75. *Tiergarten*: Berlin's central park and zoo.

[17]Redeker, *Friedrich Schleiermacher. Leben und Werk*, 42. English tr., 28.

[18]Kantzenbach, *Friedrich Daniel Ernst Schleiermacher*, 43.

[19]See for example Schleiermacher's letters to Charlotte of May 30 and Oct. 15, 1798 (*Br.* I, 175–76 and 193). In the former, the phrase "*aber die beiden von uns beiden!*" should read "*aber die Leiden von uns beiden!*" Cf. *Werden*, 106.

[20]Letter to Charlotte, Mar. 23, 1799. *Br.* I, 206–7. Emphasis added.

A year after this letter to Charlotte, Schleiermacher reiterates the theme of its final clause—the attainment of a friendship beyond love—as a theme in one of his *Confidential Letters on Lucinde*:

> A friendship between man and woman *prior* to love seems to me something unnatural and an empty, indeed even culpable, undertaking [*ein leeres, ja sogar sträfliches Unternehmen*]. . . . But on the contrary, I can grasp quite well how friendship can arise between men and women who already love—not simply for lack of something better, but rather completely naturally, with full consonance of the heart, and without any secret wishes.[21]

This passage seems a more adequate reflection of Schleiermacher's friendship with Henriette Herz than the simple assertion that their relation had "nothing to do with sensual love."

The fact is that twice in his correspondence marriage with Henriette Herz was on Schleiermacher's mind, albeit as an improbability. "If I could ever have married Herz," he writes to his sister in 1798, " I believe it would have been a capital marriage—except that it would surely have become too harmonious."[22] And again, some two years later:

> Whoever understands something about the expression of inwardness immediately recognizes in her a passionless nature, and even if I wanted to give myself merely to her outward influence, she has nothing to charm me, although her face is undeniably very beautiful. Her colossal, royal figure is so very much the opposite of mine, that if I imagine that we were both free and loved each other and married, I would always find something laughable and absurd in this discrepancy, which I could set aside only on the basis of very overweighty causes.[23]

In a letter of 1802 to Henriette Herz herself, Schleiermacher summarizes his perception of their relationship as follows:

> General sexual consciousness must always be the point from which one proceeds; how it is to be managed must first be arranged before a connection between man and woman can decide itself definitely for friendship. As this relates to you . . . , I have never seen you engage in coquettery toward me which I would want to censure; I do not know that you have ever done anything to captivate my sensuality. That I have never fallen in love with you, even without your complicity, may be attributed to two quite different factors. First, my conviction that you belonged to A.,[24] who led me to you. And second, the feeling of the immense physical disparity between us. I would have appeared laughable to myself if I had

---

[21] *Vertraute Briefe*, "Achter Brief. An Eleonore," 155–56. The letter goes on to say that Schlegel's novel knows nothing of this kind of friendship.

[22] Nov. 8, 1798. *Br*. I, 195.

[23] Letter to Charlotte, Feb. 12, 1801. *Br*. I, 261. In translating the final clause ("*worüber ich mich nur sehr überwiegender Gründe wegen hinwegsezen könnte*") I have tried to preserve Schleiermacher's amusing pun, be it intentional or Freudian.

[24] Alexander Dohna. See above, p. 113.

thought of myself in any sensual situation with you, and that is why it
struck me as so tasteless when people conjectured this sort of thing about
us.[25]

The nuances of this account, like those of Schleiermacher's *Confidential Letters*, were once again invisible to Berlin observers of the Schleiermacher-Herz relation. The amusing incongruity of their sizes, however, was not. The 1801 issue of Johannes Falk's *Pocketbook for Friends of Humor and Satire*, containing the parody of the *Confidential Letters*, included also a satirical engraving in which, along with other literary and social figures, the two Schlegels, Schleiermacher, and Henriette Herz are caricatured (Fig. D). The latter two are labeled "Jew-wives." In her memoirs, dictated late in her life, Henriette recalls this caricature of herself and Schleiermacher, and their reaction to it:

> It is understandable that people who had as much to do with one another
> as Schleiermacher and I would be seen together often outside the house
> as well. And there the contrast between me, the very tall and in those
> days still rather fully endowed *Frau*, and the small, thin, and not even
> well-formed Schleiermacher may well have had its comical aspect. Berlin
> wit even went so far as a caricature of us—in those days still a rather rare
> medium of satire in Berlin. I was walking with Schleiermacher, carrying
> him in my hand as a *Knicker*—a kind of small, collapsible parasol then in
> use—while he in turn had a similar *Knicker* in miniature, peeping out of
> his pocket.[26] This caricature did not remain hidden from us, and I believe
> that no one in Berlin laughed over it more than Schleiermacher and I
> did.[27]

Schleiermacher's overseer Sack was less amused. As early as 1798, already disturbed over Schleiermacher's social life, the Berlin Directorate of the Reformed Church under Sack's leadership had secured Schleiermacher a position as court chaplain in Schwedt, a little town some fifty miles to the northeast of Berlin. So insistent was Sack's urging of Schleiermacher to sever his Berlin connections and go to Schwedt that Schleiermacher had to refuse in writing, not once, but

---

[25]Oct. 26, 1802. *Werden*, 282.

[26]This recollection is not quite accurate. In the caricature Schleiermacher carries Henriette's parasol, and it is a copy of the *Speeches* that peeps out of his pocket. The inaccuracy may perhaps be traced to the casual, if not careless, editing of these memoirs by Henriette Herz's friend, J. Fürst. See the comment on Fürst's work *Jugenderinnerungen von Henriette Herz*, in *Mittheilungen aus dem Litteraturarchiv in Berlin, 1896*, 141. What is apparently a second public Herz-Schleiermacher caricature, different from that done by Falk, is described by Hans Landsberg, ed., *Henriette Herz. Ihr Leben und ihre Zeit*, 57.

[27]*Henriette Herz. Ihr Leben und ihre Erinnerungen*, ed. J. Fürst, 160–61. Schleiermacher perhaps deserved the cheap caricature. In 1799 he had suggested to Brinkmann a poetic counter-satire of Falk, recommending the doggerel rhyme scheme *Falk/Schalk*, *Satyre/Geschmiere* ("Falk/scoundrel, satire/smear"). Letter to Brinkmann, July 6, 1799. *Br.* IV, 51.

twice. "It is a very unpleasant feeling not to be able to make something so closely connected to the innermost person clear to a man whom I esteem and love so much . . . ," he wrote to Charlotte:

> But as you may imagine, in going there I should have been obliged to take leave of many studies I am pursuing here with so much zeal, and my scientific cultivation would have come to a standstill on account of my remoteness from all resources and the lack of literary connections. I would have entered into a luxurious little town, where society consists in parties and card playing, and I would have had to break away from my friends here without finding others.[28]

Unfortunately, an even more isolated exile from Berlin was in store for Schleiermacher. The controversy over Schleiermacher's mode of life grew steadily, fueled by the publication of his *Confidential Letters on Lucinde* in 1800, by the Falk parody and caricature, by Schleiermacher's sharp exchange of letters with Sack in 1801, and finally by Schleiermacher's increasingly intense involvement with Eleonore Grunow, which by the autumn of 1801 had reached the point of an open confrontation with the minister Grunow over Eleonore's miserable state.[29] The pressure upon Schleiermacher from his Church Directorate grew in proportion with the controversy. Finally, in the early spring of 1802, Schleiermacher yielded to the Directorate's insistence that he accept the position of court chaplain in the Pomeranian town of Stolp near the Baltic Sea (Figs. K and L), where Schleiermacher's maternal grandfather had served as court chaplain some eighty years before.[30]

Upon learning of Schleiermacher's reluctant decision to leave Berlin, Schlegel wrote to console him: "Bear in mind that you have always been able to reach your goals in science only through a sacrifice of your social needs. . . . Solitude is the mother of science and art."[31] But Dorothea, living with Schlegel in Dresden at the time, knew Schleiermacher better. She appended a note to Schlegel's letter. Upon receiving the news of Schleiermacher's transfer, she writes,

> my first move was to the map. God help us, how far away this Stolp lies! How far removed from Berlin, and from every other respectable city; so god-awful northern [*so himmelschreyend nördlich*], so far from everything beautiful. Poor friend, you have much misery before you to endure!

Dorothea's prophecy, by thus contrasting directly with Schlegel's, confirms the truth of Schleiermacher's long-standing intuition of himself: "it lies deep in my nature . . . that I shall always be more closely related to

[28]July 25, 1798. *Br.* I, 184.
[29]See the letter to von Willich, Oct. 8, 1801. *Werden*, 229.
[30]Hermann Hering, *Samuel Ernst Timotheus Stubenrauch und sein Neffe Friedrich Schleiermacher*, 11. Stolp is today Slupsk, Poland.
[31]Mar. 25, 1802. *Br.* III, 310.

women than to men, for there is so much in my mind and heart
[*Gemüth*] that the latter seldom understand."[32] Nonetheless, Sack's
masculine assessment of Schleiermacher's destination proved to be as
accurate as it was flat-footed: "Stolp can be no substitute for Berlin."[33]

"Life steals past me like a hot wind that singes everything, and my
fantasy does not rest until it hears the dirt roll on my coffin."[34] Such
was Schleiermacher's mood six months after his arrival in Stolp. Then
the loss of Eleonore Grunow struck him. Schleiermacher had left Berlin
expecting Eleonore to dissolve her marriage and come to Stolp to join
him within a year's time. Already in the summer of 1801 he had
proposed marriage, albeit in an unguarded moment and without intending to.[35] In the fall of that year Eleonore had greeted him on at least
one occasion as her "bridegroom."[36] As late as January, 1803, Schleiermacher was still expecting Eleonore to join him. But by February,
having a presentiment of the futility of their plans, Schleiermacher was
gripped by a tragic sense of identification with Novalis's loss of his
fiancée, and with that poet's early death.[37]

March, 1803, brought a letter from Eleonore conveying her anguished decision to cut herself off from him.[38] The month of June
found Schleiermacher still unable to concentrate, and for distraction,
gambling away "a great deal of money" at a local club.[39] His health,
which, as he once said, had never been supported by anything more
than "good will and good humor alone,"[40] was shattered. By August,

---

[32]Letter to Charlotte, Mar. 23, 1799. *Br*. I, 207.

[33]Letter from Sack to Schleiermacher, July 1, 1802. *Br*. III, 320. Two years later, during
which time Schleiermacher had all but perished of loneliness and anguish, Sack was to hit
the mark again: "So much is certain: Stolp is not the place that can satisfy and please you
in the long run" (letter of Jan. 17, 1804. *Br*. III, 377).

[34]Letter to von Willich, Dec. 18, 1802. *Werden*, 290. Schleiermacher's later epithets for
Stolp echo this early image, as when he refers to Stolp as "an Arabian desert" (*Briefe
Schleiermachers an A. W. Schlegel*, 773) and "a great casket" (*Briefe Schleiermachers*, ed. H.
Mulert, 194).

[35]Letter to Charlotte, July 1, 1801. Quoted in Dilthey, *Leben Schleiermachers*, ed.
Redeker, I/1, 494.

[36]Letter from Schleiermacher to von Willich, Nov. 4, 1801. *Werden*, 230.

[37]Letter to Reimer, Feb., 1803. *Werden*, 294. Novalis had died in Mar., 1801, at the age
of twenty-eight; his fiancée, Sophie von Kühn, in Mar. 1797, age fifteen.

[38]See Schleiermacher's letter to Henriette Herz, Mar., 1803. *Werden*, 297–98.

[39]Letter to Henriette Herz, June 21, 1803. *Br*. I, 369.

[40]Letter to von Willich, June 15, 1803. *Briefe Friedrich Schleiermachers an Ehrenfried und
Henriette von Willich*, 66. A perusal of Schleiermacher's correspondence reveals that
Schleiermacher suffered from an appalling list of physical ailments. There was first his
slight deformity of the upper back from childhood. In addition, between 1789 and 1804,
Schleiermacher continually feared blindness; suffered regularly from backaches, headaches,
toothaches, and stomach cramps; experienced a mysterious periodic swelling of hands and
feet; suspected tuberculosis on the basis of severe chest pains; was jaundiced by a liver
disorder, plagued by insomnia, and weakened by occasional blood lettings. At the age of
twenty-nine Schleiermacher was told by a physician that he should not expect to live past

1803, Henriette Herz honestly feared that Schleiermacher was going to die.[41]

Her fears do not seem to have been unreasonable. The topic of suicide, which Schleiermacher had long discussed with Brinkmann, begins to appear in Schleiermacher's letters from Stolp with ominous immediacy. As early as 1789, Schleiermacher had expressed his opinion that if any circumstance justifies suicide, it is "that in which a person cannot act freely, for in this consists the whole worth and real essence of life."[42] This connection between suicide and a loss of freedom, which he had defined abstractly in 1789, became all too concrete for Schleiermacher in the summer of 1803. Immersed in grief over the loss of Eleonore, Schleiermacher for a time had difficulty seeing beyond the constraints that loneliness, failing health, and now bereavement had imposed upon his freedom. Even before Eleonore's letter of farewell Schleiermacher had written to Henriette Herz, "certainly there is no more poetic suicide than a plunge into water."[43] Shortly after Eleonore's letter he wrote again: "The waters close over my head, as Kind David would say. Do you know the sensation when one is under water and unable to get one's breath? So it is with me."[44]

Schleiermacher's despair in Stolp drove him for almost the only time in his life to express himself in poetry. One poem is *Der Verlassene* ("The Forsaken"), a ballad of five stanzas, concluding with the following three:

> " *Wo mag die Braut doch bleiben? ich sehne mich so sehr—* "
> *Ach die Braut ist dir gestorben,*
> *Ist vom Feind mit List erworben.*
> *Jammre, weine nur sehr,*
> *Siehst sie nimmermehr.*
>
> " *Wo ist nun meine Freude? wo ist nun all mein Glück?* "
> *Ach die Freud' in Nacht versunken,*
> *All dein Glück in Schmerz ertrunken.*
> *Keine Freude, kein Glück*
> *Kehret dir zurück.*

---

the age of fifty. In the *Soliloquies* Schleiermacher dismisses his ailments with the remark that health "deceives those who have it; for death hides in little corners, and one day springs out and grabs them with mocking laughter. What does it hurt, then, that I already know where he lurks?" *Monologen*, 86–87. *Soliloquies*, 93.

[41]Letter to von Willich from Henriette Herz, Aug. 6, 1803. Herz, *Schleiermacher und seine Lieben*, 61–62.

[42]Letter to Brinkmann, dated to 1789 by its place of origin, Drossen. *Br*. IV, 31. Schleiermacher adds that even if under this condition he committed suicide, it would not be "in the hope of some better" life after death.

[43]Aug. 24, 1802. *Br*. I, 321.

[44]To Herz, June 10, 1803. *Br*. I, 366.

" Wo ist der Tod zu finden? wo gräbt mir wohl mein Grab?"
Wo du suchst wirst du finden,
Kannst's in Land und See dir gründen.
Bald gräbt man ein Grab
Willst du nur hinab.[45]

*   *   *   *   *   *

"Where might my bride be tarrying? I yearn so terribly — "
O your bride is dead,
Is won by the enemy's cunning.
Grieve, weep as you will,
You shall see her nevermore.

"Where now is my joy? where now is all my happiness?"
O your joy is sunk in night,
All your happiness is drowned in pain.
No joy, no happiness
Will return to you.

"Where is death to be found? where can I dig my grave?"
Where you seek you shall find,
Can inter yourself in land or sea.
A grave is quickly dug
Once you wish to go.

Imagery of drowning dominates a second poem, *An der See* ("By the Sea"). It ends:

. . . Drunten darf nichts erklingen,
Trauer ist ungestört.
Tiefe, nur du
Zur Ruh'
Schliessest die Sinne zu.[46]

*   *   *   *   *   *

. . . Down below nothing can sound,
Grief is undisturbed.
Deep, only you,
In order to give rest,
Close up the senses.

Schleiermacher's early philosophy of life was assayed in this crucible of despair. In particular, the idealistic philosophy of his *Soliloquies* was tested by the realities of his life at Stolp, and our concern in the remainder of this chapter will be to discover how well it fared. This is

---

[45]From the manuscript in the *Schleiermacher Nachlass*, Item #751. The poem is printed in full in a somewhat different form, which I would judge to be an earlier version, in Dilthey, *Leben Schleiermachers*, ed. Redeker, I/1, 309–10.

[46]Printed in full in Dilthey, ibid., 310–11.

not an arbitrary scholarly concern. It is a concern that burned in Schleiermacher's own heart in 1803. One more of Schleiermacher's poems from that unhappy year is a Petrarchan sonnet entitled *Zugabe zu den Monologen* ("Appendage to the Soliloquies"). Its sestet comments on the idealism of the *Soliloquies*, which has been the theme of the sonnet's octave:

> *So hofft ich nah dem schönen Ziel zu kommen,*
> *Ergriff mit kühnem Muth der Liebe Hand,*
> *In reine Höhen mich mit ihr zu schwingen.*
> *Jezt ist durch herbe Pein das Herz beklommen,*
> *In liebeleere Wüste streng verbannt,*
> *Wird unter Thränen wenig mir gelingen.*[47]

> *   *   *   *   *   *

> So I hoped to approach the beautiful goal,
> With audacious spirit took my beloved's hand,
> To ascend the pure heights with her.
> Now my heart is oppressed with bitter pain,
> Harshly exiled in a loveless desert,
> Amid tears, little shall I succeed.

Our question is this: How well or how poorly did the philosophy of the *Soliloquies* "succeed," in the sense of Schleiermacher's poem?

In a letter on the occasion of Schleiermacher's thirty-fifth birthday, November 21, 1803, Henriette Herz advised her friend "only to endure, not to struggle."[48] A philosophy of endurance, closely related to the philosophy of quietism we examined in the preceding chapter, had long been a part of Schleiermacher's deterministic ethical outlook. Only shortly before, in fact, he had counseled Henriette, deeply distraught over the recent departure from Berlin of both Schleiermacher and Alexander Dohna, to endure her unaccustomed loneliness with as much "serenity" as she could muster.[49] Much earlier, Schleiermacher had concluded his 1793 essay *On the Worth of Life* with a section entitled "Resignation": "In the rules of the understanding, *resignation* is everywhere life's governing command."[50] Schleiermacher tried to live by this credo of resignation. Shortly before the crisis in their relationship Schleiermacher had written to Eleonore, "Whoever seriously wants something must also want all that is necessarily connected with it."[51]

---

[47]From the manuscript in the *Schleiermacher Nachlass*, Item #752/3. The sonnet is printed in full in Dilthey, ibid., 479.

[48]Quoted in Schleiermacher's letter to Henriette, Nov. 21, 1803. *Br*. I, 382.

[49]Letter of June 6, 1802. *Werden*, 245. Upon receiving Schleiermacher's letter Henriette wrote to von Willich, "What one can say to oneself, I do; and Schleier has said it to me so beautifully. But I am by far not strong enough to endure quietly so powerful a disruption of my outer world" (June 6, 1802. Herz, *Schleiermacher und seine Lieben*, 35–36).

[50]"Denkmale," 63. Schleiermacher's emphasis.

[51]Sept. 10, 1802. *Br*. I, 334.

Such was Schleiermacher's deterministic philosophy of resignation in the abstract. Our question is how it fared in the actual crisis. Schleiermacher wanted Eleonore; he loved her where she was and for what she was. Could he also "want," that is, could he accept and resign himself to the decision Eleonore's character and circumstances eventually determined her to make? From the midst of his anguish in June, 1803, Schleiermacher writes to von Willich:

> O, dear friend, let me speak no more of myself. In and of itself my life contains nothing deserving of sympathy. I devote none to it myself; do not you do so either. *It is such that it cannot be otherwise, and therefore good.*[52]

These sentences embody Schleiermacher's determinism and the existential attitude of resignation that accompanies it. More than once Schleiermacher's correspondence even intimates a Stoic *amor fati*, love of fate, in his temperament. He had written to Eleonore in 1802, "Glory be also to these sorrows, which in this age are an unavoidable element of a beautiful life. Must not everyone to whom they are not near seek them out in the wide world, in order to become certain of his love and his faith?"[53] To Reimer, Schleiermacher describes the "rending" pain of his absence from Eleonore, but adds, "Yet these pains belong together with the enjoyment of life. Thereby the innermost self is more filled."[54]

Except for a few moments of his deepest depression, however, Schleiermacher's determinism was not fatalism— not the surrendering of one's ethical goals to fate, the abandoning of one's moral ideals because of what happens to one's life.[55] In the *Soliloquies* one finds Schleiermacher shunning resignation of a certain kind—what he calls the passive and passionless endurance of middle age: "Such calm is only the foolish transition from hope to contempt."[56] In this spirit of the *Soliloquies* Schleiermacher responds to Henriette's advice "only to endure, not to struggle":

> Take that advice back, dear Jette. Your knowledge of me has not inspired it, but only your wishes for me. For me there is no other endurance than struggling endurance; any other would only be a sullen despair. I cannot endure this without hoping. Hope that merely waits is only the hope of fools. I must struggle in order to hope, as I must hope in order to endure.[57]

---

[52]June 15, 1803. *Briefe Schleiermachers an Willich*, 67. Emphasis added.

[53]Oct. 16, 1802. *Br.* I, 343. See also *Br.* I, 349.

[54]Letter of Jan. 12, 1803. *Br.* I, 358.

[55]See Schleiermacher's definition of the "unchristian term *fate*, which always implies that the individual is determined by the cooperation of all other things without the least respect to what would have issued from his own independent existence" in *The Christian Faith*, Prop. 164.3.

[56]*Monologen*, 48. *Soliloquies*, 49.

[57]Letter of Nov. 21, 1803. *Br.* I, 382.

As we spoke of Schleiermacher's quietism as an "active" quietism, therefore, so we must speak of his resignation as an active resignation. It remains for us, in concluding this chapter, to ascertain the character of the activity, the struggle, that enabled Schleiermacher to endure.

In the *Soliloquies* Schleiermacher had written, "I shall rather choose to die than, in protracted misery, to intuit in myself an existence that annuls my humanity."[58] In the crisis of his life in 1803, he was rescued from the grim alternative of suicide by activity that constituted his "humanity" and energized his philosophy of resignation, activity having an inner and an outer component. The outward activity was the Plato project, taken over from Schlegel (see above, pp. 127ff). But as always Schleiermacher's greater attention was directed to his inner life. The inward action that sustained his will to live was his striving toward the goal of ethical life that he had defined a decade before, the practice of cultivating and molding an integral, balanced sphere of individual knowledge and desire, the art of shaping an aggregate of personal experiences into a characteristic whole.

In the *Soliloquies* Schleiermacher had spoken of the invincibility of this inward action with the full confidence of inexperience:

> Always to become more fully what I am: that is my only will. . . . As surely as I can always act, I can always act in this way. . . . Come then what may! So long as I relate everything to this goal, and every outer relation, every outer form of life, leaves me indifferent—and all are of equal worth to me if they but express [*äussern*] the nature of my being and appropriate [*aneignen*] new material for its inner cultivation [*Bildung*] . . .—just so long shall my will rule fate, and turn to its purpose all that fate may bring, with freedom [*Freiheit*].[59]

"Is this but empty illusion?" Schleiermacher asks at the end of this passage. "Does impotence hide behind this feeling of freedom?" Those are good questions. They could be tested nowhere but in the crucible of Schleiermacher's own suffering. From the midst of that suffering, in June, 1803, Schleiermacher writes to von Willich:

> Do not understand me, dear friend, as if in the real moral sense I were overcome by fate. It has little power over my nature, over my way of thinking, over my action and my love. Would it not be an affectation if I refused to admit that fate has ruined my life? Yet this only confirms that a person and a person's life are not one and the same.[60]

---

[58] *Monologen*, 85. *Soliloquies*, 92.

[59] *Monologen*, 69–70. *Soliloquies*, 71–72. Notice here again the conjunction of the three aspects of freedom we examined in Part II—expression, appropriation, and cultivation.

[60] June 15, 1803. *Briefe Schleiermachers an Willich*, 68. The word "action" here is *Thun*, which in the *Soliloquies* commonly denotes inward action, as opposed to outward *Handlung*, which I translate "activity." Fichte makes a similar distinction in his *Erste Einleitung in die Wissenschaftslehre*, 440.

Schleiermacher's philosophy of life recommends an acceptance of life's fate, then, but an active acceptance that molds fate willfully into the integral sphere of knowledge and love known as a person's heart and mind (*Gemüth*). "In the thinking of such a will," he writes in the *Soliloquies*, "the concept of fate disappears."

> I have experienced joy and pain; I know every grief and every smile; and of all I have encountered . . . , what is there from which I have appropriated nothing new for my being, from which I have not won strength that nourishes the inner life?[61]

If there is inexperienced complacency in such passages, nevertheless the philosophy of the *Soliloquies* came to Schleiermacher's service when he most needed it. In the autumn of 1803, Schleiermacher wrote to a friend who had inquired about the *Soliloquies*:

> Like every good work, this one is its own reward. You have given me occasion to look at myself once more in this mirror after a long interval. I am shocked to find myself so weakened and disfigured by sorrow and by the short space of time during which I have had to live without the presence of any friends, who are so utterly necessary to the thriving of my nature. I have found the courage not to lose myself entirely. . . . I have looked into the *Soliloquies* again with a joyful feeling. . . . It was a lucky spirit that impelled me thus to present myself—or rather my striving, the innermost law of my life. Much that is beautiful I owe to this book.[62]

Slowly Schleiermacher regathered and redirected his life. In October of 1804, after a restorative summer visit on the Baltic island of Rügen where he was reunited with many of his dearest friends, he arrived in Halle to assume his new duties as Preacher to the University and Professor *extraordinarius* of Theology.[63] He was once again entertaining the hope that Eleonore would join him and become his wife. [64] Once again that hope was to be frustrated. On Rügen, however, he had met von Willich's fiancée, Henriette von Mühlenfels, who as a widow would

[61] *Monologen*, 70, 72. *Soliloquies*, 72, 75. As with his definition of freedom (above, p. 137n), Schleiermacher's active acceptance of fate again echoes Stoic philosophy. See for example the section headed "That We Can Derive Advantage from All External Things" in Epictetus, *Discourses*, tr. Long, 241–44.

[62] Letter to Charlotte von Kathen, Aug..10, 1803. *Br.* I, 377.

[63] For details of Schleiermacher's transition from Stolp to Halle see my article "Three New Schleiermacher Letters Relating to his Würzburg Appointment of 1804," *Harvard Theological Review*, 68:3/4 (1975).

[64] See for example Schleiermacher's letter to Schlegel, Oct. 10, 1804: "Today I leave for Halle. Eleonore is once more close to the salutary separation, and if you return to Germany, perhaps it will be my pleasure to greet you under my roof and hers" (*Br.* III, 406). For Schleiermacher's completest account of his final separation from Eleonore in October of 1805, see his letter of Nov. 16, 1805, in *Fr. Schleiermacher's Briefwechsel mit J. Chr. Gass*, 38–39. See also *Braut*, 52–53, and for Schleiermacher's later perspective on his relation with Eleonore, *Braut*, 170.

in 1809 become Schleiermacher's wife (see above, p. 202). An eyewitness reports[65] that when Schleiermacher next saw Eleonore Grunow, at a large social gathering in 1819, he approached her, took her hand, and said, "Dear Eleonore, God has indeed made amends to us."

---

[65] *Br.* I, 138, where the report is relayed by Schleiermacher's daughter and step-son, who edited the first edition of *Aus Schleiermacher's Leben in Briefen*, Vols. I and II.

Chapter 6. Sympathy and Phantasy in Schleiermacher's Life

O that people knew to use this godly power of fantasy, which alone sets the spirit free, carries it out beyond every dominion and every limit, and without which a person's sphere is so narrow and anxious! . . . It supplies me with what actuality lacks; every relation in which I see another, I appropriate through fantasy.

Henrich Steffens, a natural scientist and philosopher who became Schleiermacher's closest colleague at the University of Halle, has left a perceptive verbal portrait of Schleiermacher as Steffens knew him shortly after Schleiermacher's return from his exile in Stolp:

> Schleiermacher, as is well known, was small in stature, and somewhat misshapen, although it scarcely disfigured him. In all his movements he was lively, and his features were most highly impressive. A certain sharpness in his look might perhaps strike one as repellent. Indeed he seemed to look right through one. . . . His face was longish, his features sharply drawn, his lips firmly closed, his chin protruding, his eye lively and fiery, his look continuously earnest, collected, and circumspect. I saw him in the most manifold changing relationships of life, deeply reflective and playful, jesting, mild and angry, moved by joy as by pain. Continuously an unchanging calm, greater, more powerful than the passing emotions, appeared to govern his disposition [*Gemüth*]. Yet there was nothing stiff in this calm. A soft irony played in his features, an intimate sympathy stirred him inwardly, and an almost childlike goodness permeated the evident calm. His prevailing self-possession had sharpened his senses in a wonderful way. Even while he was engaged in the most lively conversation, nothing escaped him. He saw all that went on around him; he heard all, even the soft conversation of others.[1]

Steffens' description reflects not only the quietism and resignation that have been our subjects in the preceding chapters, but also the "active" character of those qualities (above, pp. 253 and 269), the fact that there was "nothing stiff" (*nichts Starres*) in Schleiermacher's calm. Steffens' description of Schleiermacher also introduces our opening theme for this chapter, the "intimate sympathy" that "stirred him inwardly."

Sympathy—literally "feeling with" or sharing another's position in the world—is the pulse of Schleiermacher's life and ethics. To judge

---

[1]Henrich Steffens, *Was ich Erlebte*, vol. V, 141–42.

from his correspondence and the testimony of his friends, Schleiermacher had a virtually inexhaustible reservoir of sympathy for others,
and a correspondingly insatiable need for love and sympathy in return.
"O, dear Jette," he writes to Henriette Herz,

> do rightly by me and write me diligently. That is necessary for the
> preservation of my life, which absolutely cannot thrive in solitude. Truly I
> am the most dependent and least self-sufficient being on earth; I even
> doubt that I am an individual. I stretch out all my roots and leaves after
> love. I must contact it immediately, and if I cannot quaff it in full
> draughts, I quickly dry up and wither. Such is my innermost nature.
> There is no remedy for it, nor do I desire any.[2]

Written as it was from Potsdam, where in 1799 Schleiermacher suddenly
found himself isolated from the Berlin friends he had lately grown to
cherish (see above, pp. 140–141), this letter is an extreme expression of
Schleiermacher's need for sympathy, but it is not uncharacteristic. Such
expressions of need literally fill Schleiermacher's letters from the period
of his early life.

Give as well as take distinguishes Schleiermacher's need for sympathy, however. In the *Soliloquies* Schleiermacher coins a phrase to
express the twofold dynamics of sympathy: *die Gemüther Wechselan-
schauung*, "the reciprocal intuition of minds and hearts."[3] Schleiermacher richly reciprocated the sympathy he required. His capacity for
uncommonly vivid participation in another's frame of mind lies at the
heart of his genius for friendship. "Your true calling is friendship,"
Schlegel once told his Berlin roommate.[4] That Schleiermacher realized
this of himself, if there were ever any reason to doubt it, is indicated by
his acquiescence in Eleonore Grunow's opinion that he was a "virtuoso
in friendship": "It may be that you are not incorrect about that; by
God's grace I think it is true."[5]

More is involved in these assertions than a mere romantic cult of
friendship. The sympathy that animates Schleiermacher's genius for
personal friendship animates his ethical genius as well. In connection
with sympathy's ethical role, the cryptic opinion of Bettina von
Arnim—that Schleiermacher was, if not the greatest man, the greatest
human being of his day (above, p. 175)—is illumined by a distinction
Schlegel draws in his novel *Lucinde*. Schlegel suggests that what sets
human beings (*Menschen*) apart from merely men (*bloss Männer*) is the
capacity for sympathetic participation in many points of view.[6] Reading

---

[2]Feb. 15, 1799. *Br.* I, 196.
[3]*Monologen*, 80. Translated "the mutual contemplation of each other's souls" by Friess
in *Soliloquies*, 86.
[4]Letter from Schlegel to Schleiermacher, no date (1798?). *Br.* III, 92.
[5]Letter dated only "Evening" (Sep. 10, 1802?). *Br.* I, 331–32.
[6]*Lucinde*, "Allegorie von der Frechheit," 28.

Schleiermacher's correspondence, one is struck by the number of his letters that express just such participation. This does not seem to be simply an affectation or a matter of form. Schleiermacher appears to have had an instinct for sympathetic participation in the state of health, state of affairs, or state of mind of the person to whom he was writing.

Two examples, from opposite extremes of Schleiermacher's own states of mind, will serve to acquaint us with this characteristic of his correspondence. The first is a letter Schleiermacher wrote on his twenty-ninth birthday, a day he counted among the happiest of his life. It was on this day that Schlegel extracted from Schleiermacher the promise to publish something, from which the *Speeches* eventually resulted. On the same day Schlegel decided to move into Schleiermacher's quarters as his roommate, which he did a month later (see above, pp. 114–115). Earlier in the day, to Schleiermacher's complete· surprise, Henriette Herz, Friedrich Schlegel, Dorothea Veit, and two sons of the Dohna family of Schlobitten had burst into his bachelor's quarters bearing cake, chocolate, birthday gifts, and most important, their good wishes. Schleiermacher had been settled in Berlin for just over a year, and this surprise party represented a cementing of his new circle of friendships. He was deeply gratified, as we learn from a letter to his sister Charlotte in Gnadenfrei, written on the evening of the same day: "I am pervaded with gratitude and joy. How cordial all these good people were! How every word and every expression assured me of their sincere best wishes, indeed of their trust." But it is typical that, in spite of Schleiermacher's exhilaration over the events of his day, his letter postpones its good news, opining instead with a sympathetic identification with Charlotte's recent tenuous health: "For all the joy I have had today, my thoughts of you have never been without anxiety, for who knows in what sad state of health you, poor friend, may have spent the day." The letter closes similarly:

> My thoughts have been in Gnadenfrei also, occupied with cordial, warm thanks to those good souls who have shared your own joy and thoughts. What is it when joy makes us melancholy? It is the highest and most beautiful point on its thermometer, and joy has stood at that point in me today.[7]

At the other extreme of mood, Schleiermacher's first letter to his friend von Willich from Stolpe after his loss of Eleonore numbers among the most depressed he ever wrote: "The pain will not leave me. . . . This isolated life here gapes at me horribly with its infinite emptiness." Two substantial paragraphs precede the paragraph containing these despondent lines about himself, however. In the first, betraying scarcely a hint of the loss that has befallen him, Schleiermacher warmly

---

[7]Nov. 21, 1797. *Br.* I, 164–67.

congratulates von Willich on his recent ordination as a minister: "You shall discover ever more clearly the greatness and beauty of this calling. Let us diligently exchange notes and experiences, as befits friends. My heartfelt good wishes accompany you, and I rejoice in the good omens under which you enter upon your career." There then follow two pages written in sympathy with Eleonore's fate in far off Berlin:

> For her always to have the terrible feeling, in vain: that is my deepest sorrow. And this image of her life when it stands before my eyes could almost make me despair. . . . O God, why must she perish so![8]

As Schleiermacher valued sympathy personally, so also he valued it ethically, as a vessel through which moral concern can flow. This helps to account for the fact that he felt willing to sacrifice his "effectiveness in the world" if it should have proven necessary in order for him to enjoy the sympathetic intimacy of family life, where one's moral effectiveness is "significant" and "endures" (above, p. 250). "I must dedicate myself to the rights and duties of fatherhood," Schleiermacher writes in the *Soliloquies*, "so that the highest power that freedom exercises upon freedom does not remain dormant in me, so that I may show how one who believes in freedom preserves and protects reason [*Vernunft*] in the young."[9]

Yet it can also happen that the sympathies of personal friendship and an immediate family circle can restrict a person's moral concerns even as they express them. Almost insidiously, they can cut us off from sympathy for the great portion of humankind we do not contact directly. In an essay entitled *Attempt at a Theory of Social Behavior*, which Schleiermacher published anonymously at the beginning of 1799, he writes:

> Domestic life puts us into contact with only a few persons, and those always the same. In this circle, to a watchful mind [*Gemüth*], even the highest demands of morality soon become familiar. The more properly everything proceeds and the more the moral economy is day by day perfected, the more limited a person's profit becomes in manifold intuitions of humanity and human activity. So there must be a condition that enlarges and completes these two,[10] which brings the sphere of an individual into the situation of intersecting the spheres of others as multifariously as possible, which affords to each, from his own boundary, a prospect into a different and foreign world, so that gradually all the appearances of humanity become known to him, so that all the most foreign of dispositions and relations become his friends, and, as it were, his neighbors.[11]

---

[8]Apr. 1, 1803. *Briefe Schleiermachers an Willich*, 62-65. Abridged in *Werden*, 298-300; truncated in *Br*. I, 362.

[9]*Monologen*, 75. *Soliloquies*, 77–78.

[10]"These two": Schleiermacher's essay had just spoken of a person's profession in terms similar to these describing a person's domestic life.

[11]Schleiermacher, *Versuch einer Theorie des geselligen Betragens*, ed. Herman Nohl, 3–4.

As the essay's title suggests, Schleiermacher in 1799 trusted social interaction to provide the requisite broadening conditions: "This function is provided by the free interaction of reasonable, mutually cultivating persons."[12] In the *Soliloquies* of 1800, however, Schleiermacher speaks often of a human "consciousness of kind," a broader "consciousness of the whole of humankind," a concept so important for Schleiermacher's ethics as to have superseded the traditional concept of conscience.[13] No degree of social interaction, not even the ferment of the intellectual salons of Berlin in 1800, can ever provide contacts comprehensive enough to cultivate so universal a consciousness as this. We must ask how Schleiermacher thought it possible for us to broaden our sympathies beyond our sphere of immediate contacts to a comprehensive sense of moral empathy with our race.

It is evident from both his life and his *Soliloquies* that Schleiermacher's answer to this question was not chiefly in terms of activities such as wide-ranging sociability, formalized education, or the literate exchange of ideas (see above, p. 249). His chief emphasis in the widening of ethical sympathy was not upon external means of any kind. "From *within* came the lofty revelation, produced by no doctrine of virtue and no system of wisdom," Schleiermacher writes in the *Soliloquies*. "In quiet calm, in unchanging simplicity I entertain within me an uninterrupted consciousness of the whole of humankind."[14] Schleiermacher felt that the chief means of widening sympathy is the most inward of all our capacities, phantasy.

The English romantic Shelley writes:

> A man, to be greatly good, must imagine intensely and comprehensively; he must put himself in the place of another and many others; the pains and pleasures of his species must become his own. The great instrument of moral good is the imagination . . . , the organ of the moral nature of man.[15]

In a sense very near to Shelley's, Schleiermacher thought of phantasy as "the organ of the moral nature of man." In the *Soliloquies* he describes the operation by which the "nature and mode of thought" of another person, another age, or another race is "transplanted" into our own "intuition," and he attributes this operation to *die Fantasie*.[16] He regarded phantasy, under the cultivation of outward experience, as the

---

Published in *Schleiermachers Werke*, ed. Otto Braun and Joh. Bauer, II, 1–31. The essay appeared originally in the *Berliner Archiv der Zeit und des Geschmacks* (Jan.-Feb., 1799). In this instance anonymity served Schleiermacher all too well; the essay was not recognized as Schleiermacher's for over a century. See Braun and Bauer, II, xxiii–xxiv.

[12]Ibid., 4.

[13]See *Monologen*, 26–28. *Soliloquies*, 27-29.

[14]*Monologen*, 28. *Soliloquies*, 29. Emphasis added.

[15]Percy Bysshe Shelley, *A Defence of Poetry*, 11–12.

[16]*Monologen*, 73. *Soliloquies*, 76.

most vivid stimulant of moral sympathy. For of all the mind's capacities, phantasy is the most wide ranging and most free. In phantasy, therefore, the two primary rays of Schleiermacher's moral philosophy–freedom and sympathy–are gathered into a single focus.

Jacobi, in his dialogue of 1787, *David Hume on Belief, or Idealism and Realism*, quotes Hume's *Enquiry concerning Human Understanding*:

> "Nothing is more free than the imagination of man; and though it cannot exceed that original stock of ideas furnished by the internal and external senses, it has unlimited power of mixing, compounding, separating, and dividing these ideas."[17]

Schleiermacher regarded phantasy in exactly the same way, both in relation to its determination and in relation to its freedom. Compared with any other human capacity, the play of phantasy, the unbridled association of ideas, is more facile and fluent, less subject to constraints foreign to a person's nature, and thus, according to Schleiermacher's fundamental definition (above, p. 79), more *free*. We may see how sympathy and freedom combine in Schleiermacher's concept of phantasy by considering freedom once more under the three aspects developed in Part II. In relation to the aspect of self-expression, the association of ideas in phantasy brings forth what is most characteristic of ourselves, our most inward and immediate images and thoughts. Yet it is also phantasy, under the stimulation of the widest self-cultivation possible to us, that most effortlessly carries us outside our immediate circle of sensible contacts and puts us in touch with the distant, the unaccustomed, the strange. And in relation to the third of freedom's aspects, appropriation, phantasy is the most accessible of all resources from which we may appropriate ideas into the unity of heart and mind:

> O that people knew to use this godly power of fantasy, which alone sets the spirit [*Geist*] free, carries it out beyond every dominion and every limit, and without which a person's sphere is so narrow and anxious! For how much does anyone touch in the brief course of life? From how many sides would a person have to remain indeterminate and uncultivated if his inner action were limited to only the little that actually knocks against him from without? . . . And even if life were to lead him at an accelerated pace in a thousand new paths, could infinity exhaust itself in the short span of life? What such a one could never even wish for, I gain through the inner play of fantasy. It supplies me with what actuality lacks; every relation in which I see another, I appropriate through fantasy.[18]

---

[17]Friedrich Heinrich Jacobi, *David Hume über den Glauben, oder Idealismus und Realismus*, 156. Jacobi is quoting from Section V of Hume's *Enquiry*.
[18]*Monologen*, 77. *Soliloquies*, 81–82.

"The more agile the fantasy . . . ," Schleiermacher writes a little later in the *Soliloquies*, "the more wisdom and experience grow and prosper."[19]

In our final chapter we shall be concerned with the further development of phantasy's ethical function as the synthesizer of sympathy and freedom. But before we leave our more biographical discussion, let us turn our attention briefly to the "agility" of phantasy in Schleiermacher's own life. In Chapter 1 of this Part we traced the development of Schleiermacher's attitude toward phantasy (above, pp. 213-216), mentioning particularly the role of phantasy in his religious experiences as a child. As Schleiermacher grew older, and phantasy began to take on a central function in his ethical thinking, it also assumed a more welcome role in his adult life. "In the years of my childhood," Schleiermacher recollected in 1804, "I was like an old man who had already lived through the whole world and only played or dreamed at being a child. If I did not have more childish sense [*Kindersinn*] now than then, I would be a miserable man."[20] The man who on his twenty-fourth birthday had boasted, "The time of youth lies behind me; the dominion of phantasy comes to an end" (above, p. 214), in later years fills his birthday letters with a recurrent theme: the vivid emotion he feels at having his absent friends with him in phantasy. After his thirty-fourth birthday Schleiermacher writes from Stolp to Henriette Herz, "How I have embraced you in thought, my dear, my only Jette, and not without tears,"[21] and to Eleonore Grunow:

> How I have been with you in these days, dear suffering friend! I was not so fortunate as to see you in my dreams; but awake, phantasy has painted you with a vividness [*Lebendigkeit*] that could have startled me. I see you at your mother's sickbed; I see your soft, silent tears, your graceful walk, your look, in which your whole beautiful soul portrays itself.[22]

To some critics the letters exchanged within the Berlin romantic circle have appeared excessive. Surely no one can read them without being struck by the abandon of their emotions, the candor of their opinions, the freedom of their intimacies, the richness of their sympathy, the vividness of their imagination. Is it perhaps fair to say that whatever one's canons of epistolary taste, Schleiermacher's emphasis upon the roles of feeling and phantasy in religion and ethics would hardly be credible if his correspondence did not give testimony to the vitality of these forces in his life?

---

[19] *Monologen*, 89. *Soliloquies*, 96.

[20] Letter to Luise von Willich, July 29, 1804. *Briefe Schleiermachers*, ed. Hermann Mulert, 194. On the same theme see *Br.* I, 7, and *Braut*, 240.

[21] Nov. 22, 1802. *Br.* I, 347.

[22] Nov. 24, 1802. *Br.* I, 347. For similar evidence of Schleiermacher's vivid phantasy life, see *Braut*, 56, 149, and 185.

We are allowed a touching, even pathetic, look into Schleier-macher's phantasy life in a letter he wrote from Stolp to Henriette Herz after he had received Eleonore's word that she was cutting off their correspondence, and with it, Schleiermacher's hope of having her as his bride. Childlike, almost desperate with grief and fatigue, he writes:

> Last evening, completely undressed, intending to go to bed, I stood for two full hours with my arms propped on the table. It came over me in all its bitterness and harshness. . . . What shall become of me here? Every morning I have handed her tea in my thoughts, and jested with her across breakfast. . . . And how often have I looked full of yearning to the place where her writing desk should stand.[23]

"So living and close to me has been her image," he writes to von Willich,[24] "I actually have the feeling that I have already had her here, and that she is now dead."

[23] Undated (Mar., 1803). *Werden*, 297.
[24] Apr. 1, 1803. *Werden*, 299.

Chapter 7. Phantasy's Place in Ethics and Moral Education

I would that the Devil might take half of all the understanding in the world—my own quota I will also surrender over, although reluctantly—and that we could receive in return even a fourth part of the phantasy that is lacking to us on this lovely earth.

We broaden our view now from phantasy's place in Schleiermacher's life to include its place in his moral philosophy. Shelley calls imagination "the great instrument of moral good . . . , the organ of the moral nature of man." We have seen that Schleiermacher came to understand phantasy in a similar way. Shelley's word "imagination" and Schleiermacher's word "phantasy" are not the same, however, and we need to distinguish them in order to go further.

Schleiermacher's distinction between imagination and phantasy is the same as that drawn by Kant in his book of 1798, *Anthropology in a Pragmatic Point of View*—a book Schleiermacher reviewed in 1799[1] and thus knew well by the time of his *Soliloquies*. Kant defines imagination (*Einbildungskraft*) as "a faculty of intuition even without the presence of the object." Phantasy (*Phantasie*) he then defines as "the imagination insofar as it brings forth imaginations even apart from choice [*auch unwillkührlich*]."[2] The final phrase, "even apart from choice," is the crucial one here. We shall see in this chapter that Schleiermacher emphasizes the involuntary connotations of the word "phantasy" as he brings it to the fore in his moral philosophy.

"Imagination," in contrast, is a word Schleiermacher uses only rarely. In his writings after 1794, this may be because Fichte's use of the term *productive imagination* in his *Foundations of the Entire Science of Knowledge*, published in that year, had colored the word too indelibly in Fichtean hues. In Schleiermacher's 1793 treatise *On Human Freedom*, where "phantasy" designates the mental capacity for the association of ideas (see above, p. 214), the word "imagination" occurs twice, both times in contrast to phantasy by virtue of the presence of an element of

---

[1]Schleiermacher, "Anthropologie von Immanuel Kant," *Athenaeum*, II/2 (1799), 300–306.
[2]Immanuel Kant, *Anthropologie in pragmatischer Hinsicht*, 167.

deliberate choice. Imagination is our capacity to direct our attention where we choose. Thus Schleiermacher writes that "the first ground of existence of every particular activity of the understanding, namely the direction of the imagination, is nothing other than *an activity of the faculty of desire*."[3] The word "imagination" occurs once in the *Speeches* of 1799, and again it designates a voluntary act—in this instance the act of extrapolating from the behavior of a "civilized" and relatively cosmopolitan people in order to arrive at an idea of their distinguishing ethnic character.[4] Both in Schleiermacher's first collection of sermons of 1801, and in the 1804 Introduction to his edition of *Plato's Works*, "imagination" is used to designate mental activity that is not only willful but also possibly arbitrary, in the sense of being misleading or illusory. Thus, for example, he speaks of the mind's "empty imagination that it has understood what in fact it does not understand."[5]

Willful imagining plays an important role in ethical sympathy as Schleiermacher conceives of it. We shall presently see in closer detail that it is part of what Schleiermacher means when he speaks of putting oneself in the place of another. What is more, it is not clear that Schleiermacher never implies willful imagining when he uses the word "phantasy." As we have seen in Chapter 2 of this Part the *Soliloquies* do not employ their terms with systematic precision. It is clear, however, that willful imagining is not all that Schleiermacher means by his frequent use of the term *phantasy*, nor is it the principal thing he wishes to stress. Unlike Kant, Schleiermacher does not bind the "organ of the moral nature of man" to voluntary action alone.

We may clarify Schleiermacher's concept of phantasy by returning for a moment to his early treatise *On Human Freedom*. We saw in Part I how Schleiermacher, by taking the term *impulse* (*Trieb*) as the beginning point for his ethical analysis, traced the roots of our moral nature to a level deeper than that of choice (*Willkühr*). We observed that impulse, like phantasy, is by definition prior to deliberate choosing (see above, pp. 39–40). In fact Schleiermacher's terms *impulse* and *phantasy* share essentials of the same definition. In 1803 Schleiermacher defines phantasy as "the free faculty of associating and bringing forth."[6] That is very near to his 1793 definition of impulse as "the activity of the representing subject, grounded in his nature, of bringing forth representations" (above, p. 40). Impulse can be said to be a "free faculty" in the same sense as phantasy, since, as we have seen repeatedly, to be "grounded" in a person's "nature" is to be under no foreign constraints and therefore to be free. To turn this same observation around, phantasy,

---

[3] MS 24. Emphasis added. Also MS 10.
[4] *Reden*, 33. The term disappears from the later editions of the *Speeches*.
[5] Above, p. 150. Also *Predigten. Erste Sammlung*, 16.
[6] *Grundlinien einer Kritik der bisherigen Sittenlehre*, 269.

like impulse, is causally grounded in a person's nature, since for Schleiermacher as for Hume (above, p. 278), free phantasy and the hypothesis of determinism are fully compatible:

> Phantasy reproduces for us no other representations, and in its productions adds no other representations, than such as have at some previous moment been parts of a present, total representation.[7]

This passage dates from Schleiermacher's treatise of 1792, but we see the same compatibility between phantasy and determinism reflected in the wording of Schleiermacher's definition of 1803, where phantasy is called not an originating faculty but rather a faculty of "associating and bringing forth." In fact, in his lectures on Psychology from 1818 through 1834 Schleiermacher will trace all representations of the mind to a determinate origin, citing as partial evidence the fact that representations often "arise *against* the will of the one who thinks them."[8]

There is a remarkable discovery implicit in this similarity between the definitions of *impulse* and *phantasy*, and it brings our study full circle. Phantasy, whose "dominion" Schleiermacher had pronounced at an end on his twenty-fourth birthday, not only persists in his thinking after that 1792 pronouncement, but by 1800 has assumed a place at the very center of his moral philosophy. For in the treatise *On Human Freedom* the term *impulse* occupies a central place, and by the time of the *Soliloquies*, Schleiermacher's term *phantasy* shares essentially the same definition.

It is hardly surprising that phantasy required so long a time to assume its central place in Schleiermacher's ethics. What makes this development remarkable is that it happened at all. It is remarkable that Schleiermacher—a Prussian; reared and educated by Prussians; from the age of eighteen a student of Kant's consummately Prussian doctrine of moral duty; three years a tutor in the household of an authoritarian Prussian nobleman and military enthusiast[9]—ever developed a moral philosophy upon the foundation, not of duty, but of virtue (see above, p. 169), and around a keystone of idiosyncratic phantasy instead of universal law.

But how can ethics be centered in phantasy, a capacity involving the involuntary association of ideas? Is ethics not fundamentally concerned with our voluntary capacities, with what we do with our wills? At the very least one might think that of the two, imagination and phantasy, Schleiermacher would have stressed the former, more clearly voluntary faculty in his ethics. But he did not. The pulse of Schleiermacher's ethics is

---

[7]MS 23. On the connection between determinism and phantasy see also above, p. 246.

[8]Schleiermacher, *Psychologie*, 225. Schleiermacher's emphasis.

[9]See Schleiermacher's descriptions of the elder Count Alexander Dohna in his letters from Schlobitten of Dec. 17, 1790, and May 7, 1793 (*Br.* III, 32–33, and I, 113–15). The two found themselves at odds over such issues as the French Revolution and the education of children. The latter of these disagreements led eventually to Schleiermacher's dismissal from the Dohna household.

sympathy—the capacity for identifying with another person's condition and feelings, the ability to share another's frame of mind. Schleiermacher saw that we are all too often brought up to entertain no ideas and feelings except those we have been specifically trained to acknowledge. An idea not willfully selected from our own experience, according to the rules of our own education; an opinion not chosen from our repertory of the habitual and the respectable; another person's perspective, not already more or less congruent with our own: these associations of ideas are all too often screened out of our consciousness. If they happen to appear, they are all too often greeted more with suspicion than with respect. Conditioned in this way we cannot be expected to put ourselves in another's frame of mind. We cannot, by mere willing, accomplish something we are no longer constitutionally capable of doing.

"To know one viewpoint for all": this, as Schleiermacher has already observed in the *Speeches*, is the usual aim of our schooling. Thus we are trained in "the most direct way to leave the universe behind," conditioned to become "a true *glebae adscriptus* of the spot of earth on which one happens to stand" (above, p. 187). Only the free play of phantasy can lead us further toward the infinite goal of genuine moral sense, namely, the goal of "having all viewpoints for everything." Here once more Schleiermacher is similar to Schiller—perhaps to Schiller virtually alone among the German moral philosophers around the turn of the century. Without the liberating influence of "aesthetic education," Schiller writes in his *Letters* on that subject, a person

> never sees others in himself, only himself in others; and society, instead of expanding him into his species, only confines him more and more narrowly in his individualism. In this stifling limitation he errs his way through his twilit life. . . . The first appearance of reason [*Vernunft*] in a person is therefore not yet the beginning of his humanity. This is first decided through his freedom, and reason begins this liberation by making his sensible dependence unbounded. . . . On the wings of imagination a person leaves the narrow confines of the present, in which mere animality is enclosed.[10]

Schleiermacher believed that moral education, like Schiller's "aesthetic education," must encourage respect for all the associations of the mind, not only for those ideas we are accustomed to accredit or duty-bound to choose. Habit prejudices. Training in duty restricts our range of feelings and choice. Phantasy, however, if it is not squelched, provides us with an expanded consciousness of possibilities and an extended range of feelings, which may provide the basic impulses of moral sympathy and decision.

---

[10]Schiller, *Über die ästhetische Erziehung des Menschen*, Twenty-fourth Letter.

There is of course no guarantee that a person's choice from among the possibilities suggested by phantasy will be a moral one. Initial respect for the alternatives brought forth by phantasy does not mean that they will all be found to be of equal moral value. We must emphasize once more Schleiermacher's recognition that practical reason provides the ethical principles by which we choose among various alternatives. Both Schiller and Schleiermacher are in this respect pupils of Kant. Schleiermacher was both Platonic and Kantian enough (above, p. 47) to recognize that sympathy is blind without the guidance of rational moral principles.[11] There is nothing indiscriminate in Schleiermacher's romantic emphasis upon phantasy. Here again, Schleiermacher is entitled to his romanticism by virtue of his previous discipline as a student of critical rationalism. But as we have seen, Schleiermacher felt that Kant's philosophy suffered from "a deficiency of animation and a superfluity of reason." Schleiermacher was brought to his romantic emphasis upon phantasy and sympathy by the necessity of giving Kant's moral philosophy the animating transfusion of life he believed it needed.

Schleiermacher seems to have understood the interrelation of practical reason, imagination, phantasy, and sympathy in something like the following way. If we encourage and respect the free associations of phantasy, a limitless and almost infinitely variable spectrum of possibilities spreads itself in our consciousness. At points along this spectrum we shall approach the wavelengths of other persons' consciousness, and sympathetic resonances will occur. Practical reason requires us willfully to tune our moral imagination to these points of mutuality with our race, and rational principles of justice and virtue may then discriminate which vibrations to reinforce and which to suppress. If, however, we *first* limit phantasy, then our spectrum of consciousness is arbitrarily narrowed, the chances of sympathetic resonance with others are reduced, and moral decision is confined within our own private band of habit and custom.

Schleiermacher, believing that people are endowed at birth with potentially agile phantasies, shuddered to see children being schooled to discredit the strainings of phantasy as "unfruitful," simply because they do not coincide with the accustomed and expected range of experience (see above, p. 214). He had known at first hand the struggle to overcome the childhood effects of such restricting education. His writings become as angered as one ever finds them over the fact that education, by poisoning phantasy, was so often killing the root from which a child's moral sympathy might later have developed. He feared that if the fundamental impulse of moral life is caused to wilt in childhood, it is not likely to revive.

---

[11]See the characteristically fine discussion of this point in John Rawls, *A Theory of Justice*, Sections 69–72, esp. pp. 468–70 and 474–76.

Schleiermacher's passion over this issue accounts in large part for his lifelong interest in the education of children.[12] Here once more, as in so many paths of his thinking, his beginning point was Kant. The concluding section of Kant's *Critique of Practical Reason*, "Methodology," deals with practical applications of his formal moral principles (see above, p. 50). There Kant describes two stages by which a pupil's appropriation of ethical principles must proceed. In the first, Kant explains, the pupil must learn to judge all actions by the standard of the moral law, until, by repeated practice, he reaches the stage at which such judgments are "a habit, as it were." Only then, as a second stage, may the pupil's "attention be fixed upon the consciousness of his freedom"; only when disciplined to resist the "impetuous importunity of the inclinations" may the pupil be counted on to act "for the sake of the moral law" alone.[13]

From Schleiermacher's perspective, Kant's theory of moral education is standing on its head. The beginning of ethical development is not habit (*Gewohnheit*) but freedom (*Freiheit*) — that inward freedom of which phantasy is the "clearest proof" (above, p. 246). In the *Soliloquies* Schleiermacher contrasts the Kantian "world" of moral education with that of his own theory:

> Helpless is the struggle of that better person who seeks morality and cultivation in this world that recognizes only the Right, that instead of life offers only dead formulas, that instead of free action knows only rule and habit. . . . What could save me, were it not for you, divine fantasy?[14]

Schleiermacher felt that adults entrusted with the education of children should scarcely *habituate* a child to anything. To certain details of daily schedule and basic order, to be sure; but not to the "dead formula" of the Kantian moral law, and certainly not to that which is considered "respectable" by the child's society.

Schleiermacher's attitude toward social respectability would sustain a study all its own. He was an avowed opponent of conformity to social convention for its own sake. This opposition is apparent in his youthful resistance to religious convention, where, as we have seen, his attitude sometimes went beyond mere unorthodoxy in the direction of outright irreverence (above, pp. 208-209). This attitude carried over into Schleiermacher's early work on the journal *Athenaeum*. In 1799, A. W. Schlegel had to caution Schleiermacher against too much "devilment" in the pages of the new periodical.[15] Less abstractly, the involvement of Schleiermacher and his circle of male friends with married women manifests a

---

[12]For Schleiermacher's lectures and writings on pedagogy, see C. Platz, ed., *Schleiermachers pädagogische Schriften, mit einer Darstellung seines Lebens*. Also Vol. III/9 of Schleiermacher's *Sämmtliche Werke*.

[13]Kant, second *Kritik*, 159,161.

[14]*Monologen*, 59–60. *Soliloquies*, 60–61.

[15]Letter to Schleiermacher, Nov. 1, 1799. *Br*. III, 131.

disregard for social convention that even those closest to him found difficult to comprehend. In 1809, three months before their wedding, Henriette von Willich writes to Schleiermacher from Rügen:

> Among our women here a good bit of conversation has arisen about such relations as that of Jette [Herz] with Al[exander Dohna], you with E[leonore Grunow], or Fr. Schlegel with his present wife [Dorothea]. Their feelings run completely against every such relation. I am then expected to say how I feel, and although I believe I feel and see things rightly, yet I cannot venture upon an explanation, simply because it would find no acceptance. As a result I am now completely enigmatic to them, since they do not know me at all on any more casual basis. They really believe that I have adopted certain worldly principles, from which they do not exempt you either, of course, and they do not rightly know how they are supposed to reconcile this with your religious principles.[16]

Steffens reports wrinkled brows among the Halle congregation in 1804 over Schleiermacher's disregard for certain details of the deportment expected of a minister.[17]

More is involved in these examples than merely Schleiermacher's flaunting of certain canons of gossip. He states the fundamental ethical principle at issue in his 1801 letter to Sack defending his friendship with Schlegel:

> I shall never become the confidential friend of a person of reprehensible character; but neither shall I ever, out of fear of popular opinion, deny the comfort of friendship to someone despised but innocent; never shall I, because of my position, let myself be led by an appearance in the minds of others instead of acting in accordance with the true circumstances of the matter in question.[18]

In short, like many another independent thinker, Schleiermacher was opposed not to social convention but to social hypocrisy, not to respectability but to prudery.

Schleiermacher's 1799 apology for Schlegel's *Lucinde* had centered in the issues of hypocrisy and prudery. Two years later Schleiermacher returned to such issues in a dialogue *On the Respectable*—an ethical sally against "slavery" to habit (*Gewohnheit*), politeness (*Artigkeit*), or respectability (*Anstand*).[19] As the dialogue opens, Kallikles is introduced as a character with considerable notoriety for idiosyncrasy and iconoclasm. His friend Sophron encounters him in Berlin's *Tiergarten* and is surprised to find him "in the most elegant clothes and wholly transformed into the mold of a person of good breeding." It only goes to show, Kallikles

---

[16]Feb. 16, 1809. *Braut*, 341.

[17]Henrich Steffens, *Was ich Erlebte*, Vol. V, 146–50.

[18]*Br*. III, 282.

[19]Schleiermacher, *Über das Anständige*, 533, 504. The dialogue remained unpublished until 1863.

explains, that any person with his senses about him can weave at will the "web of outer customs and imagined, arbitrarily invented virtues[20] that one calls the Respectable":

> I was transformed in a few days into the man you see. In a few days I have learned the tone and the behavior which people of the elegant world take to be such infinite arts unless they are instilled from the years of childhood onward—learned them, I might almost say, as well as any of them.[21]

In other words, adults can put on conventional respectability almost as easily as they put on clothing. But Kallikles has recently become the tutor of two young children, and his argument in the dialogue proves to be that in children, canons of respectability can smother, and the stifling can inflict permanent damage to their fragile inner lives.

We must recall once more Schleiermacher's observation that in a genuine dialogue no one voice represents the whole truth, nor even the author's own opinion. We may not simply identify Kallikles' point of view with that of Schleiermacher. In the *Soliloquies* Schleiermacher writes quite positively of manners, in fact, as the "garment of inner individuality, delicately and meaningfully conforming to its noble form, disclosing the proportion of its members, and beautifully accompanying its movements."[22] But this passage goes on to denounce the "artful fraudulence" of hypocritical social conventions, and Schleiermacher's dialogue *On the Respectable* ends in agreement between Sophron and Kallikles on the latter's insistence that children must be protected from the oppression of arbitrary canons of external respectability. A child's cultivation of inner life, Schleiermacher writes in the *Soliloquies*, is commonly

> hindered by every association he enters, from the first bonds of education onward, where the young spirit, instead of winning new room for play and glimpsing the world and humanity in their entire scope, is restricted in accordance with alien ideas and early accustomed to the long slavery of life.[23]

When Schleiermacher joins condemnation of pragmatic social utilitarianism with his condemnation of arbitrary social convention, bitterness is added to indignation. The phantastic inclinations of children, he writes in the *Speeches*, are

> forcibly suppressed from the beginning. Everything supernatural and miraculous is proscribed. Phantasy should not be filled with empty images!

---

[20] "*eingebildetes willkührlich erdachter Tugenden.*" Ibid., 506. Notice the narrowing connotation of *eingebildetes*, an etymological cousin of *Einbildungskraft*, "imagination."
[21] Ibid., 505.
[22] *Monologen*, 64. *Soliloquies*, 65.
[23] *Monologen*, 59. *Soliloquies*, 60.

> One can just as easily introduce facts and provide preparations for life. So
> the poor souls who thirst for something entirely different are bored·with
> moral stories, and learn how nice and useful it is to be delicately polite and
> rational.[24]

In writing to Schlegel about his dialogue *On the Respectable*, Schleiermacher characterized its ethical opinions as *avant-coureurs*: "precursory"
or "prophetic."[25] He was not mistaken. Such satirical indignation over the
squelching of young spirits in their schooling was not to be voiced again
with equal vehemence until mid-century, with the writings of Dickens:

> Now, what I want is Facts. Teach these boys and girls nothing but Facts.
> Facts alone are wanted in life. Plant nothing else, and root out everything
> else. . . . So Mr. McChoakumchild began in his best manner . . . , not
> unlike Morgiana in the Forty Thieves: looking into all the vessels ranged
> before him, one after another, to see what they contained. Say, good
> McChoakumchild: When from thy boiling store, thou shalt fill each jar
> brimful by-and-by, dost thou think that thou will kill outright the robber
> Fancy lurking within—or sometimes only maim and distort him![26]

In his writings prior to 1805, Schleiermacher's two most concentrated
discussions of the education of children occur in the third of his *Speeches*
of 1799, "On the Cultivation of Religion," and in a sermon of October,
1800, "The Scriptural Restriction upon Our Concern for the Future." The
latter presents the more negative or critical side of Schleiermacher's
opinions:

> Are we acting rightly when we look upon all that we do and attempt to do
> during the earlier years of life, all that we instigate in behalf of the young
> spirits [*Gemüther*] who are entrusted to our guidance, only as a preparation
> for what will be required in later years? Thus in fact most people treat
> everything that we call education and cultivation. . . . To me this appears a
> great injustice . . . , and from this injustice important injuries arise. When
> we complain that even with our best care so much in the education we give
> our children does not succeed, and that our best hopes come to nothing;
> when our children complain that they enjoy so little in this most beautiful
> time of life, and that they always feel oppressed by strict shackles; when
> society complains that every lad rushes to become a boy, every boy to
> become a youth, every youth to become a man, and that in this rush, some
> beautiful spirits overrush, and then become mediocre and uselessly slack
> workers—all these complaints are fruits of these useless and vain concerns
> over a time that is not yet come. Let us not impatiently outrun the order of
> nature. Let us be convinced that . . . the best that can happen for the
> future happens when every day, at every moment, we do what is best and
> most wholesome for that moment, without regard for any still to come.

[24] *Reden*, 156. *Speeches*, 126.
[25] Letter to Schlegel, Jan. 24, 1801. *Br.* III, 258.
[26] Charles Dickens, *Hard Times*, Book I, Chs. 1 and 2.

In summary, as educators we must "think less that children will become youths, than that they should be children."[27]

How may children be allowed to be children? Schleiermacher suggests the answer in a letter of 1802 to Eleonore Grunow: "People always have to do only with reason, and indeed with reason as applied to bourgeois relations, in which alone they live and move and have their being. Even all the morality they wish to inculcate is nothing other than this. It is for this reason that I am so brutally sickened by their pedagogical books and procedures." With their utilitarian concern for affairs of the world, educators "leave heaven empty—that is, *phantasy, from which love and heaven must proceed.*"[28]

The hope of rescue, then, lies with Dickens's "robber Fancy," which we must accordingly take care not to kill, maim, or distort. Schleiermacher develops this hope positively in his *Speeches'* discussion of religious education:

> I look with great reverence upon the yearning of young spirits for the miraculous and the supernatural. Along with the finite and determinate they seek something else which they can set over against it. They grasp in every direction to see if there is not something reaching above sensible appearances and their laws. However much their senses are filled with mundane objects, it is as if besides this sense they have still others, which without nourishment must waste away. This is the first stirring of religion.

Then, in what follows, we see the remarkable presupposition underlying the religious education Schleiermacher is commending to his Prussian readers:

> Let it be supposed that the taste for grotesque figures is as characteristic of the young phantasy in religion as it is in art, and let it be richly satisfied. Indeed, let there be no concern over the fact that the earnest and holy mythology taken to be religion itself will be immediately associated with this zestful play of childhood. Suppose God, the Savior, the angels *are* but another kind of fairies and sylphs.

Yes, Schleiermacher adds, such notions might lead to a usurping of religious sense by empty speculations. A child left to develop at his own pace, however, a child whose mind is not "tainted" by education and who thus manages to "keep himself free from the yoke of understanding and disputing, will in later years more easily find his way out of this labyrinth" than his more strictly "educated" counterpart.[29]

What Schleiermacher calls "the yoke of understanding and disputing" is a significant part of the educational repression he felt many children are forced to bear. The usual theory, he writes, is that education consists

---

[27] *Predigten. Erste Sammlung,* 136–37.
[28] Aug. 12, 1802. *Br.* I, 313. Emphasis added.
[29] *Reden,* 154–56. *Speeches,* 125–26.

primarily in teaching children to understand. But "by this understanding [*Verstand*] they are cheated completely of their sense [*Sinn*]."[30]

> I would that the Devil might take half of all the understanding in the world—my own quota I will also surrender over, although reluctantly—and that we could receive in return even a fourth part of the phantasy that is lacking to us on this lovely earth.[31]

Schleiermacher's "although reluctantly" here is important. We must once more recall that Schleiermacher's romanticism had no quarrel with either reasonableness or rationality. Schleiermacher suspected "mere" or "pure" (*bloss*) rationality, and here his suspicions were all but boundless. The Devil would be wary of swapping phantasy for understanding, Schleiermacher concludes his Mephestophelean scenario, "for he must know that his Kingdom would ill endure."

Schleiermacher wanted to see children, in the course of their learning and development, encouraged to remain more-than-reasonable beings. He wanted to rescue them from the repressive watchword of Kantian moralism, "But suppose everyone did it?" The answer to that, as Kant himself fully realized, has always been "Not everyone will." But unlike Kant, Schleiermacher believed that not everyone should.[32] Ethical freedom, as Schleiermacher repeats over and over again in the *Soliloquies* and elsewhere, is not simply to toe the line of the universal and necessary but also to pursue the goal of characteristic individuality.

Out of romantic love for individuality and freedom Schleiermacher was convinced that we must not think of ourselves as merely rational beings. He believed that pure reason must not be granted exclusive legislative authority in our lives. "Poets," Shelley writes, "are the unacknowledged legislators of the world."[33] Persons of aesthetic education, writes Schiller, "are born to play great roles."[34] Schleiermacher's agreement with these judgments determined his fervent advocacy of phantasy's role in religious and moral education.

This advocacy, especially in the context of Schleiermacher's own time and place, qualifies him as a progressive in pedagogical theory. It often happens, however, that the most progressive educational theories are also the most detailed and comprehensive, and tend to become as

---

[30] *Reden*, 157.

[31] Letter to Eleonore Grunow, Sep. 29, 1802. *Br*. I, 342.

[32] See Kant, second *Kritik*, 69: "Now everyone knows very well that if one secretly permits himself to deceive, it does not follow that everyone else will do so, or that if, unnoticed by others, he is lacking in compassion, everyone else will immediately take the same attitude toward him. This comparison of the maxims of his actions with a universal natural law, therefore, is not the determining ground of his will. But such a law is still a type for the estimation of maxims according to moral principles." It is Kant's final sentence with which Schleiermacher takes issue.

[33] Percy Bysshe Shelley, *A Defence of Poetry*, 38.

[34] Schiller, *Erziehung*, note to the Twenty-first Letter.

rationalistic, even as dogmatic and rigid, as the theories they are intended to replace. In this regard Schleiermacher's romantic pedagogy recommends another means of developing individuality that might not sit well with even the most progressive educational theorists. It is the recommendation to exempt a portion of a child's education from theory altogether—to free a child from deliberate pedagogical control and entrust its education instead to the haphazard contingencies of fate.

We have seen Schleiermacher's attitude toward fate in connection with his deterministic philosophy of resignation, where he recommends an acceptance of fate in such a way as to mold the experiences it brings into a characteristic individuality. We have seen also that at times Schleiermacher says even more than this about the contingencies of fate, suggesting that we should "seek them out" (above, p. 268), that we should deliberately free ourselves from the habitual and the comfortable to let fate seek us out as it will. A passage from a work dear to Schleiermacher can illustrate this point for us, a passage that may have helped to shape Schleiermacher's pedagogical views and surely must have pleased him.

The work is Goethe's *Wilhelm Meister*. Schleiermacher had been "delighted" by Goethe's novel as early as November, 1795, immediately upon the appearance of the book's first part.[35] In the spring of 1796 he reread it with Henriette Herz. By 1801 he knew the novel well enough to review Schlegel's famous review of it (written by Schlegel in the room adjoining Schleiermacher's) in which Schlegel had ranked *Wilhelm Meister* with the French Revolution and Fichte's *Science of Knowledge* as the most important phenomena of the age.[36]

In Book II of his "cultivation novel" Goethe portrays his young protagonist Wilhelm in animated discussion with a gentleman identified only as someone possessing the "dignified mien" of a clergyman. Their subject is education—in particular, the early education of actors. The gentleman's ideas on the subject are progressive. He would have each pupil's individuality honored in the course of his training. But he believes that in the early stages, no aspect of education is insignificant, and thus none should be left to chance.[37] Educational planning should extend to every detail of a pupil's development if true excellence is to result:

> "But will not a well-disposed nature alone," Wilhelm replied, "as the first and last requisite, bring an actor, like every other artist—indeed like every person, perhaps—to so lofty a goal?"
>
> "The first and last, beginning and end it may well be and remain,"

---

[35]Letter to Alexander Dohna, Nov. 24, 1795. *Werden*, 86.

[36]Schleiermacher, *Charakteristiken und Kritiken von A. W. und F. Schlegel*, in the *Erlanger Litteraturzeitung*, II (1801), 1513–20. Also in *Br.* IV, 554–61.

[37]One is reminded here of Jean Jacques Rousseau's *Émile* of 1762, a work in which Schleiermacher appears to have expressed no interest.

replied the other; "but in the middle, much will be lacking to an artist if cultivation, and early cultivation at that, has not first made of him what he should be. . . . Let no one think he can overcome the first impressions of youth. If one has grown up in enviable freedom, surrounded by beautiful and noble objects, in intercourse with good people; if his masters have taught him what he needed to know first in order to grasp more easily what comes later; if he has learned what he never needs to unlearn; if his first actions have been so guided that later he may more easily and comfortably complete what is good, without having to disaccustom himself from anything; then this person will lead a purer, more completed, and happier life than another who has spent his youthful energies in opposition and error. So much is said and written about education; yet I see but few people who can comprehend and put into practice this simple but great concept, which includes all others in itself."

"That may very well be true," said Wilhelm, "for most people are limited enough to want to educate others to their own likeness. Happy are those, therefore, who accept fate [*Schicksal*], which educates each in his own way!"

"Fate," the other replied with a smile, "is a noble but costly tutor. I would rather always stick to the reason [*Vernunft*] of a human master. Fate, for whose wisdom I bear all reverence, has in chance [*Zufall*], through which it works, a very clumsy instrument. For chance seems very seldom to carry out precisely and purely that which fate has resolved upon."[38]

This is again good dialogue in the Platonic sense: there is truth in both points of view. But Goethe's emphasis in this passage on fate is betrayed by its underlying irony, for it is fate that has brought Wilhelm and this stranger into contact with each other. Sheer chance has interrupted the novel's plot to make room for their enlightening debate over the role of chance in education.

Schleiermacher agreed with Goethe. His suspicion of persons who want to educate "precisely and purely," his sense of the inevitable limitation of "the reason of a human master," placed him among those few who are "happy" to "accept fate, which educates each in his own way." "Disposition and phantasy must . . . for the most part be left to the unfolding of a free life," Schleiermacher was to write in his lectures on Pedagogy in 1813–14,[39] and he elaborates on this dictum in the Aphorisms he added to the margin of his lecture notes:

> Must we not let all that relates to disposition [*Gesinnung*] proceed chaotically out of life?
> The relation of education to our chaotic life is a general one. Whatever is not contained in this relation does not belong in education.[40]

In an 1803 letter to Charlotte von Kathen, later to become his sister-in-law, Schleiermacher writes:

[38]Johann Wolfgang Goethe, *Wilhelm Meisters Lehrjahre*, Book II, Ch. 9.
[39]Schleiermacher, *Zur Pädagogik*, in *Schleiermachers Werke*, ed. Braun and Bauer, III, 460.
[40]*Aphorismen zur Pädagogik*, Nos. 48 and 57.

No other woman, dear Charlotte, has ever expressed my thoughts on education as purely as you have. . . . Truly in what relates to the inner life of children . . . there is nothing to do but to look on and hold off, that they not be disturbed, and then also to see to it that the effects of love and the governance of understanding surround them in life. If things do not go well in this way, the good certainly cannot be inculcated and the bad expelled in some other. The better feeling one gains from living with young children in this way is richly worth those empty imaginations [*leere Einbildungen*] which assume that all the good in a person must be the work of education — imaginations that, by their very presupposition, destroy every higher consciousness.[41]

Not long after the conversation in *Wilhelm Meister* between Wilhelm and the stranger, the latter disappears from Goethe's novel as inexplicably as he had entered it shortly before. Laertes, one of Wilhelm's friends, remarks:

"I have been trying the whole time to recollect where I might have seen this strange man before. I fully intended to ask him about it at his parting."

"It was exactly the same with me," Wilhelm replied, "and I certainly would not have let him go until he had told us more about his circumstances. Unless I am badly mistaken, I had spoken with him somewhere before."

But Philine, the trollop of the theatrical troupe, clears up the mystery:

"And well you might be mistaken. This man really has only the false appearance of an acquaintance, because he looks like a man and not like Hans or Kunz."

"What is that supposed to mean?" asked Laertes. "Don't we all look like men?"

"I know what I am saying," Philine replied, "and if you don't understand me, than just let it be."[42]

Schleiermacher could have had no difficulty understanding Philine's meaning. Unlike Kant, he formed his ideas about education not with Man, but with individual persons, with "Hans or Kunz," in mind. Like Goethe's Wilhelm, Schleiermacher felt that the surprises of fate should be welcomed in the development of children as free and individual spirits. Too pure and precise an educational theory; too much pedagogical control, irreligiously forgetful of the infinite complexity of the processes that mold a child's character — these can maim and distort phantasy by arbitrarily restricting the environment of learning. Genuinely progressive education of children, by its graceful acceptance of fate

[41]Nov. 26, 1803. *Br.* I, 384—85. "Empty imaginations": notice once again how Schleiermacher uses this relative of *Einbildungskraft* to designate arbitrary and narrow opinion (see above, footnote 20). Charlotte von Kathen was Henriette von Willich's older sister.

[42] *Wilhelm Meisters Lehrjahre*, Book II, Ch. 10. Cf. Schleiermacher's remark, "Suppose a soul resisted being born because it wanted to be not this person or that, but rather a person in general!" *Reden*, 271. *Speeches*, 234.

"which educates each in his own way," supports individual development and thus the free play of phantasy. For "phantasy," Schleiermacher writes in 1804, "is the really individual and particular in each of us."[43]

[43] *Grundlinien einer Kritik der bisherigen Sittenlehre*, 269.

Epilogue: People as Poets

No poetry, no reality. . . . Despite all sense, there is no outer world without fantasy.

By ending our study with the year 1804 we have included the peak of Schleiermacher's romanticism, for in the second edition of the *Speeches* in 1806, and in the second edition of the *Soliloquies* in 1810, we find his romanticism somewhat in decline. Let us therefore take a final look at three of the most characteristic aspects of Schleiermacher's romanticism at its height. They are his sense for individuality, his sense for infinity, and his sense for the creative function of the most individual and infinitely variable of all our capacities, phantasy.

The early romantic preoccupations with infinity and individuality often came together in the form of a fascination for the unending inward spiral of self-reflection. Schlegel, for example, has protagonist Julius say, "I did not merely enjoy, but I also felt and enjoyed my enjoyment," and later in *Lucinde* Schlegel puts his hero in the dilemma of being "distrustful of his own distrust."[1] Perhaps the young Goethe's Werther gave the initial impetus to such maelstroms of self-contemplation: "I turn back into myself and find a world."[2]

Schleiermacher, for all his emphasis upon infinity and inwardness in the *Speeches* and the *Soliloquies*, believed that the vortex of introspection could be philosophically hazardous. In his opinion the extreme subjectivism of Fichte's early idealism—

> Attend to yourself: turn your gaze away from all that surrounds you and inward upon yourself. This is the first demand philosophy makes upon its disciple. Its concern is not with anything outside you, but solely with yourself[3]—

was one philosophical mishap for which the whirlpool of pure self-reflection was directly responsible. We have seen that the infinity holding Schleiermacher in fascination was not the inward spiral of self-

---

[1]Schlegel, *Lucinde*, "Julius an Lucinde," 8, and "Lehrjahre der Männlichkeit," 53.
[2]Goethe, *Die Leiden des jungen Werthers*, "Am 22. Mai (1771)," 12.
[3]Fichte, *Erste Einleitung in die Wissenschaftslehre*, 422.

contemplation by itself, but rather the never-ending oscillation of consciousness about the dipole of self and world. Schleiermacher's view
might be expressed by paraphrasing Goethe: I turn back into myself and
find *the* world. The world is in us as we are in it. Schleiermacher's
oscillation between idealism and realism follows the pattern of Schlegel's
famous definition of romantic poetry in the *Athenaeum* of 1798: the
romantic poet looks within and sees the world reflected in himself; he
looks without and finds himself reflected in the world; romantic poetry
is infinite reflection in this "endless row of mirrors."[4]

Schleiermacher's romanticism not only accepts Schlegel's definition
but universalizes it. Schleiermacher broadens poetry to comprehend all
the arts and sciences; he regards all artists and scientists as poets in
Schlegel's sense. Thus the opening sentence of the first chapter of the
Soliloquies asserts:

> The outer world with its most eternal laws as with its most fleeting
> appearances, like a magic mirror, reflects in a thousand delicate and
> sublime allegories the highest and most inward of our nature back upon
> us.[5]

The allegorical radiation of Schleiermacher's metaphor is of course
phantasy, "the highest and most original in a person." Thus what
Schlegel has asserted of poets, what the *Speeches* have asserted of
theologians, what Novalis has asserted of historians, the *Soliloquies* now
assert of all of us, of "our nature." We are all poets. We all perceive the
world according to the direction of our phantasy.

Not *merely* according to the direction of our phantasy. In our
interaction with the world, we half create but half perceive. Our relation
to the world is that of Pygmalion and her sculptor, except that we can
never say with finality which is which. As Schlegel's definition puts it,
the highest and most comprehensive cultivation proceeds "not merely
from within outwards, but also inward from without." The world
imposes limits and patterns upon our perception and thought which we
do not invent but must attempt to discover. Thus the synthetic and the
analytic are for Schleiermacher the irreducible dipole of human thinking.
Informed by empirical sense, synthetic phantasy invents and analytic
reason discerns. The role of imagination, as the voluntary direction of
our attention, is to regulate the oscillation between the two. How well
or how poorly imagination serves this function is a measure of a
person's degree of cultivation.

The 1780s and 1790s were dominated by what Schleiermacher
perceived to be a regulation in the direction of a "superfluity" of
enlightenment rationality. In reaction to this superfluity of analysis,

---

[4]"Fragmente," *Athenaeum*, I/2 (1798), 205.
[5]*Monologen*, 9. *Soliloquies*, 10.

Schleiermacher emphasized—perhaps sometimes overemphasized—the synthetic function of phantasy. Thus his insistent reminder that the contributing of phantasy to our perception of the world is not something we may choose to do or not to do. We are not at liberty to be poets in this sense, merely as we might wish. *Keine Poesie, keine Wirklichkeit*, he writes bluntly in the *Athenaeum* of 1798: "No poetry, no reality. . . . Despite all sense, there is no outer world without fantasy."[6] Once again Schleiermacher's philosophical point of view finds its literary expression in Novalis:

> It is too bad that poetry has a special name and that poets constitute a special guild. Poetry is nothing special at all. It is the characteristic mode of action of the human spirit. Is not every person a poet, aspiring in every moment?[7]

How serious can these romantics be? Can they really intend their theory of the role of phantasy in knowledge and education to apply to all our spheres of endeavor? One thinks of standards of scientific detachment, or of objectivity in historical research. There is nothing in Schleiermacher's romantic writings, however, to lead us to believe that he was less than wholly serious. By opening his *Soliloquies* with the mention of phantasy's role in our perception of "the outer world with its most *eternal laws* and with its most *fleeting appearances*," Schleiermacher seems to be making it implicit that scientists and historians are among those whom he is addressing.

Even if it were possible for one to put down the *Soliloquies* still unconvinced of Schleiermacher's skepticism concerning pure objectivity in the sciences, an intriguing incident in his own experience illustrates the point concretely. The book Schleiermacher published next after the *Soliloquies* was the *Groundwork to a Critique of Previous Ethical Doctrine* of 1804. He had begun planning and collecting materials for his *Critique* as early as August, 1798. It was to be at last the "regular concert" Schleiermacher had promised, following the warm-up "fantasias" of the *Speeches* and the *Soliloquies*. In short, Schleiermacher felt himself ready to produce a work of scientific thoroughness, rigor—and detachment. Three times during the year before its publication he literally boasted of as much. To Alexander Dohna he wrote, "My basic presuppositions and feelings are not the question; for the *Critique* is wholly dialectic and proceeds entirely according to the scientific form,"[8] and to Henriette Herz, "No one, not even a critical genius like Friedrich, should be able to guess my own ethics from it. . . . May God grant his blessing to its completion."[9]

---

[6]"Fragmente," *Athenaeum*, I/2(1798), 278.
[7]*Heinrich von Ofterdingen*, Ch. 8, 119.
[8]Apr. 10, 1803. *Werden*, 301.
[9]Sep. 6, 1802. *Br.* I, 328—29. "Friedrich": Schlegel. Schleiermacher expresses the same opinion in a letter to Eleonore Grunow, Sep. 3, 1802 (*Werden*, 266).

Schleiermacher's benediction was more fitting than he knew. One can understand his chagrin when approaching the end of his work on the *Critique*, he discovered that the conclusion of his almost five years of work had slipped his mind. "Today I will finish writing the conclusion of the *Critique*," he wrote to Henriette Herz,

> but in that connection a great misfortune has befallen me, which I simply cannot comprehend. The conclusion I wanted to make I have quite lost from among my thoughts. For three days I have tormented myself to find it, but in vain; and so I shall eternally remain indebted to my readers, and the end will not be worthy of the whole. *But how is it possible that one can lose a thought that no longer stands at all alone and by itself, but rather in necessary connection with a whole?*[10]

How is it possible? "Is this not some kind of madness?" Schleiermacher writes in dismay. But if one takes the *Soliloquies* seriously, it is not madness, unless to be mad and to be human are the same thing. Schleiermacher has tripped over his own romantic principle that the world does not yield its truths objectively to a detached investigator. Truths of ethics, like all others, are as much invented by "the direction of phantasy" as discovered by "wholly dialectic" scientific procedure.

Near the beginning of his *Critique* Schleiermacher writes:

> But who would like . . . to think so little of science that it could appear possible to him that the same problem could result, in accordance with the laws of science and without error, in several different solutions?[11]

One can scarcely avoid the thought that the author of the *Soliloquies* should have known better—even the young author of *On Human Freedom*, for that matter. In that early treatise, with which we began our study and Schleiermacher began his philosophical career, he wrote:

> If a given fact, which one person applies to the explanation of a correct proposition, is used by another person to confirm a prejudice; if the one develops a completely different series of clear representations from a given point, if he derives from given premises a conclusion almost completely different from that of another; if the one draws from the same grounds his own completely different inference, or takes the same results to imply completely different principles; the grounds for this can be sought nowhere else than in the faculty of desire. . . . Indeed the first ground of existence of every activity of the understanding, namely, *the direction of imagination*, is nothing other than an activity of the faculty of desire.[12]

According to his own diagnosis, then, Schleiermacher's difficulty with the conclusion of his *Critique* is attributable to the direction of his imagination. Not only had his imagination played a role in creating what

---

[10] Aug. 2, 1803. *Br.* I, 374. Emphasis added.

[11] *Grundlinien einer Kritik der bisherigen Sittenlehre*, 8.

[12] MS 24. Emphasis added.

he supposed to be a necessary scientific conclusion; that same imagination, even with the completed analysis spread out before it, was unable to come up with the conclusion a second time. It was enough to drive an aspiring dialectician to distraction—a vivid illustration of the insidiously attractive scientific mentality that Schleiermacher's own treatise of 1792 and *Soliloquies* of 1800 had warned against.

Did Schleiermacher's experience lead him to take his own warning more seriously than he had before? Or does the *Groundwork to a Critique of Previous Ethical Doctrine* mark the end of Schleiermacher's romantic emphasis upon phantasy? There are indications that the former is the case. In his discussion of analytic or deductive knowledge in his lectures on dialectics in 1814, Schleiermacher writes, "The principal thing here is the discovery of the ground of distinction. The certainty of this act can be none other than that of a provisional assumption, produced by free fantasizing."[13] In his discussion of synthetic or inductive knowledge in his lectures on Ethics in 1812–13, he writes, "Fantasy is the synthetic faculty, and indeed is so at every stage. Personal sensibility [*Sinnlichkeit*] is fantasy, and reason [*Vernunft*] is also fantasy."[14] But these are issues for a study of Schleiermacher's later life. In 1800 his opinion is clear: "A person belongs to the world he helps to make."[15] In such a world, religious, ethical, and scientific truths are not merely discovered, and an awareness of the creative activity of "living phantasy" can liberate us from the constraining assumption that they are.

[13] *Dialektik*, ed. Jonas, 250n.
[14] *Ethik*, in *Schleiermachers Werke*, ed. Braun and Bauer, II, 313.
[15] *Monologen*, 61. *Soliloquies*, 62.

BIBLIOGRAPHY

Bibliography

Allison, Henry E., *The Kant-Eberhard Controversy*. Baltimore: The Johns Hopkins University Press, 1973.

Aristotle, *Nicomachean Ethics*. Tr. Martin Ostwald. Indianapolis: Bobbs-Merrill, 1962.

Augustine, *The Confessions of St. Augustine*. Tr. John K. Ryan. Garden City, N.Y.: Image Books, 1962.

Barth, Karl, *Protestant Thought: From Rousseau to Ritschl*. Tr. Brian Cozens. New York: Clarion Books, 1969.

Beck, Lewis White, *Early German Philosophy: Kant and His Predecessors*. Cambridge: The Belknap Press of Harvard University Press, 1969.

Behler, Ernst, "Athenaeum: Die Geschichte einer Zeitschrift." Afterword to A. W. Schlegel and Friedrich Schlegel, eds., *Athenaeum. 1798–1800*. Stuttgart: J. G. Cotta'sche Buchhandlung, 1960.

Bigler, Robert M., *The Politics of German Protestantism: The Rise of the Protestant Church Elite in Prussia, 1815–1848*. Berkeley: University of California Press, 1972.

Borcherdt, Hans Heinrich, *Schiller und die Romantiker*. Stuttgart: J. G. Cotta'sche Buchhandlung, 1948.

Brandt, Richard B., *The Philosophy of Schleiermacher*. New York: Harper and Brothers, 1941.

Brinkmann, Karl Gustav von, *Briefe von Karl Gustav von Brinckmann an Friedrich Schleiermacher*. Ed. Heinrich Meisner and Erich Schmidt. In *Mitteilungen aus dem Litteraturarchive in Berlin*, VI. Berlin: Litteraturarchiv-Gesellschaft, 1912.

Camerer, Theodor, *Spinoza und Schleiermacher: die kritische Lösung des von Spinoza hinterlassenen Problems*. Stuttgart and Berlin: J. G. Cotta'sche Buchhandlung, 1903.

Chapman, J. Arundel, *An Introduction to Schleiermacher*. London: The Epworth Press, 1932.

Dawson, Jerry F., *Friedrich Schleiermacher: The Evolution of a Nationalist*. Austin: University of Texas Press, 1966.

Descartes, René, *Discourse on Method*. Tr. Laurence J. Lafleur. Indianapolis: Bobbs-Merrill, 1960.

Dilthey, Wilhelm, *Leben Schleiermachers*. 1st ed. Berlin: Georg Reimer, 1870.

Dilthey, Wilhelm, *Leben Schleiermachers*. 3rd ed. 2 vols., each in 2 half-vols. Ed. Martin Redeker. Berlin: Walter de Gruyter, 1966–70.

Eberhard, Johann August, *Sittenlehre der Vernunft. Zum Gebrauch seiner Vorlesungen*. 2nd ed. Berlin: Friedrich Nicolai, 1786.

Epictetus, *The Discourses of Epictetus*. Tr. George Long. London: George Bell and Sons, 1890.

Esselborn, Friedrich Wilhelm, *Die philosophischen Voraussetzungen von Schleiermachers Determinismus*. Ludwigshafen: J. G. Biller, 1897.

Falk, Johannes Daniel, ed., *Taschenbuch für Freunde des Scherzes und der Satire*. V (1801). Weimar: Im Verlage des Industrie-Comptiors, 1801.

Fawcett, Joseph, *Sermons Delivered at the Sunday-Evening Lecture, for the Winter Season, at the Old Jewry*. 2 vols. 2nd ed. London: J. Johnson, 1801.

Fichte, Immanuel Hermann von, *J. G. Fichte und Schleiermacher: Eine vergleichende Skizze*. In *Vermischte Schriften zur Philosophie, Theologie und Ethik*, I. Leipzig: F. A. Brockhaus, 1869.

Fichte, Johann Gottlieb, *Die Bestimmung des Menschen*. In *Sämmtliche Werke*, I/2. Berlin: Veit, 1845.

Fichte, Johann Gottlieb, *Erste Einleitung in die Wissenschaftslehre*. In *Sämmtliche Werke*, I/1. Berlin: Veit, 1845.

Fichte, Johann Gottlieb, *Philosophie der Maurerei*. Ed. Wilhelm Flitner. Leipzig: Felix Meiner, 1923.

Fichte, Johann Gottlieb, *Philosophy of Masonry*. Tr. Roscoe Pound. *Masonic Papers*, II (Sep., 1945), 11–65.

Fichte, Johann Gottlieb, *Science of Knowledge, with the First and Second Introductions*. Tr. Peter Heath and John Lachs. New York: Appleton-Century-Crofts, 1970.

Fichte, Johann Gottlieb, *The Vocation of Man*. Tr. William Smith. LaSalle, Illinois: Open Court, 1965.

Fichte, Johann Gottlieb, *Zweite Einleitung in die Wissenschaftslehre*. In *Sämmtliche Werke* I/1. Berlin: Veit, 1845.

Forstman, Jack, *A Romantic Triangle: Schleiermacher and Early German Romanticism*. Missoula, Montana: Scholars Press, 1977.

Fuchs, Emil, *Vom Werden dreier Denker: Was wollten Fichte, Schelling und Schleiermacher in der ersten Periode ihrer Entwicklung?* Tübingen and Leipzig: J. C. B. Mohr, 1904.

Fuchs, Emil, *Von Schleiermacher zu Marx*. Ed. Heinrich Fink and Herbert Trebs. Berlin: Union Verlag, 1969.

Goethe, Johann Wolfgang, *Die Leiden des jungen Werthers*. Stuttgart: Philipp Reclam, 1969.

Goethe, Johann Wolfgang, *Wilhelm Meisters Lehrjahre*. In *Gesamtausgabe*, vols. 15 and 16. 3rd ed. München: Deutscher Taschenbuch Verlag, 1969.

Grommelt, Carl and Christine von Mertens, *Das Dohnasche Schloss Schlobitten in Ostpreussen*. Stuttgart: W. Kohlhammer Verlag, 1962.

Gurwitsch, Georg, *Fichtes System der Konkreten Ethik*. Tübingen: J. C. B. Mohr, 1924.

Haym, Rudolph, *Die romantische Schule*. Berlin: Rudolph Gaertner, 1870.

Herder, Johann Gottfried, *God: Some Conversations*. Tr. Frederick H. Burkhardt. Indianapolis: Bobbs-Merrill, 1940.

Hering, Hermann, *Samuel Ernst Timotheus Stubenrauch und sein Neffe Friedrich Schleiermacher*. Gütersloh: C. Bertelsmann, 1919.

Herz, Henriette, *Henriette Herz. Ihr Leben und ihre Erinnerungen*. Ed. I. Fürst. Berlin: Wilhelm Hertz, 1850.

Herz, Henriette, *Henriette Herz. Ihr Leben und ihre Zeit*. Ed. Hans Landsberg. Weimar: Gustav Kiepenheuer, 1913.

Herz, Henriette, *Schleiermacher und seine Lieben. Nach Originalbriefen der Henriette Herz*. Magdeburg: In der Creutz'schen Verlagsbuchhandlung, 1910.

Jacobi, Friedrich Heinrich, *David Hume über den Glauben, oder Idealismus und Realismus. Ein Gespräch*. In *Werke*, II. Leipzig: Gerhard Fleischer, 1815.

Jacobi, Friedrich Heinrich, *Eduard Allwills Briefsammlung*. Leipzig: Gerhard Fleischer, 1826.

Jacobi, Friedrich Heinrich, *Friederich Heinrich Jacobi's auserlesener Briefwechsel*. Ed. Friedrich Roth. 2 vols. Leipzig: Gerhard Fleischer, 1825, 1827.

Jacobi, Friedrich Heinrich, *Sendschreiben an Fichte*. In *Werke*, III. Leipzig: Gerhard Fleischer, 1816.

Jacobi, Friedrich Heinrich, *Über die Lehre des Spinoza in Briefen an Herrn Moses Mendelssohn*. 2nd ed. In *Werke*, IV/1. Leipzig: Gerhard Fleischer, 1819.

Jaeger, Werner, *Paideia: the Ideals of Greek Culture*. Tr. Gilbert Highet. 3 vols. New York: Oxford University Press, 1943.

Kant, Immanuel, *Anthropologie in pragmatischer Hinsicht*. In *Kant's gesämmelte Schriften*, ed. Königlich Preussischen Akademie der Wissenschaften, I/7. Berlin: Georg Reimer, 1907.

Kant, Immanuel, *Beantwortung der Frage: Was ist Aufklärung*? In *Kant's gesämmelte Schriften*, ed. Königlich Preussischen Akademie der Wissenschaften, VIII. Berlin: Georg Reimer, 1908.

Kant, Immanuel, *Briefwechsel von Imm. Kant*. 3 vols. Ed. H. E. Fischer. München: Georg Müller, 1912.

Kant, Immanuel, *Grundlegung zur Metaphysik der Sitten*. In *Kant's gesämmelte Schriften*, ed. Königlich Preussischen Akademie der Wissenschaften, I/4. Berlin: Georg Reimer, 1903.

Kant, Immanuel, *Kritik der praktischen Vernunft*. In *Kant's gesämmelte Schriften*, ed. Königlich Preussischen Akademie der Wissenschaften, I/5. Berlin: Georg Reimer, 1908.

Kant, Immanuel, *Kritik der reinen Vernunft*. Ed. Raymund Schmidt. Leipzig: Felix Meiner, 1926.

Kant, Immanuel, *Die Religion innerhalb der Grenzen der blossen Vernunft*. Ed. Karl Vorländer. Hamburg: Felix Meiner, 1956.

Kant, Immanuel, *Religion within the Limits of Reason Alone*. Tr. Theodore M. Greene and Hoyt H. Hudson. New York: Harper Torchbooks, 1960.

Kant, Immanuel, *Was heisst: Sich im Denken Orientieren*? In *Kant's gesämmelte Schriften*, ed. Königlich Preussischen Akademie der Wissenschaften, VIII. Berlin: George Reimer, 1908.

Kant, Immanuel, *What is Enlightenment*? Tr. Lewis White Beck. In Kant, *Critique of Practical Reason and Other Writings in Moral Philosophy*, ed. Beck. Chicago: University of Chicago Press, 1949.

Kant, Immanuel, *What is Orientation in Thinking?* Tr. Lewis White Beck. In Kant, *Critique of Practical Reason and Other Writings in Moral Philosophy*, ed. Beck. Chicago: University of Chicago Press, 1949.

Kantzenbach, Friedrich Wilhelm, *Friedrich Daniel Ernst Schleiermacher. In Selbstzeugnissen und Bilddokumenten*. Reinbek bei Hamburg: Rowohlt Taschenbuch Verlag, 1967.

Kierkegaard, Søren, *Concluding Unscientific Postscript*. Tr. David F. Swenson and Walter Lowrie. Princeton: Princeton University Press, 1941.

Kierkegaard, Søren, *The Point of View for My Work as an Author*. Tr. Walter Lowrie. New York: Harper and Brothers, 1962.

Meisner, Heinrich, *Schleiermachers Lehrjahre*. Ed. Hermann Mulert. Berlin and Leipzig: Walter de Gruyter, 1934.

Meyer, E. R., *Schleiermachers und C. G. Brinkmanns Gang durch die Brüdergemeine*. Leipzig: Friedrich Jansa, 1905.

Niebuhr, Richard R., *Schleiermacher on Christ and Religion: A New Introduction*. New York: Charles Scribner's Sons, 1964.

Novalis (Friedrich von Hardenberg), *Heinrich von Ofterdingen*. In *Novalis Schriften*, ed. Ludwig Tieck and Friedrich Schlegel. 3rd ed. Berlin: Realschulbuchhandlung, 1815.

Oko, Adolph S., *The Spinoza Bibliography*. Boston: G. K. Hall, 1964.

Olivier, Paul, *Zum Willensproblem bei Kant und Reinhold*. Berlin: Verlag Dr. Emil Ebering, 1941.

Pascal, Blaise, *Pensées*. Tr. W. F. Trotter. *Great Books of the Western World*, ed. Robert M. Hutchins, vol. 33. Chicago: Encyclopedia Britannica, 1952.

Plato, *The Apology*. In *Plato*, tr. Harold North Fowler, vol. 1. Cambridge: Loeb Classical Library of Harvard University Press, 1971.

Plato, *Platons Werke*. Ed. Friedrich Schleiermacher. 2 vols. 3rd ed. Berlin: Georg Reimer, 1855.

Plato, *The Republic of Plato*. Tr. Allan Bloom. New York: Basic Books, 1968.

Pollock, Frederick, *Spinoza: His Life and Philosophy*. London: C. Kegan Paul, 1880.

Rawls, John, *A Theory of Justice*. Cambridge: The Belknap Press of Harvard University Press, 1971.

Redeker, Martin, *Friedrich Schleiermacher. Leben und Werk*. Berlin: Walter de Gruyter, 1968.

Redeker, Martin, *Schleiermacher: Life and Thought*. Tr. John Wallhausser. Philadelphia: Fortress Press, 1973.

Reinhold, Carl Leonhard, *Briefe über die Kantische Philosophie*. 2 vols. Leipzig: Georg Joachim Göschen, 1790, 1792.

Schelling, F. W. J., *Aus Schellings Leben in Briefen*. Ed. G. L. Plitt. 2 vols. Leipzig: S. Hirzel, 1869–70.

Schenk, H. G., *The Mind of the European Romantics*. Garden City, New York: Anchor Books, 1969.

Schiller, Friedrich, *Naive and Sentimental Poetry* and *On the Sublime*, Tr. Julius A. Elias. New York: Frederick Ungar, 1966.

Schiller, Friedrich, *On the Aesthetic Education of Man, In a Series of Letters*. Tr. and ed. Elizabeth M. Wilkinson and L. A. Willoughby. Oxford: At the Clarendon Press, 1967.

Schiller, Friedrich, *On the Aesthetic Education of Man, In a Series of Letters*. Tr. Reginald Snell. New York: Frederick Ungar, 1954.

Schiller, Friedrich, *Über Anmut und Würde*. In *Gesamtausgabe*, vol. 18. München: Deutscher Taschenbuch Verlag, 1966.

Schiller, Friedrich, *Über die ästhetische Erziehung des Menschen in einer Reihe von Briefen*. In *Gesamtausgabe*, vol. 19. München: Deutscher Taschenbuch Verlag, 1966.

Schiller Friedrich, *Über naive und sentimentalische Dichtung*. In *Gesamtausgabe*, vol. 19. München: Deutscher Taschenbuch Verlag, 1966.

Schlegel, August Wilhelm and Friedrich Schlegel, eds., *Athenaeum. 1798–1800*. Stuttgart: J. G. Cotta'sche Buchhandlung, 1960.

Schlegel, Friedrich, *Friedrich Schlegel's "Lucinde" and the Fragments*. Tr. Peter Firchow. Minneapolis: University of Minnesota Press, 1971.

Schlegel, Friedrich, *Lucinde. Ein Roman*. Ed. Karl Konrad Polheim. Stuttgart: Philipp Reclam, 1964.

Schleiermacher, Friedrich, *Aphorismen zur Pädagogik*. In *Sämmtliche Werke*, III/9. Berlin: George Reimer, 1849.

Schleiermacher, Friedrich, *Aus Schleiermachers Leben in Briefen*. 4 vols. Vols. 1 and 2, 2nd ed. Berlin: Georg Reimer, 1860–63.

Schleiermacher, Friedrich, *Briefe Friedrich Schleiermachers an August Wilhelm Schlegel*. In *Euphorion. Zeitschrift für Literaturgeschichte*, XXI/3 and 4. Leipzig: Carl Fromme, 1914.

Schleiermacher, Friedrich, *Briefe Friedrich Schleiermachers an Ehrenfried und Henriette von Willich geb. von Mühlenfels, 1801–1806*. Ed. Heinrich Meisner. In *Mitteilungen aus dem Litteraturarchive in Berlin*, IX. Berlin: Litteraturarchiv-Gesellschaft, 1914.

Schleiermacher, Friedrich, *Briefe Schleiermachers*. Ed. Hermann Mulert. Berlin: Im Propyläen-Verlag, 1923.

Schleiermacher, Friedrich, *The Christian Faith*. Tr. H. R. Mackintosh and J. S. Stewart. 2 vols. New York: Harper Torchbooks, 1963.

Schleiermacher, Friedrich, *Der christliche Glaube*. 7th ed. 2 vols. Ed. Martin Redeker. Berlin: Walter de Gruyter, 1960.

Schleiermacher, Friedrich, *Christmas Eve Celebration*. Tr. W. Hastie. Edinburgh: T. and T. Clark, 1890.

Schleiermacher, Friedrich, *Christmas Eve: Dialogue on the Incarnation*. Tr. Terrence N. Tice. Richmond: John Knox Press, 1967.

Schleiermacher, Friedrich, *Dialektik*. Ed. I. Halpern. Berlin: Mayer und Müller, 1903.

Schleiermacher, Friedrich, *Dialektik*. Ed. L. Jonas. In *Sämmtliche Werke*, III, 4/2. Berling: Georg Reimer, 1839.

Schleiermacher, Friedrich, *Ethik*. In *Schleiermachers Werke*, ed. Otto Braun and Joh. Bauer, II. Leipzig: Felix Meiner. 1913.

Schleiermacher, Friedrich, *Friedrich Schleiermachers Briefwechsel mit seiner Braut*. Ed. Heinrich Meisner. Gotha: Friedrich Andreas Perthes, 1919.

Schleiermacher, Friedrich, *Fr. Schleiermacher's Briefwechsel mit J. Chr. Gass*. Ed. W. Gass. Berlin: Georg Reimer, 1852.

Schleiermacher, Friedrich, *Grundlinien einer Kritik der bisherigen Sittenlehre*. In *Sämmtliche Werke*, III/1. Berlin: Georg Reimer, 1846.

Schleiermacher, Friedrich, *Kurze Darstellung des spinozistischen Systems*. In *Sämmtliche Werke*, III, 4/1. Berlin: Georg Reimer, 1839.

Schleiermacher, Friedrich, *The Life of Schleiermacher as Unfolded in his Autobiography and Letters*. Tr. Frederica Maclean Rowan. 2 vols. London: Smith, Elder and Co., 1860.

Schleiermacher, Friedrich, *Monologen. Eine Neujahrsgabe*. Critical ed. by Friedrich Michael Schiele. Leipzig: Verlag der Dürr'schen Buchhandlung, 1902.

Schleiermacher, Friedrich, *On Religion: Speeches to Its Cultured Despisers*. Tr. John Oman. New York: Harper Torchbooks, 1958.

Schleiermacher, Friedrich, *Predigten. Erste Sammlung.* In *Sämmtliche Werke*, II/1. Berlin: Georg Reimer, 1834.

Schleiermacher, Friedrich, *Predigten in den Jahren 1789 bis 1810 gehalten.* In *Sämmtliche Werke*, II/7. Berlin: George Reimer, 1836.

Schleiermacher, Friedrich, *Predigten über den christlichen Hausstand.* In *Sämmtliche Werke*, II/2. Berlin: Georg Reimer, 1843.

Schleiermacher, Friedrich, *Psychologie.* Ed. L. George. In *Sämmtliche Werke*, III/6. Berlin: George Reimer, 1862.

Schleiermacher, Friedrich, *Reden über die Religion.* Critical ed. by G. Ch. Pünjer. Braunschweig: C. A. Schwetschke, 1879.

Schleiermacher, Friedrich, *Schleiermacher als Mensch. Sein Werden. Familien–und Freundesbriefe 1783 bis 1804.* Ed. Heinrich Meisner. Gotha: Friedrich Andreas Perthes, 1922.

Schleiermacher, Friedrich, *Schleiermacher als Mensch. Sein Wirken. Familien–und Freundesbriefe 1804 bis 1834.* Ed. Heinrich Meisner. Gotha: Friedrich Andreas Perthes, 1923.

Schleiermacher, Friedrich, *Schleiermacher Nachlass.* Schleiermacher manuscripts, journals, papers, letters, and the like, preserved in the Literatur–Archiv der Deutschen Akademie der Wissenschaften zu Berlin. See particular titles.

Schleiermacher, Friedrich, *Schleiermacher's Introductions to the Dialogues of Plato.* Tr. William Dobson. New York: Arno Press, 1973.

Schleiermacher, Friedrich, *Schleiermachers pädagogische Schriften, mit einer Darstellung seines Lebens.* Ed. C. Platz. 2nd ed. Langensalza: 1876.

Schleiermacher, Friedrich, *Schleiermachers Sendschreiben über seine Glaubenslehre an Lücke.* Ed. Hermann Mulert. Giessen: Alfred Töpelmann, 1908.

Schleiermacher, Friedrich, *Schleiermacher's Soliloquies: An English Translation of the Monologen.* Tr. Horace Leland Friess. Chicago: Open Court, 1957.

Schleiermacher, Friedrich, *Spinozismus.* Manuscript in *Schleiermacher Nachlass*, #138. Abridged text in Hermann Mulert, "Schleiermacher über Spinoza und Jacobi," *Chronicon Spinozanum*, vol. 3. Hague: Curis Societatis Spinozanae, 1923. Additional text in Dilthey, *Leben Schleiermachers*, 1st ed., 68–69.

Schleiermacher, Friedrich, *Über das Anständige. Zwei Gespräche.* In *Aus Schleiermachers Leben in Briefen*, IV, 503–33. Berlin: Georg Reimer, 1863.

Schleiermacher, Friedrich, *Über das höchste Gut.* Abridged text in Dilthey, *Leben Schleiermachers*, 1st ed., "Denkmale," 6–19.

Schleiermacher, Friedrich, *Über den Unterschied zwischen Naturgesetz und Sittengesetz.* In *Schleiermacher's Werke*, ed. Otto Braun and D. Joh. Bauer, I. Leipzig: Felix Meiner, 1910.

Schleiermacher, Friedrich, *Über den Werth des Lebens.* In Dilthey, *Leben Schleiermachers*, 1st ed., "Denkmale," 46–63.

Schleiermacher, Friedrich, *"Über die Freiheit des Menschen."* Abridged text in Dilthey, *Leben Schleiermachers*, 1st ed., "Denkmale," 19–46. Manuscript in *Schleiermacher Nachlass*, #133.

Schleiermacher, Friedrich, *Versuch einer Theorie des geselligen Bertragens.* Ed. Herman Nohl. In *Schleiermachers Werke*, ed. Otto Braun and Joh. Bauer, II. Leipzig: Felix Meiner, 1913.

Schleiermacher, Friedrich, *Vertraute Briefe über Friedrich Schlegels Lucinde.* In *Sämmtliche Werke*, III/1. Berlin: Georg Reimer, 1846.

Schleiermacher, Friedrich, *Weihnachtsfeier.* Critical ed. by Hermann Mulert. Leipzig: Verlag der Dürr'schen Buchhandlung, 1908.

Schleiermacher, Friedrich, *Zur Pädagogik.* In *Schleiermachers Werke*, ed. Otto Braun and Joh. Bauer, III. Leipzig: Felix Meiner, 1913.

Seifert, Paul, *Die Theologie des jungen Schleiermacher.* Gütersloh: Gerd Mohn, 1960.

Shelley, Percy Bysshe, *A Defence of Poetry.* In *The Prose Works of Percy Bysshe Shelley.* Ed. Richard Herne Shepherd. Vol. 2. London: Chatto and Windus, 1888.

Sommer, Wolfgang, *Schleiermacher und Novalis. Die Christologie des jungen Schleiermachers und ihre Beziehung zum Christusbild des Novalis.* Bern: Herbert Lang, 1973.

Spiegler, Gerhard, *The Eternal Covenant: Schleiermacher's Experiment in Cultural Theology.* New York: Harper and Row, 1967.

Spinoza, Benedict de, *Ethics.* Tr. R. H. M. Elwes. New York: Dover Publications, 1951.

Steffens, Heinrich, *Was ich Erlebte. Aus der Errinerung niedergeschrieben.* 10 vols. Breslau: Joseph Max, 1841–44.

Süskind, Hermann, *Der Einfluss Schellings auf die Entwicklung von Schleiermachers System.* Tübingen: J. C. B. Mohr, 1909.

Sykes, Stephen, *Friedrich Schleiermacher.* Richmond: John Knox Press, 1971.

Tice, Terrence N., *Schleiermacher Bibliography*. Princeton: Princeton Theological Seminary, 1966.

Tuveson, Ernest Lee, *The Imagination as a Means of Grace*. New York: Gordian Press, 1974.

Ungern-Sternberg, Arthur von, *Freiheit und Wirklichkeit: Schleiermachers philosophischer Reifeweg durch den deutschen Idealismus*. Gotha: Leopold Klotz, 1931.

Walzel, Oskar, *Deutsche Romantik*. 5th ed. 2 vols. Leipzig and Berlin: B. G. Teubner, 1923.

Walzel, Oskar, *German Romanticism*. Tr. Alma Elise Lussky. New York: Capricorn Books, 1966.

Weizsäcker, Hugo, *Schleiermacher und das Eheproblem*. Tübingen: J. C. B. Mohr, 1927.

Wendland, Johannes, *Die Religiöse Entwicklung Schleiermachers*. Tübingen: J. C. B. Mohr, 1915.

Willich, Ehrenfried von, *Aus Schleiermachers Hause. Jugenderinnerungen seines Stiefsohnes*. Berlin: George Reimer, 1909.

Wizenmann, Thomas, *Die Resultate der Jacobischen und Mendelssohnschen Philosophie: kritisch untersucht von einem Freywilligen*. Leipzig: G. J. Göschen, 1786.

Wolff, Robert Paul, *The Autonomy of Reason: A Commentary on Kant's Groundwork of the Metaphysic of Morals*. New York: Harper and Row, 1973.

Zuckerkandl, Victor, *Man the Musician*. Tr. Norbert Guterman. Princeton: Princeton University Press, 1973.

Zuckerkandl, Victor, *Sound and Symbol: Music and the External World*. Tr. Willard R. Trask. New York: Pantheon Books, 1956.

INDEXES

Index of Personal Names

Albertini, Johann Baptist von, 7n.
Aristotle, 22, 89.
Arnim, Bettina von, 174–175, 274.
Augustine of Hippo, 37.
Bamberger, Hofprediger, 140–141.
Barth, Karl, 186.
Bismark, Otto von, 150n.
Boeckh, August, 129n, 132.
Brahms, Johannes, 223, 224.
Brinkmann, Karl Gustav von, 9, 10, 18, 51n, 63, 76n, 89, 115, 119n, 127n, 128n, 142, 145, 146, 147, 153, 157, 158nn, 159n, 161, 165, 166n, 166n, 167, 170, 187n, 208, 209, 212, 215, 216n, 219–220, 244, 248, 258, 262n, 265.
Buridan, Jean, 80n
Calvin, John, 1, 4, 34.
Coleridge, Samuel Taylor, 236.
Descartes, Rene, 55, 56n.
Dickens, Charles, 168, 171, 181–182, 289, 290.
Dilthey, William, 68, 69.
Dohna, Friederika, 10, 250.
Dohna, Friedrich Alexander, 10, 89, 113, 235, 236, 250, 261n, 267, 283n, 287, 292, 299.
Eberhard, Johann August, 2, 12, 13, 35, 53, 76, 89, 127.
Epictetus, 137n, 270n.
Ernst, Charlotte Schlegel, 258.
Euclid, 54.
Euler, Leonhard, 89.
Falk, Johannes Daniel, 111–112, 146, 262, 263.
Fawcett, Joseph, 104–107, 125, 149, 236.
Fichte, Immanuel Hermann, 227.
Fichte, Johann Gottlieb, 2, 53, 56, 57, 58, 59, 60, 81, 82, 119, 124, 126, 144, 147, 157–160, 161, 162, 166, 171, 187, 188, 220, 221, 227–229, 251, 281, 297.
Friess, Horace Leland, 220.
Frommann, Friedrich, 129, 130, 132.
Fürst, Julius, 262 n. 26.
Gedike, Friedrich, 18, 89.
Goethe, Wolfgang, 41, 120, 171, 233, 292, 293, 297–298.
Grunow, Eleonore, 8n, 17n, 128n, 155nn, 117–172, 182, 202, 222n, 234, 235n, 238, 239, 243, 250, 257, 263, 264, 265, 267, 268, 270, 271, 274, 275, 276, 279–280, 287, 290, 291n, 299n.
Hardenberg, Friedrich von, 153n, 234. See also Novalis.
Hazlitt, William, 104.
Hegel, Georg Wilhelm Friedrich, 147, 164, 165, 190.
Herz, Henriette, 12n, 19, 55, 82n, 86n, 90n, 113, 114, 115, 126, 127n, 128, 129nn, 130, 134n, 136n, 138n, 139n, 141n, 141n, 142nn, 144, 157, 168n, 171, 202–202, 207, 223n, 228n, 239n, 246, 247, 249, 250n, 251n, 255n, 257, 259–262, 264n, 265, 267, 268, 274, 275, 279–280, 287, 292, 299, 300.

Index of Place Names

Index of Titles